Public
Policymaking
An Introduction

Public

Policymaking

An Introduction

EIGHTH EDITION

JAMES E. ANDERSON

Texas A&M University

CENGAGE
Learning·

Australia • Brazil • Japan • Korea • Mexico • Singapore • Spain • United Kingdom • United States

CENGAGE
Learning®

Public Policymaking:
An Introduction,
Eighth Edition
James E. Anderson

Product Director: Suzanne Jeans

Product Manager:
Carolyn Merrill

Content Developer: Jean Findley

Content Coordinator:
Jessica Wang

Product Assistant: Abigail Hess

Media Developer:
Laura Hildebrand

Marketing Brand Manager:
Valerie Hartman

Rights Acquisitions Specialist:
Jennifer Meyer Dare

Manufacturing Planner:
Fola Orekoya

Art and Design Direction,
Production Management, and
Composition: PreMediaGlobal

Cover Image: [SE] © Donovan
Reese/Stone/Getty Images

> For product information and
> technology assistance, contact us at **Cengage
> Learning Customer & Sales Support, 1-800-354-9706**
> For permission to use material from this text or product,
> **submit all requests online at www.cengage.com/permissions.**
> Further permissions questions can be emailed to
> **permissionrequest@cengage.com.**

Library of Congress Control Number: 2013951258
ISBN-13: 978-1-285-73528-3
ISBN-10: 1-285-73528-5

Cengage Learning
200 First Stamford Place, 4th Floor
Stamford, CT 06902
USA

Cengage Learning is a leading provider of customized learning solutions with office locations around the globe, including Singapore, the United Kingdom, Australia, Mexico, Brazil and Japan. Locate your local office at **international.cengage.com/region.**

Cengage Learning products are represented in Canada by Nelson Education, Ltd.

For your course and learning solutions, visit **www.cengage.com.**

Purchase any of our products at your local college store or at our preferred online store **www.cengagebrain.com.**

Instructors: Please visit login.cengage.com and log in to access instructor-specific resources.

Printed in the United States of America
1 2 3 4 5 6 7 17 16 15 14 13

Contents

CHAPTER 7   *Policy Impact, Evaluation, and Change*   *290*

CHAPTER 8   *Reflections and Observations*   *341*

Preface

In *Public Policymaking: An Introduction*, Eighth Edition, the policymaking process is presented as a policy cycle—a sequence of functional activities beginning with problem identification and agenda formation, and continuing through the evaluation of policy, which may result in the continuation, modification, or termination of policy. This may restart the policy cycle in a search for alternatives for handling a problem.

The policy cycle schema is a workable and flexible approach to the study and analysis of public policymaking, whether in the United States or elsewhere. In addition, the text looks at some other ways to study policy formation (e.g., group theory and elite theory); makes some comparisons with action in other countries; and delves into some of the logistical aspects of policymaking, such as majority building, cost–benefit analysis, and decision-making.

Since the seventh edition of this book was written, various noteworthy changes or developments have occurred in American government and public policy. National budget deficits soared because of the Great Recession and then began to decline. The Patient Protection and Affordable Care Act and the Wall Street Reform and Consumer Financial Protection Act were enacted. The Democratic Party, which won control of both houses of Congress in 2008, lost control of the House of Representatives in 2010 to the Republicans, partly because of the Tea Party. The long American combat involvement in Iraq has finally ended, although violence in that country has not. The long war in Afghanistan is now winding down, at least as far as American participation is involved. In 2012, President Barack Obama decisively won a second term.

The Obama administration has a more leftward tilt than the predecessor George W. Bush administration. In Congress, however, polarization of the political parties has intensified. The increased opposition of the Republicans, especially in the House, to anything "Obama," has made stalemate commonplace in Congress, which is often referred to as a dysfunctional body.

The fundamental structure of the policymaking process remains as before. However, in the last few years not much of significance has made the journey through the policy cycle. That said, I believe the policy cycle approach remains useful. For instance, it can be used in the analysis of executive policymaking, which seems likely to gain greater usage in the Obama administration.

As the subtitle indicates, *Public Policymaking: An Introduction* is intended to be a starting point for the study of public policymaking by giving some consideration to all of the stages or phases of the policymaking process. For those who wish to explore various stages more deeply, the suggested readings and websites listed at the end of each chapter will be helpful. After decades of studying the policy process, I still have much to learn.

While I am fully equipped with opinions on policy and politics, I have tried to be impartial and objective in my treatment of the many topics covered in this book. I have been informed, and I think with considerable success, by the principle of "intended neutrality" in writing this book. Analysis rather than advocacy and teaching rather than preaching have been my goals.

Organization and Updates

I have made many changes, updates, additions, and a few deletions in this revision, taking into account new developments in public policymaking, especially at the national level in the United States. I have also benefitted from recent additions to the scholarly literature on public policy formation. The basic framework of the book, however, remains intact.

Chapter 1, "The Study of Public Policy," has new material on distributive policy, elite theory, and the application of various policy approaches to the Wall Street Reform and Consumer Financial Protection Act.

Chapter 2, "The Policy-Makers and Their Environment," surveys the political environment, or context of policymaking, and presents the official and unofficial participants in the policy process. Material has been added on political culture, social change, the President, and the communications media. I retained the Snail Darter case, because though old, it is seminal.

Chapter 3, "Policy Formation: Problems, Agendas, and Formulation," examines policy problems and agendas, agenda-setting processes, and the formulation (or crafting) of policy proposals. These are the pre-adoption aspects of the policy process. Here one will encounter new material on policy problems, issue definition, agenda denial, an updating of coal mine safety and pollution control, and a new case study of the Affordable Care Act.

Chapter 4, "Policy Adoption," centers on decision-making processes and criteria and the adoption of policies. Here one will find new and/or updated material on public opinion, filibustering in the U.S. Senate, and the Israeli election. A new case study is included on the Family Smoking Prevention and Tobacco Control Act.

Chapter 5, "Budgeting and Public Policy," discusses the national budgetary process because of its importance for the substance, implementation, and impact of public policies, which I try to make more apparent. Budgetary numbers are updated. There is a new example on the ever-popular Animal and Plant Health Inspection Service and on the budgetary process, per se. The ongoing saga of the struggle for a balanced budget, which becomes more partisan, complicated, and seemingly hopeless as time goes on, has been modified and updated.

Chapter 6, "Policy Implementation," roams over much ground to provide understanding of the implementation or administration of public policies. Changes here include new material on the President and implementation, agency rule-making, the failed Nuclear Waste Disposal Act, tax expenditures, and "libertarian paternalism."

Chapter 7, "Policy Impact, Evaluation, and Change," probes the effects of policies, their evaluation, and possible termination. Numerous limited modifications, additions, and deletions have been made here. There is more on food safety, Head Start, and policy termination. The concluding case study on airline deregulation has also been updated. Does the air traveler in coach really feel better off?

Chapter 8, "Reflections and Observations," goes beyond stating conclusions. It is, rather, an informative essay on the American policymaking process, adding new information to the topic.

Companion Website

An exciting feature of this edition is the text's companion website, which provides additional resources for instructors and students. The Instructor website includes PowerPoint slides for classroom presentations, ideas for classroom activities, suggested paper topics, and an Instructor's Manual, while the Student website has flashcards for reviewing text terms, crossword puzzles, tutorial quizzes, and chapter outlines. Access the companion website at login.cengage.com.

Acknowledgments

I wish to express my appreciation to all who have assisted in the preparation of this edition. At the request of Cengage Learning, several scholars provided pre-revision reviews. They provided many good ideas and suggestions for change and improvement. I did not agree with everything that came at me, nor was I able to respond positively to some of their recommendations. Overall, though, they helped greatly in this revision. My thanks go to the following professors for reviewing the text and offering their evaluations, comments, and suggestions:

Mike Abels (University of Central Florida)

Jeffrey M. Brauer (Keystone College)

William Doyle (Vanderbilt University)

Shankar Prasad (NYU Wagner)

Stephen Sussman (Barry University)

Various colleagues at Texas A&M University and elsewhere were providers of information and advice. Carrie Kilpatrick, in her usual pleasant and agreeable style, quickly and accurately converted my handwritten copy into good typescript. Alberta (Mrs. Anderson) kept me on track to complete the revision. She has been a source of support for my scholarly endeavors and a positive influence on my life for several decades. At Cengage Learning, Carolyn Merrill and Eireann Aspell helped to get the revision underway, kept me in motion, and otherwise helped to bring the project to a successful conclusion. Thanks go to Jeffrey M. Brauer (Keystone College), who has written the Instructor's Manual for this edition. Also, much appreciation to my development editor, Jean Findley, at LEAP Publishing Services, Inc.

Any shortcomings in the book—errors of fact or faulty judgments—are my own doing, so responsibility for them is mine. I would appreciate readers informing me about them. "Sock it to me," as President Richard M. Nixon once said on the television program *Laugh In*.

1

The Study of Public Policy

In the course of their daily lives, people are affected, directly and indirectly, obviously and subtly, by an array of public policies. Take, for example, automobile owners. When a car is purchased, the Truth in Lending Act requires provision of accurate information by a lender on the cost of credit. The vehicle features safety equipment, such as a padded dash and seat belts, required by the National Highway Traffic Safety Administration, and a catalytic converter to reduce tailpipe emissions, necessitated by Environmental Protection Agency (EPA) rules. Out on the highway, financed jointly by the state and national governments, our driver needs to be aware of state and local traffic regulations or risk direct contact with law enforcement officials. State policy requires that the automobile be insured and that both it and the driver be licensed. The price of the gasoline it consumes is indirectly affected by national energy policies and directly increased by national and state excise taxes. The vehicle's gas mileage must meet the national corporate average fuel economy (CAFE) standard or a "gas guzzler" tax will apply. Many more laws and rules apply to automobiles.

Public policies in a modern, complex society are indeed ubiquitous. They confer advantages and disadvantages; cause pleasure, irritation, and pain; and collectively have important consequences for our well-being and happiness. They constitute a significant portion of our environment. This being so, we should know something about public policies, including how they are formed, budgeted, implemented, and evaluated. There are also scientific, professional, and political reasons for studying public policies and policymaking.

Scientifically, the systematic and rigorous study of the origin, development, and implementation of public policies will enhance our knowledge of political behavior and governance, as well as of public policy per se. How is policymaking affected by federalism and the separation of powers? Were pressure groups or public opinion or the media influential in the adoption of a policy? Why did government cease to confront a problem? Concern with questions of this sort are designated as *policy study*.

Professionally, a person may pursue a career as a policy analyst or evaluator. Practitioners of *policy analysis*, which draws heavily upon economic theory and statistical and mathematical analytical techniques, have been growing in number in recent decades.[1] Policy analysis has an applied orientation and seeks to identify the most efficient alternative (i.e., the one that will yield the largest net social benefit) for dealing with a current problem, such as the control of air pollution or the disposal of household garbage. A variant of policy analysis is evaluation research, which assesses how well policies attain their goals and the other societal effects that they may have. Cost–benefit analysis and risk analysis fall into this category.

Politically, many people want to engage in *policy advocacy*, using knowledge of public policy to formulate and promote "good" public policies that will have the "right" goals, that is, goals that serve their purposes. They may think of themselves as liberals, conservatives, libertarians, communitarians, or socialists and disagree greatly in their notions of what is good or just. The research efforts of policy advocates are frequently skewed by their wish to generate data and analysis in line with their preferences. In contrast, policy study is motivated by the intent to be impartial.

This book draws on the scientific policy studies approach to develop a basic understanding of the policymaking process, which is here viewed as an inherently political process involving conflict and struggle among people (public officials and private citizens) with conflicting interests, values, and desires on policy issues. In describing and analyzing the policymaking process, the scientific policy studies approach has three basic aims.[2] First, its primary goal is to explain the adoption of a policy rather than to identify or prescribe "good" or proper policy. Analysis, rather than advocacy, is its style. Second, it searches for the causes and consequences of public policies by applying social-scientific methodology, which is not restricted to the use of quantitative data and methodology. At a minimum, it requires that one should strive to be rational, empirical, and objective. Third, this approach aims to develop reliable theories and explanations about public policies and their politics. Thus, policy studies can be both theoretical and relevant to the more practical aspects of policymaking. It has been said that nothing is as practical as a good theory.

The Plan of This Book

There is not a single process by which public policies are formed. They do not come off an assembly line as do automobiles, refrigerators, and other standard products. Rather, variations in the subjects of policies will produce variations in the style, techniques, and politics of policymaking. Foreign policy, taxation, health-care financing, surface-transportation policy, occupational licensing, and land-use zoning are each characterized by a somewhat different policy process—different participants, procedures, decision rules, political patterns, and more. There is a case to be made for the argument that policy determines politics, though I do not fully subscribe to it.

Policymaking may also take different forms, depending upon whether its organizational venue is a legislature, the White House, the judiciary, or an administrative agency. Policymaking within agencies is more likely to feature hierarchy, secrecy (or low visibility), and the involvement of experts or professionals than is legislative policymaking. Courts do not act in the same way that legislatures or executives do. And certainly one can discern different patterns in tax policy formation in the United States, Great Britain, and Greece.

This variability does not mean, however, that there are no common functions or elements and that it is impossible to formulate generalizations on policy formation. Given the diversity and complexity in policymaking processes, the development of some sort of "general theory" that has broad explanatory power is an unrealistic aspiration.[3] But we can achieve a useful start toward what political scientists call "theory building" by striving to develop sound generalizations about such topics as who is involved in policy formation, on what sorts of issues, under what conditions, in what ways, and to what effect. Nor should we neglect to ask about how policy problems develop or obtain a place on governmental agendas. Such questions are not as simple as they may first appear.

To provide a conceptual framework to guide the examination of the policy process in the ensuing chapters, I view it as a sequential pattern of activities or functions that can readily be distinguished analytically although they may be empirically more difficult to pull apart. The following categories or stages are employed (see their portrayal in Table 1.1). Some illustrative questions are included.

1. *Problem identification and agenda setting.* The focus here is on how the problems that may become the targets of public policies are identified and specified. Why only some problems, out of all that exist, receive consideration by policy-makers requires an examination of agenda setting, that is, how governmental bodies decide what problems to address. What is a public problem? Why does some condition or matter become a public problem? How does a problem get on a governmental agenda? Why do some problems not achieve agenda status?

2. *Formulation.* This encompasses the creation, identification, or borrowing of proposed courses of action, often called alternatives or options, for resolving or ameliorating public problems. Who participates in policy formulation? How are alternatives for dealing with a problem developed? Are there difficulties and biases in formulating policy proposals?

3. *Adoption.* This involves deciding which proposed alternative, including taking no action, will be used to handle a problem. In American legislatures this function is performed by majorities. How is a policy alternative adopted or enacted? What requirements must be met? Who are the adopters? What is the content of the adopted policy?

TABLE 1.1

The Policy Process

Policy Terminology	Stage 1: Policy Agenda	Stage 2: Policy Formulation	Stage 3: Policy Adoption	Stage 4: Policy Implementation	Stage 5: Policy Evaluation
Definition	Those problems, among many, that receive the serious attention of public officials	Development of pertinent and acceptable proposed courses of action for dealing with a public problem	Development of support for a specific proposal so that a policy can be legitimized or authorized	Application of the policy by the government's administrative machinery	Efforts by the government to determine whether the policy was effective and why or why not
Common sense	Getting the government to consider action on the problem	What is proposed to be done about the problem	Getting the government to accept a particular solution to the problem	Applying the government's policy to the problem	Did the policy work?

Source: Adapted from James E. Anderson, David W. Brady, and Charles Bullock III, *Public Policy and Politics in the United States*, 2d ed. (Monterey, CA: Brooks/Cole, 1984).

4. *Implementation.* (A synonym is *administration.*) Here attention is on what is done to carry into effect or apply adopted policies. Often further development or elaboration of policies will occur in the course of their administration. Who is involved? What, if anything, is done to enforce or apply a policy? How does implementation help shape or determine the content and impact of policy?

5. *Evaluation.* This entails activities intended to determine what a policy is accomplishing, whether it is achieving its goals, and whether it has other consequences. Who is involved? Who is advantaged and disadvantaged by a policy? What are the consequences of policy evaluation? Are there demands for changes in or repeal of the policy? Are new problems identified? Is the policy process restarted because of evaluation?

Within this simplified framework, the formation and implementation of policies are seen as political in that they involve conflict and struggle among individuals and groups, officials and agencies, with conflicting ideas, interests, values, and information on public-policy issues. Policymaking is "political"; it involves "politics." That is, its features include conflict, negotiation, the exercise of power, bargaining, and compromise—and sometimes such nefarious practices as deception and bribery. There is no good reason to resist or disparage this conclusion, or to imitate those who derogate policies that they do not like with such statements as "It's nothing but politics." Although it is sometimes implied or even asserted that if enough analysis were done, if enough facts and data were gathered, all "right-thinking" people would agree on the appropriate course of action to handle a problem, this is not the way the world works. Quite reasonable people can disagree on policy issues because they have differing interests, values, and affiliations. Politics is the way a democratic society resolves such differences.

The policy-process (sometimes it is called the *policy cycle*) approach to policy study has several advantages. First, and most important, the policy-process approach centers attention on the officials and institutions who make policy decisions and the factors that influence and condition their actions. We need to be concerned about more than the complexity of public problems, the goals of the polity, the general forms policy responses can take, and similar matters. Knowledge of these is clearly of value, but we also want to know who makes policy decisions and how they do it. Consequently, answers are needed for such questions as: What is the legislature's role in policymaking? How does its structure affect decision-making? What sorts of factors or considerations influence the legislators' decisions? The policy-process approach not only helps us learn about policymaking and policy, it also causes us to take a more holistic view of how government works.

Second, policymaking usually incorporates the stages or categories of activity that I have described. Its sequential nature thus helps one capture and comprehend the flow of action in the actual policy process. However, in actuality the formulation and adoption stages may blend together, as when proposed legislation on welfare reform is modified during consideration in committees and on the House and Senate floors in order to win votes needed for its enactment. Administrative agencies issue rules elaborating policy, as in the case of public-lands policy, while implementing it (see Chapter 6, "Policy Implementation"). The adoption of a policy, such as restrictions on abortion, solves a problem for some people while it creates a problem for others, who then restart the policy process in an effort to modify or repeal the disliked policy. Even in such instances, the policy-process approach can be used to analytically distinguish the various activities involved.

Third, the policy-process approach is flexible and open to change and refinement.[4] Additional stages can be introduced if experience indicates that they would strengthen description and analysis. Perhaps budgeting should be recognized as a separate stage of the process. Various forms of data collection and analysis, whether quantitative (statistical), historical, legal, or normative (value-oriented), are compatible with it. It can be used to study a single policy (e.g., the Americans with Disabilities Act) or to compare the enactment and implementation of several civil-rights laws. Group, institutional, and other approaches to policy study can be fitted into it. The group approach may help explain policy adoption; institutionalism can cast light on its implementation. Systems theory may help alert us to some of its societal consequences.

Fourth, the policy-process approach helps present a dynamic and developmental, rather than static and cross-sectional, view of the policy process. It is concerned with the evolution of policy and requires that one think about what moves action on policy from one stage of the process to another. Moreover, it helps emphasize relationships, or interactions, among the participants in policymaking. Political parties, interest groups, legislative procedures, presidential commitments, public opinion, and other matters can be tied together as they drive and help explain the formation of a policy. Further, one can seek to discover how action at one stage of the process affects action at later stages. For example, how does the design and content of legislation ease or complicate its implementation? How does implementation affect its impact?

Fifth, the policy-process approach is not culture bound. It can readily be used to examine policymaking in foreign political systems. It also lends itself to manageable comparisons such as how problems reach governmental agendas, how policies are legitimated, or how policies are implemented in various countries. Some comparisons of this sort are included in this book.[5]

We now turn to an explanation of public policy and of various ways of categorizing public policies.

What Is Public Policy?

In general usage, the term *policy* designates the behavior of some actor or set of actors, such as an official, a governmental agency, or a legislature, in an area of activity such as public transportation or consumer protection.

Public policy also may be viewed as whatever governments choose to do or not to do. Such definitions may be adequate for ordinary discourse, but because we set out in this book to do a systematic analysis of public policy, a more precise definition or concept is needed to structure our thinking and to facilitate effective communication with one another.

In this book, a policy is defined as *a purposive course of action or inaction followed by an actor or set of actors in dealing with a problem or matter of concern.* This definition focuses on what is actually done instead of what is only proposed or intended; differentiates a policy from a decision, which is essentially a specific choice among alternatives; and views policy as something that unfolds over time.

Public policies are developed by governmental bodies and officials. (Nongovernmental actors and factors may of course influence public-policy development.) The special characteristics of public policies stem from their being formulated by what political scientist David Easton has called the "authorities" in a political system, namely, "elders, paramount chiefs, executives, legislators, judges, administrators, councilors, monarchs, and the like." These are, he says, the persons who "engage in the daily affairs of a political system," are "recognized by most members of the system as having responsibility for these matters," and take actions that are "accepted as binding most of the time by most of the members so long as they act within the limits of their roles."[6] In short, public policies are those produced by government officials and agencies. They also usually affect substantial numbers of people.

There are several implications of this concept of public policy as a relatively stable, purposive course of action followed by government in dealing with some problem or matter of concern. First, the definition links policy to purposive or goal-oriented action rather than to random behavior or chance occurrences. Public policies in modern political systems do not, by and large, just happen. They are instead designed to accomplish specified goals or produce definite results, although these are not always achieved. And, unintended consequences may occur. Proposed policies may be usefully thought of as hypotheses suggesting that specific actions be taken to achieve particular goals. Thus, to increase farm income, the national government has utilized income subsidies and production controls. These programs have indeed enhanced the incomes of many farmers, but by no means all.

The goals of a policy may be somewhat loosely stated and imprecise in content, thus providing a general direction rather than precise targets for its implementation. Those who want action on a problem may differ both as to what should be done and how it should be done. Ambiguity in language then can become a means for reducing conflict, at least for the moment. Compromise to secure agreement and build support may consequently yield general phrasing and lack of clarity in the statement of policy goals.

Second, policies consist of courses or patterns of action followed over time by governmental officials rather than their separate, discrete decisions. It is difficult to think of such actions as a presidential decision to honor a movie actor or a Social Security Administration decision to award disability benefits to John Doe as public policies. A policy includes not only the decision to adopt a law or make a rule on some topic but also the subsequent decisions that are intended to enforce or implement the law or rule. Industrial health and safety policy, for example, is shaped not only by the Occupational Safety and Health Act of 1970 but also by a stream of administrative rules and judicial decisions interpreting, elaborating, and applying (or not applying) the act to particular situations.

Third, public policies emerge in response to *policy demands*, or those claims for action or inaction on some public issue made by other actors—private citizens, group representatives, or legislators and other public officials—upon government officials and agencies. Such demands may range from general insistence that a municipal government "do something" about traffic congestion to a specific call for the national government to prohibit theft of pet dogs and cats for sale to medical and scientific research organizations. In short, some demands simply call for action; others also specify the action desired.

In response to policy demands, public officials make decisions that give content and direction to public policy. They may enact statutes, issue executive orders or edicts, promulgate administrative rules, or make judicial interpretations of laws. Thus, the decision by Congress to enact the Sherman Antitrust Act in 1890 was a policy decision; another was the 1911 Supreme Court ruling that the act prohibited only unreasonable restraints of trade rather than all restraints of trade. Each was of major importance in shaping that course of action called *antitrust policy*. (The Sherman Act also prohibits monopolization and attempts to monopolize.) Such decisions may be contrasted with the innumerable relatively routine decisions that officials make in the day-to-day application of public policy. The Department of Veterans Affairs, for example, makes hundreds of thousands of decisions every year on veterans' benefits; most, however, fall within the bounds of settled policy and can be categorized as routine decisions.

Policy statements in turn usually are formal expressions or articulations of public policy. Among these are legislative statutes, executive orders and decrees, administrative rules and regulations, and court opinions, as well as statements and speeches by public officials indicating the government's intentions and goals and what will be done to realize them. Policy statements are sometimes notably ambiguous. Witness the conflicts that arise over the meaning of statutory provisions or judicial holdings, or the time and effort expended analyzing and trying to divine the meaning of policy statements by national political leaders such as the president of the United States or the chair of the Federal Reserve Board. Different levels, branches, or units of government may also issue conflicting policy statements, as on such matters as environmental pollution or liability for consumer products.

Fourth, policy involves what governments actually do, not merely what they intend to do or what officials say they are going to do. If a legislature enacts a law requiring employers to pay no less than a stated minimum wage, but nothing is done to enforce the law, and subsequently little change occurs in economic behavior, it seems reasonable to contend that public policy actually takes the form of nonregulation of wages.

Relevant here is the concept of *policy outputs*, or the actions actually taken in pursuance of policy decisions and statements. This concept focuses our attention on such matters as amounts of taxes collected, miles of highway built, welfare benefits paid, restraints of trade eliminated, traffic fines collected, and foreign-aid projects undertaken. These can usually be enumerated with little difficulty. Examining policy outputs, we may find that a policy differs somewhat or even greatly from what policy statements indicate it should be.

Policy outputs should be distinguished from *policy outcomes*, which focus on a policy's societal consequences. For example, do longer prison terms reduce crime rates? Do air pollution control programs improve public health? Outputs can be counted; outcomes are often difficult or impossible to measure.

Fifth, a public policy may be either positive or negative. Some form of overt governmental action may deal with a problem on which action is demanded (positive), or governmental officials may decide to do nothing on some matter on which government involvement was sought (negative). In other words, governments can follow a policy of laissez-faire, or hands off, either generally or on some aspects of economic activity. Such inaction may have major consequences for a society or some groups, as in the late 1970s, when the national government decided to cease regulating commercial airline rates and routes.

Inaction becomes a public policy when officials decline to act on a problem—that is, when they decide an issue negatively. This choice differs from nonaction on a matter that has not become a public issue, has not been brought to official attention, and has not been considered or debated. A slightly ludicrous example is the lack of governmental action on the taking of earthworms—the activity has no seasons and no bag limits. Is this a public policy? The answer is no because it is not an issue and no decisions have been made.

Finally, public policy, at least in its positive form, is based on law and is authoritative. Members of a society usually accept as legitimate the facts that taxes must be paid, import controls must be obeyed, and highway speed limits must be complied with, unless one wants to run the risk of fines, jail sentences, or other legally imposed sanctions or disabilities. Thus, public policy has an authoritative, legally coercive quality that the policies of private organizations do not have. Indeed, a major characteristic distinguishing government from private organizations is its monopoly over the legitimate use of coercion. Governments can legally incarcerate people; private organizations cannot.

Some public policies may be widely violated even though they are authoritative, such as national prohibition in the 1920s and many highway speed limits. Moreover, enforcement may be limited, piecemeal, or sporadic. Are these still public policies? The answer is yes because they were on the statute books and enforcement was provided for. Whether such policies are effective or wise is another matter. Authoritativeness is a necessary but not a sufficient condition for effective public policy.

Categories of Public Policies

Governments at all levels in the United States—national, state, and local—have been increasingly active in producing public policies. Every year a large volume of laws and ordinances flows from the nation's national, state, and local legislative bodies. That volume of laws in turn is greatly exceeded by the quantity of rules and regulations produced by administrative agencies acting on the basis of legislative authorizations. This proliferation of public policies has occurred in such traditional areas of governmental action as foreign policy, transportation, education, welfare, law enforcement, economic regulation, and international trade. Much activity has also come in areas that received little attention until recent decades: economic stability, environmental protection, equality of opportunity, medical care, and consumer protection. (Table 1.2 illustrates the variety of laws passed.)

During the 112th Congress (2011–2012), 238 public laws were enacted. A great many involved naming public buildings and technical or limited changes in existing laws. Despite substantial partisan conflict, Congress was able to adopt several important statutes. Collectively, they dealt with a broad range of topics. All of them incorporate biases or preferences that benefit some groups and disadvantage or disappoint other groups. Only rarely does a public policy make everyone better off.

Given the large number and complexity of public policies in the United States, the task of trying to make sense of them is enormous. This section will

TABLE 1.2

Major Congressional Legislation, 2008

Economic Stimulus Act
Ensuring Continued Access to Student Loans Act
Extension of Higher Education Programs
Food, Conservation, and Energy Act (The Farm Bill)
Foreign Intelligence Surveillance Act Amendments
Consumer Product Safety Improvement Act
Americans with Disabilities Act Amendments
National Aeronautics and Space Administration Authorization Act
Emergency Economic Stabilization Act
Housing and Economic Recovery Act
Global AIDS Relief Reauthorization Act
Medicare Improvements for Patients and Providers Act
Rail Safety Improvement Act (included AMTRAK reauthorization)
Post-9/11 Veterans Educational Assistance Act
Energy Improvement and Extension Act
Mental Health Party and Addiction Equity Act
United States-India Nuclear Cooperation Act

Source: United States Statutes at Large 2008

summarize a number of general typologies that political scientists and others have developed for categorizing public policies. These typologies will prove much more useful in distinguishing among and generalizing about policies than some of the more traditional and widely used categorization schemes, such as by issue area (labor, welfare, civil rights, and foreign affairs), institution (legislative policies, judicial policies, and departmental policies), and time (New Deal era, post–World War II, and late nineteenth century). Although these categories are convenient for designating various sets of policies and organizing discussions about them, they are not helpful in developing generalizations because they do not reflect the basic characteristics and content of policies. The discussion of typologies will also provide the reader with a notion of the scope, diversity, and different purposes of public policies.

Constituent, Distributive, Regulatory, Self-Regulatory, and Redistributive Policies

This typology differentiates policies on the basis of their effects on society and the relationship among those involved in their formation.[7] We begin with constituent policies. (*Constituent* is used here in the sense that it involves the composition or makeup of government.) As Professor Theodore Lowi states: "Constituent policies are policies formally and explicitly concerned with the establishment of government structure, with the establishment of rules [or procedures] for the conduct of government, of rules that distribute or divide power and jurisdictions within which present and future government policies might be made."[8] This is sometimes referred to as "state-building."

A structural example of constituent policy is the creation of the Department of Homeland Security. In June 2002, President George W. Bush, who had argued that an executive department to manage counterterrorism programs was unnecessary, reversed course (or "flip-flopped") and called on Congress to create a Department of Homeland Security. Members of Congress previously had advocated setting up such a department, as had a presidential commission appointed by President Bill Clinton. Congress responded quickly to the president's recommendation, passing the Homeland Security Act in November 2002.

The new Department of Homeland Security pulled together functions from twenty-two units in other executive departments. These included the Immigration and Naturalization Service (Justice), Customs Service (Treasury), Coast Guard (Transportation), and Secret Service (Treasury), among others. No intelligence agencies (e.g., the Central Intelligence Agency and the National Security Agency) were included. By having these units lodged in the same vast and sprawling department (170,000 employees), it was believed that they would be able to act in a more unified and effective manner to protect the nation's internal security against terrorist attacks. Melding them into a coherent and effective operating department proved to be a difficult task.

A procedural example of constituent policy is the federal Administrative Procedure Act (APA) of 1946. This important statute, a response to the growth of administrative agency discretion in the early twentieth century, prescribes procedures to be used by agencies in notice and comment or informal rule-making. For example, APA requires notice of the proposed rule-making opportunity for interested persons to participate in the proceeding through oral or written submissions, publication of a proposed rule at least thirty days before it becomes effective, and opportunity for interested persons to petition for issuance, amendment, or repeal of a rule. The act's requirements for adjudication are much more detailed, but in both instances it is intended to ensure openness and fairness in agency decision-making.

Another example of a procedural policy is the requirement that an environmental impact statement (EIS) be prepared by federal agencies proposing major actions affecting the environment by the National Environmental Policy Act (NEPA). Its purpose is to cause agencies to give consideration to environmental effects before making their decisions. In itself NEPA adds nothing to the substance of policy; it neither prohibits nor requires particular agency actions toward the environment. Rather, it specifies what agencies must do when making a decision affecting the environment.

Constituent policies also include such matters as personnel practices and budgetary actions. Because they are concerned with government organization, procedures, and processes, constituent policies can have important substantive consequences. That is, how something is done or who has responsibility for acting may help determine what is actually done. Governmental procedures can be used here briefly to indicate the importance of constituent policies in this respect.

Frequently, efforts are made to use procedural issues to delay or prevent adoption of substantive decisions and policies. An agency's action may be challenged on the grounds that improper procedures were followed, as under APA, when it is really the substance of the action that is being resisted. Some Washington lawyers have become highly skilled in manipulating procedural rules to delay or negate agency action. Thus, because of procedural delays and complications (most of them produced by the maneuverings of the defendant company), it took the Federal Trade Commission thirteen years to complete a case compelling the manufacturer to remove the word *liver* from a product named "Carter's Little Liver Pills." (The product has no effect on one's liver.) If an agency becomes entangled with procedural requirements, it may lose the capacity for timely and effective action.

Distributive policies involve the allocation of benefits or services, at no charge, to particular segments of the population—individuals, groups, companies, or communities. These include subsidies, grants, loans, technical assistance, information (as on the weather), contracts, and river and harbor improvement actions. The federal departments of Agriculture, Commerce, Energy, and Transportation administer a wide range of distributive policies. Distributive policies may variously serve to enhance prices or incomes, reduce the cost or risk of actions, encourage research or economic development, stimulate economic activity, and provide recreational opportunities, tourism, and more. Perhaps needless to state, the expenditure of public funds is usually involved, although not in the case of protective tariffs or import limitations.

Typically, distributive policies do not impose costs upon any specific group. Rather, the costs are paid by the public treasury, which means taxpayers generally. Thus distributive policies appear to create only winners and no specific losers, although obviously someone does stand for their financial costs.

Although many distributive policies are of low political visibility, there are exceptions. One example is the successful automobile industry bailout in 2009. To help stave off their collapse and the loss of hundreds of thousands of jobs, the government ultimately loaned General Motors and Chrysler (Ford was in better shape), their finance companies, and many of their suppliers $82 billion. Also, $3 billion was put into a Cash for Clunkers program for consumers to encourage them to swap gas guzzlers for newer models. Many Republicans and Conservatives were opposed to these efforts. However, the companies survived. The government made a billion dollars on its loan to Chrysler but is likely to lose several billion dollars on the General Motors deal.[9]

Another example is Future Gen. In 2003, the government initiated a competitive program to construct a coal-fired electric power generating plant, using carbon capture and storage technology that would have no CO_2 emissions. A consortium focused on Mattoon, Illinois, was the winner. Because of its high cost, the Bush administration decided to cancel the project. The Obama administration decided the project should go forward. It should be completed by the time you read this.[10]

A discussion of distributive policies would not be complete without attention to pork barrel projects ("earmarks"). The Office of Management and Budget defines "pork" or an earmark as "funds provided by Congress for projects or programs where congressional direction (in bill or report language) circumvents Executive Branch merit-based or competitive allocation processes, or specifies the location or recipient, or otherwise curtails the ability of the Executive Branch to manage critical aspects of the funds allocation process." So defined, OMB identified nearly 9,200 earmarks in 2010 appropriations bills worth $11 billion.[11] Most states and congressional districts shared in the bacon. Funds were directed to highway projects, research activities, public buildings, tourist attractions, and more.

Scattered around the country, these projects have little connection with one another, which supports Professor Theodore J. Lowi's contention that distributive policies "are virtually not policies at all but are highly individualized decisions that only by accumulation can be called a policy."[12] Each locality and its supporters usually seek designated money for their own project without challenging the right of others to do the same. Most projects thus have some friends and no enemies in Congress, and presidents usually choose to leave them alone. Very recently, as earmarks came under sharp criticism as "wasteful spending," their numbers greatly diminished. Even skilled congressional "porkers" halted their efforts.

Regulatory policies impose restrictions or limitations on the behavior of individuals and groups. That is, they reduce the freedom or discretion to act of those regulated, whether bankers, utility companies, meat-packers, or saloonkeepers. In this sense they clearly differ from distributive policies, which increase the freedom or discretion of the persons or groups affected.

When we think of regulatory policies, we usually focus on business regulatory policies, such as those pertaining to control of pollution or regulation of transportation industries. Among others, these sorts of policies were the focus of the movement for deregulation. The most extensive variety of regulatory policies, however, is that which deals with criminal behavior against persons and property. What are called social regulatory policies deal with such topics as affirmative action, school prayer, gun control, pornography, and abortion, and involve the regulation of personal behavior.[13]

The formation of regulatory policy usually features conflict between two groups or coalitions of groups, with one side seeking to impose some sort of control on the other side, which customarily resists, arguing either that control is unnecessary or that the wrong kind of control is being proposed. Amid this opposition, regulatory decisions involve clear winners and losers, although the winners usually get less than they initially sought. (When the winners are public-interest groups, they may not gain direct material benefits from policies that, like the Clean Air Act, provide broad social benefits.) It is often difficult, however, to identify all the purposes and consequences of regulatory policies. Regulatory policies take several forms.

Some regulatory policies set forth general rules of behavior, directing that actions be taken or commanding that others not be taken. The Sherman Act (which is a favorite of mine) in effect tells businesses, "Thou shalt not monopolize or attempt to monopolize or act to restrain trade." These prohibitions are enforced by actions brought in the federal courts against violators. In contrast, public-utility regulation by state governments involved detailed control of entry into the business, standards of service, financial practices, and rates charged by electric, telephone, and other utility companies. Comparatively, antitrust regulation entails much less restriction of business discretion than does public-utility regulation.

Consumer-protection policies illustrate other variations in regulatory policies. Some statutes, such as the Pure Food and Drug Act of 1906 and the Drug Amendments of 1962, set standards for quality that drug manufacturers must comply with. Thus, before new drugs can be put on the market, they must be shown to meet the standards for safety in use and efficacy for the purposes intended. Other consumer legislation, such as the Consumer Credit Protection Act, requires creditors to provide borrowers with accurate information on interest and other financing costs for credit purchases. The first sort of policy is intended to prevent products that do not meet designated standards from entering the marketplace; the second type is meant to provide consumers with enough information to make informed decisions.

Some regulatory policies, such as those that restrict entry into a business such as television broadcasting or electric power distribution, are implemented by decisions that confer benefits on some and deny them to others. Of the several applicants for a television broadcast license for a city that may be before the Federal Communications Commission, only one can be propitiated. These can be called *competitive regulatory policies* because they limit the number of providers of specific goods and services. They also may regulate the quality of services that can be provided to consumers.[14]

Self-regulatory policies are similar to competitive regulatory policies in that they involve restricting or controlling some matter or group. Unlike competitive regulatory policies, however, self-regulatory policies are usually more controlled by the regulated group as a means of protecting or promoting the interests of its members. Several hundred professions and occupations, ranging from tree surgeons and auctioneers to lawyers and physicians, are licensed in one or more states; about sixty are licensed in a majority of states. Commonly licensed health professionals include chiropractors, dentists, dental hygienists, emergency medical technicians, optometrists, pharmacists, physicians, podiatrists, practical and registered nurses, psychologists, sanitarians, and social workers.[15]

The usual policymaking pattern here is for a professional or occupational group acting on its own to seek licensing legislation from the state legislature. Outside the ranks of the interested group, interest in the matter usually is slight. The result is enactment of a licensing law, whose implementation is delegated to a board dominated by members from the licensed group. In time, entry into the licensed occupation or profession may be restricted, and the prices charged for its specialized services may increase. It is unclear to what extent licensing improves the quality of services available to the public.[16]

Redistributive policies involve deliberate efforts by the government to shift the allocation of wealth, income, property, or rights among broad classes or groups of the population, such as haves and have-nots, proletariat and bourgeoisie. "The aim involved is not use of property but property itself, not equal treatment but equal possession, not behavior but being."[17] In American society, redistributive policies ultimately involve disagreements between liberals (pro) and conservatives (con) and tend to be highly productive of conflict.

The usual pattern in redistributive policy shifts resources from haves to have-nots. It is possible, however, for the flow to reverse. Farm subsidy payments under the agricultural income-support programs go mostly to large commercial farmers; small-scale farmers derive few benefits, yet everyone who pays taxes contributes to financing of these programs. Typically, however, such instances are not debated as redistributive,[18] perhaps because of reluctance to acknowledge that sometimes the haves benefit at the expense of the have-nots.

Redistributive policies are difficult to enact precisely because they involve the reallocation of money, rights, or power. Those who possess money or power rarely yield them willingly, regardless of how strenuously some may discourse upon the "burdens" and heavy responsibility attending their possession. Because money and power are good coinage in the political realm, those who possess them have ample means to resist their diminution.

Policies that have (or have had) some redistributive influence include the graduated income tax, Medicare and Medicaid, the War on Poverty, the Voting Rights Act, and legislative reapportionment. The Johnson administration's War on Poverty represented an effort to shift wealth and other resources to blacks and poor people. Encountering much resistance from conservatives and lacking strong presidential support, it was gradually dispersed and dismantled, but not without effect. Although most of the individual antipoverty programs (such as Head Start and the community action or service programs) still function, they have lost much of their redistributive quality. The Voting Rights Act, which on the whole has been enforced with considerable strength by the Justice Department, has helped to produce a substantial increase in black voter registration, voting, and state and local officeholding in the South.

The graduated income tax, which is based on the principle of ability to pay (those who have more income can fairly be expected to pay at progressively higher rates), has now lost some of its redistributive potential. The top marginal rate once was as high as 91 percent. In the early 1980s, the rates ranged from 14 to 50 percent over a dozen income brackets, which still held out the possibility of considerable redistribution. The Tax Reform Act of 1986, enacted by Congress with strong support from President Reagan, who believed that high marginal tax rates both infringed on individual liberty and discouraged economic growth, provided for only two tax brackets at 15 and 28 percent.[19] Brackets of 31, 36, and 39.6 percent were added in the 1990s, however. These marginal tax rates were reduced over the next several years by tax-reduction legislation enacted in 2001 at the urging of the George W. Bush administration. In 2008, there were six rates: 10, 15, 25, 28, 33, and 35 percent. The top rate was restored to 39.6 percent in 2012 for high-income people.

Redistributive policies are not only difficult to obtain, they are also hard to retain, as the discussion of the income tax indicates. Equality of result or condition (i.e., equality in income or standard of living) is not overly appealing to most Americans, whatever they think about equality of opportunity.

Material and Symbolic Policies   Public policies may also be described as either material or symbolic, depending upon the kind of benefits they allocate.[20] Material provide tangible resources or substantive power to their beneficiaries, or impose real disadvantages on those who are adversely affected. Legislation requiring employers to pay a prescribed minimum wage, appropriating money for a public-housing program, or providing income-support payments to farmers is material in content and effect.

Symbolic policies, in contrast, have little real material impact on people. They do not deliver what they appear to deliver; they allocate no tangible advantages and disadvantages. Rather, they appeal to people's cherished values, such as peace, patriotism, and social justice. A historic example of a symbolic policy is the Kellogg-Briand Pact of 1928, by which the United States and fourteen other countries agreed to outlaw war. Comment on its impact seems unnecessary.

Burning of the U.S. flag as a symbolic form of political protest has agitated members of Congress for many years. In 1989, the Flag Protection Act provided criminal penalties for any person who "knowingly mutilates, defaces, physically defiles, burns, maintains on the floor or ground, or tramples upon any flag of the United States." Quickly challenged, the act was declared unconstitutional by the U.S. Supreme Court as an infringement on the freedom of expression protected by the First Amendment. The Court's ruling touched off a public and political furor. Beginning early in the 1990s, the House several times has approved a constitutional amendment banning "physical desecration" of the flag.[21] Each time, it has failed by a few votes to get the necessary two-thirds approval of the Senate. This is an issue that has emotional appeal for many Americans, especially conservatives.

Occasionally a policy that appears to be mostly symbolic may turn out to have important consequences. The Endangered Species Act of 1973, which is intended to help ensure the survival of rare animals and plants, initially appeared to be a statement of good intentions with few costs. Little opposition attended its enactment. As implemented, however, the act has had important effects, sometimes being used to block construction projects, timber cutting, and other activities that would threaten or destroy the habitats of endangered species, such as spotted owls, California gnatcatchers, and the red-cockaded woodpecker.[22]

Most policies are neither entirely symbolic nor wholly material. The symbolic and material categories should instead be viewed as the poles of a continuum, with most policies being ranged along the continuum depending upon how symbolic or material they are in practice. The Sherman Act, as an instrument for "trust busting," for breaking up large monopolistic companies, has long been symbolic. With the exception of AT&T, no trusts have been broken up since the Progressive Era. On the other hand, beginning with the Carter administration and continuing on into the Clinton administration and the Obama administration, the Sherman Act has been applied with some vigor against collusive behavior such as price fixing, bid rigging, and market allocation. Here it has had substantial material impact.

Policies that are ostensibly material as labeled by legislative language may be rendered essentially symbolic by administrative action or by the legislature's failure to provide adequate funds for their implementation. The goals of the Housing Act of 1949 and later laws were made substantially symbolic by the subsequent failure of Congress to provide the authorized level of funding for public-housing construction.[23] On the other hand, policies may move from the more symbolic to the more material category. Professor Bruce I. Oppenheimer argues that policy for controlling oil pollution was largely symbolic during the years 1947 to 1966.[24] Legislation was on the books, but little was done to enforce it. Since 1966, as the environmental movement gained strength and public concern about pollution intensified, enforcement became much stronger and additional legislation, such as the Oil Pollution Act, was passed. Oil spills now draw strong responses. Witness what occurred following the massive April 2010 spill in the Gulf of Mexico at a BP drilling operation.

The material–symbolic typology is especially useful to keep in mind when analyzing effects of policy because it directs attention beyond formal policy statements. It also alerts us to the important role of symbols in political behavior.

Policies Involving Collective Goods or Private Goods Public policies may also involve the provision of either collective (indivisible) goods or private (divisible) goods.[25] The nature of collective goods is such that if they are provided for one person, they must be provided for all. Moreover, one person's consumption of a collective good does not deny it to others. A standard example is national defense: There is no effective way to provide it for some citizens and exclude others from its benefit, enjoyment, or other consequences, nor to calculate that some citizens benefit more from it than others. Thus, an economically rational person would never voluntarily pay for national defense, clean air, or mosquito control, choosing rather to be a free rider and let others stand the costs. Hence, defense must be provided, if we want it, by government and financed by taxation. Other examples of collective goods are public safety, traffic control, and scenic beauties.

Private goods, in contrast, may be broken into units and purchased or charged by the individual user or beneficiary, and are available in the marketplace. Others may be excluded from their use. Various social goods provided by government (garbage collection, postal service, medical care, museums, public housing, and national parks) have some characteristics of private goods. Charges and fees are sometimes, but not always, levied on users. Whether such goods, which conceivably could be provided by the market economy, will be provided by the government is a function of political decisions influenced by tradition (parks), notions of the proper functions of government (the post office), the desire of users or beneficiaries to shift some of their costs to others (federal crop insurance), and the like.

Some argue that only collective goods should be the subject of public policy. The tendency, however, has been more and more to convert private goods into social goods by government action. Many consider ill health, unemployment, environmental pollution, industrial accidents and disease, and misrepresentation in the marketplace to be collective, rather than individual, problems—matters affecting the entire population, hence involving public goods for which the entire society should pay. Generally, the more something is thought to have the qualities of a public good, the more likely people are to accept its provision by government. If it seems clear that some benefit more directly than others, there may also be a desire to levy charges, fees, or taxes on the direct beneficiaries to cover part of the cost. Thus, we encounter user fees at national parks, tuition at public colleges, rent in public-housing projects, and tolls for some bridges and highways.

The privatization movement, encouraged in the 1980s by the Reagan administration, represented a counterforce to the long-run tendency to expand the scope of social goods. Based on free-market economic theory, privatization supports transferring many government assets or programs to the private sector and contracting with private companies to handle many public services, whether the collection of garbage or the operation of prisons. "The private sector, it is argued, will perform these functions more efficiently and economically than the public sector."[26] Sometimes it actually does.

The results of the privatization movement at the national level are mixed. A successful example is the sale of Conrail, which operated several railroads in the Northeast and Midwest, to a private corporation. Nothing, however, came out of proposals by the Reagan administration and others to sell public lands in the western states to private buyers.[27] Even western ranchers and other supporters of the "sagebrush rebellion," which promoted transferring ownership of public lands to state and local governments, lost interest in privatization. Their access to public grazing lands with low lease rates would have been jeopardized by privatization. Congress was also quite skeptical about the sale of public lands.

Approaches to Policy Study

Political and social scientists have developed many models, theories, approaches, concepts, and schemes for analyzing policymaking and its related component, decision-making. Indeed, political scientists have often displayed more facility and zeal for theorizing about public policymaking than for actually studying policy and the policymaking process. Nonetheless, theories and concepts are needed to guide the study of public policy, to facilitate communication, and to suggest possible explanations for policy actions. Those who aspire to systematically study the policymaking process need some guidelines and criteria of relevance to focus their effort and to prevent aimless meandering through the fields of political data. What we find when we engage in research depends partly upon what we are looking for; policy concepts, models, and theories give direction and structure to our inquiry.

This section will survey several theoretical approaches to the study of public policy. But first we must distinguish between policymaking and decision-making, a distinction that students of public policy do not always make with clarity, if at all.

Decision-making, which will be treated in the chapter titled "Policy Adoption," involves making a discrete choice from among two or more alternatives, such as whether or not to read further in this book. Theories of decision-making deal with the criteria and processes used in making such choices.

A *policy*, as defined earlier, is "a purposive course of action or inaction followed by an actor or set of actors in dealing with a problem or matter of concern." Policymaking thus typically encompasses a flow and pattern of action that extends over time and includes many decisions, some routine and some not so routine. Rarely will a policy be synonymous with a single decision. Here is a mundane illustration: It would not be accurate for a person to state that it was his policy to take a bath on Saturday night if in fact he did so infrequently, however, elegant and thoughtful the decision-making process that led to his doing so on a rare Saturday. It is the course of action, the pattern or regularity, that defines policy, not an isolated event. In the example, the policy is best thought of as going dirty.

The theoretical approaches discussed here include political systems theory, group theory, elite theory, institutionalism, and rational-choice theory. Although most of these approaches were not developed specifically for analyzing policy formation, they can readily be bent to that purpose. In addition, all of them can be fitted into the policy-process framework. They are useful to the extent that they direct our attention to important political phenomena, help clarify and organize our thinking, and suggest explanations for political activity or, in our case, public policies. Limitations and criticisms are mentioned as the discussion proceeds.

Political Systems Theory

Public policy may be viewed as a political system's response to demands arising from its environment.

The political system, as Easton defines it, comprises those identifiable and interrelated institutions and activities (what we usually think of as governmental institutions and political processes) in a society that make authoritative allocations of values (decisions) that are binding on society. The environment consists of all phenomena—the social system, the economic system, and the biological setting—that are external to the boundaries of the political system. Thus, at least analytically one can separate the political system from all the other components of a society.[28]

Inputs into the political system from the environment consist of demands and supports. Demands are the claims for action that individuals and groups make to satisfy their interests and values. Support is rendered when groups and individuals abide by election results, pay taxes, obey laws, and otherwise accept the decisions and actions undertaken by the political system in response to demands. The amount of support for a political system indicates the extent to which it is regarded as legitimate, or as authoritative and binding on its citizens.

Outputs of the political system include laws, rules, judicial decisions, and the like. Regarded as the authoritative allocations of values, they constitute public policy. The concept of feedback indicates that public policies (or outputs) made at a given time may subsequently alter the environment and the demands arising therefrom, as well as the character of the political system itself. Policy outputs may produce new demands, which lead to further outputs, and so on in a never-ending flow of public policy (see Figure 1.1).

FIGURE 1.1

A Model of the Political System

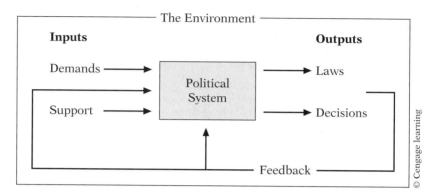

The usefulness of systems theory in studying public policy is limited by its highly general and abstract nature. It does not, moreover, say much about the procedures and processes by which decisions are made and policy is developed within the "black box" called the political system. Indeed, systems theory depicts government as simply responding to demands made upon it, and its results are sometimes characterized as "input-output studies." (For an illustration, see the discussion in Chapter 2 in the section headed Socioeconomic Conditions.) Nonetheless, this approach can be helpful in organizing inquiry into policy formation. It also alerts us to some important facets of the political process, such as these: How do inputs from the environment affect the content of public policy and the operation of the political system? How in turn does public policy affect the environment and subsequent demands for policy action? How well is the political system able to convert demands into public policy and preserve itself over time?

Group Theory   According to the group theory of politics, public policy is the product of the group struggle. One writer states, "What may be called public policy is the equilibrium reached in this [group] struggle at any given moment, and it represents a balance which the contending factions or groups constantly strive to weight in their favor."[29] Many public policies do reflect the activities of groups. Examples include the AFL-CIO and minimum-wage legislation, farm groups and agricultural subsidies, the National Rifle Association and gun-control policies, and the National Education Association and federal aid to public schools.

Group theory rests on the contention that interaction and struggle among groups are the central facts of political life. A group is a collection of individuals that may, on the basis of shared attitudes or interests, make claims upon other groups in society. It becomes a political interest group "when it makes a claim through or upon any of the institutions of government."[30] And many groups do just that. The individual is significant in politics only as a participant in or a representative of groups. It is through groups that individuals seek to secure their political preferences.

A central concept in group theory is that of *access*. To have influence and to be able to help shape governmental decisions, a group must have access, or the opportunity to contact and express its viewpoints to decision-makers.[31] Obviously, if a group is unable to communicate with decision-makers, if no one in government will listen, its chances of affecting policymaking are slim. Access may result from the group's being organized, from its having status, good leadership, or resources such as money for campaign contributions. Social lobbying—the wining, dining, and entertaining of legislators and other public officials—can be understood as an effort to create access by engendering a feeling of obligation to the groups involved. Then, when a group wishes to discuss policy matters with an official, it will have an opportunity to present its case or have its telephone calls returned. Contributions to legislators by political action committees (PACs) are also often justified as a way of acquiring or maintaining access.

In the nature of things, some groups will have more access than others. Public policy at any given time will reflect the interests of those who are dominant. As groups gain and lose power and influence, public policy will be altered in favor of the interests of those gaining influence against the interests of those losing it.

The role of government ("official groups") in policy formation is described by one proponent of group theory:

> The legislature referees the group struggle, ratifies the victories of the successful coalitions, and records the terms of the surrenders, compromises, and conquests in the form of statutes. Every statute tends to represent compromises because the process of accommodating conflicts of group interests is one of deliberation and consent. The legislative vote on any issue tends to represent the composition of strength, i.e., the balance of power, among the contending groups at the moment of voting.... Administrative agencies of the regulatory kind are established to carry out the terms of the treaties that the legislators have negotiated and ratified. . . . The judiciary, like the civilian bureaucracy, is one of the instrumentalities for the administration of the agreed rules.[32]

Group theory focuses on one of the major dynamic elements in policy formation, especially in pluralist societies such as the United States, but it seems both to overstate the importance and power of groups and to understate the independent and creative role that public officials can play in the policy process. Indeed, many groups have been generated by public policies. The American Farm Bureau Federation, which developed around the agricultural extension program, is a notable example, as is the National Head Start Association. Public officials also may acquire a stake in particular programs and act as an interest group supporting their continuance. In the United States some welfare-agency employees, including social workers, prefer current programs, with their emphasis on supervision and services (as well as benefits), to a guaranteed annual income, which would probably eliminate some of their jobs.

Another shortcoming of group theory is that in actuality many people (e.g., the poor and disadvantaged) and interests (such diffuse interests as natural beauty and social justice) are either not represented or only poorly represented in the group struggle. As Professor E. E. Schattschneider remarks about the underorganization of the poor, "The flaw in the pluralist heaven is that the heavenly chorus sings with a strong upper-class accent."[33] Those who are not represented will have little voice in policymaking and thus their interests are likely to be slighted therein.

Finally, from a methodological perspective, it seems misleading and inefficient to try to explain politics and policymaking solely in terms of interests and the group struggle. This bias leads to neglect of many other factors, such as ideas and institutions, that abound and that independently affect the development of policy. The reductionism or unicausal explanation that results when all political phenomena are crammed into the group concept should therefore be avoided.[34]

Elite Theory

Approached from the perspective of elite theory, public policy can be regarded as reflecting the values and preferences of a governing elite. The essential argument of elite theory is that public policy is not determined by the demands and actions of the people or the "masses" but rather by a ruling elite whose preferences are carried into effect by public officials and agencies.

Professors Thomas Dye and Harmon Zeigler provide a summary of elite theory:

1. Society is divided into the few who have power and the many who do not. [Only a small number of persons allocate values for society; the masses do not decide public policy.]

2. The few who govern are not typical of the masses who are governed. Elites are drawn disproportionately from the upper socioeconomic strata of society.

3. The movement of non-elites to elite positions must be slow and continuous to maintain stability and avoid revolution. Only non-elites who have accepted the basic elite consensus can be admitted to governing circles.

4. Elites share a consensus on the basic values of the social system and the preservation of the system. [In the United States, the elite consensus includes private enterprise, private property, limited government, and individual liberty.]

5. Public policy does not reflect demands of the masses but rather the prevailing values of the elite. Changes in public policy will be incremental rather than revolutionary. [Incremental changes permit responses to events that threaten a social system with a minimum of alteration or dislocation of the system.]

6. Elites may act out of narrow self-serving motives and risk undermining mass support, or they may initiate reforms, curb abuse, and undertake public-regarding programs to preserve the system and their place in it.

7. Active elites are subject to relatively little direct influence from apathetic masses. Elites influence masses more than masses influence elites.[35]

So stated, elite theory is a challenging theory of policy formation. Policy is the product of elites, reflecting their values and serving their ends, one of which may be a desire to provide in some way for the welfare of the masses. Dye argues that development of civil-rights policies in the United States during the 1960s can be suitably explained by elite theory. These policies were "a response of a national elite to conditions affecting a small minority of Americans rather than a response of national leaders to majority sentiments." Thus, for example, the "elimination of legal discrimination and the guarantee of equality of opportunity in the Civil Rights Act of 1964 was achieved largely through the dramatic appeals of middle-class black leaders to the conscience of white elites."[36]

This interpretation presents a narrow perspective on both who is affected by or interested in civil-rights policies and the explanation for adoption of the Civil Rights Act of 1964. Certainly leadership in Congress and the executive branch was very important, but so too were civil-rights protests and marches, public opinion, and support from an array of nonblack organizations. The civil-rights movement of the 1960s was far more than an effort by black leaders to appeal to the conscience of white elites.

Elite theory focuses our attention on the role of leadership in policy formation and on the reality that in any political system, a few govern the many. Whether elites rule and determine policy, with little influence from the masses, is a difficult proposition to handle. It cannot be proved merely by assertions that the "establishment runs things," which has been a familiar plaint in recent years. Political scientist Robert Dahl argues that to defend the proposition successfully, one must identify "a controlling group, less than a majority in size, that is not a pure artifact of democratic rules . . . a minority of individuals whose preferences regularly prevail in cases of differences of preferences on key political issues."[37] It may be that elite theory has more utility for analysis and explanation of policy formation in some political systems, such as developing or Eastern European countries, than in others, such as the pluralist democracies of the United States and Canada. Sociologist William Domhoff has long argued, however, that there is an American upper class, based on the ownership and control of large corporations, which is in fact a governing class.[38] There is a case to be made for his viewpoint. Since the early 1980s, the income and wealth of the top 1 percent of taxpayers has soared. Billionaires have become numerous; many choose to become politically active. On the other hand, the income of most of the population has stagnated. Then in 2010, the U.S. Supreme Court declared unconstitutional, as a violation of freedom of speech, legislation restricting campaign spending by corporations and others.[39] In 2012, some persons and corporations spent tens of millions of dollars on political campaigns, mostly to defeat the reelection of Barack Obama or Democratic candidates.

Institutionalism The study of government institutions (or organizations) is one of the oldest concerns of political science. This is not surprising since political life generally revolves around governmental institutions such as legislatures, executives, courts, and political parties; public policy, moreover, is authoritatively determined and implemented by these institutions.

Traditionally, the institutional approach concentrated on describing the more formal and legal aspects of governmental institutions: their formal structure, legal powers, procedural rules, and official functions or activities. Formal relationships with other institutions might also be considered, such as legislative–executive relations. Usually little was done to explain how institutions actually operated as opposed to how they were supposed to operate, to analyze public policies produced by the institutions, or to discover the relationships between institutional structure and public policies.

Subsequently, political scientists turned their attention in teaching and research to the political processes within governmental or political institutions, concentrating on the behavior of participants in the process and on political realities rather than formalism. In the study of the legislatures, interest shifted from simply describing the legislature as an institution to analyzing and explaining its operation over time, from its static to its dynamic aspects. In the academic curriculum, the course on the legislature often came to be about the legislative process.

Institutionalism, with its emphasis on the formal or structural aspects of institutions, can nonetheless be usefully employed in policy analysis. An institution is, in part, a set of regularized patterns of human behavior that persist over time and perform some significant social function or activity. To describe institutions as "rules," as some do, is to oversimplify. It is their differing patterns of behavior that really distinguish courts from legislatures, from administrative agencies, and so on. These regularized patterns of behavior, which we often call rules or structures, can affect decision-making and the content of public policy. Rules, structural arrangements, and other institutional features are usually not neutral in their effects; rather, they tend to favor some interests in society over others and some policy results over others.

It is contended that some of the Senate rules (and traditions, which often have the effect of rules), such as those relating to unlimited debate and action by unanimous consent, favor the interests of legislative minorities over majorities. Many actions in the Senate, such as bringing bills up for consideration and closing off debate on them, are done by unanimous consent. Thus, one senator, so inclined, can block action by the Senate.

In the American federal system, which allocates governmental power among the national and state governments, several arenas of action are created. Some groups may have more influence if policy is made at the national level, whereas others may benefit more from state policymaking. Civil-rights groups, for example, have received a better response in Washington, DC, than in the capitals of the southern states. Groups advocating adoption of English as the nation's official language, however, have fared better at the state level. Since 1983 some twenty states adopted such laws, but Congress has been unsympathetic. Indeed, the Voting Rights Act provides that in some states ballots must be printed in foreign languages as well as in English.

In summary, institutional structures, arrangements, and procedures often have important consequences for the adoption and content of public policies. They provide part of the context for policymaking, which must be considered along with the more dynamic aspects of politics, such as political parties, groups, and public opinion, in policy study. By itself, however, institutional theory can provide only partial explanations of policy. It has little to say about what drives the policy process, the dynamic forces of politics.

Rational-Choice Theory   The rational-choice theory, which is sometimes called *social-choice*, *public-choice*, or *formal theory*, originated with economists and involves applying the principles of micro economic theory to the analysis and explanation of political behavior (or non-market decision-making). It has now gained many adherents among political scientists.

One of the earliest uses of rational-choice theory to study the political process is Anthony Downs's *Economic Theory of Democracy*.[40] In this influential book, Downs assumes that voters and political parties act as rational decision-makers who seek to maximize attainment of their preferences. Parties formulated whatever policies would win them most votes, and voters sought to maximize the portion of their preferences that could be realized through government action. In attempting to win elections, political parties moved toward the center of the ideological spectrum to appeal to the greatest number of voters and maximize their voting support. Thus, rather than providing voters with "meaningful alternatives," parties will become as much alike as possible, thereby providing an "echo rather than a choice."

Let us now look more closely at the major components of rational-choice theory. One of its basic axioms is that political actors, like economic actors, act rationally in pursuing their own self-interest. Thus, economist James Buchanan, a leading proponent of rational-choice theory, contends that politicians are guided by their self-interest rather than by an altruistic commitment to such goals as statesmanship or the national interest. "This should be no surprise," says Buchanan, "because governments are made up of individuals, and individuals operate from self-interest when they are engaged in a system of exchange, whether this is in the market economy or in politics."[41]

Individuals who are engaged in decision-making exchanges or transactions, such as voting, also have preferences that vary from person to person. Being rational, it is argued, individuals can comprehend and rank their preferences from most to least desired. In making decisions (whether economic or political), they are guided by these preferences and will seek to maximize the benefits they gain. In short, people are self-interested utility maximizers, not the uninformed, confused, or irrational choice-makers often depicted in analyses of political behavior.

A second basic axiom of rational-choice theory involves methodological individualism. The individual decision-maker is the primary unit of analysis and theory. The individual's preferences or values are assumed to be more important than other values—collective, organizational, or social. Conversely, rational-choice theorists argue that the actions of organizations and groups can be satisfactorily explained in terms of the behavior of a model individual. Nothing substantial will be lost by so doing in explaining the behavior of all persons.

For example, a rational-choice explanation of why Congress delegates discretionary power to administrative agencies begins with the assumption that the preference of members of Congress is to get reelected.[42] To this end, legislators delegate power to agencies, knowing that in exercising that power the agencies will create problems for their constituents. Legislators will then be called on by their constituents to assist them with their bureaucratic problems, and in return for assistance, the grateful constituents will vote to reelect the legislators. The pursuit of self-interest by the members of Congress thus explains the delegation of power and the growth of bureaucracy.

Some rational-choice theorists have explored the effects of incomplete or imperfect information and uncertainty on policymaking.[43] Political decision-makers are said to be possessed of differing amounts of information (a condition called *information asymmetry*) and are uncertain about the outcomes or consequences of laws and policies when they are implemented. In Congress, legislative committee members, as policy specialists and the basic developers of legislation, are best informed about the relationship between a proposed policy and its likely consequences. In comparison, the rank-and-file members of Congress, who make the final decisions on the enactment of legislation, have only limited knowledge of the policy–consequences relationships. Conceivably, this information asymmetry would permit committee members to act strategically and secure the enactment of policies of benefit primarily to themselves (and their constituents).

Various rules and practices in Congress, however, help ensure that legislators will have incentives both to specialize in analyzing public problems and crafting policies and to make information generally available to the members of Congress. The problem is to identify the institutional arrangements that help reduce uncertainty. This "information-theories" variant of rational choice continues to assume that legislators are utility maximizers with differing interests. Their utility, however, is determined by policy outcomes rather than by policies per se. About outcomes, as we have seen, there is uncertainty.

Rational-choice studies of political behavior are often characterized by rigid and narrow assumptions, mathematical equations, abstractions, and remoteness from reality. Even William C. Mitchell, an early enlistee in the rational-choice movement, remarks that as it appears in textbooks, rational-choice theory "hardly involves government, politicians, bureaucrats, and interest groups. Little of the exposition ... has anything to do with the fiscal or regulatory lives of the community or state."[44] A more positive view holds that "in its pure form it is one, but only one, useful, partial explanation of politics."[45]

Rational-choice theory both alerts us to the importance of self-interest as a motivating force in politics and policymaking and provides a better understanding of decision-making processes. Many contend, however, that politics is not nearly as devoid of altruism and concern for the public interest as the rational-choice theorists assume. The adoption of "good public policy," for example, is frequently a goal of members of Congress.[46] And public-interest groups, such as the National Wildlife Federation, are motivated by more than immediate self-interest.[47]

Commentary   Because individual political scientists often manifest strong preference for one or another of these theoretical approaches (or others, such as incrementalism, which is presented as a decision-making theory in the chapter titled "Policy Adoption"), there is no consensus on which is the "best" or the most satisfactory. Each approach focuses attention on different aspects of policymaking and politics, and thus seems more useful for understanding some situations or events than others.

Group theory and elite theory are mutually exclusive explanations of how the policy process operates and, most important, of who controls or dominates and benefits from it. Or, succinctly: Who rules? Sharp intellectual catfights have been waged between group (or pluralist) theorists and elite theorists about who controls decision-making on public policy in American communities. Much heat, if not light, was generated by this controversy, which has quieted down without the issue having been fully resolved.[48]

Systems theory and institutionalism both focus on the process of policymaking, albeit in different ways, and are not incompatible. Institutionalism can be used to help explain what goes on within the "black box" (the political system), which is neglected by systems theory. Because neither theory directly confronts the question of who rules, either group or elite theory could be combined with them to some degree.

Rational-choice theory, because of its narrow focus, must stand pretty much by itself. Institutions appear as the individual writ large; little attention is given to the policy environment, how issues are brought to the attention of government, or how policy preferences are developed. Like institutionalism, however, rational-choice theory does show much interest in how rules and structures help determine the outcomes of decision-making. Rational-choice scholars often occupy themselves with demonstrating how the manipulation of rules could produce preferred decisions.

On the question of who rules, rational-choice theory asserts that democratically elected officials will promote their own interest rather than the people's.

This conviction frequently leads to the normative (and conservative) conclusion that less government is better government. Group theorists feel that the interests of dominant groups (however determined) prevail, and for elite theorists, the few (a ruling class) govern in their own interest, perhaps with some concern for the condition of the masses.

The various theories thus raise some controversial questions about politics and the policymaking process. They also tend to skew research findings. Not surprisingly, pluralists find groups in control, elite theorists detect dominance by an elite, and rational-choice theorists find that self-interest dominates. These theories are therefore not merely neutral alternatives for guiding analysis. What one finds in policy research depends in important part on what one is looking for, just as those who go about town "looking for trouble" are more apt to find it than are more peaceful citizens.

The differing concerns of these theoretical approaches can be further clarified by briefly observing how their proponents might look at the recent struggle to adopt financial regulatory legislation. Bands and other financial institutions were firmly regulated from the Great Depression until the 1970s. Then, as free-market ideology and the economic deregulation movement gained traction, regulation was weakened or eliminated. Also, a "shadow" financial system not subject to regulation evolved. This inadequately restrained financial system led eventually to the near collapse of the financial system and the Great Recession. Strong pressure developed for regulatory legislation to prevent future financial crises.

In 2010, after months of partisan conflict, Congress enacted the Dodd-Frank Wall Street Reform and Consumer Protection Act by votes of 237–192 in the House and 60–39 in the Senate. Only three Republicans in each house voted for the complex, 2,300-page Act. It prohibited future bailouts of financial institutions, regulated over-the-counter sale of derivatives, restricted proprietary trading by banks, abolished the Office of Thrift Supervision, created a Consumer Financial Protection Bureau, and much more. In all, it greatly increased national financial regulation.[49]

A group theorist would view this titanic struggle to adopt financial regulation as a contest for advantage among various financial interests, regulatory advocates, and consumer groups, as well as the political parties and the Obama administration. Lobbying and other group tactics would be scrutinized. An institutionalist, in comparison, would focus on the problems presented by congressional structure and procedure in securing the enactment of legislation. These could include getting the bill to the House floor for debate, overcoming filibusters in the Senate, resolving differences in House and Senate versions of the bill, and avoiding a presidential veto. Much attention would be given to how a bill becomes law.

A rational-choice proponent would see members of Congress calculating how the content of reform legislation would affect the ability to raise campaign money and to get reelected. Another of his or her concerns would be strategic behavior, as when opponents propose amendments that, if adopted, would make the bill unacceptable to some of its supporters (a "poison pill"), or when reformers craft amendments to help gain or retain supporters. Self-interest would be seen as informing legislative behavior.

An elite theorist would see the legislative struggle here as one of interest primarily to top-level legislative and political leaders. Both proponents and opponents of reform would contend that what they were trying to do was best for the public. The elitist would hold that the mass public was neither interested nor informed, especially on the details of legislation.

Finally, a systems theorist would likely rivet on how government action was influenced by inputs (demands, pressures, and information) from its political, social, and economic environment. Limited attention at best would be devoted to the details of how a bill becomes law. In time the systems theorist would be attentive to how the government's decisions on campaign-finance reform affected its operation and future demands on it.

To conclude, the lesson here is that it is advisable to avoid becoming too dogmatically or rigidly attached to a particular model or theory. As a rule, eclecticism and flexibility should be preferred in selecting theories and concepts for explanatory use. The policy analysts' goal should be the objective explanation of the political behavior under scrutiny, rather than the validation of a favored model or theoretical approach. Each of the theories here discussed can, if used skillfully and fairly, contribute to a fuller comprehension of policymaking.

Methodological Difficulties in Studying Public Policy

Methodological problems afflict all research, although social scientists appear both more self-conscious about their methodology and more intellectually inclined to batter themselves for methodological infirmities than do natural and physical scientists. Policy research, especially given the complexity of its subject matter, has its full share of methodological problems. Such problems may impede or limit policy research, and may make it more than a little frustrating at times, but they neither prevent it nor negate the need for it. An awareness of some of these problems, however, may help prevent wasted efforts, needless errors, unsound conclusions, and insomnia.

Solid, conclusive evidence, facts, or data, as one prefers, on the motives, values, and behavior of policy-makers, the nature and scope of public problems, the impact of policies, and other facets of the policy process are often difficult to acquire or simply not available. The urge to convert assumptions or speculations about what happened into facts is something to be resisted, along with the uncritical acceptance of the often self-serving statements or incomplete explanations emanating from public officials and other participants in the policy process.

Sometimes numerical measures of political phenomena such as policy impacts are used without sufficient care in determining their validity. Is the number of infant deaths (in their first year) per 1,000 live births a good indicator of the general level of health care in a society that has much income inequality? Do salary levels and similar data really measure the professionalism of civil servants? The acquisition of hard facts about who did what, why, and with what effect should be the goal of research. We need to be able to say with some certainty why members of Congress respond to constituency interests on some issues and not others, or what role the media play in setting agendas.

In explaining behavior in the policy process, one needs empirical data that will permit the demonstration or sound inference of cause-and-effect relationships. Once a person gets involved in quantitative data–based analysis, it is important to resist the notion that collecting empirical data is of prime importance and that the more data one has, the more one can explain. One can drown in a sea of data as well as thirst for lack thereof. To account for or explain behavior, theory is needed that will guide analysis in potentially fruitful directions, as well as good judgment in the selection of policy measures. As much as possible, hypotheses about cause-and-effect relationships need to be developed and tested on the basis of the best available evidence.

The notion that policy analysis is worthwhile only when it involves the analysis of quantitative data with statistical techniques—the higher powered the better—should also be resisted. There is no reason to assume that if something cannot be counted, it does not count. Some policy areas and problems have not been very amenable to rigorous quantitative measurement and analysis, although this may not always continue to be the case. Many aspects of social welfare and economic regulatory policies currently fit into this category. How does one measure the comparative influence of pressure groups, agency values, and economic analysis on rule-making by the EPA or OSHA? The prosecution of insider traders by the Securities and Exchange Commission? The total benefits of a public-housing program? And how does one appraise the power of ideas, as distinct from interests, in developing programs for the handicapped? Such questions present real puzzles.

Yet it should be stressed that explicit theory, quantitative data, and careful, rigorous analysis have not been as frequently utilized in studying policy as would be possible or desirable. Thus, political scientist Marver H. Bernstein's hoary contention that regulatory agencies pass through a four-stage life cycle (gestation and birth, youth, maturity, and old age), frequently culminating in their "capture" (which is not well-specified) by the regulated groups, is often cited as though it were a clearly supported phenomenon.[50] Bernstein provides impressionistic support but by no means strong proof for his life-cycle theory. (He does not follow a single commission through all of the stages of the cycle.) It still lacks systematic empirical support. Conventional wisdom of this sort frequently rests on a rather frail intellectual foundation. Another example, also in the regulatory area, is economist George Stigler's theory of economic regulation. It holds that, as a rule, regulation is sought by the affected industry and operated for its benefit.[51] This theory will not do much to explain a raft of consumer protection, industrial health and safety, and environmental programs, or the deregulation legislation of the late 1970s and early 1980s.

Many perceptive and informative studies of policy formation employ little or no statistical analysis. Examples are Barbara J. Nelson's *Making an Issue of Child Abuse*, I. M. Destler's *American Trade Politics*, Adam Sheingate's *The Rise of the Agricultural Welfare State*, and Paul Milazzo's *Unlikely Environmentalists*.[52] The quality of intellectual analysis and careful use of sound data (or information) are more important than whether and to what extent quantitative analysis is employed when it comes to determining the worth of a study.

To be rigorous, analysis does not have to be quantitative, and not all quantitative analysis is rigorous. Those who use quantitative techniques have been known to quarrel with enthusiasm and even some rancor over the reliability or appropriateness of their techniques, the quality of their data, and the validity of their findings. (In the chapter titled "The Policy-Makers and Their Environment," there is a discussion on whether socioeconomic or political variables better explain policy.) Also, to be fair-minded, one should avoid developing a phobia for quantitative or statistical analysis, as some did in reaction to the behavioral movement in political science. Much can be learned through quantitative analysis.

Data gained by interviews and questionnaires administered to public officials and other players in the policy process are often invaluable and may not otherwise be available to researchers. Care is required, however, in using both such techniques and the data acquired. Questions must be properly framed to elicit the needed information. Questions that are "loaded" and therefore bias responses, or that are so general as to create strong doubt about their intent, need to be avoided. Officials and others may not always respond fully or candidly to questions, their memories may be hazy, and they may overstate their own role in events. Data gained from these sources obviously should not be viewed as gospel. Rather, they should be checked against other sources, used with care, and regarded as representing particular viewpoints on some event. Good judgment is called for.

Many studies of policymaking take the form of case studies; that is, they focus on particular programs, statutes, or areas of public policy. Case studies have been the butt of much criticism because, being narrowly based, they do not permit sound generalization. "What is a case study a case of?" is a common gibe. Preferred studies are those dealing with all the cases in a universe, such as all regulatory commissions or sunset laws, or a meaningful sample thereof, such as Supreme Court decisions on the rights of the accused or the benefit decisions made by a welfare agency. These afford a better basis for generalizations. Case studies, however, do have a variety of uses.[53] They can be used to test theories; to develop new theories; to provide detailed, contextual analysis of events; to analyze deviant cases that contradict our generalizations; and to help provide an "intuitive feel" for the subtleties and nuances of the policy process and the practice of politics. There is plenty of room in the study of policy for both case studies and more general and comparative studies. And, as someone once remarked, the plural of anecdote is data.

For Further Exploration

- *www.care2.com/causes/politics/*

  The Policy Action Network site provides numerous links to liberal think tanks and foundations devoted to a variety of public-policy issues such as economic, health, education, and media policies.

- *http://www.jointcenter.org*

  This site for the Joint Center for Political and Economic Studies provides a wide range of information on policy issues and other matters relating to racial and ethnic groups.

- *http://www.ncpa.org*

  Although it is conservative in nature, the homepage of the National Center for Policy Analysis (NCPA) provides a wealth of descriptive material on specific domestic- and foreign-policy issues.

- *http://www.pbs.org/newshour/*

  The Online NewsHour provides a site titled "Forum," where several current policy issues are debated each month. This site also contains transcripts of the various policy discussions and roundtable issues that were broadcast on The NewsHour with Jim Lehrer.

Test Your Knowledge

Log on to the student companion website at

> *login.cengage.com*

to access tutorial quizzes, chapter outlines, crossword puzzles, and glossary flashcards that review chapter concepts and terminology.

Suggested Readings

Carl E. Van Horn, Donald C. Baumer, and William T. Gormley Jr., *Politics and Public Policy*, 3rd ed. (Washington, DC: CQ Press, 2001). Six policy domains—boardroom, bureaucratic, cloakroom, chief executive, courtroom, and living room politics—are utilized in a wide-ranging examination of the policy process.

Frank R. Baumgartner and Beth L. Leech, *Basic Interests: The Importance of Groups in Politics and Political Science* (Princeton, NJ: Princeton University Press, 1998). No one interested in groups and politics should ignore this outstanding analysis of group theory and the literature on groups.

Kevin B. Smith and Christopher W. Larimer, *The Public Policy Theory Primer*, 2nd ed. (Boulder CO: Westview Press, 2013). This is a weighty, up-to-date exposition of public-policy theories and the study of public policy.

Michael E. Kraft and Scott R. Furlong, *Public Policy: Politics, Analysis, and Alternatives* (3rd ed. Washington, DC: CQ Press, 2010). This readable book combines an examination of the policy process with a discussion of several areas of domestic policy.

Paul A. Sabatier, ed., *Theories of the Policy Process*, 2nd ed. (Boulder, CO: Westview Press, 2007). The challenging essays in this anthology present a variety of theoretical lenses for studying the policy process.

Theodore J. Lowi, *Arenas of Power* (Boulder, CO: Paradigm Publishers, 2009). This long-awaited study by the leading public policy guru draws on history, analysis, and case studies to provide deep understanding of the policy process.

Thomas R. Dye, *Top Down Policymaking* (New York: Chatham House, 2001). This controversial examination of the policymaking process in the United States argues that it is dominated by a national elite.

Notes

1. On policy analysis, see Robert D. Behn, "Policy Analysis and Politics," *Policy Analysis*, Vol. VII (Spring 1981), pp. 199–226; Peter J. May, "Politics and Policy Analysis," *Political Science Quarterly*, Vol. 101 (Spring 1986), pp. 109–125; and Michael C. Munger, *Analyzing Policy* (New York: Norton, 2000).

2. Thomas R. Dye, *Understanding Public Policy*, 7th ed. (Englewood Cliffs, NJ: Prentice-Hall, 1992), p. 7.

3. See David Easton, *The Political System* (New York: Knopf, 1953), Chap. 2.

4. See, generally, Richard Rose, "Concepts for Comparison," *Policy Studies Journal*, Vol. I (Spring 1973), pp. 122–127.

5. For criticisms of the sequential-process approach, see Charles E. Lindblom and Edward J. Woodhouse, *The Policy Making Process*, 3rd ed. (Englewood Cliffs, NJ: Prentice-Hall, 1993), pp. 10–12; and Paul A. Sabatier and Hank Jenkins-Smith, eds., *Policy Change and Learning: An Advocacy Coalition Approach*, (Boulder, CO: Westview, 1993), Chap. 1.

6. David Easton, *A Systems Analysis of Political Life* (New York: Wiley, 1965), p. 212.

7. The basic typology is from Theodore J. Lowi, "American Business, Public Policy Case Studies, and Political Theory," *World Politics*, Vol. XVI (July 1964), pp. 677–715. The self-regulatory category is from Robert Salisbury, "The Analysis of Public Policy," in Austin Ranney ed., *Political Science and Public Policy* (Chicago: Markham, 1968), pp. 151–175.

8. Theodore J. Lowi, *Arenas of Power* (Boulder CO: Paradigm Publishers, 2009), p. 15.

9. Mark Zandi, *Paying the Price* (Upper Saddle River, NJ: FT Press, 2013), Chap. 4.

10. Michael J. Graetz, *The End of Energy* (Cambridge, MA: MIT Press, 2011), pp. 193–194.

11. http://earmarks.omb.gov/public/2010-appropriations-by-spendcom/summary.html

12. Lowi, *American Business*, op. cit. p. 690
13. Raymond Tatalovich and Byron W. Daynes, eds., *Moral Controversies in American Politics: Cases in Social Regulatory Politics* (Armonk, NY: M. E. Sharpe, 1998).
14. Randall B. Ripley and Grace A. Franklin, *Congress, the Bureaucracy, and Public Policy* (Pacific Grove, CA: Brooks/Cole, 1991), pp. 20–21.
15. Kenneth J. Meier and E. Thomas Garman, *Regulation and Consumer Protection*, 3rd ed. (Houston: Dome Publications, 1998), pp. 41–42.
16. For a discussion of licensing, see ibid., Chap. 3.
17. Lowi, op.cit., p. 691. On redistributive policies, see Ripley and Franklin, op. cit., Chap. 6.
18. Randall B. Ripley, *Policy Analysis in Political Science* (Chicago: Nelson Hall, 1985), pp. 68–69.
19. Paul E. Peterson and Mark Rom, "Lower Taxes, More Spending, and Budget Deficits," in Charles O. Jones, ed., *The Reagan Legacy: Promise and Performance* (Chatham, NJ: Chatham House, 1988), pp. 218–221.
20. On the symbolic aspects of policies, see Murray Edelmann, *The Symbolic Uses of Politics* (Urbana: University of Illinois Press, 1964), Chap. 2; and Charles D. Elder and Roger W. Cobb, *The Political Uses of Symbols* (New York: Longman, 1983).
21. *Congressional Quarterly Weekly Report*, Vol. 53 (July 1, 1995), p. 1933.
22. Brian Czech and Paul R. Krausman, *The Endangered Species Act* (Baltimore: Johns Hopkins University Press, 2001).
23. Richard O. Davis, *Housing Reform During the Truman Administration* (Columbia: University of Missouri Press, 1966), Chap. 10.
24. Bruce I. Oppenheimer, *Oil and the Congressional Process* (Lexington, MA: Heath, 1974), pp. 130–145.
25. Cf. L. L. Wade and R. L. Curry Jr., A *Logic of Public Policy* (Belmont, CA: Wadsworth, 1970), Chap. 5; and Charles L. Cochran and Eloise F Malone, *Public Policy* (New York: McGraw-Hill, 1995), pp. 17–19.
26. Ronald C. Moe, "Exploring the Limits of Privatization," *Public Administration Review*, Vol. XLVII (November–December 1987), p. 453.
27. R. McGregor Cawley, *Federal Land, Western Anger* (Lawrence: University Press of Kansas, 1993).
28. David Easton, "An Approach to the Analysis of Political Systems," *World Politics*, Vol. IX (April 1957), pp. 383–400; and Easton, op. cit.
29. Earl Latham, *The Group Basis of Politics* (New York: Octagon Books, 1965), p. 36.
30. David Truman, *The Governmental Process* (New York: Knopf, 1951), p. 37.
31. Alan C. Isaak, *Scope and Methods of Political Science* (Chicago: Dorsey Press, 1988), pp. 269–270.
32. Latham, op. cit., pp. 35–36, 38–39.
33. E. E. Schattschneider, *The Semisovereign People* (New York: Holt, Rinehart and Winston, 1960), p. 35.
34. See, generally, Frank R. Baumgartner and Beth L. Leech, *Basic Interest: The Importance of Groups in Politics and Political Science* (Princeton, NJ: Princeton University Press, 1998).
35. Thomas R. Dye and L. Harmon Zeigler, *The Irony of Democracy*, 10th ed. (Belmont, CA: Wadsworth, 1996), pp. 4–5. See also Thomas R. Dye, *Top Down Policymaking* (New York: Chatham House, 2001).
36. Dye, op. cit., pp. 59–63.

37. Robert A. Dahl, "A Critique of the Ruling Elite Model," *American Political Science Review*, Vol. LII (June 1958), p. 464.
38. G. William Domhoff, *Who Rules America?* (Englewood Cliffs, NJ: Prentice-Hall, 1967); G. William Domhoff, *The Power Elite and the State: How Policy Is Made in America* (New York: Walter deGruyter, 1990).
39. *Citizens United* v. *Federal Election Commission*, 558 U.S. (2010). See also Jeffrey Toobin, *The Oath* (New York: Doubleday, 2012), passim.
40. Anthony Downs, *An Economic Theory of Democracy* (New York: Harper & Row, 1957).
41. Roger Lewin, "Self-Interest in Politics Earns a Nobel Prize," *Science*, Vol. CCXXXIV (November 21, 1986), p. 941.
42. Morris P. Fiorina, *Congress: Keystone of the Washington Establishment*, 2nd ed. (New Haven, CT: Yale University Press, 1989).
43. This discussion leans heavily upon Keith Krehbiel, *Information and Legislative Organization* (Ann Arbor: University of Michigan Press, 1992); and Thomas W. Gilligan and Keith Krehbiel, "Asymmetric Information and Legislative Rules with a Heterogeneous Committee," *American Journal of Political Science*, Vol. XXXIII (May 1989), pp. 459–490.
44. William C. Mitchell, "Textbook Public Choice: A Review Essay," *Public Choice*, Vol. XXVIII (1982), p. 99.
45. Louis F. Weschler, "Methodological Individualism in Politics," *Public Administration Review*, Vol. XLIII (May–June 1982), p. 294.
46. See Richard J. Fenno Jr., *Congressmen in Committees* (Boston, MA: Little, Brown, 1973). Fenno indicates that members of Congress are variously influenced by the desires to be reelected, to help enact good public policy, and to acquire influence in the House.
47. Those wishing to explore rational-choice theory further can begin with Kenneth A. Shepsle and Mark S. Bonchek, *Analyzing Politics: Rationality, Behavior, and Institutions* (New York: Norton, 1997). For a critique, see Donald P. Green and Ian Shapiro, *Pathologies of Rational Choice Theory* (New Haven, CT: Yale University Press, 1994).
48. See Philip J. Trounstine and Terry Christensen, *Movers and Shakers: The Study of Community Power* (New York: St. Martin's, 1982).
49. For a concise summary and discussion of the Dodd-Frank Act, see Allen Blinder, *After the Music Stopped: The Financial Crisis, the Response, and the Work Ahead* (New York: Penguin Press, 2013), Chap. 11.
50. Marver H. Bernstein, *Regulating Business by Independent Commission* (Princeton, NJ: Princeton University Press, 1955), pp. 74–95.
51. George Stigler, "The Theory of Economic Regulation," *Bell Journal of Economic and Management Science*, Vol. 2 (Spring 1971), pp. 3–21.
52. Barbara J. Nelson, *Making an Issue of Child Abuse* (Chicago: University of Chicago Press, 1984); I. M. Destler, *American Trade Politics*, 4th ed. (Washington, DC: Institute of International Economics, 2005); Adam Sheingate, *The Rise of the Agricultural Welfare State* (Princeton: NJ: Princeton University Press, 2001); and Paul Charles Milazzo, *Unlikely Environmentalists: Congress and Clean Water, 1945–1972* (Lawrence, KS: University Press of Kansas, 2006).
53. See Harry Eckstein, "Case Study and Theory in Political Science," in Fred I. Greenstein and Nelson W. Polsby, eds., *The Handbook of Political Science, Vol. 7, Strategies of Inquiry* (Reading, MA: Addison-Wesley 1975), pp. 79–137.

2

The Policy-Makers and Their Environment

In the American political system, political power is fragmented and dispersed by constitutional prescription and political practice. Many points of official decision-making exist, and a multitude of officials share in the exercise of political power and the formation of public policy. At the national level, the Framers of the Constitution provided for the separation of power, distributing it among the legislative, executive, and judicial branches of the national government. Thus, Article I provides that "all legislative Powers herein granted shall be vested in a Congress of the United States. . . ." Article II states that "the executive Power shall be vested in a President of the United States of America." In turn, Article III declares that "the judicial Power of the United States, shall be vested in one supreme court and such inferior Courts as the Congress may from time to time ordain and establish." This separation was reinforced by the provision of different selection processes for officials in each branch. Thus, the House of Representatives was to be chosen by the voters, the Senate by the state legislatures (changed to the voters by the Sixteenth Amendment), the president by the Electoral College, and the judges by the president with the consent of the Senate. The Constitution also prohibits anyone from being a member of more than one branch at the same time.

The separation of powers was not rigidly imposed, however. By the corollary principle of checks and balances, the Framers gave each branch some means for interfering with—checking—the exercise of power by the other two branches. As James Madison stated in *Federalist* no. 51: "Ambition must be made to counteract ambition." Thus, Congress is given primary responsibility for the enactment of legislation, but the president is authorized to recommend matters for its attention and to veto laws, although the veto can be overcome by a two-thirds vote in both houses. Many presidential appointments, including those to the federal courts, require Senate approval. The Supreme Court can declare actions by the other branches unconstitutional, but Congress can regulate the jurisdiction of the courts and the kinds of cases they may hear. What the Framers really created was a set of separate institutions sharing

37

power. Professor Charles Jones puts it somewhat differently when he states that "these separated institutions often *compete* for shared powers!"[1]

The Framers' intent was to use the principles of separation of powers and checks and balances to prevent the abuse of power and the intrusion by government on individual liberty. Whatever their influence in these respects, these principles have had other consequences. One is the decentralization of power. Another is creation of the need for cooperation and deference among the branches in order for the government to act effectively. Indeed, if each branch were to insist on the fullest exercise of its prerogatives, the government would end in deadlock. A third is to make American government inefficient in its operation. Much time and effort are often required to make policy decisions, and the content of the resulting policy is often diluted and moderated.

Conventional wisdom holds that the national government performs more effectively when both houses of Congress and the presidency are controlled by the same party. However, divided governments, where one party controls the White House (usually the Republicans) and the other party controls one or both houses of Congress, existed for all but twelve years during the 1969–2014 period. This condition is thought to contribute to gridlock, a situation in which partisan, ideological, and other differences make it difficult for the government to deal effectively with important problems. If one believes that the government should act decisively on all problems soon after they reach the policy agenda, something of a case could be made for the gridlock contention. In actuality, it has frequently taken the government many years, even decades, to adopt legislation on such contentious matters as federal aid to education, medical care, civil rights, and welfare reform.

Further doubt on the divided government-gridlock contention was cast by Professor David R. Mayhew's study of the 1946–1990 era.[2] Using as his criteria the enactment of important legislation and the conduct of major congressional investigations of alleged misconduct in the executive branch, he finds that there are no major differences in governmental output between periods of divided and unified government. Mayhew was not concerned with whether presidents got what they wanted from Congress or with the ideological hue of legislation.

However, another study determined that, when seriously considered, more important legislation failed to be enacted under divided government than under unified government. Legislation opposed by the president was especially likely to fail under divided government.[3] These studies leave one uncertain as to the validity of the argument that unified party control is a requisite for effective national governance.

Power in the American political system is further dispersed by the principle of federalism, which created separate national and state governments, each deriving its power from the Constitution. Essentially, the Constitution assigns delegated and implied powers to the national government and unspecified reserved powers to the state governments. The basic arrangement is summarized by the Tenth Amendment: "The powers not delegated to the United States by the Constitution, nor prohibited by it to the States, are reserved to the States respectively, or to the people."

Before moving on, it should be pointed out that the Constitution also divides power between government and the populace. Note that phrase in the Tenth Amendment, "or to the people." The Bill of Rights places a variety of matters beyond the reach of government, such as freedom of speech, press, religion, and assembly. These are not absolute, however. Other limitations are found in the main body of the Constitution. American government is limited government, even if it comes to be called "big government."

Article I, Section 8 of the Constitution delegates to Congress such powers as those to tax and spend for the general welfare, to regulate interstate and foreign commerce (the "commerce clause"), to coin money and regulate the value thereof, to establish post offices and post roads, to raise and support armies and a navy, and to declare war. Congress is also authorized "to make all laws which shall be necessary and proper for carrying into execution" these and other powers assigned to the national government. The "necessary and proper" clause has served to significantly enhance the scope of the national government's power.

As usually interpreted, the Constitution does not reserve any specific policy areas for the states. Consequently, the national government can deal with any or all matters where action can be justified as exercises of its delegated and implied (necessary and proper) powers. Constitutional "habits" persist, however, and help impose political limits on the national government. Constitutional support could likely be found for a national uniformed police force but that would not make it politically acceptable to most Americans.

The reach and power of the national government have undergone continual expansion since the Constitution's adoption, albeit more rapidly in some eras than others. Today the national government is vastly more active and powerful than it was in 1850, 1900, or even 1950. National policies now apply to many areas once regarded as the domain of the states; examples include public education, social welfare, highway construction and maintenance, and environmental protection.

Much of what the national government does is constitutionally based on the commerce clause—the authority to regulate interstate and foreign commerce. Since the 1930s, the commerce clause has been given an expansive interpretation by the Supreme Court. In 1995, however, the Court, by a 5–4 majority, declared unconstitutional the Gun-Free School Zones Act of 1990. This law, which made possession of a gun within 1,000 feet of a school a federal crime, was held to be "a criminal statute that by its terms has nothing to do with 'commerce' or any sort of economic enterprise, however broadly one might define those terms." Not since 1936, when it struck down a law regulating wages and hours in the coal industry, had the Court declared a congressional action unconstitutional as in excess of the commerce clause. In 2000, the Court held unconstitutional the Violence Against Women Act, which made gender-motivated violence a crime. It too was held to exceed congressional power under the commerce clause.[4]

Notwithstanding the national government's growth, the state governments (and their local governments) continue to be important policy-makers in many areas, including law enforcement, definition and protection of property rights, public education (both higher and lower), land-use regulation, construction and maintenance of highways and streets, occupational licensing, gambling, mental-health services, and public sanitation services. Indeed, some observers contend that there has been a "resurgence of the states" as a consequence of institutional, legislative reapportionment; increased cooperation among the states; and distrust and lack of confidence in the national government.[5]

In the nineteenth century, the dominant conception of national–state relationships was that called *dual federalism.* Each level of government had its distinct functions that it handled independently of the other. In the twentieth century, dual federalism gave way to *cooperative federalism*, where all levels of government—national, state, and local—cooperate in the development and implementation of public policies. Thus, the state and the local governments play a major role in the enforcement of national environmental pollution-control and welfare programs. One would be hard-pressed to identify a policy area in which they have no involvement or effect.

Although the Constitution does not require the states to employ the principle of separation of powers in organizing their governments, they all do so. And only the state of Nebraska has chosen to have a one-house legislature. The states have created many local governments (more than 89,000 separate entities in 2012; see Table 2.1) to handle the local administration of state functions, such as law enforcement and public education, and to provide for local self-government. In practice, local governments frequently operate with only limited supervision and control by the state agencies and officials. Along with the states they provide additional arenas for policymaking and implementation.

The existence of this multitude of governments—national, state, and local—together with the separation of powers enables interest groups and others to engage in "arena shopping." Those dismayed with policy produced by one level or branch of government may look elsewhere for satisfaction. Thus,

TABLE 2.1

Local Governments, 2012

Counties	3,031
Municipalities	19,522
Townships	16,364
Special districts	37,203
School districts	12,884
Total	89,004

Source: United States Bureau of the Census: *2012 Census of Governments.*

environmental groups in the 1960s and 1970s shifted their attention from the state level to Washington and to the judiciary in search of pollution control and environmental protection. However, after the early 1990s, when the national government became unresponsive, environmental groups shifted focus and sought favorable action from the Pacific Coast and Northeastern states. Economic development interests generally have found state and local governments more inclined to do their bidding. State governments often tumble all over themselves offering incentives to entice new businesses.

In recent years, business groups have become dissatisfied with the diversity of state laws on product liability and the large monetary awards sometimes granted to aggrieved consumers by state courts. Although product liability traditionally has been handled by the states, organized business has turned to Washington for succor, where they have drawn support from the Republicans in Congress. Their goal is a national product liability law that would preempt state laws, limit awards for actual and punitive damages, and make it more difficult for plaintiffs to win damage suits. Congress passed such a bill in 1996 only to have it vetoed by President Bill Clinton. The struggle continues.

Describing and analyzing policymaking at all three levels of government is a task too extensive for one book. Hence, the remainder of this book will focus on the national government's action on domestic issues but will not wholly exclude foreign policy, American state and local governments, or other political systems. This chapter will begin by examining the environment in which policymaking occurs and which helps to shape its actions—something that tends to be overlooked by rational-choice theory but to which we are alerted by systems theory. Then we will survey the official and unofficial participants in the policymaking process.

The Policy Environment

Policymaking cannot adequately be studied apart from the environment or context in which it occurs. According to systems theory, demands for policy actions stem from problems and conflicts in the environment and are transmitted to the political system by groups, officials, and others. At the same time, the environment both limits and directs what policy-makers can effectively do. The environment, broadly viewed, includes geographic characteristics such as climate, natural resources, and topography; demographic variables such as population size, age distribution, racial composition, and spatial location; political culture; social structure, or the class system; and the economic system. Other nations become an important part of the environment when foreign and defense policies are involved. The discussion here focuses on a pair of these environmental factors that have received much attention from political scientists (although not always from a policy-studies' perspective): political culture and socioeconomic conditions.

Political Culture   Every society has a culture that differentiates its members' values and lifestyles from those of other societies. The anthropologist Clyde Kluckhohn defined *culture* as "the total life way of a people, the social legacy the individual acquires from his group. Or culture can be regarded as that part of the environment that is the creation of man."[6] Most social scientists seem to agree that culture shapes or influences social action but does not fully determine it. Culture is only one of many factors that may give form and direction to human behavior.

We are interested here in the portion of the general culture of a society that can be designated political culture: widely held values, beliefs, and attitudes on what governments should try to do, how they should operate, and relationships between the citizen and government.[7] Political culture is transmitted from one generation to another by socialization, a process in which the individual, through many experiences with parents, friends, teachers, political leaders, and others, learns politically relevant values, beliefs, and attitudes. Political culture, then, is acquired by the individual, becomes a part of his or her psychological makeup, and is manifested in his or her behavior. Within a society, variations among regions and groups may result in distinctive subcultures. In the United States, variations are noticeable in political culture (subcultures) between North and South, black and white, and young and old.

A society's political culture is not static; it changes and evolves over time, though the pace of change among its components will vary. As a consequence of the Great Depression and the New Deal, most Americans tolerate or support much more government intervention in the economy than they once did. In recent decades, attitudes have changed greatly on commercial gambling. Once viewed as evil and criminal, it was generally banned. (Nevada was an exception, having legalized gambling in 1931.) Now only three states do not have some form of legal gambling—lotteries, casinos, parimutuel betting, and so forth. Gambling is entertainment and a way to raise needed government revenue.

On the other hand, Americans continue to be distrustful or skeptical of government. The Constitution was framed and adopted in an era when people distrusted government. Hence, federalism and the separation of powers were used to disperse governmental power and prevent its abuse. "Distrust of government is as American as apple pie," says Professor Samuel Huntington. "It has historically been a central, continuing, and distinctive element of the American political tradition and the idea that people *should* trust their government is a radical departure from that tradition."[8]

Professor Paul Starr argues that "it is the anti-governmental attitude on the [political] right that particularly distinguishes Americans' political culture. American conservatives have been far more anti-statist than European conservatives, who have often played a central role in expanding the welfare state."[9] The Tea Party, which emerged soon after the inception of the Obama administration, appears to be an especially strong expression of distrust of government rather than an indication of cultural change.

Political scientist Daniel J. Elazar contends that there are three identifiable political cultures—individualistic, moralistic, and traditionalistic—and mutations thereof scattered throughout the United States.[10] The individualistic political culture emphasizes private concerns and views government as a utilitarian device to be used to accomplish what the people want. Politicians are interested in holding office as a means of controlling government's favors or rewards.

The moralistic political culture views government as a mechanism for advancing the public interest. Government service is considered public service. More governmental intervention in the economy is accepted, and there is much public concern about policy issues. Moralistic political culture is strong in states like Minnesota and Wisconsin, whereas individualistic political culture is dominant in Illinois, New York, and Louisiana.

The traditionalistic political culture takes a paternalistic and elitist view of government and favors its use to maintain the existing social order. Real political power centers in a small segment of the population, and most citizens are expected to be relatively inactive in politics. Traditionalistic political culture has been strong in some southern states, which have been marked by low levels of political participation. Such variations in political culture clearly compound the tasks of political description and analysis.

No attempt is made here to fully describe the political culture of the United States or that of any other society. Rather, the discussion is confined to indicating and illustrating some of the implications and significance of political culture for policy formation.

The sociologist Robin M. Williams identifies a number of "major value orientations" in American society, including individual freedom, equality, progress, efficiency, and practicality.[11] Values such as these—and others, such as democracy, individualism, and humanitarianism—clearly have significance for policymaking. For example, the American approach to regulating economic activity has been practical or pragmatic rather than ideological. It has emphasized particular solutions to present problems rather than long-range planning or ideological consistency. Moreover, demand for individual freedom has created a general presumption against policies restricting private activity and in favor of the broadest scope possible for private action.

Political culture also conditions the implementation of regulatory policies. This is well illustrated by Steven Kelman in his study of the enforcement of industrial health and safety policies in Sweden and the United States. Swedish political culture, which encourages deferential and accommodationist behavior, enables Swedish officials to use informal, consensual methods in rule enforcement. In contrast, America's self-assertive or adversarial political culture stimulates officials to be formal, aggressive, and inclined to "go by the book" and to develop an "us versus them" stance toward businesses. Executives are likely to share these attitudes. American safety inspectors are much more inclined to levy penalties (though they are not very stiff) than are their Swedish counterparts, who are disposed to make informal recommendations to employers on how to improve safety conditions. Kelman estimated that there was not a large difference in compliance rates between the two countries.[12]

Stress on individualism and private property finds expression in the notion (often departed from in practice) that people should generally be free to use their property as they see fit. Land-use controls and municipal zoning demonstrate that this notion is subject to limitations. The American emphasis on individualism has both slowed the development of welfare programs and, once they have come into being, helped to keep them limited and made them subject to much criticism and complaint. Large numbers of Americans believe that people should be expected to take care of themselves.

Differences in public policy and policymaking in various countries can be accounted for at least partially by variations in political culture. Public programs for medical care are of longer standing and are more numerous and extensive in Western Europe than in the United States because there public expectation and acceptance of such programs are greater. Again, more people in Great Britain approve of governmental ownership than in the United States, where support for it is quite narrow.[13] Thus, we find considerably more governmental ownership of business and industry in Great Britain. Americans much prefer governmental regulation to ownership when control seems necessary. For example, dislike for "nationalization," even if temporary, deterred the Obama administration from taking over some large banks during the 2008–2009 financial crisis. It would have been a reasonable and more effective response to the situation.

Professor Karl W. Deutsch suggests that people's time orientation—their view of the relative importance of past, present, and future—has implications for policy formation. A political culture oriented more to the past than to the present or future may better encourage preserving monuments than making innovations, and may help stimulate the enactment of legislation on old-age pensions years before expanding public higher education. Great Britain adopted an old-age pension law in 1908 but did not significantly expand public higher education until after 1960. In contrast, Deutsch notes that the United States, with a more future-oriented culture, adopted legislation providing support for land-grant colleges in 1862 and for social security in 1935.[14]

Gabriel A. Almond and Sidney Verba differentiate among parochial, subject, and participant political cultures.[15] In a parochial political culture, citizens have little awareness of or orientation toward either the political system as a whole, the input process, the output process, or the citizen as a political participant. The parochials expect nothing from the system. It is suggested that some African chiefdoms, kingdoms, and tribal societies as well as modern Italy illustrate parochial political cultures.

In a subject political culture like that of Germany, the citizen is oriented toward the political system and the output process, yet has little awareness of input processes or of the individual as a participant. He or she is aware of governmental authority and may like or dislike it, but is essentially passive. The person is, as the term implies, a subject.

In a participant political culture, which Almond and Verba say exists in the United States, many citizens have a comparatively high level of political awareness and information along with explicit orientations toward the political system as a whole, its input and output processes, and meaningful citizen participation in politics. They also more likely understand how individuals and groups can influence decision-making.

Some of the implications of these differences in political culture for policy formation seem readily apparent. Citizen participation in policy formation in a parochial political culture is essentially nonexistent because government matters little to most citizens. Individuals in a subject political culture may believe that they can do little to influence public policy, whether they like it or not. This belief may lead to passive acceptance of governmental action that may be authoritarian in style. In some instances, frustration and resentment may build until redress or change is sought through violence. In the participant political culture, individuals may organize themselves into groups and otherwise seek to influence governmental action to rectify their grievances. Government and public policy are thus viewed as controllable by citizens. It can also be assumed that more demands will be made on government in a participant political culture than in either a parochial or a subject culture.

Let us return to an earlier point. Political culture helps shape political behavior; it "is related to the frequency and probability of various kinds of behavior and not their rigid determination."[16] Common values, beliefs, and attitudes inform, guide, and constrain the actions of both decision-makers and citizens. Political cultural differences help ensure that public policy will be more likely to favor economic competition in the United States, where individual opportunity is a widely held value, but it is more likely to tolerate industrial cartels in Germany, where economic competition has not been highly valued. Some political scientists shy away from using political culture as an analytic tool because they see it as too imprecise and conjectural, resistant to quantification, and subject to varying interpretations. This undervalues the usefulness of political culture for the analysis and explanation of policy.

Socioeconomic Conditions

The term *socioeconomic conditions* is used here because it is often impossible to separate social and economic factors as they impinge on or influence political activity. The levels of educational attainment in a society, for instance, have both social and economic qualities and effects. For instance, people with more education are more likely to earn more and to vote than those with less education.

Public policies often arise out of conflicts among groups of people, private and official, with differing interests and desires.[17] This origin especially applies to regulatory and redistributive policies. One of the prime sources of conflict, particularly in modern industrial societies, is economic activity. Conflicts may develop between the interests of big business and small business, employers and employees, wholesalers and retailers, bankers and securities dealers, hospitals and medical-insurance companies, farmers and agricultural-commodity importers, and consumers and manufacturers.

Groups that are underprivileged or dissatisfied with their relationships with other groups in the economy may seek governmental assistance to improve their situation. Thus, it has been labor groups, dissatisfied with the wages resulting from interacting with corporate employers, that have sought minimum-wage legislation. Consumer groups, who feel disadvantaged in the marketplace, have sought protection against unwholesome foods and hazardous products. In a private conflict, it is customarily the weaker or disadvantaged party, at least in a comparative sense, who seeks to expand the conflict by bringing government into the fray. The dominant group, which can achieve its goals satisfactorily by private action, has no incentive to bring government into the conflict and instead usually seeks to privatize the conflict by contending that governmental action is unnecessary, improper, or unwise.

Satisfactory relationships between groups may be disrupted or altered by economic change or development. Those who feel adversely affected or threatened may then demand government action to protect their interests or establish a new equilibrium. Rapid industrialization and the growth of big business in the United States in the latter part of the nineteenth century produced new economic conditions. Farmers, small-business operators, reform elements, and other aggrieved groups called for government action to control big business (also known as "the trusts"). The eventual results were the enactment by Congress of the Sherman Act in 1890 and the Clayton and Federal Trade Commission Acts in 1914. More recently, American manufacturing companies, economically threatened by an increasing volume of less costly imported products, have sought and sometimes obtained both voluntary and mandatory import quotas. The Omnibus Trade and Competitiveness Act of 1988 authorizes retaliation against countries discriminating against the sale of American products while themselves benefiting from American market opportunities.

It is a truism that a society's level of economic development will impose limits on what government can do in providing public goods and services to its citizens. Nonetheless, this fact is occasionally overlooked by those who assume that the failure of governments to act on problems is invariably due to official recalcitrance or unresponsiveness or citizens' reluctance to pay higher taxes, rather than to limited resources. Clearly, one factor affecting what governments can provide in the way of welfare programs is the availability of economic resources.

A scarcity of economic resources (actual or perceived) will, of course, be more limiting in many of the developing countries than in an affluent society such as the United States, although even American governments do not have the funds to do everything that everyone wants. National health-insurance legislation, which seemed highly likely to be adopted in the 1970s, lost its appeal in an earlier era of large budget deficits. So, too, has there been delay in improving and repairing highways, bridges, and other parts of the transportation infrastructure because of the large costs entailed.

Within the United States, economic resources are very unequally distributed among state and local governments, affecting their capacity to deal with such social problems as inadequate public education, poverty, overcrowded prisons, and congested traffic. Consequently, among the states variations are substantial in welfare spending, and within the states educational expenditures (as measured by expenditures per student) differ among school districts. Pressed for funds, cities devote most of their resources to police and fire protection and street maintenance while cutting back on "amenities" such as libraries, parks, and recreation programs. In some states, unequal funding among school districts is a divisive and seemingly intractable political issue.

The ways in which socioeconomic conditions influence or constrain public policies in the states have been extensively analyzed by political scientists. Controversy has developed over the relative influence of political and socioeconomic variables on policy. One of the most prominent examinations of this question is Thomas R. Dye's study of policy outputs in the fifty states,[18] which is guided by systems theory. Dye contends that the level of economic development (as measured by such variables as per capita personal income, percentage of urban population, median education, and industrial employment) had a dominant influence on state policies (as measured by expenditures) on such matters as education, welfare, highways, taxation, and public regulation. Comparing the effects of economic development with those of the political system, he found that political variables (voter participation, interparty competition, political-party strength, and legislative apportionment) had only a weak relationship to public policy. Dye summarized the findings of his sophisticated statistical analysis:

> Much of the literature in state politics implies that the division of the two-party vote, the level of interparty competition, the level of voter participation, and the degree of malapportionment in legislative bodies all influence public policy. Moreover, at first glance the fact that there are obvious policy differences between states with different degrees of party competition, Democratic dominance, and voter participation lends some support to the notion that these system characteristics influence public policy. ...
>
> However, partial correlation analysis reveals that these system characteristics have relatively little independent effect on policy outcomes in the states. Economic development shapes both political systems and policy outcomes, and most of the association that occurs between system characteristics and policy outcomes can be attributed to the influence of economic development. Differences in the policy choices of states with different types of political systems turn out to be largely a product of differing socioeconomic levels rather than a direct product of political variables. Levels of urbanization, industrialization, income, and education appear to be more influential in shaping policy outcomes than political system characteristics.[19]

Dye did not argue that political variables had no influence whatsoever on state policies; rather, in his estimation they were clearly subordinated to socioeconomic factors in explaining differences in state public policies.

But is public policy really primarily an outcome of some kind of socioeconomic determinism? Two scholars cautioned against "simple acceptance" of such a conclusion.[20] Not discounting socioeconomic factors' influence on policy outputs, they pointed out a number of problems and limitations in these studies.

First, there is a tendency to exaggerate the strength of the economy-policy relationship. Thus, they state, "Dye reports 456 coefficients of simple correlations between policy measures and his four economic measures of income, urbanism, industrialization and education, but only 16 of them (4 percent) are strong enough to indicate that an economic measure explains at least one-half the interstate variation in policy."[21] This result leaves quite a bit unexplained statistically. Second, the political variables used in such studies have been limited in scope, focusing on only a few aspects of the political process. Third, there is a tendency to overlook variations in the influence of economic factors on policymaking. Officials in local governments appear more strongly influenced by economic factors than are state officials.

Another limitation is that most of these studies only consider statistical relationships among various political and socioeconomic variables and public policies. If, when condition A exists, policy B usually occurs, and the relationship is not caused by some third factor, then we can predict that when A exists, B will occur. Predictions are not explanations, however, and we are still left with the task of explaining how political decisions are actually made. If per capita income is directly related to the level of welfare spending, then we must try to account for the relationship. This task is neither insignificant nor easy. Obviously, policy decisions are made by public officials and not socioeconomic variables. No one has identified the pathways by which socioeconomic variables are translated into public policies.

Two conclusions can be fairly drawn from this discussion. One is that to understand how policy decisions are made and why some decisions are made rather than others, we must take into account social and economic as well as political factors. The second is that whether socioeconomic factors are more important than political factors in shaping public policy remains an open question. Though Dye's findings have been criticized, they have not been directly refuted.[22] Most research along this line has been focused on the American states, and it is less than conclusive. Political scientists continue to spend most of their time studying the policy effects of political variables, with which they are most comfortable.

Social change, and the conflict that often accompanies it, stimulates demands for governmental action. The employment of a large number of women outside the home, the women's movement, and increasing interest in women's rights in the post–World War II era produced demands for favorable governmental action on women's issues. In consequence, greater protection has been provided for women's rights, including equal pay for equal work, equal employment opportunity, equal support for women's athletic programs in colleges and universities, the right to terminate pregnancies by abortion, and, in some states, comparable pay for comparable work and parental leave. A major set-back occurred in the early 1980s when the Equal Rights Amendment fell three votes short of ratification by the states.

The use of narcotic drugs was legal in the United States until the Harrison Act of 1914 and the Marijuana Act of 1936.[23] Efforts to combat drug usage intensified. Then in the 1960s the spread of the drug culture, especially among the middle and upper classes, led to the lessening of penalties for the possession and use of marijuana. Many people, including prominent conservatives, advocated legalization of marijuana and other drugs. A revival of strong antidrug sentiment occurred in the 1980s, however, partly because of the highly publicized drug-induced death of a college basketball star. Stiff penalties were imposed for drug usage. A vigorous antidrug enforcement campaign was launched. Indeed, a "war on drugs" was declared. The nation's prisons were filled with persons convicted of drug law violations. Strong value conflicts exist, and persist, on issues like these, and public officials find themselves hard-pressed to craft acceptable policy responses.

Many scientific and technological developments enable people to live longer, more satisfactory, and more productive lives. The downside, however, is that they also provide opportunities for undue enrichment or create ethical or moral dilemmas when all cannot afford, or benefit, from new drugs or devices, for example. Demands may arise for government to provide support or impose restraints. Human cloning and the production of genetically modified agricultural plants are a case in point.

In 1997, Scottish cloning researchers created Dolly the sheep. Soon after, President Bill Clinton issued an executive order banning federal funding of research on human cloning. The next year a bill to prohibit human cloning failed in the Senate because opponents believed its terms were too sweeping. A distinction is often made between therapeutic cloning, intended to produce embryos for medical research, and cloning for reproductive purposes.[24] Medical researchers and their supporters believe that therapeutic cloning can contribute to the development of new treatments for diseases. Right-to-life groups, who have been joined by some environmental groups, favor an across-the-board ban on human cloning. The controversy continues.

Genetically modified farm plants, made possible by recombinant DNA research and experimentation, became commercially available in the mid-1990s. Resistant to plant diseases, adverse weather conditions, and pesticides, these transgenic plants such as corn and soybeans grow faster and yield more. They promise large profits to the companies developing and distributing them and to farmers growing them. Genetically modified crops are now extensively grown in this country. Supporters say they have great potential for increasing the world's food supply. Others, however, see a dark side to bioengineered crops, fearing they may have unanticipated adverse ecological and human consequences, sometimes referring to products made from them as "Frankenfoods." European countries have banned their importation. In the United States, the Department of Agriculture, the Food and Drug Administration, and the Environmental Protection Agency share jurisdiction to ensure the safety of transgenic crops. Critics, including the National Academy of Sciences, question the adequacy of the agencies' efforts.[25]

The Official Policy-Makers

Official policy-makers have the legal authority to engage in the formation of public policy. (Of course, some who have the legal authority to act may in fact be significantly influenced by others, such as important constituents or pressure groups.) These include legislators, executives, administrators, and judges. Each performs policymaking tasks that are at least somewhat functionally different from those of the others.

It is useful to differentiate between primary and supplementary policy-makers. Primary policy-makers have direct constitutional authority to act; for example, Congress does not have to depend upon other government units for authorization to enact legislation. Supplementary policy-makers, such as national administrative agencies, however, operate on the basis of authority granted by others (primary policy-makers). This puts secondary policy-makers in a dependency relationship. Administrative agencies, such as the Federal Trade Commission and the Bureau of Land Management, that derive their operating authority from congressional legislation will typically need to be responsive to congressional interests and requests. Congress may retaliate against unresponsive agencies by imposing restrictions on their authority or reducing their budgets. On the other hand, Congress has little need to be solicitous about agency interests.

The following survey of official policy-makers is intended to convey a notion of their general role in policy formation, not to catalogue all their powers, activities, and impacts.

Legislatures   The easy response to the question "What do legislatures do?" is that they legislate—that is, they are engaged in the central political tasks of lawmaking and policy formation in a political system. It cannot be assumed, however, that a legislature, merely because it bears that formal designation, actually has independent decision-making functions. This is a matter to be determined by empirical investigation rather than by recourse to definition.

Unlike those in most other countries, legislatures at all levels in the United States do typically legislate in an independent decisional sense. At the national level, policies on such matters as taxation, civil rights, social welfare, consumer protection, economic regulation, and environmental protection tend to be shaped in substantial degree by Congress through the enactment of substantive and appropriations legislation. The committee and subcommittee system and legislative norms (accepted rules of conduct) encouraging members to concentrate on particular policy areas have provided Congress with its own policy specialists. Specialization, in turn, gives members more opportunity to influence policy in their areas of expertise, whether tax policy, welfare programs, or banking regulation.

The capacity of Congress to engage effectively in policymaking has been much enhanced by its expanded staff assistance. As the issues that members are called upon to resolve become more complex, so their need for technical and expert assistance becomes greater. Congressional staff assistance falls into three categories:

1. *Personal staff:* These people work for the individual members of Congress, either in Washington or in their home districts and states. More than 11,000 persons serve as staff aides to members. The average House member has a full-time staff of fourteen; senators' staffs are typically larger. Some staffers handle routine office duties and constituency matters; others have important legislative responsibilities. Legislative assistants, for instance, write speeches, draft bills, monitor committee hearings, negotiate with other staffs and lobbyists, suggest policy initiatives, and otherwise assist members in handling their policymaking responsibilities.

2. *Committee and subcommittee staffs:* Members of these staffs proliferated in the past two or three decades and now number in the thousands. The professional members of committee staffs, usually subject-matter experts, often have much influence on the development of legislation— drafting bills, developing political support, working with agency officials, fashioning compromises on disputed provisions, and the like. A committee's staff is divided between the majority and minority members, with the majority getting the lion's share. Complaints that committee staffs had become too large and were contributing to congressional inefficiency culminated in action in 1995 by the new Republican majority to reduce by one-third the size of House committee staffs. They have since regained some of their size.

3. *Institutional staff:* Agencies providing information services to Congress include the Congressional Research Service (part of the Library of Congress), the Government Accountability Office, and the Congressional Budget Office. These agencies, which are expected to perform in a nonpartisan and objective manner, provide members of Congress with research studies, policy evaluations, and budgetary data. Another agency, the Office of Technology Assessment, was created to provide members of Congress with needed objective analysis of complex scientific and technical issues. When the Republicans took over in 1995, they ill-advisedly opted to abolish OTA as an economy measure. Subsequently, the GAO established a technology assessment unit.

This extensive staff assistance strengthens the policymaking capacity of Congress and reduces its dependency upon others—the executive, administrative agencies, and interest groups—for information. Also, some staff members may act as policy entrepreneurs, scouting for matters on which Congress could legislate or problems that might be investigated, or working to hinder proposals with which they disagree. Some members of Congress, especially senators, overburdened with committee and subcommittee assignments or other duties, may become overly dependent upon staff and become their captives.

Democratic government in modern societies is representative government. Only in small communities can people directly govern themselves. Consequently, at the national level, democratic theory assigns to Congress the task of representing the people in the governing process.[26] People expect their representatives to allocate benefits (public buildings, highways, and research facilities) to their districts and states; to assist them in resolving their difficulties with Social Security, veterans' benefits, and regulatory and other government programs; and to represent their interests in the course of making policy on matters both large and small. It is this third aspect of representation that is of concern to us in this book.

In enacting legislation, the members of Congress try to take care of state and local interests as well as promote broad national or public interests. Former Speaker of the House Thomas ("Tip") O'Neill often said that "all politics are local." Some critics allege that many of the members of Congress are much too caught up in local, or parochial, interests, acting more as local ambassadors than national legislators. Certainly, many members of Congress do experience many demands and pressure from some of their constituents and narrowly based interests.

However, they are also under pressure from the White House and from congressional leaders to act on behalf of more general and national interests. As a result, members find themselves squeezed between conflicting demands. Professor Walter A. Rosenbaum portrayed the effects of this condition on energy policymaking in this manner: "Thus, representatives and Senators must fashion a national energy policy within a vortex of competing political powers and pressures: national interest versus local interests, and commitments to party or congressional leaders versus loyalty to local power centers."[27] Legislators, of course, also have their own values, policy preferences, and reelection to think about in making decisions.

Congressional representation of the people on the whole is uneven. The politically active, the powerful, and the well-to-do are more likely to have their needs and interests responded to than are the politically quiescent, the weak, and the poor or disadvantaged. These and other factors—such as the pounding Congress has taken on radio and television talk shows and the perception that it has not dealt adequately with major problems such as the national debt, immigration, and the drug traffic—have generated cynicism and distrust toward Congress and the government. In a nationwide opinion survey taken in 1999, 75 percent of the respondents agreed with the statement that the government "is run by a few big interests looking out for themselves." Only 43 percent believed that the government paid at least some attention "to what the people think when it decides what to do."[28]

In the states, the legislature's role often varies with the type of issue. Many state legislatures, because of their limited sessions, rather "amateur" membership, and inadequate staff assistance, often cannot act with much independence on complex, technical legislative matters. They may simply enact bills agreed upon elsewhere. In a fairly typical case several years ago, the Texas legislature passed a law on pooling (or unitization) for the common development of oil fields. It was introduced after being agreed to and drafted by representatives of the major and independent petroleum producers' organizations and enacted with little change; the legislature did not really have the capacity to do otherwise. On other issues, such as criminal legislation, the legislature clearly does "legislate." It does not require any special skills to make decisions, for example, on the penalty for embezzlement or automobile theft. Such questions do not demand scientific or technical determination.

The British Parliament has been said merely to consent to laws that are originated by political parties and interest groups, drafted by civil servants, and steered through the House of Commons by "the government" (the prime minister and the cabinet). This view, however, is oversimplified. The government usually gets what it wants from Commons partly because it knows what Commons will accept and requests only measures that are acceptable. Conversely, what is recommended by the government helps make it acceptable to its members in Commons. In the course of approving legislation, Commons performs the vital functions of deliberating, scrutinizing, criticizing, and publicizing governmental policies and activities and their implications for the public. The legislative process in Congress also performs these functions.

To conclude, legislators are more important in policy formation in democratic than in authoritarian countries. In the latter, the legislature may simply be a form of political theater used to convey the impression of public representation in policymaking. In the democratic category, legislatures generally have a larger role in presidential systems (like the United States) than in parliamentary systems (like Great Britain). Some countries, such as Oman and Saudi Arabia, have no legislature; public policies are executive or monarchic products handed down to the people.

The Executive   We live in an "executive-centered era," in which the effectiveness of government substantially depends upon executive leadership and action in both the formation and execution of policy. This is clearly true for the United States. Our attention now turns to the president.

The president's authority to exercise legislative leadership is both clearly established by the Constitution and legislation, and accepted as a practical and political necessity. The fragmentation of authority in Congress stemming from the committee system and the limitations on party leadership renders that body incapable of fashioning a comprehensive legislative program. Congress in the twentieth century came to expect the president to present to it a program of legislative recommendations. Presidents have acted accordingly. Whether the Congress does what the president recommends is another matter.

The president cannot command Congress; he or she can urge Congress to act, and try to persuade and bargain, and appeal to the public for support, but he or she cannot compel. Indeed, Professor George Edwards contends that the essence of successful presidential leadership is skill in identifying and exploiting existing opportunities to obtain desired action, not in creating them through persuasion.[29]

Presidents have varied in their success in gaining congressional support. A standard measure of success is the percentage of votes won on issues in Congress on which the president has taken a clear stand.[30] This does not mean that the legislation involved was enacted into law. (It should be noted that the president takes a stand only on a small percentage of the matters voted on.) In the past half-century, Lyndon Johnson was most successful, winning 82 percent of the issues on which he took a stand. Jimmy Carter, in contrast, had difficulty getting what he wanted from Congress, even though his party controlled both houses. After getting much of what he wanted during his initial year in office, Ronald Reagan's success rate declined to less than 50 percent in 1987–1988, when the Democrats controlled both houses.

In his single term in office, George Bush managed to prevail in 51 percent of the issues on which he took a stand. Bill Clinton's relationship with Congress, which was largely successful during his first two years in office, took a nosedive in 1995 after the Republicans gained control of both houses of Congress for the first time since 1954. Subsequently, Clinton's relationship with Congress recovered somewhat, hovering in the 50 percent range.

George W. Bush took over the presidency following an election campaign in which he said much about being "a uniter, not a divider," and his capacity for bipartisan leadership. Overall, in his eight years in office, he prevailed on 68 percent of the issues on which his position was apparent. Some of his victories were bipartisan, as on No Child Left Behind, but more were due to a high degree of unity among Congressional Republicans, as Congress became more polarized. Bush's success rate plummeted after the Democratic 2006 takeover of Congress to 38 percent in 2007 and 48 percent in 2008. This was the poorest presidential performance on this measure in several decades.

Barack Obama did exceptionally well in his first two years in office, scoring 96 percent in 2009 and 86 percent in 2010. Democrats controlled both houses of Congress. The Republicans, capitalizing on aversion for Obama's legislative achievements, and boosted by the Tea Party, gained a House majority in the 2010 elections. Obama's support score fell to 56 percent in 2011.

Although the presidency may be a lonely place, the president does not act alone on policy matters. The Executive Office of the President (EOP) comprises several staff agencies whose raison d'être is advising and assisting the president in handling his responsibilities, including development and implementation of policy (see Table 2.2). The White House Office includes many personal aides and advisers, such as the chief of staff, the special assistant on national security affairs, the press secretary, and the counsel to the president. The Office of Management and Budget assists the president

TABLE 2.2

Executive Office of the President

White House Office
Council of Economic Advisers
Council on Environmental Quality
National Security Council
Office of Administration
Office of Management and Budget
Office of National Drug Control Policy
Office of Policy Development
  Domestic Policy Council
  National Economic Council
Office of Science and Technology Policy
Office of the United States Trade Representative

Source: United States Government Manual, 2012.

in preparing the annual budget, supervising expenditures, and managing the executive branch. Set up in 1947 to help the president coordinate foreign, military, and domestic policies relating to national security, the National Security Council has become a major player in developing and conducting foreign policy. The Council of Economic Advisers, staffed by a handful of professional economists, provides the president with information and advice on issues of micro- and macroeconomic policy. These agencies and other EOP units have taken shape in response to expanded presidential duties and responsibilities in recent decades. Collectively, they have enhanced the president's capacity to act, and frequently to act effectively, as a policy-maker.[31] They help ensure that the president will make informed decisions, if not always wise decisions.

The president is able to take direct action on many matters because of his constitutional executive authority and power delegated to him by Congress. Foreign trade legislation gives the president discretionary power to raise or lower tariffs on imported goods. Presidents have taken both kinds of actions. The Antiquities Act authorizes the president by executive order to set aside public lands of historic and scientific interest as national monuments. President Bill Clinton created several national monuments, including the 1.9 million-acre Grand Staircase-Escalante National Monument in Utah. Some Utahans were outraged by this and called it a "land grab." Near the end of his term, President George W. Bush created a national monument in the Southwest Pacific covering 195,000 square miles. The area had few inhabitants and there was little interest in its exploitation. Environmentalists were highly pleased. The ability to take direct action sometimes permits the president to circumvent the balkiness of Congress.

Perhaps the most extensive delegation of power came with the Economic Stabilization Act of 1970, which gave the president a blank check to impose wage and price controls for combating inflation. President Nixon said he did not want this authority and would not use it if it were granted. Concerned about the state of the economy and its importance for his reelection, he subsequently changed his mind and surprised the nation with a ninety-day price-wage freeze in August 1971. This decree was followed by systems for mandatory and voluntary price and wage controls until the whole unpopular effort was abandoned in 1974. Congress repealed the statute.

In foreign and military policy, which often merge, the president has greater constitutional authority and operating freedom than in domestic policy. Foreign policy of the United States is largely a product of presidential leadership and action. American policy toward Vietnam, as we well know, was shaped by the presidents in office between 1950 and 1975. The decision to seek more open and friendly relations with the People's Republic of China in the early 1970s was President Nixon's; the decision to go to war with Iraq in 2003 was made by President George W. Bush, with the help of his neoconservative advisers. Much of foreign policy is the domain of the executive, not only in the United States but also elsewhere in the world, as events in the Middle East continue to demonstrate.

In recent decades, though, Congress has sought to expand its role in foreign policy. One manifestation was the War Powers Resolution of 1973, which was stimulated by the Vietnam War. Enacted over President Nixon's veto, the resolution requires the president to consult with Congress in "every possible instance" involving use of American armed forces in hostile situations. The president must report to Congress within forty-eight hours after using the forces. Unless Congress provides otherwise, military action must be halted within sixty to ninety days. Presidents have been highly critical of the resolution as an improper intrusion in their constitutional domain, and their compliance with it has been spotty at best.[32] Congress was also the source of much opposition to the Reagan administration's military and financial involvements in Central America. No longer can presidents count on bipartisan support for military and foreign-policy actions as they could in the first decade or two after World War II. By no means is Congress simply a rubber stamp for presidential initiatives. The following Somali case is illustrative.

In early December 1992, shortly before he left office, President George Bush sent several thousand U.S. troops to Somalia as part of a multination humanitarian effort to relieve famine in that nation.[33] He explained that the troops were being sent only to ensure that food supplies were moved to the starving people; the troops would not be used to "dictate political outcomes" or to "engage in hostilities." Subsequently, the conduct of the Somali operation became the responsibility of the Clinton administration. Unfortunately, hostilities did erupt. In June 1993, twenty-three Pakistani peacemakers were killed. Four U.S. soldiers were killed in August when their vehicle struck a land mine. Then, early in October, eighteen U.S. soldiers died and scores more were wounded during a botched raid on a Somali warlord. (This was the basis for the movie *Black Hawk Down*.)

As these events occurred, Congressional support for the Somali mission dissipated and Congress, with strong bipartisan support, began to consider legislation calling for the withdrawal of the American troops. So pressured, President Clinton announced that the troops would be withdrawn by March 31, 1994. He and Congress were then able to agree on a compromise that was enacted into law. The legislation provided that no funds could be used for military operations in Somalia after March 31, 1994, unless authorized by Congress. However, funds could be used after that date to support protection of American diplomatic facilities and citizens. All troops were to be under U.S., rather than United Nations, control. Several days before the March 31 deadline, almost all of the U.S. troops departed from Somalia.

Reflective of the important policymaking role of the American executive is that in evaluating an executive—whether the president, a governor, or a mayor—our emphasis is on policymaking rather than administrative accomplishments. Presidents, for their part, are more interested in policy initiation and adoption rather than administration because policies enable presidents to build more visible and measurable records of achievement.

Administrative Agencies   Administrative systems throughout the world differ in such characteristics as size, complexity, hierarchic organization, and degree of autonomy from the other branches of government. Although it was once common doctrine in political science that administrative agencies only carried into effect, more or less automatically, policies determined by the "political" branches of government, now it is axiomatic that politics and administration are inseparable, and that administrative agencies are often significantly involved in the formation of public policies. This is particularly apparent, given the concept of policy as encompassing what government actually does over time concerning a problem or situation.

Administration can make or break a law or policy that was made elsewhere. In the eighteenth century, Catherine II of Russia decreed that a large part of the institution of serfdom was to be abolished. However, the landowning aristocracy, which really controlled the administration of the government, was largely able to prevent this decision's implementation. In the United States, the effectiveness of state and national pollution-control laws has often been blunted by heel-dragging and inadequate enforcement by the administering agencies.

Especially in complex, industrial societies, the technicality and complexity of many policy matters, the need for continuing control of matters, and legislators' lack of time and information have caused the delegation of much discretionary authority, which often includes extensive rule-making power, to administrative agencies. Consequently, agencies make many decisions and issue many rules that have far-reaching political and policy consequences. Illustrations include the choice of most weapons systems by the Department of Defense, the development of air-safety regulations by the Federal Aviation Agency, the location of highways by state highway departments, and the regulation of motor vehicles by the National Highway Traffic Safety Administration and the Environmental Protection Agency. Professor Norman C. Thomas comments, "It is doubtful that any modern industrial society could manage the daily operation of its public affairs without bureaucratic organizations in which officials play a major policymaking role."[34]

Administrative agencies are an important source of legislative proposals and ideas in the American political system. Because of their experience and specialized knowledge, agency officials are able to identify needed changes in existing policies, perhaps to eliminate loopholes, as well as new problems, that, in their view, are appropriate targets for legislation. Specific proposals to deal with such matters, including statutory language, may either be conveyed directly to Congress or channeled through the White House as part of the president's legislative program.

Agencies also actively lobby and otherwise strive to win acceptance of legislation they favor or kill that which they oppose.[35] Officials frequently testify before congressional committees on legislative and budgetary issues. They provide requested information to members and help them prepare speeches. Projects and federal grants-in-aid may be allocated to states and districts with an eye to building support for the agency. Many agencies have congressional liaison offices to regularize contacts with Congress. The Department of State, for example, has an assistant secretary for legislative affairs; the Environmental Protection Agency has an associate administrator for congressional and intergovernmental relations.

There are also myriad informal contracts between the agencies and Congress. Much of this can accurately be called *lobbying*: "the stimulation and transmission of a communication, by someone other than a citizen acting on his own behalf, directed to a governmental decision-maker with the hope of influencing his decision."[36] In years past, the Congress has occasionally become irritated about administrative lobbying and has adopted legislation banning it.[37] This ban essentially has been ignored. Extensive administrative-congressional communication has become accepted as a legitimate part of the policymaking process.

The Courts   Nowhere do the courts play a greater role in policy formation than in the United States. The courts, notably the national and state appellate courts, have often greatly affected the nature and content of public policy by exercising the powers of judicial review and statutory interpretation in cases brought before them.

Judges are sometimes thought to be nonpolitical, merely "following the law" or previous decisions, but in fact they are often deeply and willingly involved in policy politics (as distinguished from party or partisan politics). That is, they are judicial activists. Their selection, whether by appointment or election, typically hinges on their party affiliation and their policy preferences and values. Once in office, values and preferences deeply affect their decisions.

Professors Robert Carp and Claude Rowland, in their exhaustive study of federal district judges, found that judges appointed by President Lyndon Johnson, who deliberately appointed civil-rights supporters to the bench, in actuality were considerably more likely to render pro-civil-rights decisions than were judges appointed by Presidents Dwight Eisenhower and Richard Nixon.[38] That the Ronald Reagan and George Bush administrations took great care to appoint staunch Republican conservatives to federal judgeships is familiar recent history.[39] The George W. Bush administration followed suit. Both Bill Clinton and Barack Obama were more inclined to appoint moderates.

Essentially, judicial review is the power of courts to determine the constitutionality of actions by the legislative and executive branches, and to declare them null and void if they are ruled to be in conflict with the Constitution. Clearly, the Supreme Court was making policy when, in various cases before 1937, it held that no legislature, state or national, had constitutional authority to regulate minimum wages. After 1937, the Constitution was found (i.e., interpreted) to permit such legislation. Clearly, too, the Court has helped shape public policy by holding that segregated school systems, official prayers in public schools, and malapportionment of state legislatures are unconstitutional. The course of policy is strongly affected by such decisions.

Although the Court has used its power of judicial review somewhat sparingly, the very fact that it has such power may affect the policymaking activities of the other branches. Congress may hesitate to act on a matter if there is expectation that its action will be found unconstitutional. State supreme courts also have the power of judicial review but frequently have less discretion in its exercise because most state constitutions are detailed and specific.

The courts are often called upon to interpret and decide the meaning of statutory provisions that are ambiguously or unclearly stated and open to conflicting interpretations. When a court accepts one interpretation rather than another, it gives effect to the policy preference of the winning party. In 1984, in the *Grove City* case, the meaning or intent of Title IX of the 1972 Education Act Amendments was at issue.[40] This provision prohibited discrimination on the basis of sex by educational institutions receiving federal aid "for any program or activity." Did this ban on discrimination apply to the entire institution being aided, as many members of Congress and civil-rights groups contended? Or did it apply only to the specific "program or activity" receiving funding, as the Reagan administration argued? A majority on the Supreme Court took the latter position, much restricting the effect of the 1972 statute and three other civil-rights laws with similar provisions.

After this ruling, a legislative campaign was initiated to correct what many critics thought was an improper interpretation of the 1972 law. It culminated in the Civil Rights Restoration Act of 1988, enacted into law over President Reagan's veto.[41] The act overcame the Court's *Grove City* decision by clearly specifying that if one part of an institution received federal funds, then the ban on sex discrimination applied to the entire institution. This was the view of the 1972 law's scope that had prevailed prior to the Court's decision.

As clarified, Title IX has produced a vast expansion of women's athletic programs in American colleges and universities. This, in turn, has had a similar impact on public school athletic programs.

We turn now to the case of Lilly Ledbetter, who for many years suffered pay discrimination at the hands of the Goodyear Tire and Rubber Company. Men doing the same work were paid considerably better. When she finally learned of this, she sued Goodyear for pay restitution under the Civil Rights Act of 1964. Ledbetter won at the federal district court level only ultimately to lose before the Supreme Court. The majority ruled that Ledbetter's case was "untimely," interpreting the Civil Rights Act to require initiation of action within 180 days of the first discriminatory paycheck.[42] The minority argued that this changed the accepted interpretation of the Civil Rights Act.

Critics of the decision in Congress (mostly Democrats) quickly introduced legislation to overcome the Goodyear's decision. Because the 110th Congress (2007–2008) failed to enact this legislation, it became an issue in the presidential campaign. Barack Obama supported the legislation, which was opposed by John McCain. When Congress met in January 2009, the Democratic majorities within the month enacted the Lilly Ledbetter Equal Pay Act, providing that the statute of limitations applied to each discriminatory paycheck rather than to the first instance of discrimination. The Act's supporters said that this restored the intended meaning of the Civil Rights Act.[43]

The judiciary has also played a major role in forming economic policy in the United States. A substantial portion of the law relating to such matters as property ownership, contracts, corporations, and employer–employee relationships has been developed and applied by the courts in the form of common law and equity. These are systems of judge-made law fashioned over the years on a case-to-case basis. They originated in England, but American judges have adapted them to American needs and conditions. Much of this law was developed by the state courts, and much of it is still applied by them.[44]

Today the courts are not only becoming more involved in policy formation but are also playing a more positive role, specifying not only what government cannot do but also what it must do to meet legal or constitutional requirements. For instance, in *Roe* v. *Wade* (1973), the Supreme Court declared unconstitutional a Texas statute prohibiting abortion as a violation of the privacy protected by the First and Fourteenth Amendments.[45] The right to an abortion was held to be a "fundamental right," one that could not be readily regulated or limited by governments. The majority went on to specify the standards future abortion laws would have to meet to comply with the Constitution. During the first trimester of pregnancy, abortion was left to the decision of a woman and her physician. During the second trimester, abortion could be regulated to protect the mother's health. During the third trimester, however, after the fetus gained viability, abortion could be prohibited except when necessary to protect the mother's life or health. This ruling clearly had a legislative-like quality. It also touched off a major, continuing political controversy.

In 1989, the Court, which had become more conservative because of three Reagan appointees, partially overruled *Roe* v. *Wade*. In *Webster* v. *Reproductive*

Health Services, the Court upheld a Missouri state law that prohibited the performance of abortions in public hospitals and clinics and the use of state funds for counseling women about abortion.[46] Also, testing was required before performing an abortion after twenty weeks to determine whether the fetus was viable outside the womb. This decision, by giving state legislatures more authority to regulate abortions, made the abortion issue even more contentious and thrust it back into the legislative arena in the fifty states.

The Supreme Court came to grips with abortion again in 1992 in *Planned Parenthood of Southeastern Pennsylvania* v. *Casey.* At issue was state law imposing various restrictions on a woman's right to end a pregnancy. The five-justice majority reaffirmed a woman's right to have an abortion in the early stages of pregnancy but upheld all provisions of the state law except one requiring spousal notification. Only two justices, however, continued to view abortion as a fundamental right.[47] The Court's 1992 decision did nothing to reduce the intensity of the abortion issue.

In more recent cases, the Court has upheld some state laws requiring a minor to notify parents of a planned abortion unless a judge grants a waiver. The Court has also upheld some restrictions on the actions of antiabortion protesters, such as congregating, picketing, or demonstrating within thirty-six feet of the property line of an abortion clinic.[48] The judicial struggle over abortion rights is unlikely to soon abate. Moral issues of this sort are not easy to resolve. State legislatures, especially in the South, continually contrive and pass laws in efforts to reduce abortions.[49]

Several factors guarantee continued judicial involvement in policy formation: the growing influence of government on people's lives, the failure or refusal of the legislative branches to act on some problems, the dissatisfaction that often arises when they do act, the willingness of the courts to become involved, and the increasing litigiousness in at least some segments of the population. Americans have become quite adept at converting political issues into legal issues that the courts are then called on to decide. Judicial activism more than judicial restraint characterizes the response of the courts.

Although courts in such other Western countries as Canada, Australia, and Germany have some power of judicial review, they have had less influence on policy than American courts. In the developing countries, the courts appear to have no meaningful role. The American practice of settling many important policy issues through judicial action, including such technical matters as standards for clean air and industrial health and safety, remains unique.

Nongovernmental Participants

The official policy-makers are joined by many other participants in the policy process, including interest groups, political parties, research organizations, communications media, and individual citizens. They are designated here as nongovernmental participants because however important or dominant they may be in various situations, they themselves do not usually have legal authority to make binding policy decisions. They provide information, they exert pressure, they seek to persuade, but they do not decide. That is the prerogative of official policy-makers.

Interest Groups   Interest groups appear to take an important part in policy-making in practically all countries. Depending upon whether they are democratic or dictatorial, modern or developing, countries may differ in how groups are constituted and how legitimate they are. Thus, groups appear to be more numerous and to operate much more openly and freely in the United States or Great Britain than in Austria or Nigeria. In all systems, however, groups may perform an interest-articulation function; that is, they express demands and present alternatives for policy action. They may also supply public officials with much information, often technical, and perhaps not available from other sources, about the nature and possible consequences of policy proposals. In doing so, they contribute to the rationality of policymaking.

Interest groups representing labor, agriculture, business, education, health, and other areas of society are a major source of demands for public-policy action in the United States. Because American society is pluralist, pressure groups are many and diverse in their interests, organization, size, and modes of operation. Their numbers have expanded greatly in recent decades. The *Encyclopedia of Associations* (a standard source) listed 5,843 associations in 1959; this number had grown to 23,298 by 1995.[50] One major growth area has been health. In 1975, there were 90 health groups, whereas currently there are around 750. "You name a disease, there's probably a Washington lobby for it," says an official of the American Heart Association.[51]

The Obama administration's health-care reform effort brought out organized interests in full force. In 2009, more than 1,750 companies, trade groups, and other organizations hired some 4,500 lobbyists and spent $1.2 billion to influence the policy process.[52]

The explosion in the size of the group system does not mean, however, that some societal interests are not poorly represented by groups. Poor people, migrant workers, and the homeless are cases in point. They do not fare well in the group struggle.

Typically, although most groups have a variety of interests, they want to influence policy on specific subjects, such as minimum wages, derivatives trading, or health-care financing. Because groups often have conflicting desires on policy issues, public officials confront the need to choose from, or reconcile, conflicting demands. Groups that are well organized, large in size, and skillfully led are likely to fare better than those that are poorly organized, poorly financed, and low in social status. The group struggle is not a contest among equals.[53]

"Single-issue" interest groups have proliferated in recent years. They focus on one issue or set of related issues such as gun control, milk prices, or legislation on abortion. The National Rifle Association and the National Abortion and Reproductive Rights Action League are illustrative. The proliferation of subcommittees in Congress with narrow jurisdictions stimulated the development of such groups and contributed to their importance by permitting concentration of their efforts. Among the single-issue groups that substantially affected public policy in the past were those advocating abolition of slavery, suffrage for women, and nationwide prohibition.

Public-interest groups are also important players in the policy process. Whereas most pressure groups represent interests of direct, material benefit to their members, public-interest groups usually represent interests that in their absence would go unrepresented, such as those of consumers, nature lovers, environmentalists, and "good-government" proponents. Frequently, these interests involve intangible matters such as honesty, beauty, and safety.[54] The members of public-interest groups usually do not benefit selectively and materially from the interests they advocate, and indeed may not benefit at all in an immediate sense. Members of groups advocating the abolition of the death penalty do not expect to be in personal jeopardy. Public-interest groups include the Sierra Club and the National Wildlife Federation, which support environmental protection and wilderness programs; Common Cause, which advocates more open and accountable government; and the Pacific Legal Foundation (PLF), which engages in litigation supporting free enterprise and economic development. Not all public-interest groups are liberal in their policy inclinations, as is sometimes assumed, and as the PLF indicates.

At the national level, many associations of state and local governmental officials routinely seek to influence the content of national policies. Three factors seem to have been especially significant in generating this "intergovernmental lobby."[55] One is the increasing professionalism in state and local governments. The second is growth in federal grants-in-aid to state and local governments, which amounted to $468 billion in 2012, or approximately 28 percent of state expenditures. Third are the many regulations and requirements that these and other federal programs impose on the states and localities and that are open to modification.

Some of these associations represent elected or appointed officials with executive and legislative duties, such as the National Conference of State Legislators, the U.S. Conference of Mayors, and the National Association of Counties. Others involve functional specialists in highways, education, recreation, and other matters, such as the American Association of State Highway and Transportation Officials, the Council of Chief State School Officers, and the National Association of County Park and Recreation Officials. They gain influence from their expertness and the support of state and local politicians.

Many individual states, cities, counties, and public universities also have their own Washington lobbyists or representatives. As with other interest groups, the intergovernmental lobby is not a monolithic force: its component groups frequently disagree among themselves. Thus, the highway officials want more funding for interurban highways, and city officials see a need for more spending on mass-transit systems.

The amount of influence that interest groups have upon decisions depends on a number of factors, including (subject to the rule of *ceteris paribus*—other things being equal) the size of its membership, its monetary and other resources, its cohesiveness, the skill of its leadership, its social status, the presence or absence of competing organizations, the attitudes of public officials, and the site of decision-making in the political system. (On this last item, recall the discussion of institutionalism in the chapter "The Study of Public Policy") With other things again being equal, a large, well-regarded group (e.g., the American Legion) will have more influence than a smaller, less well-regarded group (e.g., Friends of the Earth), and a labor union with a large membership will have more influence than one with few members. Also, as a consequence of the factors enumerated here, a group may have strong or controlling influence on decisions in one policy area and little in another. Whereas the National Association of Manufacturers has much influence on some economic issues, it has little impact on the area of civil rights.

Much of the work in promoting pressure-group interests in the policy process is performed by group representatives, or lobbyists. Although *lobbyist* is the more popular term, *group representative* seems more descriptive, given the many and varied activities in which these people engage. Table 2.3, which is based on a survey of more than 700 group representatives, conveys a notion of both the array of activities undertaken by group representatives and the relative importance they attribute to the various activities. Once a group makes a decision to try to influence government on some matter, it is then confronted with deciding how it can best accomplish that goal. Should emphasis be on lobbying—directly seeking to inform and persuade officials? Should emphasis be on providing written information and testimony to officials? How should the efforts of competing groups be countered? Typically, there is no clear road to success.

In recent years, groups have made considerable use of "outside lobbying" techniques, which try to persuade ordinary citizens to serve as their front-line advocates.[56] Prominent here are "grass-roots" and "grass-tops" lobbying. Grass-roots lobbying strives to mobilize legislators' constituents to call, write, e-mail, and otherwise deluge them with communications. Some groups, such as the Sierra Club and the NRA, have genuine grass-roots memberships. In other instances, professional lobbyists may be hired to create grass-roots movements, or at least their semblance. These mobilization efforts may be done in conjunction with televised advertising campaigns.

Grass-tops lobbying strives to favorably energize an elite rather than the masses. People who are likely to be influential with a member of Congress are identified and then persuaded to convey the preferred message to the member. These forms of lobbying are important because, except for elections, they are the means by which "elite policymakers . . . experience pressure in the form of popular participation. Were it not for outside lobbying from interest groups, many policy decisions would take place among a relatively insulated group of Washington insiders."

TABLE 2.3

Importance Rating of Group Representatives' Tasks

Task description	% reporting task was of great or considerable importance
Government regulations	
1. Monitoring changes in rules, regulations, or laws	62
2. Providing written information to officials	52
3. Maintaining general relations with officials	64
4. Maintaining informal, substantive contacts with officials	62
5. Drafting legislation or rules	27
6. Alerting client organization about issues	84
Interest-group networks	
7. Mobilizing grass-roots support	41
8. Maintaining contacts with allies	50
9. Monitoring interest groups	29
10. Political fund-raising (PACs)	19
11. Maintaining contacts with adversaries	18
12. Resolving conflicts within organization	23
Public presentation	
13. Testifying at official proceedings	27
14. Preparing official testimony	47
15. Commenting for press, publications, or speeches	44
16. Developing policy positions or strategies	83
Litigation	
17. Pursuing litigation aimed at changing policy	17
18. Working on and filing amicus briefs	5

Source: From "Lawyers and the Structure of Influence," by Robert L. Nelson and John P. Heinz with Edward O. Laumann and Robert H. Salisbury, in *Law & Society Review*, Vol. 22:2 (1988), pp. 237–300. As found in John P. Heinz, Edward O. Laumann, Robert L. Nelson and Robert H. Salisbury, *The Hollow Core: Private Interests in National Policymaking* (Cambridge, MA: Harvard University Press, 1993), p. 99. Reprinted by permission of Law and Society Association.

The relatively open and fluid pressure system in the United States is markedly different from the neocorporatist pattern of group relationships in some Western European countries, such as Austria, Norway, Sweden, and the Netherlands, which combine democratic politics with a formally structured group system.[57] In the neocorporate scheme of things, access to policy-makers is controlled by the government. Policies are adopted after close consultation, bargaining, and compromise between the government and groups that are the officially recognized representatives of farmers, labor unions, and employers. Groups can withdraw from this partnership with the government, but they may lose influence as a consequence. Some groups, such as those representing consumer and environmental interests, find it difficult to gain access to the government. Neocorporatism has found little support in the United States.

Political Parties   In the United States, political parties are organizations interested primarily in contesting elections in order to control
the personnel of government. They care more, in short, about power than
about policy. Elections are contested more on the basis of constituency, service, media imagery, and negative attacks on opponents rather than on policy
differences. This situation has often led to the complaint that the Republican
and Democratic Parties do not present a meaningful choice for the voters
and consequently, that for public-policy formation, it makes little difference
which party is in office. Although the parties are not highly policy-oriented,
such complaints ignore both the fact that many people do believe that the
parties are different and the substantial impact that the parties do have
on policy. Moreover, since the 1990s, the parties in Congress became more
united, polarized, and policy oriented. This is especially true for the House of
Representatives.

Clearly, the parties appeal to different segments of society. The Democratic
Party draws disproportionately from big-city, labor, minority, and ethnic voters; the Republican Party draws disproportionately from rural, small-town,
and suburban areas, fundamental religious groups, and businesspeople and
professionals. In the South, where for many decades it was the heavily dominant party, the Democratic Party has yielded much ground to the Republican
Party in national elections since the 1960s.

The parties often come into conflict on such issues as welfare programs, labor legislation, business regulation, public housing, taxation, and agricultural
income-support legislation. The reader should not have much difficulty in dif-
ferentiating between the parties on these issues. Given such policy inclinations
and the fact that party members in Congress often vote in accordance with
party policy positions, which party controls Congress or the presidency has
important policy implications.

In the American state legislatures, political parties vary greatly in importance from one state to another. In some states, it is obvious that parties exercise little discipline over legislative voting, and the party has little, if any, effect
on policymaking, as in the Alabama and Louisiana legislatures. In such states,
factions within the dominant party may be more important. By contrast, in
states such as Connecticut and Michigan, both parties are active and cohesive
and have considerable influence on legislative decision-making. When conflict
over policy occurs in such states, the parties' function is to provide alternatives. In many cities, an effort has been made to eliminate political-party influence on policy by running nonpartisan elections for city officials. Policy is
supposed to be made "objectively." An unintended consequence of the policy
of nonpartisanship in city elections is reduced interest and participation in
politics.

In modern societies generally, political parties often perform the function
of interest aggregation; that is, they seek to convert the particular demands of
interest groups into general policy alternatives. The way in which parties

"aggregate" interests is affected by the number of parties. In predominantly two-party systems, such as the United States and Great Britain, the parties' desire to gain widespread electoral support "will require both parties to include in their policy 'package' those demands which have very broad popular support and to attempt to avoid alienating the most prominent groups."[58] In multiparty systems, on the other hand, parties may do less aggregating and act as the representatives of fairly narrow sets of interests, as they appear to do in Israel, France, and Spain. Generally, parties have a broader range of policy concerns than do interest groups; hence, they act more as brokers than as advocates for particular interests in policy formation. In some one-party systems, such as that of Mexico, they are the predominant force in policymaking.

Research Organizations   Private research organizations, frequently and inelegantly referred to as "think tanks," are another set of important players in policymaking. One researcher reports that there are 120 private, nonprofit research organizations in the Washington, DC, area and another 170 scattered among the American states.[59] These organizations are staffed with full-time policy analysts and researchers, some of whom are ex-government officials, perhaps hoping to return to office once their party regains power in Washington. They are mostly funded by private foundations, businesses, and rich people. Their studies and reports provide basic information and data on policy issues, develop alternatives and proposals for handling problems, and evaluate the effectiveness and consequences of public policies. Their personnel testify at congressional committee hearings, communicate informally with public officials, and write articles for the op-ed pages of newspapers. Collectively, they add substance and alternatives to policy debates (see Table 2.4).

TABLE 2.4

Some Prominent Research Organizations

American Enterprise Institute
Brookings Institution
Cato Institute
Council on Foreign Relations
Economic Policy Institute
Heritage Foundation
Manhattan Institute
Progressive Policy Institute
RAND Corporation
Resources for the Future
Urban Institute
Worldwatch Institute

Most of these research organizations have policy biases and distinct ideological leanings. The intent is often to justify policy alternatives. The orientations of the American Enterprise Institute and the Economic Policy Institute, for example, are widely regarded as conservative and liberal, respectively. The Brookings Institution and Resources for the Future occupy a middle-of-the-road position. In addition to their policy-analysis activities, these organizations may also engage in policy advocacy.

Research organizations once provided "expert but neutral" information to policy-makers, which contrasted with the biased or self-interested information developed by pressure groups. In recent years, however, many research organizations with strong liberal, conservative, or libertarian inclinations have entered the policy lists as advocates.[60] Andrew Rich and Kent Weaver describe this situation:

> Think tanks, especially the more ideologically focused ones, have been active and visible participants in contentious and divisive debates associated with every contemporary policy issue, from national struggles over welfare reform to regional squabbles over school finances and performance. In these policy battles, expertise has frequently been used, and viewed by many participants, more as ammunition for partisan and ideological causes than as balanced or objective information that can and should be widely acceptable among policy-makers.[61]

This "politicization of expertise," according to Rich and Weaver, has "jeopardized the reputation of think tanks as sources of neutral expertise."

Many universities have policy or research centers that produce policy studies and evaluations on national, state, and local issues. Several, for instance, house groups that concentrate on coastal and marine resources. Individual university researchers also occasionally produce studies of direct value to policy-makers, sometimes under contract with government agencies, and participate in issue networks comprising many researchers, officials, and others interested in particular policy areas.

The usefulness of the findings of academic researchers is reduced because it is often written in technical jargon and published in little-known journals. Research "brokers," such as think tanks and congressional staff members, may be needed to increase the accessibility of scholarly output for policy-makers.[62] One way or another, academic ideas contribute to the rationality of policy.

Communications Media   The communications media—newspapers, news magazines, network and cable television, radio (including talk shows), and the Internet—are involved in policymaking as suppliers and transmitters of information; and as agenda setters in that they help people decide what to think about and, whether intentionally or otherwise, what to think.[63] Although the television networks and newspapers are still the most used news sources, reliance on them has declined substantially in the last couple of decades. New media have gained importance, including cable news (CNN, MSNBC, and Fox News), talk radio, and online news. Also, the proliferation of cell phones and other handheld electronic devices should be noted. They can be used to transmit political information in addition to personal messages and drivel. This fragmentation of news outlets provides news consumers with a wide range of choices, including ideological diversity and disinformation.

Complaints about bias in media coverage and reporting of public affairs are common, as are contentions that public officials (e.g., in the White House) are managing or manipulating the news. However valid these charges, they attest to the impact the media are thought to have in politics and policymaking. A "favorable press" is much sought after.

With good reason, Washington officials are quite sensitive to what is reported by the national media, which means newspapers such as *The New York Times* and *The Washington Post* and the major television networks. A survey found that more than 70 percent of senior federal officials believed a positive press increased the likelihood that they would attain their goals and negative coverage would reduce their chances of doing so. Here the perceived power of the media does not involve changing policy but rather influences the capacity of officials to convert their ideas into policy. However, the substance of policy may also be affected.[64] Unfavorable coverage of the Reagan administration's attempts to tighten eligibility requirements for Social Security disability benefits, for example, contributed to the eventual abandonment of the effort.

For the most part, the media provide minimal coverage of policy matters.[65] The issues receiving coverage are likely to be those judged to have high public appeal—Social Security reform, some consumer-protection topics, the environment—because they are "interesting" or "relevant." The politics of policy rather than the details of policy content receive emphasis. Except for some specialized media (such as the *National Journal*, *CQ Weekly*, and trade journals), policy on such topics as labor, agriculture, housing, financial regulation, and trade relations do not get much attention. The emergence of cable network venues, talk-show radio, the Internet, and other news media has done little to remedy this situation. Persons who rely on the general media for their policy information are likely to be woefully underinformed. As for the impact of the media on the policy process, beyond helping to set the policy agenda (see the "Policy Formation" chapter), that is problematical.[66]

Officials, of course, are not simply acted upon by the media but also strive to use the press for their own purposes. With interviews, press releases, and news "leaks," they seek to use the media to test and influence the attitudes among both the general public and other officials toward particular proposals or actions. Those who oppose a decision may "leak" premature or adverse information in an effort to kill it. This tactic was applied in the George Bush administration to a proposal for securing funds to bail out bankrupt savings and loan institutions by imposing a tax on all savings and loan depositors. The proposal was abandoned, and the costs of the bailout, which amounted to around $150 billion, were imposed on taxpayers. Few seemed to care or to be aware of this.

President Reagan was often referred to as the "great communicator" because of his ability to use radio and television addresses to shape public opinion in support of his purposes. He used this ability to put income-tax reform on the national agenda and build support for its enactment. Speaker of the House O'Neill, who was not personally inclined to support tax reform, felt the pressure generated by the president's speeches. "I have to have a bill, the Democratic party has to have a [tax] bill . . . ," he was quoted as saying. "If we don't we'll be clobbered over the head by the President of the United States."[67] Used appropriately, the presidency may be a "bully pulpit," as Theodore Roosevelt once observed.

The Individual Citizen   In discussions of policymaking, the focus typically is on legislatures, interest groups, and other prominent players; little or nothing is said about individual citizens. This bias is unfortunate, however, because individuals often do seem to make a difference. In various instances, citizens can participate directly in decision-making. In most states constitutional amendments are submitted to the voters for approval, and in many local jurisdictions bond issues and tax increases require their authorization. In some American states and in some countries (such as Switzerland), the initiative process enables citizens to vote directly on legislation.

The initiative is a policy innovation dating from the Progressive Era. Progressive reformers viewed the initiative, along with the referendum and recall, as a way of transferring power from politicians to the people. The initiative exists in half of the states and several hundred cities, especially in the western half of the United States. On the basis of a petition signed by a specified number of voters, a policy proposal is placed on the ballot. If approved by a majority of those voting on it, it becomes law without any action of the state legislature or the city council. In 1998, voters approved thirty-six of sixty-one initiatives on the ballot in several states. The successful initiatives "ended affirmative action, raised the minimum wage, banned billboards, decriminalized a wide range of hard drugs and permitted thousands of patients to obtain prescriptions for marijuana, restricted campaign spending and contributions, expanded casino gambling, banned many forms of hunting, prohibited some abortions, and allowed adopted children to obtain the names of their biological parents" in various states.[68] Two states in 2012 legalized use of marijuana. The initiative has become a means by which many contentious social and economic issues are put on the ballot.

In actuality, the initiative process frequently departs from the image of informed and activated citizens taking charge of policymaking. In many instances, the process is dominated by powerful interest groups. They hire professional organizations to solicit the needed signatures and wage expensive campaigns for and against the proposals. For example, California Indian tribes spent $66 million in support of an initiative to expand casino gambling. Nevada gambling interests, who saw this as detrimental to their business, spent $25 million on their losing cause.[69] Whether dominated by monied interests or reflecting populist action, the initiative produces a policymaking process markedly different from that featured in this book.

Whether because of inertia or indifference, most people do not take these opportunities to engage directly in shaping public policy. Moreover, many people do not vote, engage in political-party activities, join pressure groups, or otherwise display much interest in politics. Survey research tells us the voters are often little influenced by policy issues when voting for candidates for public office. Given the inaction and indifference, however, it still does not hold that citizens have no influence on policy except in the situation discussed in the preceding paragraphs. Some other possibilities for citizen impact are reviewed here.

Even in authoritarian regimes, the interests or desires of common citizens are consequential for public policies.[70] The old-style dictator will pay some attention to what his or her people want just to keep down unrest. A Latin American dictator is supposed to have said, "You can't shoot everyone." Modern authoritarian regimes such as the People's Republic of China also seem to respond to citizens' preferences even as they exclude citizens from more direct participation in policy formation.

Elections in democratic countries may indirectly reinforce official responsiveness to citizen interests. Professor Charles E. Lindblom summarizes:

> The most conspicuous difference between authoritarianism and democratic regimes is that in democratic regimes citizens choose their top policymakers in genuine elections. Some political scientists speculate that voting in genuine elections may be an important method of citizen influence on policy not so much because it actually permits citizens to choose their officials and to some degree instruct these officials on policy, but because the existence of genuine elections put[s] a stamp of approval on citizen participation. Indirectly, therefore, the fact of elections enforces on proximate policy makers a rule that citizens' wishes count in policy-making.[71]

The "rule" Lindblom refers to is sometimes expressed in the aphorism that citizens have a right to be heard and that officials have a duty to listen. The effect of such considerations on policy-makers is worth thinking about; although public sentiments are not amenable to rigorous measurement in the present state of political science, they do appear to have an effect on political behavior.

Some presidential elections in the United States have been classified as "critical" because they produce major realignments in voter coalitions and shifts in public policy. The presidential election of 1932 is a prime example. The Republican and Democratic candidates differed substantially on how they proposed to deal with the crisis of the Great Depression. The voters gave Franklin D. Roosevelt and the Democrats an overwhelming victory. The flood of New Deal legislation that followed produced major changes in government–economy relationships and in government's role in American society generally. In such instances, large numbers of newly elected officials, chosen because of their stand on the critical question, enact legislation consistent with their party's stand. Through the electoral process the voters help to produce basic changes in public policy. Other critical elections were those of 1860 and 1896.[72]

Initially, some observers thought the election of 1980, in which the Republican Party elected Reagan and gained control of the Senate, might have been a critical election, but it turned out not to be. The Democratic gains in the 1982 congressional elections indicated that no basic realignment in voters' allegiances had occurred. The Democratic Party remains the majority party among voters having a party preference. "Landslide" elections are thus not necessarily critical elections. Following the Republican victories in the 1994 congressional elections, speculation again arose as to whether this marked the beginning of a realignment.[73] In subsequent elections, however, the Democrats regained some of the seats that they had lost. They took control of Congress in 2006 and the Presidency as well in 2008. So much for a Republican realignment.

Some citizens, through their intellectual and agitational activities, contribute new ideas and directions to the policy process. Thus, Rachel Carson, with *Silent Spring*, and Ralph Nader, with *Unsafe at Any Speed*, considerably influenced policy on pesticide control and automobile safety, respectively. In a 1947 article in *Foreign Affairs* under the byline X, diplomat George Kennan outlined a proposal for a policy of containment to prevent expansion of the Soviet Union's influence and domination. This became the basic United States approach in dealing with the Soviet Union in the international arena. Only in the last few years before the collapse of the Soviet Union did the United States begin to develop new responses to the Soviets. The effect of Kennan's article was much greater than he had anticipated.

Others may substantially affect policy action through their political activism. Social Security legislation in the 1930s was certainly affected by the activities of Dr. Francis Townsend, who advocated that every person over sixty should be paid a monthly pension of $200, and the large following he gathered. In December 1955, Rosa Parks, a black seamstress, refused to give up her seat to a white passenger on a crowded segregated city bus in Montgomery, Alabama. She was arrested. Her simple act of defiance touched off the Montgomery bus boycott, which succeeded and helped spur desegregation throughout the South. In the 1960s, Reverend Martin Luther King, Jr., provided leadership for the civil-rights movement and impetus for civil-rights legislation. A small group of women whose husbands were killed in the terrorist attack on the World Trade Center towers was instrumental in causing Congress to create in 2002 the National Commission on Terrorist Attacks upon the United States. The commission investigated and reported on intelligence failures preceding the attacks.

Levels of Politics

All the participants in policymaking discussed in this chapter are not involved in every policymaking or decision-making situation. Some matters create much attention and attract a wide range of participants. Others are less visible or affect only a few people and consequently stir little attention and participation. Professor Emmette S. Redford identifies three levels of policies based on the scope of participation normally characteristic of each and, to a lesser extent, the kind of issue involved: micropolitics, subsystem policies, and macropolitics.[74] These merit attention.

Micropolitics involves efforts by individuals, companies, and communities to secure favorable governmental action for themselves. Subsystem politics focuses on functional areas of activity—such as air-pollution control, coalmine safety regulation, or river and harbor improvements—and involves relationships among congressional committees, administrative agencies (or bureaus), and interest groups. Macropolitics occurs when "the community at large and the leaders of government as a whole are brought into the discussion and determination of [public] policy."[75] The controversies over how to handle airport security and the reductions in military spending are examples of macropolitics.

Micropolitics   Micropolitics often occurs when an individual seeks a favorable ruling from an administrative agency or a special bill offering an exemption from a requirement of the immigration laws, when a company seeks a favorable change in the tax code or a television broadcasting license, or when a community seeks a grant for the construction of an airport or opposes the location of a public-housing project in its area. In each of these instances one finds the specific, differentiated, and intense interest of one or a few in a society of many individuals, companies, and communities. They require or seek a decision applicable to one or a few. Typically, only a few persons and officials are involved in or even aware of such decision-making situations, however important they may be for those seeking action, and whatever the ultimate consequences of such decisions or a cluster of them may be.

In the short run at least, micropolitical decisions appear to be distributive and can be made without considering limited resources. That is, such decisions appear to affect only those immediately interested and are usually made on the basis of mutual noninterference, each claimant seeking its own benefits (or subsidies) and not opposing or interfering with others' efforts to do likewise. Benefits received by one individual or group do not appear to be won at the expense of other individuals or groups.

Micropolitics is exemplified by the congressional enactment of private legislation.[76] Almost every year Congress enacts several bills into law that apply only to a person, company, or governmental unit specifically designated in the law. A private law may exempt someone from a provision of the Immigration and Nationality Act, or provide for the payment of a monetary claim against the government, as when a government agency has caused damage to someone's property. Such legislation arouses little attention on its way through the legislative process and becomes law with the public unaware of its existence. Each party in the House does have a three-member "objector committee" whose task is to screen private bills for controversial provisions. For whatever reason, many more private bills are introduced during a session than become law.

As governmental programs become more numerous and complex, and as they make more benefits available for, or impose more requirements or restrictions on, individuals, groups, companies, and communities, both the opportunity and the incentive to engage in micropolitics increase. As this happens, the likelihood of favoritism and unequal treatment for persons and groups increases. Those who have more political resources (e.g., information, influential contacts, and money) are more likely to become the beneficiaries of micropolitics, whatever the justness or soundness of their cause. We now consider them in more detail.

Subsystem Politics

In a frequently quoted passage, political analyst Ernest S. Griffith, in 1939, called attention to the existence of political subsystems and the value of studying them:

> One cannot live in Washington for long without being conscious that it has whirlpools or centers of activity focusing on particular problems. ... It is my opinion that ordinarily the relationship among these men—legislators, administrators, lobbyists, scholars—who are interested in a common problem is a much more real relationship than the relationship between congressmen generally or between administrators generally. In other words, he who would understand the prevailing pattern of our present governmental behavior, instead of studying the formal institutions or even generalizations in the relationships between these institutions or organs, important though all these things are, may possibly obtain a better picture of the way things really happen if he would study these "whirlpools" of special social interests and problems.[77]

In the decades since Griffith made that statement, political scientists and others have devoted much attention to examining political subsystems (also variously called subgovernments, policy clusters, and policy coalitions).

For many years, subsystems were usually designated as *iron triangles* (or *cozy little triangles*, or *triple alliances*). An iron triangle ideally involves a pattern of symbiotic relationships among some congressional committees (or subcommittees), an administrative agency or two, and the relevant interest groups centered on a policy area (Figure 2.1).[78] All have a direct, material interest in the policy matters being treated. A classic iron triangle was focused on rivers and harbors development activity. It comprised the Army Corps of Engineers (who still handle many civilian water projects), the congressional committees with jurisdiction over public works, and the National Rivers and Harbors Congress, an interest group.[79] This triangle, which was resistant to wider participation, dominated policymaking on water projects. As with other triangles, the participants preferred policy to be made cooperatively and quietly.

FIGURE 2.1

A Possible Iron Triangle

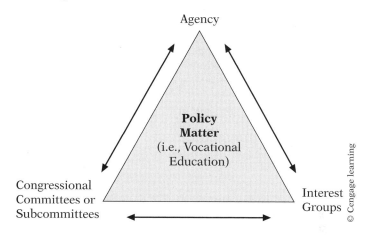

The national government was often alleged to be (and sometimes continues to be) heavily populated with iron triangles.[80] Although these arrangements provided participants with continuing access and influence on the content of policy, those who were excluded—policy experts (often within the academic community), groups adversely affected by their policies, and others—were very critical of them. Iron triangles were charged with contributing to governmental fragmentation, causing lack of policy coordination, and acting contrary to the public interest. Moreover, the governmental agencies involved were frequently alleged to have been captured by the dominant groups; the Civil Aeronautics Board (now defunct) and the Interstate Commerce Commission (also defunct) were called captives of the commercial airlines and railroads, respectively. The Office of the Comptroller of the Currency currently seems unduly responsive to the interests of the banking industry. Although frequently bandied about, the notion of capture has not been well explained. Usually it appears to mean that, for whatever reasons, an agency has become—the person alleging capture believes—too responsive to the interests of an industry or its clientele.

The iron-triangle concept came under attack several years ago by political scientist Hugh Heclo, who contended that it was "not so much wrong as it was disastrously incomplete." The concept, he said, "suggests a stable set of participants coalesced to control fairly narrow public programs which are in the direct economic interest of each party to the alliances."[81] Heclo's view was that other, larger sorts of arrangements also exist, which he referred to as "issue networks." He went on to explain that an issue network includes many participants who constantly move into and out of the network, including public officials, interest-group representatives, political activists, and technical or policy experts from universities, research organizations, and elsewhere. Within these somewhat cloudlike or amorphous configurations, no one seems to be in control of the policies and issues.

What, then, does an issue network look like? Let Professor Heclo answer:

> It is difficult to say, precisely, for at any given time only one part of a network may be active, and through time the various connections may intensify or fade among the policy intermediaries and the executive and congressional bureaucracies. For example, there is no single health policy network but various sets of people knowledgeable and concerned about cost control mechanisms, insurance techniques, nutritional programs, pre-paid plans, and so on. At any one time these experts in designing a nationwide insurance system may seem to be operating in relative isolation, until it becomes clear that previous efforts to control costs have already created precedents that have to be accommodated in any new system, or that the issue of federal funding for abortions has laid land mines in the path of any workable plan.[82]

Many of those involved in a network will not have direct material interests at stake; rather, their ideas and beliefs about proper public policy will be the basis for their participation.

Political scientists have enthusiastically embraced the concept of issue networks despite a dearth of empirical data on the actual presence and operation of networks. The political science literature is replete with references to networks and to how they have replaced iron triangles in the policy process. In reality, some iron triangles probably survive, especially in distributive policy.[83]

There is no need to assume that only one kind of subsystem can exist at a time. (That was not Heclo's position.) Why not rather assume that subsystems take various forms that can be arrayed along a continuum? At one pole, we could put classic iron triangles, with their limited participation, resistance to external influences, and preoccupation with material interests. At the other pole, we could put the issue network with its amorphousness, wide and changing participation, issue experts, and ambiguity about who is in control. Other forms of subsystems could be appropriately arrayed between the poles.[84]

What I call a policy community is broader and more open in participation than an iron triangle but less amorphous and more under identifiable control than an issue network. Thus, the antitrust community includes the Antitrust Division of the Department of Justice and the Federal Trade Commission, the House and Senate Judiciary Committees (or their antitrust subcommittees), the relevant appropriations subcommittees, writers of books and journal articles on antitrust, the private antitrust bar, and the federal courts that rule on antitrust cases. State attorneys general have become members in recent years. This community has much influence on the nature and implementation of antitrust policy as long as important new legislation is not involved. Significant changes in antitrust policy were achieved through variations in the interpretation and enforcement of laws by executive and judicial members of the antitrust community in the 1980s. The Reagan administration's attempt to have these changes enacted into statutory law failed, however. Clinton administration's antitrust officials soon acted administratively to reverse some of the Reagan and George Bush administrations' antitrust practices.

Within a subsystem, especially if it is large and complex, advocacy coalitions may develop.[85] An advocacy coalition is a set of people within a subsystem who share basic values, perceptions of problems, and policy preferences, and who cooperate to advance attainment of their policy goals and interests. Often there are two or more advocacy coalitions in a subsystem. The policy area of air-pollution control provides an illustration.

The air-pollution control subsystem is complex, comprising the Environmental Protection Agency (EPA), various congressional committees, other agencies with overlapping jurisdictions, polluting companies, state and local pollution-control agencies, makers of pollution-control equipment, many health and environmental groups, other countries (as on acid rain), and more. Two advocacy coalitions are identifiable in this subsystem: the clean-air and the economic-feasibility coalitions.

The clean-air coalition consists of EPA air-pollution officials, environmental and health groups, some labor unions, some state and local air-pollution control officials, some researchers, and some members of Congress. This coalition asserts the primacy of health over economic development, contends that the market cannot adequately deal with pollution problems, and favors a traditional regulatory approach to pollution control.

The economic-feasibility coalition includes industrial sources of air pollution, energy companies, their allies in Congress, a few labor unions, some state and local pollution-control officials, and a number of economists. The economic-feasibility coalition stresses the need to balance health and economic development and efficiency, doubts that the health problems are as serious as some contend, and favors more deference to market arrangements and the use of economic incentives to reduce pollution.

Inside the air-pollution control subsystem, rule-making and implementation actions will be shaped by the interaction of these advocacy coalitions and will rest ultimately upon the EPA's legal authority. What advocacy coalitions obviously desire is to help shape the exercise of discretionary authority of the agency or agencies that are the focal point of their subsystem. The adoption of major air-pollution control legislation, such as the Clean Air Act Amendments of 1990, however, will take place in the macropolitical arena. Rulemaking by the EPA may also become the focus of macropolitical struggle, as in the instance of the arsenic rule for drinking water.

Whatever their form or style, subsystems are influential in policy development and implementation in the American political system.[86] Perhaps issue networks are more important in new or unsettled areas of public policy, such as the disposal of hazardous waste, computer network communications, and the control of terrorism. Policy communities or iron triangles are likely to be more common in stable areas of policy such as shipping regulation, vocational education, and veterans' benefits. There has been a tendency for subsystems to become broader in scope. Thus, the iron triangle once centered on rivers and harbor projects gave way to a wider policy community as many environmental groups became interested in this policy area. As a consequence, political life was made more complex for the Army Corps of Engineers, which has become more amenable to environmental interests.

Subsystems, of course, are part of the larger (macro) political system. As such, they are subject to intervention and control by the president, Congress, and other non-subsystem actors. Some resources that subsystems need can come only from the larger political system—namely, legislation, appropriations, and political-level appointments. Those who are aggrieved by subsystem action may carry appeals for redress to the larger system. Consequently, subsystem autonomy is a conditional phenomenon. It may last only so long as subsystem actions are routine, accepted, and within the bounds of existing legislative authority. Even then, an external event, such as a change in presidential administrations or congressional majorities, may focus unwanted attention on some subsystems. The boundary lines between a subsystem and the macropolitical system are not distinct and, in practice, they are difficult to specify.

Macropolitics   Some policy issues attract enough attention or become sufficiently controversial to be ripe for action in the macropolitical areas. Some issues are "born" to be macropolitical, such as escalation of the war in Vietnam, the Clinton administration's health-care reform proposal, George W. Bush's successful call for a trillion-dollar tax cut, and the financial crisis of 2007–2009. Because of their consequences for large numbers of people and the controversy enveloping them, they attracted wide interest and participation from rank-and-file citizens and political elites alike.

Many other issues may be moved from the subsystem to the macropolitical level by the action of public officials or other interested parties, perhaps because of dissatisfaction with subsystem actions. Moreover, policy proposals developed within subsystems often require approval by the larger political system. Then, because of their importance or magnitude, they draw extensive interest and participation. So it went with the Job Partnership Training Act and the legislation strengthening the Fair Housing Act. In other instances, however, bills emerging from subsystems may move through Congress with little attention or deliberation.

CASE STUDY   *The Endangered Snail Darter*

Some matters may begin political life at the micropolitical level and then escalate into macropolitical issues because of their symbolic, scandalous, or substantive characteristics. Consider the classic case of the snail darter (a species of minnow), which was accorded protection under the Endangered Species Act (ESA) of 1973. Its designation as endangered by the U.S. Fish and Wildlife Service was initially a routine instance of policy implementation. What followed was not, as this summary reveals:

> The discovery of the snail darter in the Little Tennessee River in eastern Tennessee in August 1973, its subsequent listing as endangered in October 1975, and the designation of its critical habitat in April 1976 led to a major conflict with the Tennessee Valley Authority's [TVA's] Tellico project, a multipurpose water resource development project that was to provide economic development, hydroelectric, flood control, and recreation benefits. The conflict turned into litigation that went as high as the Supreme Court, resulting in front[-]page headlines across the nation in mid-1978. The Supreme Court ruling that the ESA prohibited completion of the project led to amendments to the act that established an interagency panel to review projects for possible exemptions from the act's provisions. [A group of high-level officials, it became known as the "god squad" because it could determine the fate of species.] In January 1979, the panel ruled that the Tellico project should not be exempted because the project was "ill-conceived and uneconomic . . ." However, by attaching a rider onto an omnibus public works appropriation bill, Tennessee congressmen were able to sneak through a provision that directed the TVA to complete the project. Citing political problems and the difficulty of vetoing a bill that would fund numerous other projects, President Carter signed the bill "with regret" in September 1979.[87]

Thus did the little snail darter and the ESA become the focus of a macropolitical struggle. It was later discovered that there were other colonies of snail darters. The Tellico Dam was completed, but many of the benefits promised by its proponents, including TVA, were never realized.[88]

Several other listings, or possible listings, or species as endangered have also precipitated macropolitical conflicts. These include the spotted owl in the Pacific Northwest and salmon in the Columbia River system. The polar bear, as global warming modifies its icy habitat, could become a macropolitical focus. Mostly, however, political conflicts over endangered species have been waged within the boundaries of a policy subsystem.[89] ■

The central participants in macropolitics include the president, party and congressional leaders (who often overlap), and the executive departments. The communications media, who can drum up public attention on an issue, and various group leaders usually are also deeply involved. This level of politics attracts most attention in studies of policymaking because it is often quite visible and salient as well as sharply conflictual and sometimes sensational.

Decisions made in the macropolitical arena may differ considerably from what they would have been if made at one of the other levels. Among other things, when an issue moves, say, from the subsystem to the macropolitical arena, the conflict is expanded in scope. More players take part, and, as E. E. Schattschneider suggests, expanding the conflict often changes the substance of the settlement, that is, the policy decision.[90] Broad public interests are likely to receive fullest consideration at the macropolitical level.

A distinctive characteristic of macropolitics is presidential involvement, which draws the attention of many policy participants. Whether the president more adequately represents national interests than does the Congress, as some contend, is open to debate. What is certainly true, however, is that those interests that are represented by the president enjoy an advantage in the macropolitical arena. Because of the centrality and visibility of the office, the capacity to formulate policy alternatives, and the resources that can be drawn upon in support of his or her proposals, the president can be the policy leader here if he or she so chooses.

Presidential actions can substantially affect the content and direction of public policies. This is illustrated by the case of the "global gag rule," which prohibited provision of federal money to international organizations that advocated or provided abortion services. An executive order, it was put in place by President Ronald Reagan and continued by President George Bush. It was quickly repealed by President Bill Clinton and just as quickly reinstated by President George W. Bush. President Barack Obama revoked the order during his first week in office.

In the chapter titled "Policy Formation: Problems, Agendas, and Formulation," we look at the emergence and definition of public problems, agenda setting, and the formulation of policy proposals, especially as they occur in the macropolitical arena.

For Further Exploration

▮ *http://www.house.gov/*
    The homepage of the U.S. House of Representatives provides information regarding individual representatives, committee hearing schedules, the current House calendar, and roll-call votes on legislation since 1990.

▮ *http://www.nga.org/*
    The National Governors' Association official homepage contains information on key policy issues currently affecting the various states.

▮ *http://www.senate.gov/*
    This is the homepage of the U.S. Senate. Information regarding individual senators, recent legislative activity, appropriations bills, committee hearing schedules, and Senate history is provided.

▮ *http://www.state.gov/*
    The U.S. State Department's website contains a link regarding current and salient foreign-policy issues and provides audio recordings of press briefings that were issued over the course of several years.

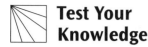

Test Your Knowledge

Log on to the student companion website at

login.cengage.com

to access tutorial quizzes, chapter outlines, crossword puzzles, and glossary flashcards that review chapter concepts and terminology.

Suggested Readings

Allen J. Cigler and Burdett A. Loomis, eds., *Interest Group Politics*, 8th ed. (Washington, DC: CQ Press, 2011). A strong collection of essays that provides much information and insight into the role of groups in American politics.

Anthony Nownes, *Total Lobbying* (New York: Cambridge University Press, 2006). This is a comprehensive overview of lobbying and its impact on the policy process.

Garry Wills, *A Necessary Evil: A History of American Distrust of Government* (New York: Simon & Schuster, 1999). Distrust of government, which is a basic feature of American political culture, gets comparative, historical examination in this solid volume.

George C. Edwards III, *Overreach: Leadership in the Obama Presidency* (Princeton, NJ: Princeton University Press, 2012). This is a challenging and thorough examination of policymaking during the first two years of the Obama administration.

J. Leiper Freeman, *The Political Process*, 2nd ed. (New York: Random House, 1965). This small volume is the seminal work on political subsystems.

Kenneth M. Murchison, *The Snail Darter Case*. (Lawrence, KS: University Press of Kansas, 2007). A thorough and readable analysis of the Snail Darter case and its meaning for American environmental law.

Louis Fisher, *Constitutional Conflicts Between Congress and the President*, 5th ed. (Lawrence, KS: University Press of Kansas, 2007). Fisher, a leading student of American government, offers the reader much information about the national policy process in his examination of constitutional conflicts.

Robert M. Emtman, *Projection of Power* (Chicago, IL: University of Chicago Press, 2004). A good analysis of the impact the communications media has on American politics and policy.

Notes

1. Charles O. Jones, *The Presidency in a Separated System* (Washington, DC: Brookings Institution, 1994), p. 16. His emphasis.
2. David R. Mayhew, *Divided We Govern: Party Control, Lawmaking, and Investigations, 1946–1990* (New Haven: Yale University Press, 1991).
3. George C. Edwards III, Andrew Barrett, and Jeffrey Peake, "The Legislative Impact of Divided Government," *American Journal of Political Science*, Vol. 41 (April 1997), pp. 545–563.
4. *United States* v. *Lopez*, 514 U.S. 549 (1995) and *United States* v. *Morrison*, reported in *The New York Times*, May 16, 2000, pp. 1, A14.
5. Ann O. M. Bowman and Richard C. Kearney, *The Resurgence of the States* (Englewood Cliffs, NJ: Prentice-Hall, 1986), pp. 10–22.
6. Clyde Kluckhohn, *Mirror for Man* (Greenwich, CT: Fawcett, 1963), p. 24.
7. For an extended discussion of political culture, see Gabriel A. Almond and Sidney Verba, *The Civic Culture* (Boston, MA: Little Brown, 1965); and Donald J. Devine, *The Political Culture of the United States* (Boston, MA: Little Brown, 1972).
8. The quotation is from Joseph S. Nye and Philip Zelikow, eds., *Why People Don't Trust Government* (Cambridge, MA: Harvard University Press, 1997), pp. 88–89.
9. Paul Starr, *Remedy and Reaction* (New Haven, CT: Yale University Press, 2011), p. 8.
10. Daniel J. Elazar, *American Federalism: A View from the States* (New York: Harper & Row, 1984), Chap. 4.
11. Robin M. Williams Jr., *American Society*, 3rd ed. (New York: Knopf, 1974), Chap. 11.
12. Steven Kelman, *Regulating America, Regulating Sweden* (Cambridge, MA: MIT Press, 1981), Chaps. 5, 6.
13. Devine, op. cit., pp. 210–211.
14. Karl W. Deutsch, *Politics and Government* (Boston, MA: Houghton Mifflin, 1970), p. 207.
15. Almond and Verba, op. cit., pp. 11–26.
16. Deutsch, op. cit., p. 207.
17. Cf. E. E. Schattschneider, *The Semi-Sovereign People* (New York: Holt, Rinehart and Winston, 1960), Chap. 1.
18. Thomas R. Dye, *Politics, Economics, and the Public Policy Outcomes in the Fifty States* (Chicago, IL: Rand-McNally, 1966). Dye uses the term *policy outcome* to designate what was described as policy outputs in the chapter titled "The Study of Public Policy."
19. Ibid., p. 293. See also Thomas R. Dye, *Understanding Public Policy*, 10th ed. (Upper Saddle, NJ: Prentice-Hall, 2002), Chap. 12; and Michael Lewis-Beck, "The Relative Importance of Socio-economic and Political Variables in Public Policy," *American Political Science Review*, Vol. 62 (June 1977), pp. 559–566.
20. Ira Sharkansky and Richard I. Hofferbert, "Dimensions of State Policy," in Herbert Jacob and Kenneth N. Vines, ed., *Politics in the American States*, 2nd ed. (Boston, MA: Little Brown, 1972), esp. pp. 318–323.
21. Ibid., p. 320.
22. They are, in effect, defined away in Robert S. Erikson, Gerald C. Wright, and John P. McIver, *Statehouse Democracy: Public Opinion and Policy in the American States* (New York: Cambridge University Press, 1993), pp. 8–10.

23. Peter Andreas, *Smuggler Nation* (New York: Oxford University Press, 2013), Chap. 14.
24. *Congressional Quarterly Weekly Report*, Vol. 60 (January 26, 2002), p. 243.
25. *Wall Street Journal*, February 22, 2002, p. B3; *The New York Times*, February 22, 2002, p. A18. See Robert L. Paarlberg, *The Politics of Precaution* (Baltimore, MD: Johns Hopkins University Press, 2001).
26. Leroy N. Rieselbach, *Congressional Politics: The Evolving Legislative System*, 2nd ed. (Boulder, CO: Westview, 1995), p. 13.
27. Walter A. Rosenbaum, *Energy, Politics, and Public Policy*, 2nd ed. (Washington, DC: CQ Press, 1987), p. 51.
28. Center on Policy Attitudes, *The Polling Report*, February 15, 1999.
29. George C. Edwards III, *Overreach: Leadership in the Obama Administration* (Princeton, NJ: Princeton University Press, 2012).
30. Norman J. Ornstein, Thomas E. Mann, and Michael J. Malbin, *Vital Statistics on Congress, 1993–1994* (Washington, DC: Congressional Quarterly, 1994), pp. 195–196.
31. William M. Lunch, *The Nationalization of American Politics* (Berkeley, CA: University of California Press, 1987), pp. 122–123. See also John Hart, *The Presidential Branch*, 2nd ed. (Chatham, NJ: Chatham Press, 1995).
32. Richard J. Harknett and Norman C. Thomas, "The Precedence of Power: Determining Who Should Authorize Military Force," *Presidential Studies Quarterly*, Vol. 25 (Spring 1998), pp. 1–21.
33. This discussion draws on ibid., pp. 153–154; and *Congressional Quarterly Weekly Report*, Vol. 51 (October 16, 1993), pp. 2823–2827.
34. Norman C. Thomas, *Rule 9: Politics, Administration, and Civil Rights* (New York: Random House, 1966), p. 6.
35. Rieselbach, op. cit., pp. 212–214.
36. Lester W. Milbrath, *The Washington Lobbyists* (Chicago: Rand-McNally, 1963), p. 8.
37. Abraham Holtzman, *Legislative Liaison: Executive Leadership in Congress* (Chicago, IL: Rand-McNally, 1970), Chap. 3.
38. Robert A. Carp and Claude K. Rowland, *Policy-Making and Politics in the Federal District Courts* (Knoxville, TN: University of Tennessee Press, 1983).
39. See, for example, Ronald Stidham and Robert A. Carp, "Judges, Presidents, and Policy Choices: Exploring the Linkage," *Social Science Quarterly*, Vol. 68 (June 1987), pp. 395–404.
40. *Grove City College v. Bell*, 465 U.S. 555 (1984).
41. *Congressional Quarterly Weekly Report*, Vol. 46 (January 23, 1988), pp. 160–163; Vol. 46 (March 26, 1988), pp. 774–776.
42. *Ledbetter v. Goodyear Tire & Rubber Co.*, 550 U.S. 618, 2007.
43. *CQ Weekly Report*, Vol. 67 (January 12, 2009), p. 83 and Vol. 67 (February 2, 2009), p. 259.
44. Emmette S. Redford, *American Government and the Economy* (New York: Macmillan, 1965), pp. 53–54.
45. *Roe v. Wade*, 410 U.S. 113 (1973). Also *Griswold v. Connecticut*, 381 U.S. 479 (1958).
46. *Webster v. Health Reproductive Services*, 492 U.S. 490 (1989). Also *The New York Times*, July 4, 1989, pp. A1, A8–A12.
47. *Planned Parenthood of Southeastern Pennsylvania v. Casey*, 112 S. Ct. 931 (1992).

48. *Madson* v. *Women's Health Center*, 114 S. Ct. 2516 (1994). See generally, Ruth Ann Strickland, "Abortion: Prochoice v. Prolife," in Raymond Tatalovich and Byron W. Daynes, *Moral Controversies in American Politics* (Armonk, NY: M.E. Sharpe, 1998), Chap. 1.

49. *The New York Times*, March 30, 2013, pp. A18, A19, April 4, 2013, p. A13; and June 18, 2013, pp. 1, 3.

50. Frank R. Baumgartner and Beth L. Leech, *Basic Interests* (Princeton, NJ: Princeton University Press, 1998), p. 103.

51. Quoted in Roger H. Davidson and Walter J. Oleszek, *Congress and Its Members*, 8th ed. (Washington, DC: CQ Press, 2002), p. 350.

52. Edwards, op. cit., p. 155.

53. See, generally, John P. Heinz, Edward O. Laumann, Robert L. Nelson, and Robert H. Salisbury, *The Hollow Core: Private Interests in National Policy Making* (Cambridge, MA: Harvard University Press, 1993).

54. This discussion is based on Kay Lehman Scholzman and John T. Tierney *Organized Interests and American Democracy* (New York: Harper & Row, 1986), pp. 28–35.

55. Thomas J. Anton, *American Federalism and Public Policy* (New York: Random House, 1989), pp. 94–95; Scholzman and Tierney, op. cit., pp. 55–57.

56. Ken Kollman, *Outside Lobbying: Public Opinion and Interest Group Strategies* (Princeton, NJ: Princeton University Press, 1998). The quotation is on p. 8. See also Alison Mitchell, "A New Form of Lobbying Puts Public Face on Private Interest," *The New York Times*, September 30, 1998, pp. A1, A14.

57. Graham K. Wilson, *Business and Politics: A Comparative Introduction*, 3rd ed. (Chatham, NJ: Chatham House, 2003), Chap. 6.

58. Gabriel A. Almond and G. Bingham Powell Jr., *Comparative Politics: A Developmental Approach* (Boston, MA: Little Brown, 1966), p. 103.

59. Andrew Rich, "Think Tanks and the Politics of Expertise in the States," paper presented at the Conference on the Study of Politics in the American States, Texas A&M University, College Station, TX, March 2–3, 2001.

60. Louis Jacobson, "Tanks on the Roll," *National Journal*, Vol. 27 (July 8, 1995), pp. 1767–1771.

61. Andrew Rich and R. Kent Weaver, "Think Tanks and the Politicization of Expertise," in Allan J. Cigler and Burdett A. Loomis, eds., *Interest Group Politics*, 5th ed. (Washington, DC: CQ Press, 1996), p. 237.

62. David M. Ricci, *The Transformation of American Politics* (New Haven, CT: Yale University Press, 1993), p. 163.

63. Timothy E. Cook, *Governing with the News* (Chicago: University of Chicago Press, 1998).

64. Martin Linsky *Impact: How the Press Affects Federal Policy-Making* (New York: Norton, 1986), pp. 114–115.

65. But see Cary Coglianese and Margaret Howard, "Getting the Message Out: Regulatory Policy and the Press," *Press/Politics*, Vol. 3 (Summer 1998), pp. 39–55.

66. Cf. Richard Davis and Diana Owen, *New Media and American Politics* (New York: Oxford University Press, 1998), Chaps. 3, 10.

67. Steven B. Roberts, "A Most Important Man on Capitol Hill," *The New York Times Magazine*, September 22, 1984, p. 48.

68. David S. Broder, *Democracy Derailed: Initiative Campaigns and the Power of Money* (New York: Harcourt, 2000), pp. 4–5.

69. Ibid., p. 164.
70. This discussion draws on Charles E. Lindblom, *The Policy-Making Process* (Englewood Cliffs, NJ: Prentice-Hall, 1968), p. 44.
71. Ibid., p. 45.
72. For further discussion, see James R. Sundquist, *Dynamics of the Party System: Alignment and Realignment of Party Systems in the United States* (Washington, DC: Brookings Institution, 1972); David W. Brady, "Critical Elections, Congressional Parties and Clusters of Policy Changes," *British Journal of Political Science*, VIII (January 1978), pp. 79–99; and Warren E. Miller and J. Merrill Shanks, "Policy Directions and Presidential Leadership: Alternative Interpretations of the 1980 Presidential Election," *British Journal of Political Science*, XII (July 1982), pp. 299–358. For a dissenting view, see David R. Mayhew, *Electoral Realignment: A Critique of an American Genre* (New Haven, CT: Yale University Press, 2002).
73. Walter Dean Burkham, "Realignment Lives: The 1994 Earthquake and Its Implications," in Colin Campbell and Burt A. Rockman, eds., *The Clinton Presidency: First Appraisals* (Chatham, NJ: Chatham House, 1995), Chap. 12.
74. Emmette S. Redford, *Democracy in the Administrative State* (New York: Oxford University Press, 1969), p. 107.
75. Ibid., p. 53.
76. Walter J. Oleszek, *Congressional Procedure and the Policy Process*, 3rd ed. (Washington, DC: CQ Press, 1989), pp. 117–118.
77. Ernest S. Griffith, *The Impasse of Democracy* (New York: Harrison-Hilton Books, 1938), p. 182.
78. The subsystem concept is discussed in J. Leiper Freeman, *The Political Process*, rev. ed. (New York: Random House, 1965). See also Jeffrey M. Berry, *The Interest Group Society*, 2nd ed. (Chicago: Scott, Foresman, 1989), Chap. 8.
79. Arthur Maass, *Muddy Waters* (Cambridge, MA: Harvard University Press, 1951).
80. Many introductory American government textbooks contain discussions of iron triangles. Examples include Karen O'Connon and Larry J. Sabato, *American Government: Continuity and Change* (New York: Longman, 2004), pp. 332–334; John R. Bond and Kevin B. Smith, *The Promise and Performance of American Democracy* (Boston, MA: Wadsworth, 2012), pp. 528–529; and James A. Morone and Rogan Kersh, *By the People* (New York: Oxford University Press, 2013), p. 429.
81. Hugh Heclo, "Issue Networks and the Executive Establishment," in Anthony King, ed., *The New American Political System* (Washington, DC: American Enterprise Institute, 1978), pp. 87–124.
82. Ibid., p. 104.
83. Randall B. Ripley and Grace A. Franklin, *Congress, the Bureaucracy, and Public Policy*, 6th ed. (Pacific Grove, CA: Brooks/Cole, 1991), Chap. 6.
84. For a similar suggestion, independently arrived at, see John Creighton Campbell with Mark A. Baskin, Frank R. Baumgartner, and Nina P. Halpern, "Afterword on Policy Communities: A Framework for Comparative Research," *Governance: An International Journal of Policy and Administration*, II (January 1989), pp. 86–94.
85. This discussion relies on Paul A. Sabatier, "Policy Change over a Decade or More," in Paul A. Sabatier and Hank Jenkins-Smith, eds., *Policy Change and Learning: The Advocacy Coalition Approach* (Boulder, CO: Westview, 1993), Chap. 2.
86. Cf. Frank R. Baumgartner and Bryan D. Jones, *Agendas and Instability in American Politics* (Chicago, IL: University of Chicago Press, 1993), Chaps. 2, 3.

87. Steven Lewis Yaffee, *Prohibitive Policy: Implementing the Federal Endangered Species Act* (Cambridge, MA: MIT Press, 1982), p. 165.

88. Kenneth M. Murchison, *The Snail Darter Case* (Lawrence: University Press of Kansas, 2007), Chaps. 4, 7.

89. An example is the pygmy owl discussed in Christopher McGrory Klyza and David Sousa, *American Environmental Policy, 1990–2006* (Cambridge, MA: MIT Press, 2008), pp. 163–168.

90. Schattschneider, op. cit., Chap. 4.

3

Policy Formation: Problems, Agendas, and Formulation

U ntil the New Deal years, government paperwork (forms, reports, information requests) was not perceived as a public problem. Up to that time the national government had only limited direct contact with citizens. The great expansion of governmental programs in the 1930s, however, "dramatically increased the need for data and unleashed a wave of forms and surveys upon the land."[1] World War II programs generated more needs for information, and complaints about the burdens imposed on citizens and companies became more frequent. Paperwork now came to be perceived as a public problem by some people.

Congress responded to this new problem with the Federal Reports Act, which authorized agencies to collect from citizens information that was necessary for agency operations unless other agencies were already gathering the information. The law rested on the assumption that agency officials could properly decide what information they needed and that any burdens imposed upon citizens were an acceptable inconvenience.[2]

The Federal Reports Act did not improve the popularity of paperwork, however. Complaints and criticisms continued and grew in volume as paperwork requirements escalated in the 1960s and early 1970s with the proliferation of national social welfare and economic regulatory programs. Soon after he became president in August 1974, Gerald Ford put regulatory reform and paperwork reduction on the national policy agenda. His public speeches and statements contained many remarks about needless paperwork, the "paperwork mountain," and the high costs of paperwork. At his request, Congress created a Commission on Federal Paperwork, which subsequently estimated that federal paperwork cost "more than $100 billion a year, or about $500 for each person in the country."[3] By now, paperwork was no longer merely an inconvenience; it was perceived as a costly and unnecessary burden; its benefits for the operation and effectiveness of the administrative process were slighted. Information collection lost quite a bit of its legitimacy.

The Carter administration continued the campaign to control paperwork, first through an executive order and then by urging Congress to legislate on the problem. The result was the Paperwork Reduction Act (a constituent policy), signed into law late in 1980 by President Jimmy Carter despite strong objections from several executive departments and agencies. The act specified that all agency requests for information had to be cleared through the Office of Management and Budget (OMB) and that OMB should act to reduce the burden of information collection by 25 percent by October 1, 1983. Apparently this goal was met.[4]

The struggle against paperwork has continued, however, and the Paperwork Reduction Act periodically has been renewed, most recently in 1998, when it received strong bipartisan support in Congress. Further reductions in the paperwork burden were called for. However, two Senate amendments that would have reduced the paperwork burden imposed by Congress on federal agencies through extensive reporting requirements were dropped from the final act.[5] In 2002, Congress passed the Small Business Paperwork Relief Act, easing the burden on small businesses.

It was estimated that the paperwork burden exceeded 9.6 billion burden hours—a burden hour being the basic unit of measurement here. Much of this burden is necessary and serves useful purposes. More than three-fourths of the burden hours are accounted for by the Internal Revenue Service, which needs to collect information from taxpayers and employers to determine taxes owed. The burden is increased by the complexity of the Internal Revenue Code, much of which can be laid on Congress's doorstep. Many other agencies need to collect information to improve their operations or to evaluate their effectiveness. Although the government has struggled to reduce it, the volume of paperwork has grown.[6]

Paperwork reduction has symbolic appeal, whatever its practical effects. (It has been used to exert substantive control over agency actions, as by OMB delay or disapproval of paperwork requests.) The paperwork burden, or "red tape," is something that almost everyone can criticize, however little they may be affected by it or benefit from its reduction. If agencies are hampered by paperwork reduction requirements, so much the better is the view of many people. The "savings" resulting from paperwork reduction are in actuality both conjectural and, for most people, insignificant. Nonetheless, the "good fight" against paperwork continued during the Obama administration.

This chapter launches the analysis of the policymaking process as a sequence of functional activities, as illustrated by federal paperwork reduction. Three interrelated aspects of policy formation are taken up: the nature of public problems, agendas and the process of agenda setting, and the formulation of proposed policies (or alternatives) to resolve problems. The adoption of policies is the focus of the chapter titled "Policy Adoption."

The meaning of a couple of terms that appear throughout the book need clarification here. *Policy formation* denotes the total process of creating, adopting, and implementing a policy. This can also be called the *policy process*.

Policy formulation, in contrast, refers only to the crafting of alternatives or options for dealing with a problem. For example, the policy formulator is concerned with developing a proposed course of action to reduce the number of high school dropouts or lessen the volume of federal paperwork.

The legislature is the primary institutional focus of this chapter, although the other branches of government also get involved in setting agendas and formulating policy proposals. The U.S. Supreme Court, for instance, sets its own agenda when it determines which of the thousands of cases appealed to it will be heard and decided. Again, much policy (or rule) formulation occurs in the context of the administrative process as agencies exercise their delegated authority to make rules on air pollution, motor-vehicle safety, trade practices, and other matters.

It should be kept in mind that defining problems, setting agendas, and formulating proposals, together with adoption of policies, are functional categories. Although they can be analytically separated, in actuality they frequently are interrelated and smudged together. For instance, those who want action on a problem may try to define it broadly, as affecting large numbers of people, to help ensure that it gets on a legislative agenda. Again, those formulating a policy proposal will often be at least partly guided in their efforts by the need to build support for the adoption of their proposal. Particular provisions may be included, modified, or excluded in an attempt to win the support or reduce the opposition of some groups or officials.

Policy Problems

Older studies of policy formation devoted little attention to the nature and definition of public problems. Instead, problems were taken as "givens," and the discussion moved on from there. However, it is now conventional wisdom that if policy study does not consider the characteristics and dimensions of the problems that stimulate government action, it is incomplete.[7] It is important to know both why some problems are acted on and others are neglected and why a problem is defined in one way rather than another. This helps one determine where power lies in the political system. Moreover, whether a problem is foreign or domestic, a new item or the outgrowth of an existing policy, or specific or broad in scope helps to determine the nature of the ensuing policymaking process. Evaluating a policy also requires information on the substance and dimensions of the target problem in order to appraise the policy's effectiveness.

For our purposes, *a policy problem* can be defined as a condition or situation that produces needs or dissatisfaction among people and for which relief or redress by governmental action is sought. All problems are not public problems. What characteristics or qualities make a problem public? Most people would agree that John Smith's car's being out of gasoline is a private problem, however irritating it might be to Smith and his passengers. In contrast, the widespread and continued shortage of gasoline in a city or region is likely to be perceived as a public problem. What distinguishes the two situations? Essentially, public problems are those affecting a substantial number of people and having broad effects, including consequences for persons not directly involved.[8] They are also likely to be difficult or impossible to resolve by individual action.

Such occurrences as dirty air, unwholesome food, free-roaming bison, the practice of abortion, urban traffic congestion, crowded prisons, and global warming are conditions that become public problems if they produce sufficient anxiety discontent, or dissatisfaction to cause many people to seek governmental remedies. Conditions abound in society.

Moreover, new conditions develop or are identified, and become candidates for problem status. To name a few: feral cats in town and feral pigs in the country, sinkholes, bacterial infections in hospitals, obesity, and Asian carp (an invasive species). Sometimes a problem can be contrived to justify action for another purpose. Voter fraud or misrepresentation is an example. Cases of voter fraud have essentially been nonexistent for years. Some Republican-controlled state legislatures, however, enacted laws requiring voters to have specified picture identification to be able to vote. This was said to be necessary to prevent voter fraud. Most likely, it would reduce voting by racial and ethnic groups tending to vote Democratic.[9]

For a condition to be converted into a problem, people must have some value or standard by which the troubling condition is judged to be unreasonable or unacceptable and appropriate for government to handle. Something needs to lead people to the conclusion that they do not need to put up with polluted streams, free-roaming dogs in the city, or a rapidly increasing price level. If, however, people believe that a condition, such as substantial income inequality, is normal, inevitable, or desirable, then nothing is likely to happen because it will not be perceived as a problem.

Conditions thus do not become problems unless they are defined as such, articulated, and then brought to the attention of government. This action can be, and frequently is, taken by public officials who are often scouting around for problems that they can claim credit for solving. Problem definition can be either a top-down or a bottom-up process.

As stated, to be converted into a problem, a condition must also be seen as an appropriate topic for governmental action and, further, as something for which there is a possible governmental remedy or solution (see Figure 3.1). Those who oppose governmental action to ban smoking in public places may argue that tobacco smoke is not harmful or that smoking is a matter of individual choice and should not be regulated. Such argumentation is variously designed to prevent the controversial condition from being viewed as a problem, to keep it off a governmental agenda, or, failing that, to prevent adoption of a smoking regulation. Professor Aaron Wildavsky contends that officials are unlikely to deal with a problem unless it is coupled with a solution. As he states, "A problem is a problem only if something can be done about it."[10]

FIGURE 3.1

Problem Creation

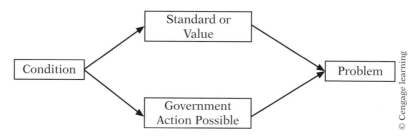

Hurricanes and earthquakes as such are not likely to become public problems because government can do nothing to prevent them. However, the conditions of human distress and property destruction caused by hurricanes do become public problems. Relief programs, building regulations, and early-warning systems are devised to prevent or reduce hurricanes' adverse consequences. Quite a few conditions will not be transformed into problems because they do not qualify as matters that government can handle appropriately and effectively. "Putting a man on the moon became a problem for policy-makers only after it became technically possible to do so in the late 1950s."[11]

Conditions can be defined as problems, and redress for them can be sought by persons other than those who are directly affected.[12] In the mid-1960s, poverty was identified as a public problem, and the Johnson administration declared a War on Poverty more because of the actions of public officials and publicists than those of the poor themselves. Legislators are frequently looking for problems that they can mitigate or solve so as to enhance their reputations and/or help themselves win reelection. Of course, there is always the possibility that others will define a problem differently than those directly affected.

Indeed, problems frequently are defined or perceived differently by various persons and groups. One's perceptions will be shaped by one's values, information, and experiences. Put differently, how a problem is defined depends not only on its objective dimensions but also on how it is socially constructed.[13] A wealthy person who has never lacked or needed a good job may see little to worry about when unemployment rates rise and, in fact, may regard an increase in unemployment as good, as necessary to prevent inflation, which he/she sees as the real cause for alarm. However, industrial workers for whom unemployment is an omnipresent fear may perceive increasing joblessness as a major threat to their well-being. There is no single correct way to assess a condition and define a problem, although many people will have strong views and preferences on some matters. Problem definitions compete for acceptance.

To amplify this point, currently some 45 million Americans were not covered by health insurance in 2009. How was this condition perceived? Many portrayed it as a private problem resulting from how people chose to spend their incomes. Others saw the lack of health insurance by so many people as a public problem but disagreed about its cause. Explanations include the lack of national health insurance, the inadequacies of private health insurance companies, the excessively high costs of medical care and health insurance, and the extensive poverty and income inequality in American society. There was also disagreement as to what form a policy solution should take, if any. Conflicting perceptions or definitions of a problem, and disagreement over remedies, reduce the likelihood of positive action. In this instance, however, after much struggle, the Patient Protection and Affordable Care Act was written into law. (See more on this topic in the Case Study later in the chapter.)

Although many problems are persistent, how they are defined may change as values and conditions change. We can use alcoholism (drunkenness) as an illustration. In the nineteenth century, drunkenness was viewed as a personal problem, as the product of one's evil, wicked, or sinful ways, and therefore as one's just punishment. In the early decades of the twentieth century, it became more common to view drunkenness as a social problem that arose from the response by some individuals to the social, family, and other pressures that played upon them. Counseling and other social services were seen as appropriate responses.

More recently, alcoholism (no longer called drunkenness) has been defined as an illness (i.e., a pathological condition) requiring medical treatment and deserving health-insurance coverage, whatever its immediate social causes. This medical definition reduces the individual's responsibility and the stigma attached to the condition. Public policy, however, has not fully caught up with the modern definition, and many problem drinkers continue to be dealt with through the regular law-enforcement processes, especially if they combine drinking and driving. Mothers Against Drunk Driving (MADD) takes a tough enforcement stance on this issue.

Conditions that in one era are accepted as the normal order of things may later, because of social change, be treated as problems.[14] For centuries, wife-beating, child abuse, and other forms of family violence were thought to be private matters except, perhaps, when the regular criminal laws, as against homicide, were violated. They are no longer so treated. Changes in public attitudes, media attention, the women's movement, and other factors changed our notions about acceptable conduct in family matters. A variety of national and state laws pertaining to family violence now are on the statute books. There is still uncertainty as to the pervasiveness of family violence, however.

The definition of problems is often a political process whose outcome will help determine appropriate solutions. Is access to public transportation for the physically handicapped a transportation problem or a civil-rights problem? Identifying it as a transportation problem means that the handicapped should have adequate transportation available to them, by regular modes or any practical means, such as special van service. Defining it as a civil-rights problem, however, means that the handicapped should have equal access to regular transportation facilities, which might require installing elevators at subway stations, fitting buses with loading ramps for wheelchairs, and making other expensive modifications in transportation facilities. After some wavering between the two alternatives, public policy moved toward the availability-of-transportation solution in the 1980s under the Reagan administration.[15] We will now focus on some dimensions of public problems.

An important aspect of problem definition is causation. A condition may be defined as a problem, but what causes the condition? Many problems—crime, poverty, inflation, and air pollution—have multiple causes. For example, inflation, the upward movement of prices at an unacceptable rate as measured by the consumer price index, is a public problem. But what is its cause? Is it the underproduction of goods and services? Excess demand for goods and services (i.e., too many dollars chasing too few goods)? Too much money in circulation? The product of inflationary psychology, where people expect prices to continue to climb? To deal effectively with a problem, one must treat its causes rather than its symptoms. For many problems, the underlying causes are not easy to diagnose or evaluate. Identifying the causes of a problem and getting agreement on them may be a hard task for policy-makers. Defining the problem then itself becomes a problem.

The nature and scope of some public problems may be difficult to specify because they are diffuse or "invisible." Because measurement may be quite imprecise, policy-makers may be uncertain about the magnitude of the problem and in turn about effective solutions, or even whether there is a need for governmental action. In the 1980s, growing numbers of homeless people were sleeping in public and private shelters, in the streets, under bridges, and in other places not suitable for human habitation. Estimates of the number of homeless people in the United States ranged from 250,000 to 3 million.[16] Anywhere from 10 to 47 percent of them were thought to be chronically mentally ill. These wide ranges reflect the difficulty in getting an accurate count of the homeless and their characteristics. The causes of homelessness are also poorly understood. The Stewart B. McKinney Homeless Assistance Act of 1987 called for better collection of data on the homeless by the states while also expanding federal assistance for services to this group. Other problems that are difficult to define or measure include child abuse, learning disabilities among schoolchildren, illegal immigration, and the amount of income not reported on federal income-tax returns.

Homelessness has declined markedly in the last couple of decades. In 2010, the United States Interagency Council on Homelessness set a goal of ending homelessness between 2015 and 2020. Various federal programs, including funds from the American Recovery and Reinvestment Act, have contributed to the decline. The expansion of Medicaid may also help achieve the stated goal. This aptly leads into the matter of tractability.

Another dimension of public problems is their tractability, or amenability to solution. Some problems, for instance, require much less behavioral change than others. Thus, the elimination of discrimination in voting registration in southern states was fairly quickly accomplished under the Voting Rights Act. Essentially, what was required to correct the problem was either altering the behavior of a comparatively small number of voting registrars or bypassing them by the appointment of federal registrars. School desegregation proved much more difficult because it involved large numbers of people and strongly established social patterns. Desegregation was strongly resisted, sometimes in violent ways. Nearly six decades after *Brown* v. *Board of Education* (1954), some public schools continue to have manifestations of racial discrimination.[17]

Tractability is also affected by whether problems are tangible or intangible. Tangible problems, such as scarce jobs, poorly managed public-housing projects, or an overburdened criminal-justice system, can be eased by improving the incentives and resources available to people and agencies. Other inner-city problems—racism, inadequate job skills, or despair—are intangible, involving values. According to Professor James Q. Wilson, such problems "are hard to address by money alone because they make whites less likely to invest or extend opportunities and blacks less likely to take advantage of opportunities."[18]

The tractability of a problem is further affected by its magnitude and complexity. Terrorism is a prime example here. Broadly defined, terrorism involves the use of violence, sabotage, and intimidation by extremist groups against civilian populations to achieve their goals. Following the September 11, 2001, terrorist attack on the World Trade Center towers in New York City, the George W. Bush administration declared "war" on world terrorism. Some simple questions, which defy easy answers, indicate the enormity of the task confronting the administration. Who are the terrorists? Where are they located? Who supports them? Where are their targets? What means will they use? How long will the terrorists persist? Other problems, such as the farm problem and the energy problem, which have troubled policy-makers for years, pale in comparison to the world terrorism problem.

Severity is a fourth dimension of problems. How serious is a problem and its consequences for individuals? Society? The environment? How much risk of harm does it present? Does it deserve space on a crowded policy agenda?

The consensus among scientists and environmental experts is that global warming (or climate change) is a very serious problem, a looming disaster for planet earth. The various reports of the United Nations Intergovernmental Panel on Climate Change document this and identify human production of greenhouse gases as the major culprit. The Kyoto Protocol (1998) represented an international effort to deal with it. Efforts continue. There are dissenters, deniers, and contrarians. A U.S. senator, James Inhofe (R, Oklahoma), contends that it is "the greatest hoax ever perpetrated on the American people." Congressman Tom Delay (R, Texas) states that "only nature can change the climate—like a volcano." What does the reader believe?

Experts and the public sometimes evaluate the severity and risks of problems quite differently. Generally, the public views hazardous waste sites as a major problem requiring strong, immediate action. Environmental experts, however, contend indoor radon gas, which is formed by the disintegration of uranium naturally found in the soil, to be a much more serious problem. It receives little attention from rank-and-file citizens, even if they know what it is.

Some of the problems that are acted on by governments are really private problems. To a large extent, the micropolitical level of politics discussed in the chapter "The Policy-Makers and Their Environment" focuses on private problems. Private bills passed by Congress that apply only to the persons named in them deal with private problems, such as immigration-law difficulties. Much of the time of many members of Congress and their staffs is also devoted to "casework," providing assistance to individual constituents in their personal problems with administrative agencies. This activity does help "humanize" government by making it more responsive to the problems of private citizens.

This review leads to the question "Why are some matters, apart from their scope or effect on society, seen as public problems requiring governmental action while others are not?" Some answers to this question are provided in the following discussion of the policy agenda and the process of agenda setting.

The Policy Agenda

One frequently reads about demands being made by this group or that individual or some public official for action by a governmental body on some problem, whether it be rough streets or crime therein, disintegration of the family, or waste and fraud in defense contracting. Of the thousands of demands made upon government, only a small number will receive serious consideration at any given time by public policy-makers. In other words, each problem must compete for official attention because legislators and executives have limited time and resources. Decisions to consider some problems mean that others will not be taken up, at least for the time being. The demands that policy-makers choose to or feel compelled to act on, or at least appear to be acting on, constitute the policy agenda,[19] which is thus distinguishable from political demands generally. It should also be distinguished from the term *political* (or *policy*) *priorities*, which designates a ranking of agenda items, with some matters being considered more urgent or pressing than others. Sometimes a problem will be labeled as a "crisis," as in "the health-care crisis," in an effort to secure higher agenda status and help ensure action. *Crisis* conveys notions of importance and urgency.

To achieve agenda status, a public problem must be converted into an issue, or a matter requiring governmental attention (see Figure 3.2). Political scientist Robert Eyestone states, "An issue arises when a public with a problem seeks or demands governmental action, and there is public disagreement over the best solution to the problem."[20] A rising crime rate may be viewed as a public problem, but disagreement over what, if anything, government should do about it creates an issue. In recent years, important public issues have included such matters as prayer in public schools, illegal drug traffic, illegal immigration, research on and treatment of AIDS, and how the United States should deal with terrorism. Many stands may be taken or alternatives proposed on such issues, thereby demonstrating the inadequacy of the old saw that there are two sides

FIGURE 3.2

The Agenda-Setting Process

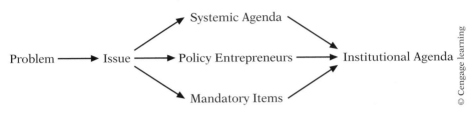

© Cengage learning

to every issue. Issue definition, or "framing" as it is also named ("spinning" is another synonym), is an important aspect of the competitive struggle for advantage in policy conflicts. A frame, says Professor George Edwards, "is a central organizing idea for making sense of an issue or conflict and suggests what the controversy is about and what is at stake."[21] The people who work for a president, for example, strive to frame issues, such as gun control or global warming, so as to give an edge to the president's preferences.

Of the number of policy agendas that can be identified in a political system, Professors Roger W. Cobb and Charles D. Elder specify two basic types: the systemic agenda and the institutional, or governmental, agenda. The systemic agenda as they define it "consists of all issues that are commonly perceived by members of the political community as meriting public attention and as involving matters within the legitimate jurisdiction of existing governmental authority."[22] A systemic agenda will exist for every national, state, and local political system. Some items may appear simultaneously on many systemic agendas, such as environmental protection, drug abuse, and crime in the streets. Other issues, such as the international trade deficit or the building of a new convention center in a city, will appear only on the national and a local agenda, respectively.

The systemic agenda is essentially a discussion agenda; it comprises matters that people are talking and fretting about. Most of the items on it will be general or abstract; technical details and specific solutions probably will not be probed. Many items on a systemic agenda will "go nowhere," so far as governmental action is concerned. To have a chance to be acted upon, a problem will have to be moved to an institutional or governmental agenda, which is where things get done—if they do.

An institutional or governmental agenda includes the problems to which legislators or other public officials feel obliged to give active and serious attention. Many of the issues or problems that draw the attention of legislative or administrative policy-makers are not likely to be widely discussed by the general public. The public's cognizance of policy issues is often rather low; awareness and information are mostly confined to a narrow segment of the public, that is, to the "attentive public." The latter may have strong interests in particular issues and access to specialized sources of information. Many of the issues that are handled by legislatures involve minor legislation or make technical or incremental changes in current laws, and are essentially unknown to rank-and-file citizens. They are likely to go unreported by the general news media.

Because policy decisions can be made at a variety of points in the political system, there are also several institutional agendas. At the national level one can identify legislative, executive, administrative, and judicial agendas. An institutional agenda is basically an action agenda and thus will be more specific and concrete in content than a systemic agenda. Whereas crime in the streets may be of systemic concern, Congress will be confronted with more fully developed proposals for action in this policy area, such as a program of financial aid to local law-enforcement agencies or a proposal for constructing additional prisons. Appearance on an institutional agenda does not guarantee that a topic will be acted upon, although it clearly increases its chances. Professor John W. Kingdon makes a useful distinction between subjects on the governmental (or institutional) agenda that are getting attention and those on the "decision" agenda, which "are up for an active decision."[23]

Institutional agenda items range from mandatory to discretionary.[24] Much congressional time is devoted to considering matters it is required (or strongly expected) to handle, including the reauthorization of current public programs (such as the foreign-aid and Head Start programs); the president's budget requests; and, for the Senate, approval of treaties and presidential appointments. Other items, notably proposals for new legislation, whether originating with members, pressure groups, administrative agencies, or other sources, are more discretionary. Congressional leaders and members exercise more control over whether these will be taken up for consideration and decision.

Discretionary items are classifiable as minor and major. Many bills passed by Congress make technical or incremental changes in existing policies. Some of them emerge from policy subsystems. Most receive little coverage by the media. Readers likely are not familiar with the Sonny Bono Copyright Term Extension Act. Passed by Congress in 1998, it extends the length of copyrights for books, songs, motion pictures, and other creations for an additional twenty years. Materials copyrighted by an individual are now protected for the life of the author or artist plus seventy years; copyrights held by corporations extend for ninety-five years. (The Constitution states that patents and copyright shall run for "limited times." These time periods appear to be a stretch.) The act resulted from the intense lobbying efforts of a group of large entertainment corporations led by the Walt Disney Company. Disney faced losing its valuable exclusive rights to Mickey Mouse, Pluto, Goofy, Donald Duck, and other cartoon characters.[25] Although often thought of as "minor," legislation of this sort can be very important and valuable to its proponents.

Major discretionary items on the congressional agenda can include such matters as tax increases or reductions, disaster relief, new consumer-protection measures, or significant alterations in environmental policies. Such items, although technically discretionary, may take on a mandatory image because of presidential or societal pressures, or the appearance of "crisis" conditions.

This was the case with Social Security reform in the early 1980s and again in the late 1990s. Members of Congress felt compelled to act. However, when President George W. Bush called for more change in Social Security early in his second term, nothing was done. After 2009, the so-called national debt crisis again gave Social Security a prominent agenda spot.

The number of people affected and the intensity of their interest will vary across the issues on an agenda. Some matters will attract much interest from the broad range of citizens and officials; others will attract the attention primarily of policy specialists and those who have a direct stake in them. Professor Barbara Sinclair suggests that an agenda "is best conceptualized as roughly pyramidal" in form. A "limited number of highly salient issues" will be at the top; as one moves toward the base, there will be "an increasing number of progressively less and less salient issues."[26] Those at the top would likely qualify for Kingdon's decision agenda, although many of them will attract little attention from the public or the media.

To conclude, a policy agenda is not a matter of precision or fixed content. It would probably not be possible to secure complete agreement on the content of any policy agenda, at least if it is somewhat complex, whether it is that of Congress or a city council. Clues to the content of the congressional agenda, for example, are provided by presidential messages, legislation singled out by party leaders for attention, issues discussed in the communications media, and the like. Inability to enumerate readily all the items on a policy agenda does not destroy the usefulness of the concept for studying policy.

The Agenda-Setting Process

How, then, do problems reach the agendas of governmental organizations such as Congress? A prominent answer to this query has been supplied by Professor John Kingdon.[27] In an analysis that has captivated many political scientists, he holds that agenda setting can be viewed as comprising three mostly independent streams of activity (problems, proposals, and politics), which occasionally converge, opening a "policy window" and permitting some matters to reach a governmental agenda (see Figure 3.3).

The problems stream consists of matters on which policy players, either inside or outside of the government, would like to secure action. In the health area, for instance, people may be worried about the cost of health care, access to care, the adequacy of disease-prevention programs, or the need for more biomedical research.

The policy-proposals stream comprises possible solutions for problems. Public officials, congressional committee staffs, bureaucrats, academics, group representatives, and others develop proposals. "They each have their pet ideas or axes to grind; they float their ideas up and the ideas bubble around in . . . policy communities. In a selection process, some ideas or proposals are taken seriously and others are discarded."[28] Solutions that survive await problems

FIGURE 3.3

Kingdon's Agenda-Setting Model

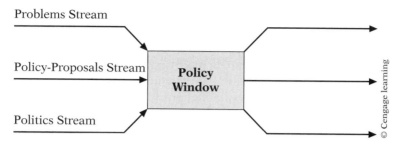

to which to attach themselves. Sometimes, according to Kingdon, those with "pet" solutions look for problems that can be solved with them. For example, mass transit has been proposed to redress several problems, including energy supply, traffic congestion, air pollution, and highway maintenance.

The politics stream includes such items as election results, changes in presidential administrations, swings in public moods, and pressure-group campaigns. Occasionally, these three streams converge, and for a short time, a policy window opens; that is, "an opportunity for advocates of proposals to push their pet solutions, or to push attention to their special problems" becomes available. Sometimes the window opens predictably, as when a law comes up for renewal; in other instances, it happens unpredictably.[29]

Kingdon's streams theory seems to make agenda setting a rather random or chancy process; much depends upon timing and luck. Without denying that timing and luck play a part in agenda setting, especially for large or basic changes in public policy, the process is more predictable, manipulable, and orderly than he implies. Following is an alternative view of agenda setting.[30]

At any given time, many problems and issues will be competing for the attention of public officials, who will also have their own preferred ideas to push. Only a portion of these problems will succeed in securing agenda status, however, because officials lack the time, resources, interest, information, or will to consider many of them. Agenda building is thus a competitive process, and various factors can determine whether an issue gets on an agenda, including how the problem at issue is defined.

One factor is suggested by political scientist David B. Truman, who says that interest groups seek to maintain themselves in a state of reasonable equilibrium and that if anything threatens this condition, they react accordingly.

> When the equilibrium of a group (and the equilibrium of its participant individuals) is seriously disturbed, various kinds of behavior may ensue. If the disturbance is not too great, the group's leaders will make an effort to restore the previous balance. . . . This effort may immediately necessitate recourse to the government. Other behaviors may occur if the disturbance is serious to the point of disruption.[31]

Thus, American steel producers and ethanol producers, seeing cheaper imported steel and Brazilian ethanol as contrary to a satisfactory price and profit situation, obtained limitations on imports. Companies threatened by unfriendly take-overs have likewise sought governmental restrictions on corporate acquisitions. Moreover, when one group gets what it wants from government, this gain may cause a reaction by other groups, as with organized labor's continued efforts to secure first the repeal of and then modifications to some of the restrictions in employee relations and collective bargaining imposed on them by the Taft–Hartley Act. For years, automobile manufacturers were similarly successful in delaying imposition of fuel-economy standards set by legislation on energy conservation. Interest groups thus successfully strive to place issues on an institutional agenda, but by no means do they account for all issues achieving agenda status.

Political leadership is another important factor in setting agendas. Political leaders, whether motivated by thoughts of political advantage, the public interest, or their political reputations, may seize upon problems, publicize them, and propose solutions. Of particular importance here is the president because of his prominent role as an agenda setter in American politics. Presidents can use the State of the Union, the budget, and special messages to set the congressional agenda. Media events may accompany these messages and bring them to the attention of the general public as well. Presidential ini-tiative here tends to be limited by the notion that Congress can handle only a few major initiatives at a time. Jimmy Carter was criticized for flooding Congress with legislative proposals and thereby reducing his effectiveness as a legislative leader. (In actuality, President Carter got much of what he sought from Congress.) In contrast, Ronald Reagan successfully focused on tax cuts and expenditure reductions during his initial year in office.

In his study of presidential agenda setting, Professor Paul Light found that in selecting major domestic issues on which to advocate action, presidents are motivated by three primary considerations.[32] The first is electoral benefits, which are especially important during a president's first term. Certain issues are seen as critical to electoral success and as vital in building and maintaining electoral coalitions. There is also a feeling that issues stressed during a cam-paign should be acted on.

The second concern is historical achievement. Because history surrounds the office, and the Washington community and others constantly compare presidents, a president often becomes mindful of greatness, of his or her place in history. Issues are singled out with which the presidents want to "mark" their administrations.

The third consideration is good policy. Presidents enter office with ideolog-ical leanings and personal commitments that may dispose them to act on some matters even in the face of congressional hostility and bureaucratic resistance. The importance of some issues, moreover, makes such action imperative. Light concludes, "Presidents do have notions of what constitutes good public policy." This was certainly true for both Ronald Reagan and Barack Obama, although many people did not agree with what they considered good policy.

Presidents are successful in getting many of their major policy proposals placed on the congressional agenda. Presidential proposals, however, have to compete with congressional proposals for agenda space. In their study of presidential agenda setting, Professors George Edwards and Andrew Barrett found that for the 1953–1996 period, presidential proposals made up a third of the congressional agenda. Fewer than half of the presidential proposals were eventually enacted into law, although presidential proposals fared better than those of Congress in this regard.[33] By no means, then, does securing agenda status guarantee enactment. Presidents are more likely to get action on what they want when the government is unified.

The president's role as an agenda setter for Congress is diminished when it is controlled by the opposition party.[34] The majority party leaders are then reluctant to accept the president's agenda as the "starting point for policy dialogue." They take on more responsibility for agenda setting, drawing issues from the complex of matters under examination in committees and elsewhere in Congress. In selecting issues, they are influenced by public opinion, congressional support, triggering events, and other criteria.

Members of Congress also may serve as agenda setters. In a study of agenda setting in the U.S. Senate, Professor Jack L. Walker concludes that there are some "activist legislators, motivated by a desire to promote social change, and anxious to gain reputations as reformers [who] constantly search for issues that might be transformed into new items on the Senate's discretionary agenda."[35] Senator Ted Kennedy (D, Massachusetts) was instrumental in putting health-care reform legislation on the congressional agenda, if not in securing its enactment. In the House, Representative Henry Waxman (D, California) has been a strong proponent of legislation to control acid rain and other forms of air pollution.

Members of Congress, interest-group representatives, agency officials, and citizens who push policy proposals are often referred to as *policy entrepreneurs*. Much time, energy, and resources may be devoted by entrepreneurs to keeping an issue alive, building support for it, getting it on an agenda, and securing action on it. Alfred Kahn, an economist who became head of the Civil Aeronautics Board, used his position successfully to generate support for airline deregulation and the abolition of his agency. The role of Ralph Nader in bringing about automobile-safety legislation is familiar history. Professor John Kingdon observes that policy entrepreneurs may be motivated by "their straightforward concern about certain problems, their pursuit of such self-serving benefits as protecting or expanding their bureaucracy's budget or claiming credit for accomplishment, their promotion of their policy values, . . . their simple pleasure in participating," or some combination of these.[36]

Governmental entities often serve as agenda setters for one another. The case of highway speed limits is a good example. In 1974, as an energy-saving measure, Congress adopted the National Maximum Speed Law, which stipulated that states would lose some federal highway funds if they did not reduce their speed limits to 55 miles per hour. This put the speed-limit issues on the agendas of state legislatures; 55-miles-an-hour speed limits sprung up across the nation. More agenda setting on speed limits occurred in the late 1980s, when Congress permitted the speed limit on rural interstate highways to rise to 65, and again in 1995, when the maximum speed law was repealed.

Supreme Court decisions have often helped put items on the congressional agenda.[37] Congress has tried (unsuccessfully) to overcome the Court's decision that prayer in public schools is unconstitutional by proposing a constitutional amendment. Several provisions have also been included in legislation to restrict use of federal funds to pay for abortions as a consequence of the Court's decision in *Roe* v. *Wade* (see the Budget Execution section in the "Budgeting and Public Policy" chapter). More frequently, Court decisions interpreting and applying legislation trigger congressional responses to overcome their effects. The Civil Rights Act of 1991 offset several Court decisions that had made it more difficult for job discrimination victims to successfully sue for damages.

Some matters may achieve agenda status and be acted upon as a consequence of some sort of crisis—an industrial accident, an airplane crash, or a natural disaster. Professor Thomas Birkland calls these "focusing events"— events that are "sudden; [are] relatively uncommon; can be reasonably defined as harmful or revealing the possibility of potentially greater future harms; have harms that are concentrated in a particular geographical area or community of interest; and . . . [are] known to policy makers and the public simultaneously."[38] Such events dramatize an issue and draw wide attention, causing public officials to feel compelled to respond in some manner. There may previously have been discussion and advocacy of the need to be prepared to act on some matter, but without a sense of urgency. A focusing event pushes the matter onto a policy agenda where action seems likely to occur.[39]

The September 11, 2001, attack by Islamic terrorists on the World Trade Center towers in New York City and the Pentagon in Washington, DC, elevated terrorism to the top of the national agenda. For a time, domestic issues—immigration, health care, bankruptcy, energy—were shouldered aside as national officials enacted legislation on terrorism and its consequences. Events of the magnitude of the terrorist attack that cause concern to intensify are rare.

The slaughter of twenty grade-school children and six educators in Newtown, Massachusetts, by a deranged person in December 2012, put the issue of gun control, which had been languishing, on the decision agendas of various governments—national and state. Political analyst Norman Ornstein commented that before the slaughter, there seemed no likelihood of Congressional action on gun control. Now it was a possibility. The Senate, he said, appeared more likely than the House to impose new controls.[40]

In April 2013, the Senate voted, 68 to 32, to allow debate on gun control legislation to proceed. The Senate leadership decided that 60 votes would be needed to approve anything. All of the proposed amendments to a gun bill failed, although many had majority support.[41] Minority rule and the anti-gun control lobby prevailed once more.

Protest activity, which may include actual or threatened violence, is another means by which problems may be brought to the attention of policy-makers and put on a policy agenda.[42] During the 1960s, such actions as the sit-in movement, the voters' rights march in Selma, Alabama (and the brutal reaction by the Selma police), and the 1963 march on Washington helped keep civil-rights issues at the top of the national policy agenda. Riots in many northern cities were also contributory. In more recent years, groups concerned with women's rights have utilized various kinds of demonstrations in their efforts to move their concerns onto policy agendas, and with some success. Gays, lesbians, and antiabortion protesters have also taken to the streets and engaged in protest activities to call attention to their problems.

Some problems or issues attract the attention of the communications media and, through their reportage, can be either converted into agenda items or, the more likely result, if already on an agenda, given more salience. A classic example is the highly colored and often inaccurate reporting of the Pulitzer and Hearst newspapers in the 1890s in making Spain's treatment of its colonies, particularly Cuba, a major issue and thus doing much to cause the United States eventually to declare war on Spain.[43] More recently, the media helped make nuclear safety a continuing concern by extensive coverage of such major events as the meltdown at the Three Mile Island nuclear-power plant in Pennsylvania in 1979 and the explosion of a nuclear reactor at Chernobyl in the Soviet Ukraine in 1986, as well as lesser nuclear-safety incidents. This contributed to the decline of the nuclear power industry in the United States. The April 2010 nuclear disaster at Fukushima Daiichi in Japan, although caused by an earthquake-generated tsunami, focused attention again on nuclear safety. It was a setback for the nuclear power industry, which had been experiencing something of a revival as a clean energy alternative.

Whether the news media are motivated by a desire to "create" news, report all that is newsworthy, stimulate sales, or serve the public interest is not the question here. Whatever their motives, as important opinion shapers they help structure policy agendas. Although notions about proper news-media operations and the compelling force of some events limit somewhat the discretion the media have in selecting the events (the "news") they bring to the public's attention, they nonetheless do have much leeway. The media do not so much tell people and policy-makers what to think as they do what to think about.

Changes in statistical indicators also produce awareness of problems and help move them onto agendas.[44] Governmental agencies and others regularly collect data on many activities and events, such as consumer prices, the foreign-trade balance, highway deaths, disease rates, infant-mortality rates, and industrial-accident rates. Health-care cost containment has been an important issue in Washington because statistics indicate that the costs of health care are rising rapidly. Conversely, as the rate of increase in the consumer price index remained low in the 1990s, so, too, did public concern about inflation.

Although the Federal Reserve Board continued to worry about inflation (reflecting its policy orientation), most Washington officials became more interested in other problems.

Political changes, including election results, changes in administrations, and shifts in the public mood, may make possible moving onto an agenda items that previously were unlikely candidates for inclusion.[45] Lyndon Johnson's landslide election in 1964, together with the election of favorable majorities in both houses of Congress, opened the doors for enacting a flood of social-welfare legislation. These doors partly closed two years later when the voters, reacting negatively to the administration's ventures in Vietnam, turned many of Johnson's supporters out of office.

Political change can also reduce the agenda opportunities for some items. The Reagan administration's preference for cutbacks in the government's role in society made major new spending and regulatory programs difficult to obtain, and few were proposed. The Republican takeover of Congress in 1995 brought to the fore many proposals for reducing or eliminating national government programs, though their success was limited.

The 2009 arrival of the Obama administration in Washington shifted agenda opportunities from what they had been under the George W. Bush administration. Environmental and labor interests, for example, now found doors open that previously had been minimally ajar, at best. Access does not necessarily mean policy success, however, but it will certainly help.

Finally, items may gain agenda status in rather arcane or peculiar ways. Take the instance of occupational safety and health. Robert Hardesty, one of President Lyndon Johnson's speechwriters, had a brother who worked in the Department of Health, Education, and Welfare's (HEW's) Bureau of Occupational Safety and Health, a research unit. At his urging, Hardesty would occasionally insert references to occupational safety and health in the president's speeches. Although HEW and the labor movement were indifferent to occupational safety, the Department of Labor saw in the speech references an opportunity to propose a program that would win presidential approval. A draft occupational safety and health bill was included in a package of legislative ideas that Labor sent to the White House in late 1967. With little urging from Labor, it was accepted and became part of the Johnson administration's 1968 legislative program. It did not win congressional approval that year, but it stayed on the agenda and became law as the Occupational Safety and Health Act of 1970.[46]

Although all the possibilities have not been sketched here, my purpose has been to show that problems can follow a variety of routes in reaching a policy agenda.[47] Moreover, a number of factors may be instrumental in a given instance. Thus, political leadership, media coverage, and statistical analysis converged to place Social Security solvency on the national agenda in the late 1990s. Of course, all problems do not find a place, or a prominent place, on a policy agenda. Those opposing action on a problem typically strive to block its consideration so as to deny it agenda status.

Agenda Denial Competition for agenda space occurs not only among those touting favored proposals but also between those favoring and opposing action on a problem. Those opposing action and wanting to maintain the status quo—business groups and conservative organizations are often involved here— tend to be advantaged in the agenda-status struggle. They have ample resources, and time is on their side. Moreover, public officials may be risk averse or more concerned with other matters.

Various tactics may be used by the opponents of agenda status for a problem.[48] They may deny that a problem exists, as the tobacco companies did for decades concerning the use of cigarettes and other tobacco products. As late as the mid-1990s, tobacco companies testified to Congress that cigarette smoking was not addictive. Research was sponsored denying adverse effects of smoking.

Secondly, arguments may be presented that a given problem is not appropriate for government action, or that it is beyond the power of government, or both, for good measure. Opponents of sex education contend that it has no place in the public school curriculum, being a matter properly left to church or family.

Third, fears may be expressed (and attempts may be made to create them) about the negative consequences of a proposed policy. Opponents of the Clinton administration's health-care reform plan, depicting it as excessively costly, productive of red tape, unduly bureaucratic, and restrictive of individual choice, prevented it from being voted on in Congress.

Fourth, it is sometimes argued that a problem can adequately be handled by non-governmental means. Opponents of boating-safety legislation have often argued successfully that most people do not need to be told by government to wear life jackets and to refrain from the use of alcohol while boating. Agricultural animals—veal calves, farrowing sows, laying hens—are often confined in spaces so small they can barely move. Agricultural groups deny this is cruel and contend that farmers do not need animal welfare organizations to tell them what to do.

Fifth, another ploy is to call for the creation of a commission or task force to gain more information on a problem, such as pornography, traffic congestion, or global warming. At least for a time this can delay action by seeming to do something about a problem. The Reagan administration used this tactic to fend off calls for action on acid rain (or deposition).

Sixth, recourse may be directed to the election process. The National Rifle Association, with its extensive grassroots organization, has often succeeded in keeping gun control off legislative agendas. Its actions in supporting opponents of gun control and opposing its proponents seem to intimidate many legislators. This happens notwithstanding public-opinion surveys that indicate substantial support for various forms of gun control.

Also of use in understanding why some problems, or potential problems, such as increasing income inequality in the United States, do not achieve agenda status, is the concept of nondecision. We now turn to it.

Nondecisions

Nondecision-making is defined by Professors Peter Bachrach and Morton S. Baratz as "a means by which demands for change in the existing allocation of benefits and privileges in the community can be suffocated before they are even voiced; or kept covert; or killed before they gain access to the relevant decision-making arena; or failing all these things, maimed or destroyed in the decision-implementing stage of the policy process."[49] Problems may be kept off a systemic or institutional agenda in various ways. At the local level, particularly, force may be utilized, as in the South during the 1950s and 1960s by white groups to stifle black demands for equal rights. Another possibility is that prevailing values and beliefs—political culture—may also operate to deny agenda status to problems or policy alternatives. Our beliefs about private property and capitalism kept railroad nationalization from ever becoming a real agenda item—even late in the nineteenth and early in the twentieth centuries, when railroad policy was being developed—except when facets of railroad operations, such as passenger service (witness Amtrak), became unprofitable for private enterprise.

A third possibility is suggested by Professor E. E. Schattschneider. "The crucial problem in politics," he states, "is the management of conflict. No regime could endure that did not cope with this problem. All politics, all leadership, all organization involves the management of conflict. All conflict allocates space in the political universe. The consequences of conflict are so important that it is inconceivable that any regime would survive without making an attempt to shape the system." To survive, then, political leaders and organizations must prevent problems or issues that would threaten their existence from reaching the political arena (i.e., from achieving agenda status). The kinds of problems that they resist will depend upon what kinds of leaders and organizations they are—whether, for example, they are conservative Republicans or independent commissions. They will, in any case, resist considering some problems, for, as Schattschneider contends, "all forms of political organization have a bias in favor of the exploitation of some kinds of conflicts and the suppression of others because organization is the mobilization of bias. Some issues are organized into politics while others are organized out."[50]

In studying public policymaking, it is important to know why some problems are dealt with and others are neglected or suppressed. Recall that public policy is determined not only by what government does do but also by what it deliberately does not do. Take the situation of migratory farm workers, whose problems usually receive short shrift from public officials. Why? What does an answer to this question tell us about who gets what and why from the policy process? Is the neglect of migrant workers at least partly due to nondecision-making? Notwithstanding the somewhat imprecise nature of the concept of nondecision, it has utility for analyzing the policy process.

The Loss of Agenda Status

Problems that reach agendas may also disappear from agendas. Action may be taken on a problem, or a decision may be made not to take action, not to enact a law or adopt a rule on a matter. Policy-makers may then believe that the problem has been taken care of and turn their attention to other issues. Whether to levy user fees on commercial companies and other users of inland waterways, such as the Mississippi and Ohio Rivers, which require maintenance by the Army Corps of Engineers, was a hot issue for a time.[51] Once legislation imposing user fees was enacted, the issue quickly dropped from view. The fees are still collected.

Another example is military conscription (the draft), which existed from 1940 to 1973. A salient and divisive issue during the Vietnam War because of inequities in its administration, its authorization lapsed in 1973 and an all-voluntary military came into being. In 1980, legislation was passed requiring all males to register with the Selective Service System when they reached the age of eighteen. No inductions have occurred.

A third example is silicosis, a deadly respiratory illness that afflicts workers in stone quarries, foundries (that make metal castings), and other dusty workplaces. It received much attention in the early decades of the twentieth century. After World War II, however, silicosis became defined "as a disease of the past that could be adequately addressed by medical researchers and engineers working with an enlightened business community."[52] This was an overly optimistic appraisal. Silicosis continues to be a serious but neglected health threat to workers in the "dusty trades."

Factors that may push items from an agenda include changes in or disappearance of the conditions that created a problem, the emergence of new and more pressing problems, people becoming accustomed to a condition (e.g., construction noise) and no longer calling it a problem, and social or culture change, as that which converts gambling from an evil into a source of government revenue.

Policy analyst Anthony Downs suggests that an "issue-attention cycle" causes some public problems to fade from public view.[53] The cycle has five stages that vary in duration:

1. The pre-problem stage. At this time a quite undesirable social condition exists but has not received much public notice. Some specialists and interest groups may have become concerned about it.

2. Alarmed discovery and euphoric enthusiasm. Something causes the public to become aware of and alarmed about the problem. There is a strong desire to quickly solve the problem, which reflects the notion that most obstacles to improvement are external. Hence, the solution does not appear to necessitate fundamental change in society.

3. Realization of the cost of significant progress. Awareness spreads that solving the problem will entail high costs. People realize that part of the

problem stems from arrangements, such as the millions of cars that cause traffic congestion, that benefit many people. The nation's most pressing social problems usually involve intended or unconscious exploitation of one social group by another.

4. Gradual decline in the intensity of public interest. As people realize how difficult and costly it will be to solve the problem, many become discouraged, others feel threatened, and some become bored. Attention to the issue wanes, and moreover, by now another issue may be reaching stage 2.

5. The post-problem stage. The issue moves into a "twilight realm" of less attention. The agencies, policies, and programs created to help solve it persist and usually have some impact. A supportive subsystem may develop.

Not all major problems go through the "issue-attention cycle." Those which do likely possess three qualities in some degree: First, they affect a numerical minority, as in poverty and unemployment. Second, they involve social arrangements beneficial to a majority or a powerful minority. Thus, car owners and highway lobbies benefit from the ban on using motor-fuel taxes for mass-transit systems that would aid the urban poor. Third, there are no longer exciting events associated with problems, such as television coverage of race riots or NASA space shots. The space program, the War on Poverty, the farm program, and labor–management relations policy all seem to have experienced this cycle. Downs predicted that environmental protection was an issue unlikely to fade quickly because its support was constantly being renewed. Time appears to have validated his opinion. What will happen to the "war on drugs"? To reduction of the national budget deficit? To the imposition of term limits on elected public officials?

Two Cases in Agenda Setting

To provide further perspective on the agenda-setting process, we can consider how two regulatory problems of quite different scope, content, and societal impact achieved agenda status. The first is coal-mine safety, which today directly affects only a small segment of the workforce and is likely to be unfamiliar to many readers. Annually, hundreds of workers are killed or severely injured in coal-mine accidents. Many more suffer from the ravages of black-lung disease.[54] The second is environmental-pollution control, which has been an important item on government agendas since the early 1970s.

CASE STUDY *Coal-Mine Safety*

Coal mining has long been a highly hazardous occupation marked by high rates of accidental injury and death. Coal-mine fatalities averaged more than 1,000 annually in the 1930s and the 1940s. Underground (or shaft) coal mines, which until after World War II produced most of the nation's coal, tend to be deep, dark, dusty, and dangerous. Regulatory activity to protect miners was first undertaken by the state governments early in the twentieth century.[55] Because of dissatisfaction with the ineffectiveness of state regulation, however, federal regulation was sought by miners and their supporters. After decades of struggle, Congress enacted the Coal Mine Safety Act of 1952.

Enforcement of the act was entrusted to the Bureau of Mines (this agency was abolished in 1996) in the Department of the Interior. The bureau, which also had responsibility for promoting the economic well-being of the mining industry was often criticized as being too responsive to the mine owners' interests. Frequent accidents and deaths continued to occur in the coal mines. For nearly two decades nothing really effective was done to strengthen policy on mine safety, even though technology was available to improve safety conditions without a major decline in production. One reason for the inactivity was that underground coal mining is concentrated in a few areas of the country, such as West Virginia and southern Illinois, and most people are both relatively unaffected by and unaware of the miners' problems. Also, mine union leaders were more interested in economic issues.

This situation changed, however, on November 20, 1968, when an explosion occurred at the Consolidation Coal Company's No. 9 mine in Farmington, West Virginia. Seventy-nine miners were trapped below the surface, and all died before rescue workers could reach them. This major tragedy, well reported by the national news media, focused the nation's attention on the miners' plight, including not only explosions and other accidents but also black-lung disease, a chronic and deadly ailment caused by continued inhalation of coal dust. Demanding remedies, the miners staged protest meetings, engaged in wildcat strikes, and conducted other activities, including a march on the West Virginia state capitol. In March 1969, the West Virginia legislature enacted legislation providing compensation for victims of black-lung disease.

The miners and their leaders continued to press for national legislation as well, repeatedly threatening a nationwide coal strike if action was not forthcoming. President Nixon responded by sending Congress a special message, along with a draft bill, on coal-mine safety. The bill was stronger than one proposed a year earlier, prior to the explosion, by President Johnson. In October 1969, the Senate passed a mine-safety bill by a 73 to 0 vote, and a few weeks later the House did so by a 389 to 4 vote. Signed into law by President Nixon, the federal Mine Safety and Health Act of 1969 provided for health standards and stronger safety standards for mines and authorized a black-lung compensation program. The Bureau of Mines continued to have responsibility for enforcing the health and safety standards.[56]

Mine safety did not drop off the congressional agenda with the adoption of the new law, however, as frequently happens in such matters, although it did become less salient. Interested members of Congress continued to monitor the mine-safety act's enforcement by the Bureau of Mines, which was criticized as being too responsive to the mining industry, too willing to trade safety for more production, and generally lax in enforcing the law. Early in 1973, several bills providing for transfer of mine safety away from the Bureau of Mines were introduced in Congress. Before action could be taken on them, however, the secretary of the interior unexpectedly set up a new Mine Enforcement and Safety Administration (MESA) in the department to handle the mine-safety program separately from the Bureau of Mines.[57] This ploy was obviously intended to fend off congressional action.

Because accidents and deaths continued to occur in the coal mines, some members of Congress transferred their unhappiness with the quality of mine-safety enforcement from the Bureau of Mines to MESA. The Department of the Interior was viewed as being lax on health and safety matters. Discontent peaked in 1977, and mine safety returned to the congressional decision agenda. Amendments to the federal Coal Mine Safety Act transferred mine-safety enforcement from MESA to a new Mining Safety and Health Administration (MSHA) in the Department of Labor, which was viewed as a more hospitable locale for the program. The 1969 act was also revised in an effort to expedite setting health and safety standards and imposing penalties for their violation. Metal and nonmetal mines were also put under the jurisdiction of MSHA. Strongly supported by organized labor, the 1977 legislation was strenuously opposed by the coal-mining industry.

Enforcement of the mine-safety legislation, which was never stringent, waned under the Reagan administration.[58] A former coal-mine operator was appointed to head MSHA, and revisions were made in mine-safety regulations that generally accorded with coal-industry recommendations. Also, legislation was proposed by the administration that, it was said, would reduce the regulatory burden on mine operators without reducing safety protection for workers. No action was taken by Congress.

In 1987, as a consequence of multiple-death mine accidents and studies critical of mine-safety enforcement, the issue once again hit the congressional agenda. Hearings were held by both House and Senate committees. At a hearing before the Senate Labor and Human Resources Committee, witnesses decried the laxity of enforcement and supported the creation of a new, independent agency to handle all mine-safety enforcement duties. The committee chair, Senator Orrin Hatch (R, Utah), and its ranking Democratic member, Senator Edward Kennedy (D, Massachusetts), joined in assailing MSHA for weakening safety standards and enforcement programs. No legislation resulted. The Reagan administration, however, did agree to hire about 100 additional mine inspectors, and a rule that had reduced criminal convictions of negligent operators was rescinded.[59]

The number of coal-mine deaths has greatly declined in recent years, in part because the number of workers employed in underground mines has declined as more of the nation's coal is produced by surface (or strip) mining. Less hazardous for miners, surface mining is more hazardous for the environment, which is a problem that President Carter and Congress sought to deal with by the Surface Mining Control and Reclamation Act of 1977.

Critics of MSHA, taking advantage of the antiregulatory atmosphere created by the new Republican majorities in Congress, put the agency on the agenda again in 1995. Supported by the owners and operators of coal mines in eastern Kentucky, which were "among the most dangerous and latest targets" of MSHA, legislation was launched to reduce MSHA's inspection and enforcement powers and then abolish it through a merger with the Occupational Safety and Health Administration.[60] Called reform legislation, it readily cleared the House Education and the Workforce Committee. It was not further acted upon during that term of Congress and then dropped off the congressional agenda.

The enforcement of coal-mine safety rules has fluctuated with control of the White House. Whereas under the Clinton administration, efforts were made to strengthen safety rules, under the George W. Bush administration, enforcement slackened. MSHA, under the leadership of a former coal-industry executive, moved to weaken some of the rules.

Several coal-mine accidents in early 2006 gave coal-mine safety a prominent place on the national policy agenda. Within a few months negotiations among Democrats and Republicans in Congress, mining companies, and mine unions yielded enactment of the Mining Improvement and New Emergency Response Act (the MINER Act). Mine companies were directed to develop new emergency response plans, to provide more emergency oxygen supplies, to install wireless underground communications systems, and to have certified rescue teams at the ready. Stronger penalties were provided for health and safety violations.[61] Violations, accidents, and deaths continue to occur.

Narratives similar to that of coal-mine safety could be written for many other relatively "obscure" public problems and the low-visibility policies involving them. The protection of wild horses in the western states, the Indian health services program, the regulation of national credit unions, the Department of Agriculture's animal damage control program, and the regulation of ocean dumping are examples of policies that are not widely known. One will rarely encounter coverage of them in the communication media.

Collectively, such policies and the problems at which they are directed comprise a significant part of the work of modern government. Each is of importance to particular segments of the population, who can be counted on to stoutly support their continuation. Unless something out of the ordinary happens, for example, a scandal or an accident, to stir the public's consciousness, they will be handled by political subsystems. Few members of Congress or White House officials will worry about them.

Now, however, we turn to a complex problem that has drawn widespread attention from citizens and officials—environmental pollution and its control. ■

CASE STUDY *Environmental Pollution Control*

Environmental pollution has long been a condition in American society. The nation's air, waters, and soil were commonly used as free or inexpensive means for disposing of wastes. Not until the 1960s, however, did pollution begin to be widely perceived as a major public problem. Whereas belching factory smokestacks once were thought to be emblematic of economic progress, now they are usually viewed as deplorable matters requiring control. The national and state governments have enacted a large volume of legislation designed to control pollution and protect the environment, often in the face of considerable resistance from economic development interests. Topics include air, water, drinking water, hazardous waste, acid rain, pesticides, and solid waste.

Several factors have contributed to making pollution control an important item on the policy agendas. Early on, a number of triggering events raised public awareness about the adverse consequences of pollution. The publication in 1962 of Rachel Carson's *Silent Spring* called attention to the detrimental effects of the extensive application of chemical pesticides on wildlife and human beings.[62] An oil-well blowout off the California coast near Santa Barbara in 1969 polluted miles of beaches and received extensive coverage by the news media. The first Earth Day, which occurred on April 22, 1970, elicited the participation of millions of people on college campuses and elsewhere. It represented a tremendous expression of popular interest in protecting the environment. Earth Day continues to be observed on a lesser scale.

Environmentalist J. Clarence Davies argues that underlying the attention to pollution is the affluence of American society. He explains,

> The massive growth in production and in the availability of resources which have characterized the American economy ... affect the problem of pollution in several ways. The increase in production has contributed to an intensification of the degree of actual pollution; the increase in the standard of living has permitted people the comparative luxury of being able to be concerned about this; and the availability of ample public and private resources has given the society sufficient funds and skilled manpower to provide the potential for dealing with the problem.[63]

People who are compelled to continually worry about whether they will be able to secure the basic necessities of life are likely to have little time or inclination to fret about pollution. In the developing countries concern about the problem is still limited; indeed, it is probably not perceived as a problem by many of their inhabitants. In an affluent society, in comparison, favorable conditions of life contribute to a growing belief in the need to control pollution. More time for leisure leads to greater demand for recreational resources and aesthetic pleasures, and a higher level of education enables people to more readily understand the nature and dangers of pollution and the need to protect the natural environment. There is considerable accuracy to the contention that pollution control is a "middle-class issue," a characteristic that contributes to government's willingness to respond favorably.

Pollution and its consequences, however, do affect everyone, and that helps make it an attractive public issue. Pollution control, in turn, can be depicted as an activity that does something for everyone, which enhances its political appeal. Politicians supporting pollution control can portray themselves as on the side of the angels and as protectors of the public interest. Although many business groups and industries are opposed to tough environmental-protection programs, they are handicapped by the issue's broad appeal and attractiveness. Not much support can be won by appearing to favor dirtier air or water. Rather, opposition to stringent control must be indirectly expressed, as by contending that the cost of controlling pollution will increase the cost of doing business, cost jobs, or add to inflation. This sort of argumentation has an abstract quality that reduces its public effectiveness.

Another factor contributing to the political attractiveness of environmental protection is its strong link to public health. Pollution is not benign. Chemicals and other wastes discharged into the environment have a variety of adverse consequences for the health of people (and other creatures), consequences that if not always well understood are much feared. The situation is much like the sentiments expressed in an old song: "Everybody wants to go to heaven, but nobody wants to die."

Finally government action to control pollution has created a dynamic that produces demands for additional and stronger action. We can draw on Davies again for an explanation:

> The issue is given publicity and "respectability" by governmental recognition, and the public learns that something can be done to alleviate the problem. Once an official agency has been established to control pollution, that agency becomes a focal point for bringing the issue to the attention of the general public as well as of other government officials. The members of the agency have a vested interest in drawing attention to the problem. If they are successful, private interest groups will take up the call for action and new groups will be created for the specific purpose of doing something about pollution. This public concern will in turn strengthen the hand of the governmental agency. The concern with pollution thus becomes institutionalized and the pressure to take action becomes constant.[64]

For more than four decades, the control of environmental pollution has been prominent on national systemic and governmental agendas. New environmental issues, often of a global nature, continue to arise: acid rain (or deposition), depletion of the stratospheric ozone layer, sustainable development, and world population growth. Disastrous crude-oil spills have focused public attention on threats to the environment. First, there was the blowout of an oil well offshore from Santa Barbara, California, then the grounding of the oil tanker Exxon *Valdez* in Prince William Sound, Alaska; later came an oil spill in Michigan's Kalamazoo River. In April 2010, the "mother" of all oil disasters occurred: the oil platform Deepwater Horizon operating in the Gulf of Mexico exploded, releasing an estimated 4.9 million barrels of oil.

International diplomatic events have also focused attention on the environment. Examples include the United Nations Conference on Environment and Development (the "Earth Summit") in Rio de Janeiro in June 1992 and the negotiation of the 1998 Kyoto Protocol on Climate Change (global warming). The periodic reports of the United Nations Intergovernmental Panel on Climate Change must also be noted.

Focusing events of these sorts help ensure that pollution will remain on policy agendas at all levels of government in the United States, as well as in international venues, for years to come.

Also, the impact of the environmental movement merits attention. Many hundreds of national, state, and local organizations keep a watchful eye on the environment and government actions and policies affecting it. As an astute observer remarked: "The many groups marching under the environmental banner continue to grow in number, sophistication, and political aggressiveness."[65] They can be counted on to continue to strive to put new environmental problems on the agenda or to revive some that have lost salience. For example, Congress in 1978 banned the sale of interior lead-based paint because of its adverse health effects. It remains, however, on the walls and woodwork of many homes and apartments, especially in lower-income areas. In recent years, it has been identified as a cause of lead poisoning in children, who ingest paint dust or flakes.[66] Remedial action has been called for.

Now it is time to turn our attention to the formulation of policy proposals intended to resolve or ameliorate policy problems. ■

The Formulation of Policy Proposals

Policy formulation involves developing pertinent and acceptable proposed courses of action (often called alternatives, proposals, or options) for dealing with public problems. Policy-makers may be confronted with several competing proposals for dealing with a problem, or they may have to struggle with devising their own alternative. Policy formulation does not always culminate in a law, executive order, or administrative rule. Policy-makers may decide not to take positive action on a problem, but instead to leave it alone, to let matters work themselves out. Or they may be unable to agree on what to do. For example, because Reagan administration officials could not agree on how to revise an executive order on affirmative action in hiring by governmental contractors, the existing order was left intact. It continues to define national policy. In short, that a public problem reaches a policy agenda does not mean positive action will be taken or, if it is, that it will be soon in coming. Decades of complaints, recommendations, studies, and failed attempts preceded the enactment by Congress of the Family Support Act (FSA) of 1988 to reform the nation's welfare system. FSA satisfied the demand for welfare reform only for a short while, being replaced in 1996 by the Personal Responsibility and Work Opportunity Act. Awareness of a problem does not guarantee positive governmental action, although unawareness or lack of interest pretty much ensures inaction.

Those who formulate alternatives to resolve or ameliorate problems— for example, water pollution, catastrophic health care, corporate financial practices, or telecommunications regulation—typically do not have to start from scratch. Over time, a vast pool of policy ideas has been developed. Some have been enacted into law; many have not. All, however, are available, perhaps in modified form, to would-be formulators, who often ask how similar problems have been dealt with. Mimicry is a common form of policy formulation. Policy proposals are likely intended to make incremental changes in existing policy. Radically innovative proposals are scarce. To paraphrase King Solomon, there is not much new under the sun (Ecclesiastes 1:9).

Policy formulators need to keep several factors in mind that will affect their chances of producing a successful policy. First, is the proposal technically sound? Is it directed at the problem's causes to the extent that they can be ascertained? To what extent is the proposal likely to resolve or ameliorate the problem? If recession is the problem, as in 2009, will spending programs or tax cuts provide more economic stimulus? If taxes are cut, will people spend the proceeds? Or will they save the money or use it to pay off existing debts, which will not do much to revive the economy?

Second, are the budgetary costs of the proposal reasonable or acceptable? This will not be a significant concern for many regulatory proposals, at least insofar as direct governmental costs are at issue. But what about the compliance costs imposed on private entities? Currently, the high cost of covering the many millions of people without health care coverage is bedeviling policy-makers.

Third, is the proposal politically acceptable? Can it gain enough support from legislators or public officials to be adopted? Can it win bipartisan support if that is thought necessary or important? The addition or deletion of various provisions may be warranted in order to gain support.

Fourth, if the proposal becomes law, will it be acceptable to the public? Will those affected be inclined to comply? A classic case involved a rule promulgated by the National Highway Traffic Safety Administration (NHTSA) requiring that new cars be equipped with an ignition interlock system that prevented starting the motor unless the driver's seat belt was buckled. Public reaction to the rule was quick, strong, and adverse. Congress hastily enacted legislation repealing the rule. NHTSA's attention turned to airbags, another idea that had been circulating in the automobile safety policy community. In time this idea gained public acceptance (and that of the automobile industry). Airbags have now become standard equipment in cars, and most people have become wise enough to buckle up.

Who Is Involved? In discussing who is involved in developing policy proposals, we focus primarily on the national level in the United States. In the twentieth and twenty-first centuries, the president, together with his chief aides and advisers in the Executive Office of the President, has been the leading source of initiative in forming major policy proposals. (At the state level, governors usually play the same role.) The origins of these proposals are many. Some may have originated in the EOP agencies; more likely, however, they bubbled up from the bureaucracy or had been floating around Congress and the Washington community for some time and were taken over by the president.

The members of Congress and the public have come to expect the president to present policy recommendations to Congress for consideration. Years ago, President Dwight Eisenhower was the target of much criticism, even from members of his own party, when in his first year in office he chose not to submit a legislative program to Congress. Moreover, the members of Congress have come to expect the chief executive to present them with draft bills embodying his recommendations. What the members of Congress want is "some real meat to digest," not merely some good ideas to consider. "Don't expect us to start from scratch on what you want," a committee chair told an Eisenhower official. "That's not the way we do things here—you draft the bills, and we work them over."[67] As this quotation implies, Congress does not always proceed kindly in handling the president's proposals (far from it), but presidential recommendations do, among other things, help Congress set its agenda and indicate where the president stands on some major issues, which is useful information to members of Congress.

GOVERNMENTAL AGENCIES Many policy proposals are developed by officials—both career and appointed—in the administrative departments and agencies. Continually working with governmental programs in agriculture, health, welfare, law enforcement, foreign trade, and other areas, they become aware of new policy problems, or deficiencies in existing laws, and develop proposals to deal with them. These plans are then transmitted to the executive and, if in accord with the president's policies and programs, sent on to Congress. Agency officials, because of their specialization, expertise, and continued involvement in particular policy areas, are in a good technical position to engage in formulating policy.

Many agency proposals are designed to modify or strengthen existing laws, typically to the benefit or advantage of the proposing agency. During their administration, loopholes, weaknesses, or omissions may have been identified. A large, complex piece of legislation, the Tax Reform Act of 1986, which reduced income-tax rates, contained numerous technical errors when it was passed, typical of such legislation. Two years were required for Congress to pass "corrective" legislation: the Technical and Miscellaneous Tax Act of 1988. The reason for the delay lay not in correcting the technical errors, which were readily taken care of. Rather, problems arose in reaching agreement on new substantive provisions, some raising revenue and others providing tax breaks for various individuals, companies, and groups that senators and representatives wanted to put into the tax law. The need to correct the 1986 law provided them with an opportunity and a legislative vehicle for additional tax action.

PRESIDENTIAL ORGANIZATIONS Temporary organizations, sometimes called "adhocracies," may be established by the president to study particular policy areas and to develop policy proposals.[68] These include presidential commissions, task forces, interagency committees, and other arrangements. Except for interagency committees, their memberships may include both legislative and executive officials as well as private citizens.

The President's Commission on Privatization, set up by President Reagan, recommended that various services provided by the U.S. Postal Service and some federal prisons be turned over to private contractors. The commission also supported previous proposals by the administration to sell some governmental petroleum reserves and marketing administrations for electric power. Advisory commissions of this sort are variously employed to develop policy proposals, to win support for those proposals through the endorsement of their usually prestigious members, or to create the appearance of government concern with some problem.

Presidential commissions, however, may not always produce the sorts of policy recommendations preferred by their appointer. The Brady Commission was appointed by the Reagan administration to investigate the stock-market collapse of October 19, 1987, and to make recommendations for preventing future recurrences. To the administration's surprise, the commission recommended tighter governmental control, preferably by the Federal Reserve Board, of trading activities on the stock and futures markets. Finding such advice uncongenial, the administration appointed an interagency committee, which drew its members from the various financial regulatory agencies, to review the recommendations of the Brady Commission and others. The interagency committee (formally, the White House Working Group on Financial Markets), composed of conservative administration officials, subsequently favored making only minimal changes in regulatory policies, which was in line with presidential preferences.[69] Doing little or nothing is often a preferred policy option, notably among conservatives, on economic regulatory problems.

President Lyndon Johnson made extensive use of task forces to develop legislative proposals, appointing more than 100 of these groups during his tenure.[70] He believed that task forces, composed of outstanding private citizens and top administration officials, would be more innovative and imaginative in developing proposals for new policies than would the national bureaucracy. He was quite pleased with the results. His successors in the 1970s and 1980s made little use of task forces, perhaps because they were less activist in their policy inclinations.

Another arrangement is a committee jointly composed of executive officials, members of Congress, and perhaps private citizens appointed by the president and legislative leaders to devise a solution for a program. The National Bipartisan Commission on the Future of Medicare is an example. Created by statute in 1997, it consisted of seventeen legislators and health-care policy experts selected by the president and congressional leaders. Its task was to make recommendations on Medicare's long-term structural and financial problems, matters on which Congress had been unable to devise acceptable answers. The commission conducted extensive deliberations. When its March 1999 deadline for reporting came, however, it was unable to agree on a reform proposal, which required approval of at least eleven of its members. Many of Medicare's problems remain unresolved.

President Barack Obama created by executive order the National Commission on Fiscal Responsibility and Reform, consisting of three Democrats and three Republicans from each house of Congress and six presidentially appointed civilians. Its task was to make recommendations "to bring the budget into primary balance and to meaningfully improve the long-run fiscal outlook." The commission prepared an extensive report but failed to win enough votes from its members to be acted upon. (For more, see Chapter 5 on Budgeting and Public Policy.)

LEGISLATORS   In the course of congressional hearings and investigations, through contacts with administrative officials and interest-group representatives, and on the basis of their own interests and activities, legislators receive suggestions for action on problems and formulate proposed courses of action. The capacity of members of Congress to engage in formulating policy has been strengthened by the creation of the House and Senate Offices of the Legislative Counsel and the Congressional Research Service (a part of the Library of Congress). Increased staff resources for both individual members and committees also have had a positive effect. Indeed, much of the work in drafting legislation is handled by Congressional staff, who possess the requisite knowledge.

In some policy areas, Congress has done much of the formulation: environmental protection, agriculture, welfare reform, and energy conservation are examples. Both the Clean Air Act of 1970 and the Clean Air Act Amendments of 1990, in final form, were primarily legislative products.[71] They represent markedly different styles in formulation. The landmark 1970 act takes up forty-seven pages in the statute books. Focused mostly on setting goals for the reduction of air pollution, it accorded much discretion to the Environmental Protection Agency (EPA) and industry in achieving them. In contrast, the 1990 Clean Air Act Amendments are several hundred pages in length and are studded with many specific requirements, timetables, and "hammers" (tough provisions intended to compel action). For example, the act designated 189 hazardous chemicals that the EPA is to regulate. All of the detail is intended to limit the discretion of administrative officials in implementing the act. In part, this reflects distrust of Republican-appointed administrators and federal judges by Democratic congressional majorities. But also, it signifies the willingness and capacity of Congress to enact more detailed legislation and to engage in what some call "micromanagement" of the implementation process.

Much of the actual writing of legislation is handled by congressional staff members possessing expertise in agricultural, environmental, taxation, or other policy areas. They worry about the details of legislation—the choice of words or phrases, the inclusion of particular provisions, and whether if enacted it will do what its supporters want done. House and Senate staff members also do much of the bargaining over legislative details. Also, each house of Congress has an Office of Legislative Counsel. Collectively, these units employ several dozen lawyer-technicians to perform the technical work in drafting legislation, including fitting it into the existing body of law.[72]

INTEREST GROUPS Interest groups have a major role in policy formation, often going to the legislature with specific proposals for legislation. They may also work with executive and legislative officials to develop and enact an officially proposed policy, perhaps with some modifications to suit their interests. Environmental, agricultural, and pesticide manufacturers were major players in formulating the legislation in 1988 that amended and reauthorized the Federal Insecticide, Fungicide, and Rodenticide Act (FIFRA). The act is intended to protect the public against harm from hazardous pesticides used on farm crops. Another example is the Israeli lobby, which consists of a number of groups and has been very influential and successful in shaping American financial aid to Israel.

At the state level, interest groups may play a big part in formulating legislation, especially on complex and technical issues, because state legislators frequently lack the time and staff needed to cope with such matters. It is reported that the Illinois legislature customarily enacts legislation in labor–management relations only after it has been agreed to by representatives of organized labor and industry.[73] Thus, by custom, private groups can become the actual formulators of policy.

Competing proposals for responding to a problem may emanate from several of these sources, as in the case of medical care. Cooperation is also a possibility. Another alternative is to draw on a favored source. George W. Bush administration officials worked with petroleum industry representatives, while paying little attention to environmental groups, in developing its 2001 energy proposal. It was not enacted into law until 2005, perhaps because of its complexity and the controversy stirred by its origins. Increasing domestic energy production was its main concern. In contrast, when the Obama administration moved on financial regulation, the bill it sent to Congress was put together within the administration. Congress, of course, made extensive changes before its enactment.

Formulators can also draw on the experiences of other governments, foreign and domestic, for policy ideas and to gain notions of what works and what does not work. For better or worse, the American states sometimes mimic one another. Obama administration officials, in developing proposals to deal with the Great Recession in 2009, looked at what Japan had done in the 1990s when confronted with a severe economic downturn. Japanese policy-makers had refused to take sufficiently strong action to counter the decline, so it persisted.

Policy Formulation as a Technical Process

Policy formulation involves two markedly different sorts of activities. One is to decide generally what, if anything, should be done about a problem. Thus, in the earlier illustration we find the question "What kind of national health-insurance system should we have?" In other instances, the question may be "What sorts of restrictions should be imposed on the practice of abortion?" or "What should be the minimum-wage level, and who should be covered by it?" Answers to these questions take the form of general principles or statements. Once such questions have been resolved, the second type of activity comes into play. Legislation or administrative rules must be drafted that, when adopted, will appropriately carry the agreed-upon principles or statements into effect. Often new legislation must be appropriately tied into existing statutes. This is a technical and rather mundane but nevertheless highly important task. The way a bill is written and the specific provisions it includes can substantially affect its administration and the actual content of public policy. Poor drafting can result in a statute like the one enacted by the Kansas legislature early in the twentieth century. It provided that when two trains met on the same track, each should get off onto a siding until the other had passed. (Think about this.)

An informative historical illustration of what can result from careless formulation is provided by the National Defense Education Act of 1958, enacted after the launching of the Soviet Sputnik and intended to help the United States "catch up with the Russians" in scientific and engineering education. This illustration also provides a glimpse into how the fear of communism affected politics and policymaking in the United States during the Cold War years. A provision in the act stating that students receiving graduate-fellowship assistance had to sign a noncommunist affidavit, or "loyalty oath," quickly produced a great deal of controversy.

Liberals criticized the oath requirement as an affront to the patriotism of students and as unnecessary, among other things. To them it was an important public problem requiring redress. Conservatives defended the loyalty oath as a necessary means of preventing financial aid from going to Communists (who were then much out of favor in the United States) and wondered why any loyal American would balk at signing such an oath. In short, they saw no problem. Some universities announced they would not participate in the fellowship program if the oath requirement were retained. Apparently, few graduate students who qualified for fellowships, practical souls that they were, declined to sign the oath and give up the money. Eventually, the oath was replaced by a milder and more acceptable "loyalty affirmation." Symbolic language is important.

Despite the controversy sparked by the oath requirement, there had been no discussion of it either in the committee hearings or during the floor debates on the act. No one had advocated its inclusion. How, then, did it find its way into the law? The answer to this question is not very dramatic, but so it goes with answers to many public-policy questions. The person drafting the formal language of the act copied some of its fellowship provisions from an existing statute; one of these provisions (it can be called "boilerplate") was the loyalty-oath requirement. It had caused no dispute under the earlier law. But when it was discovered in the 1958 act, the spat began. One moral that can be drawn from the story is that often it is easier to get a provision into a law than it is to remove it later. Bill drafters frequently borrow language from laws already on the books when they write new legislation.

The writing of laws and rules has to be done skillfully because as soon as these laws or rules go into effect, people will begin looking for loopholes or trying to bend the meaning of the language to their advantage.

The Emergency Economic Stabilization Act of 2008 authorized the expenditure (or investment) of up to $700 billion to alleviate the nation's financial crisis. It established the Troubled Assets Relief Program (TARP) to buy bad mortgage-related assets from banks, who had unwisely invested in large amounts of them. Somewhere along the way to adoption, the phrase "or other financial instruments" was added to the act. Consequently, when the Treasury Department switched from buying troubled assets to providing capital to banks (The Capital Purchase Program), it had legal authority to do so, much to the dismay of many members of Congress and others. Many banks chose to hoard their new capital rather than lending, as was intended.

Clarity in phrasing and intent also may help protect laws and rules against unfavorable judicial interpretations and provide clear guidance to those assigned the task of implementation. Congress and most of the state legislatures now have bill-drafting services to assist them in writing legislation. They also draw on the expert services of committee staffers, bureaucrats, and interest-group representatives.

Confronted with the task of interpreting a law that is unclear in meaning or intent, judges traditionally have sought guidance by examining the law's legislative history: hearings, committee reports, and congressional debates recorded in the *Congressional Record*. This contextualist approach often serves to clarify the meaning of the law. Sometimes attempts are made in Congress to construct legislative histories that will support favored interpretations. Floor statements and colloquies are used for this purpose. The president of the American League of Lobbyists states: "Often a bill is written too broadly and Congress says, 'We'll fix it up with legislative history.' Lobbyists frequently suggest terminology, phrases, ideas, concepts."[74] Legislative history needs to be read with care and some skepticism.

Conservative judges led by Justice Antonin Scalia of the U.S. Supreme Court express strong doubts about using legislative history to comprehend congressional intent. Scalia contends that it is a judge's duty to interpret the text of statutes, not to attempt to discover legislators' intentions by reading legislative history.[75] Should this textualist, or "plain meaning," approach to statutory interpretation catch on—and it has quite a bit of support from conservative judges appointed by the Ronald Reagan and George Bush administrations—it would put pressure on congressional bill drafters to produce legislation with a minimum of loose, ambiguous, or sloppy provisions.

Of course, as we saw in Chapter 2, titled "The Policy-Makers and Their Environment," if Congress disagrees with judicial interpretation of its intent, the court's action can be overcome by enacting legislation clarifying the meaning of the law. Between 1967 and 1990, Congress enacted laws reversing or modifying at least 220 lower court and 120 Supreme Court rulings.[76] All of this makes the courts an integral part of the legislative process.

CASE STUDY *Formulating Policy: The Patient Protection and Affordable Care Act*

Since the end of World War II, national medical care issues have frequently appeared on the national policy agenda. President Harry Truman called for "compulsory national health insurance." Some members of Congress introduced legislation to accomplish this. Strong opposition, especially from the then-powerful American Medical Association, which erroniously called the proposal "socialized medicine," caused its demise. At the same time, however, increased federal spending for hospital construction and medical research easily passed muster.[77]

The Johnson administration succeeded in persuading Congress to enact legislation creating the Medicare (for the elderly) and Medicaid (for low-income people) programs. The Nixon and Carter administrations advocated legislation expanding health-care coverage, as did Senator Ted Kennedy (D, Massachusetts), a noted policy entrepreneur on this topic. Nothing came of these various efforts.

Health-care reform, which had retained a spot on the national agenda, was a major issue during the 1992 presidential campaign. Soon after taking office, the Clinton administration appointed a Task Force on National Health Care Reform chaired by Hillary Rodham Clinton. In the course of several months, assisted by some 500 public-and-private-sector health-care specialists, the task force produced a complex, 1,300-page bill. Provisions included mandatory employer-based coverage, health-insurance purchasing cooperatives, limits on consumer expenses, and partial funding by an increase in tobacco taxes.

Various other health-care reform plans, including one for universal national health insurance, were crafted and introduced by members of Congress. Strong opposition to the Clinton plan quickly surfaced from various health-care organizations, notably the Health Insurance Association of America. Members of Congress were unable to agree on anything. So, once more, the status quo prevailed. The Clinton plan failed to reach the floor of Congress.

In 1995, President Clinton and the new Republican-controlled Congress focused on holding down the cost of the Medicare and Medicaid programs. That did not work out very well, either. The George W. Bush administration demonstrated little interest in general health-care reform. It did produce Medicare Part D, which provided limited coverage for prescription drug expenses.

In the 2008 presidential campaign, Barack Obama initially showed a meager grasp of health matters. As the campaign wore on, his knowledge increased and by the time he won election, he was committed to general health-care reform. We pause now to look at the health-care situation in the United States in 2009.

Many people, especially those opposed to health-care reform, that is, most Republicans and conservatives, often proclaimed that the United States has "the greatest health-care system in the world." At its best, American health care is excellent, especially for those with lots of money and/or premium health insurance. Some 46 million people had no health insurance; others had inadequate coverage. The United States was the only industrialized democracy that did not in some way have universal health-care coverage.[78] Yet the United States spent 16 percent of its Gross Domestic Product on health care, considerably more than any other country. Moreover, on various health care measures, the U.S. did not do well, ranking fifteenth on avoidable deaths and twenty-fourth on healthy living expectancy. The British, the Canadians, and the French, for instance, spent less and had higher-rated health-care systems.

The preceding paragraph makes a case for needed improvement in health. Here we will look at something that makes change difficult—what Professor Paul Starr labels the "health policy trap." Although an increasing number of Americans have no health insurance or inadequate financial protection against illness, the health-care system satisfies enough people to make reform hard to achieve. Starr explains:

> The key elements of the trap are a system of employer-provided insurance that conceals its true costs from those who benefit from it; targeted government programs that protect groups such as the elderly and veterans, who are well organized and enjoy wide public sympathy and believe that, unlike other claimants, they have earned their benefits; and a financing system that has expanded and enriched the health-care industry, creating powerful interests adverse to change.[79]

The Obama administration and Democratic majorities in Congress were able to circumvent this trap. The price was considerable political capital and willingness to agree to more limited legislation than many preferred.

Rather than present a complete presidential plan to Congress as President Clinton had done, Obama left most of the details to Congress. In various speeches and statements, he did set forth some goals for health-care reform. These included expanding access to health insurance and medical services; regulating the private insurance business to curb some of its bad practices, such as denying coverage for "existing conditions"; raising new revenue and cutting the costs of existing programs to pay for expanded coverage; and lessening the rate of growth in health-care spending, both public and private.[80]

Early on in the health-care policy struggle, the president, administration officials, and congressional leaders met and negotiated with representatives of health-care organizations to lessen their opposition. In time, bargains were arrived at. One involved the lobbying group for the drug industry—the Pharmaceutical Research and Manufacturers of America (PhRMA). PhRMA agreed to provide $80 billion in cost savings for drugs under government programs and to sponsor advertising in support of reform. In return, PhRMA got a pledge that the government would not permit the importation of lower-cost drugs or engage in negotiations over Medicare drug prices, among other things. This was worth a lot of money for the drug companies. The hospital associations agreed to payment reductions that would save the government $155 billion over ten years. The hospitals were spared more stringent cost controls and would benefit from the additional revenue they would gain from expanded health insurance coverage.

In the House, three committees—Energy and Commerce, Ways and Means, and Education and Labor—considered and approved versions of health-care legislation, which were then melded into a single bill. Features of the bill included a national health insurance exchange, a public insurance option, an individual mandate to purchase insurance, subsidies for lower-income people, and a requirement that most medium and large employers offer insurance coverage or pay a substantial penalty.

The 255-member Democratic majority in the House was a mixture of liberals, moderates, and conservatives. Speaker Nancy Pelosi strove mightily, drawing on all of her legislative skills, to construct a 218-member majority. The Republicans offered lots of criticism and opposition to the bill, but only one vote (a Louisiana Republican). As summer wore on into fall, Pelosi found herself a few votes short of the needed majority. Consequently, she decided she had no choice other than to negotiate with Representative Bart Stupak (D, Michigan). Stupak was both a strong supporter of health-care reform and an intense opponent of abortion. He wanted strong antiabortion language in the bill, contending that lacking this, he and several other Democrats would vote against. After much bargaining failed to satisfy both sides of the issue, Pelosi gave in and let Stupak offer an antiabortion amendment, which was adopted with a vote of 240 to 194 (64 Democrats and 176 Republicans in favor). The health-care reform bill then passed, 220 to 215, with 39 mostly Blue Dog Democrats joining the Republicans in voting no. We now turn to the Senate.

In the Senate, health-care reform bills were handled by the Health, Education, Labor, and Pensions committee (HELP) and the Finance committee. HELP, chaired by Senator Chris Dowd (D, Connecticut), who had taken over for the ailing Senator Ted Kennedy (D, Massachusetts), reported out a bill in July. Senator Max Baucus (D, Montana), chair of the Finance committee, wanted to put together a bill that would draw bipartisan support. To this end, he put together a group from his committee that became known as the "Gang of Six," consisting of himself, two other Democrats, and three Republicans. With the acquiescence of Senate Democratic leader Harry Reid (D, Nevada) and the White House, the Gang of Six engaged in meetings and negotiations for four months. It became obvious, however, that they would not produce a bipartisan bill. Baucus then decided to use the regular committee process and mark up a bill. This was done and it was reported out by a 14-to-9 vote after several days of debates and amendments. The only Republican voting for the bill was Olympia Snowe (R, Maine). (She eventually crawfished and voted against health-care reform.) Republicans offered a stew of amendments intended to weaken or gut the bill. Since they were in the minority, they fared poorly.

Majority leader Reid cobbled together a compromise bill from the two committee versions to appeal to the various segments of his party. The House operates by majority rule, but in the Senate 60 votes are needed because of the filibuster. In July 2009, Reid had those 60 votes following the decision that Democrat Al Franken had won the contested Minnesota Senate race. These votes included two independents—Bernard Sanders of Vermont and Joseph Lieberman of Connecticut—who caucused with the Democrats.

Because Reid could not lose a single vote, unlike Pelosi who had some to spare, individual senators had strong leverage to bargain for preferences, if they so chose. And some did. Senator Mary Landrieu of Louisiana was kept on board by the "Louisiana Purchase," the promise of funds to offset the impact of Hurricane Katrina in 2005 on health-care funding. The "Cornhusker Kickback," which would send extra Medicaid money to Nebraska, was used to secure the vote of Senator Ben Nelson. These deals received much criticism, especially from Republicans, though they were not uncommon in congressional bargaining.

Then there was the unpredictable Joe Lieberman, who wanted and got assurance from Reid that the bill would include neither a public option (a government-sponsored insurance plan) nor permit people in the 55–64 age bracket to "buy in" to Medicare. The Medicare option was favored by some liberals as an alternative to the public option, which by then had been much watered down.

Having 60 votes in hand, Reid brought the health-care reform bill to the Senate floor on December 18. Over the next few days, three successful cloture votes were needed as the Republicans did their best to obstruct the proceedings. Finally, on December 24, the reform bill passed, 60 to 39. The Democrats were very pleased, even though some of them had not gotten all that they wanted included in the bill.

The second action involved enactment of the reconciliation (or supplemental) bill that made changes in the Affordable Care Act wanted by the House and made the Senate bill more progressive. The "Cornhusker Kickback" was deleted, so Senator Ben Nelson was now free to follow the dictates of his conscience. After some forty Republican amendments were rejected, by a vote of 56 to 43 the Senate passed the bill. The House then cleared the bill by a 220-to-207 vote. A few days later, President Obama signed the Health Care and Education Reconciliation Act into law.

Before turning to a summary of the Affordable Care Act, some explanation of the appearance of "education" in the Reconciliation Act is in order. By this act, the federal government became the only provider of student loans; federal guarantees of loans by private lenders were not longer available. This was estimated to save the government about $61 billion over ten years, much of which would be used for Pell grants and other education programs. The gravy train of risk-free loans would no longer be on track for private lenders.

A brief summary of the Affordable Care Act follows.[81] Most persons without health insurance were required to purchase it or pay tax penalties (the "individual mandate"). Subsidies were available to help lower income people. The states were expected to set up health insurance exchanges to assist those needing to buy insurance. Employers did not have to offer health benefits, but penalties would be imposed on many who did not. Insurance companies could no longer refuse to cover preexisting conditions, contrive ways to cancel coverage, or put limits on annual or lifetime coverage. Children were covered by their parents' plan until they turned twenty-six. Medicaid was expanded to cover all persons with incomes below 133 percent of the federal poverty level. If a state chose to participate, the federal government would pay the total cost for three years and 90 percent thereafter. The cost of the Affordable Care Act would be met by a variety of taxes, mostly on upper income people, and reduced payments to Medicare providers. The Congressional Budget Office (CBO) estimated that the ten-year cost of the program would be $940 billion; another $138 billion would be available for deficit reduction. (The effective dates of various provisions of the act were spread over several years.)

In January 2010, soon after the holiday recess, an unexpected event occurred. Republican Scott Brown won the special election in Massachusetts to complete the term of the late Senator Ted Kennedy. This meant the Democrats no longer had the sixty votes needed to block filibusters. Conservatives gleefully predicted that the health-care reform bill was dead. Many Democrats became panicky. What could be done to salvage health-care reform? Some said a slimmed-down bill should be passed. Others favored passing several small bills that might lessen Republican opposition.

After some reflection, cooler heads prevailed. President Obama and the Democratic leadership decided success was too near for them to give up. The President began to speak strongly in favor of reform and to rebut the Republican arguments against it. He also presented a specific plan for health-care reform, which was similar to the Senate bill. At a "bipartisan healthcare summit" organized by the White House, it became clear that the Republicans would provide neither support nor useful ideas. Some simply wanted to "start over."

The Democrats then developed a strategy to get health-care reform adopted. Fortuitously, the Democrats in early 2009 had passed a budget reconciliation resolution under the Congressional Budget Act. This permitted budgetary action to be taken by majority vote, thereby eliminating the likelihood of a Republican filibuster. (The Republicans had used this procedure to pass George W. Bush's tax cuts.)

It was decided that the House would pass the Senate bill without making any changes. Representative Stupak at this point got a "second bite of the apple." The Senate bill, he insisted, did not have sufficiently strong antiabortion language. He was mollified when President Obama issued an executive order affirming the Hyde amendment. The House then passed the Senate bill, 219 to 212. Thus, when the President signed it, the Patient Protection and Affordable Care Act became law.

Following its enactment, the struggle over the Affordable Care Act moved into the judicial, state government, and administrative arenas. The U.S. Supreme Court, in *National Federation of Independent Business* v. *Sebelius*, upheld its constitutionality in a 5 to 4 decision, based on government's power to tax and spend for the general welfare.[82] The struggle to implement the act is ongoing.

A Concluding Comment

Problem identification, agenda setting, and policy formulation constitute the predecision segment of the policy process in that they do not involve formal decisions on what will become public policy. They are important, however, because they help determine which issues will be considered, which will be given further examination, and which will be abandoned. Thus, they involve political conflict and help set the terms for additional conflict. E. E. Schattschneider comments:

> Political conflict is not like an inter-collegiate debate in which the opponents agree in advance on the definition of the issues. As a matter of fact, the definition of the alternatives is the supreme instrument of power. . . . He who determines what politics is about runs the country, because the definition of the alternatives is the choice of conflicts, and the choice of conflicts allocates power.[83]

In actuality, it is often difficult neatly to separate policy formulation from policy adoption, the subject of the "Policy Adoption" chapter. Analytically, they are distinct functional activities that occur in the policy process. They do not, however, "have to be performed by separate individuals at different times in different institutions."[84] Most often, as the Affordable Care Act case study demonstrates, those who formulate courses of action will be influenced by the need to win adoption of their proposals. Some provisions will be included, others excluded, and words and phrasing will be carefully chosen in an attempt to build support for a proposed policy. Looking further ahead, the formulators may also be influenced by what they think may happen during the administration of the policy once adopted. Possible reactions may be anticipated and taken into account in an effort to help ensure that the policy will accomplish its intended purposes. Such strategic actions help tie together the different stages of the policy process.

For Further Exploration

▮ *http://www.epi.org/*

The Economic Policy Institute is a liberal organization that is committed to promoting public policies that lead to economic growth and foster economic equality. Reports are provided on such subjects as the standard of living, the role of government in the economy, foreign trade, and the nature of public opinion.

▮ *http://www.heritage.org/*

The Heritage Foundation is a conservative "think tank." This website has provided news reports since May of 1997 on a variety of current domestic and foreign-policy issues.

▮ *http://rollcall.com/*

This congressional-oriented site contains a link titled "Policy," in which members of Congress and other governmental officials discuss current policy issues facing the nation.

▮ *www.csg.org*

The official homepage of the Council of State Governments (CSG) provides daily news articles reported in major newspapers on the current status of state policies. There are also valuable links to other websites that devote attention to specific state issues.

Test Your Knowledge

Log on to the student companion website at

login.cengage.com

to access tutorial quizzes, chapter outlines, crossword puzzles, and glossary flashcards that review chapter concepts and terminology.

Suggested Readings

Barbara J. Nelson, *Making an Issue of Child Abuse* (New York: Basic Books, 1984). This is a perceptive and absorbing account of how child abuse became a major social-welfare issue in the United States.

Bryan D. Jones and Frank M. Baumgartner, *The Politics of Attention* (Chicago, IL: University of Chicago Press, 2005). The dynamic duo have struck again, this time on the processes by which government sets priorities on problems.

Frank R. Baumgartner and Bryan D. Jones, *Agendas and Instability in American Politics*. 2nd ed. (Chicago, IL: University of Chicago Press, 2004). A systematic, empirical examination of how policy issues rise and decline and the consequences of this for the policy process.

John Gaventa, *Power and Powerlessness* (Urbana, IL: University of Illinois Press, 1980). This compelling study of political power in an Appalachian valley looks at the various dimensions of power, including nondecisions.

John W. Kingdon, *Agendas, Alternatives, and Public Policies*, 2nd ed. (New York: HarperCollins, 1995). In this important study of agenda setting, it is argued that separate streams of problems, policies, and politics sometimes converge to create opportunities to set the policy agenda.

Paul Starr, *Remedy and Reaction: The Peculiar American Struggle Over Health Care Reform* (New Haven, CT: Yale University Press, 2011). One of the many virtues of this book is its treatment of the enactment of the Affordable Health Care Act.

Roger W. Cobb and Charles D. Elder, *Participation in American Politics*, 2nd ed. (Baltimore, MD: Johns Hopkins University Press, 1983). This is a leading study of agenda setting in American politics.

Thomas A. Birkland, *Lessons of Disaster* (Washington, DC: Georgetown University Press, 2006). An examination of disasters and their consequences for agenda setting and policy change.

Notes

1. Janet A. Weiss, "The Powers of Problem Definition: The Case of Government Paperwork," *Policy Sciences*, Vol. 22 (January 1989), pp. 99–100.
2. Ibid.
3. *A Report of the Commission on Federal Paperwork: Final Summary Report* (Washington, DC: Government Printing Office, October 3, 1977), p. 5.
4. House Committee on Government Operations, Hearings on *Implementation of the Paperwork Reduction Act Amendments of 1983*, 98th Cong., 2nd Sess., April 1983, pp. 27–28.
5. *Congressional Quarterly Weekly Report*, Vol. 53 (April 8, 1995), p. 1205.
6. *The New York Times*, July 13, 2009, p. A13.
7. See John Dewey, *The Public and Its Problems* (Denver, CO: Swallow, 1927), pp. 12, 15, and 16.
8. For an extended discussion of policy problems, see David A. Rochefort and Roger W. Cobb, eds., *The Politics of Problem Definition: Shaping the Policy Agenda* (Lawrence, KS: University Press of Kansas, 1994).
9. Jeffrey Toobin, "Casting Votes," *The New Yorker*, January 14, 2013, pp. 17–18.
10. Aaron Wildavsky, *Speaking Truth to Power* (Boston, MA: Little, Brown, 1979), p. 42.
11. George C. Edwards III and Ira Sharkansky, *The Policy Predicament* (San Francisco: W. H. Freeman, 1978), p. 90.
12. David G. Smith, "Pragmatism and the Group Theory of Politics," *American Political Science Review*, LVIII (September 1964), pp. 607–610.
13. Murray Edleman, *Constructing the Political Spectacle* (Chicago, IL: University of Chicago Press, 1988), Chap. 2.

14. See Barbara J. Nelson, *Making an Issue of Child Abuse* (Chicago, IL: University of Chicago Press, 1984); and Elizabeth Pleck, *Domestic Tyranny* (New York: Oxford University Press, 1987).

15. Robert A. Katzmann, *Institutional Disability* (Washington, DC: Brookings Institution, 1986).

16. General Accounting Office, *Homeless Mentally Ill: Problems and Options in Estimating Numbers and Trends* (Washington, DC, 1988).

17. Charles S. Bullock III and Charles M. Lamb, eds., *Implementation of Civil Rights Policy* (Monterey, CA: Brooks/Cole, 1984), Chaps. 2, 3.

18. James Q. Wilson, "How to Teach Better Values in Inner Cities," *Wall Street Journal,* May 18, 1992, p. A14.

19. Cf. Layne Hoppe, "Agenda-Setting Strategies: The Case of Pollution Problems." Unpublished paper presented at the Annual Meeting of the American Political Science Association (September 1970).

20. Robert Eyestone, *From Social Issues to Public Policy* (New York: Wiley, 1978), p. 3.

21. George C. Edwards III, *Overreach: Leadership in the Obama Administration* (Princeton, NJ: Princeton University Press, 2012), p. 67.

22. Roger W. Cobb and Charles D. Elder, *Participation in American Politics: The Dynamics of Agenda-Building,* 2nd ed. (Baltimore, MD: Johns Hopkins University Press, 1983), p. 85.

23. John W. Kingdon, *Agendas, Alternatives, and Public Policies,* 2nd ed. (New York: HarperCollins, 1995), p. 4.

24. See Jack L. Walker, "Setting the Agenda in the United States Senate: A Theory of Problem Selection," *British Journal of Political Science,* VII (October 1977), pp. 423–446.

25. *The New York Times,* February 20, 2002, p. B1.

26. Barbara Sinclair, *The Transformation of the U.S. Senate* (Baltimore, IL: Johns Hopkins University Press, 1989), p. 51.

27. Kingdon, op. cit., Chap. 4.

28. Ibid., p. 87.

29. Ibid., p. 165.

30. For yet another view of agenda setting, see Frank R. Baumgartner and Bryan D. Jones, *Agendas and Instability in American Politics* (Chicago, IL: University of Chicago Press, 1993).

31. David B. Truman, *The Governmental Process* (New York: Knopf, 1951), p. 30.

32. Paul Light, *The President's Agenda, rev.* ed. (Baltimore, MD: Johns Hopkins University Press, 1991), Chap. 3. The quotation is on p. 69.

33. George C. Edwards III and Andrew Barrett, "Presidential Agenda Setting in Congress," in Jon R. Bond and Richard Fleisher, eds., *Polarized Politics: Congress and the President in a Partisan Era* (Washington, DC: CQ Press, 2000), Chap. 6.

34. John B. Bader, *Taking the Initiative: Leadership Agendas in Congress and the "Contract with America"* (Washington, DC: Georgetown University Press, 1996), Chap. 1.

35. Walker, op. cit., p. 431.

36. Kingdon, op. cit., p. 204.

37. Beth M. Hensikin and Edward I. Sidlow, "The Supreme Court and the Congressional Agenda-Setting Process." Unpublished paper presented at the Annual Meeting of the Midwest Political Science Association (April 1989); and Roy B. Flemming, B. Dan Wood,

and John Bohte, "Policy Attention in a System of Separated Powers: An Inquiry into the Dynamics of American Agenda Setting." Unpublished paper presented at the Annual Meeting of the Midwest Political Science Association (April 1995).

38. For more on the consequences of natural and industrial disasters, see Thomas A. Birkland, "Focusing Events, Mobilization, and Agenda Setting," *Journal of Public Policy*, Vol. 18 (January–April 1998), pp. 53–74.

39. Cf. Cobb and Elder, op. cit., p. 25.

40. Norman Orstein, National Public Radio.

41. *The New York Times*, April 18, 2013, pp. 1, 15.

42. See Michael Lipsky "Protest as a Political Resource," *American Political Science Review*, Vol. 67 (December 1968), pp. 1144–1158.

43. This subject is discussed in fascinating style in W. A. Swanberg, *Citizen Hearst* (New York: Scribner's, 1961), pp. 79–169.

44. Kingdon, op. cit., pp. 95–99.

45. Ibid., pp. 152–160. See, generally, James A. Stimson, *Public Opinion in America: Moods, Cycles, and Swings*, 2nd ed. (Boulder, CO: Westview Press, 1999).

46. Joseph A. Page and Mary Winn O'Brien, *Bitter Wages* (New York: Grossman, 1973), Chap. 7.

47. Those who wish to pursue this topic further should consult the highly informative study by Cobb and Elder, op. cit.

48. This discussion owes much to Roger W. Cobb and Marc H. Ross, eds., *Cultural Strategies of Agenda Denial* (Lawrence, KS: University Press of Kansas, 1997), Chap. 2.

49. Peter Bachrach and Morton S. Baratz, *Power and Poverty* (New York: Oxford University Press, 1970), p. 44. See also John Gaventa, *Powerlessness: Quiescence and Change in an Appalachian Valley* (Urbana, IL: University of Illinois Press, 1980).

50. E. E. Schattschneider, *The Semi-Sovereign People* (New York: Holt, Rinehart and Winston, 1960), p. 71.

51. T. R. Reid, *Congressional Odyssey: The Saga of a Senate Bill* (San Francisco, CA: W. H. Freeman, 1980).

52. David Rosner and Gerald Markowitz, *Deadly Dust: Silicosis and the Politics of Occupational Disease in Twentieth-Century America* (Princeton, NJ: Princeton University Press, 1991). Chapter VI is titled "Last Gasp: The Death of the Silicosis Issue." The quotation is on p. 179.

53. Anthony Downs, "Up and Down with Ecology: The Issue-Attention Cycle," *Public Interest*, XXXII (Summer 1972), pp. 38–50.

54. Duane Lockard, *Coal: A Memoir and Critique* (Charlottesville, VA: University Press of Virginia, 1998), Chap. 4.

55. William Graebner, *Coal Mining Safety in the Progressive Period* (Lexington, KY: University of Kentucky Press, 1976). Also, John Bartlow Martin, "The Beast in Centralia No. 5: A Mine Disaster No One Stopped," *Harpers Magazine* Vol. 196 (March 1948), pp. 193–220.

56. Daniel J. Curran, *Dead Laws for Dead Men: The Politics of Federal Coal Mine Health and Safety Legislation* (Pittsburgh, PA: University of Pittsburgh Press, 1993), Chap. 5.

57. *The New York Times*, May 8, 1973, p. 21.

58. Laurence E. Lynn Jr., *Managing Public Policy* (Boston, MA: Little, Brown, 1987), pp. 254–256.

59. *The New York Times*, March 12, 1987, p. 11; *Wall Street Journal*, June 1, 1987, pp. 1, 10.

60. David Maraniss and Michael Weisskopf, "OSHAs Enemies Find Themselves in High Places," *The Washington Post*, July 24, 1995, pp. A8–A9.

61. *CQ Almanac 2006* (Washington, DC: Congressional Quarterly, Inc., 2007), pp. 18-4–18-5.

62. See Phillip Shabecoff, *A Fierce Green Fire: The American Environmental Movement* (New York: HarperCollins, 1993), pp. 106–111.

63. J. Clarence Davies, *The Politics of Pollution*, 2nd ed. (Indianapolis, IN: Bobbs-Merrill, 1975), p. 7. This discussion relies considerably on Davies.

64. Ibid., pp. 8–9.

65. Walter A. Rosenbaum, *Environmental Politics and Policy*, 5th ed. (Washington, DC: CQ Press, 2005), p. 39.

66. Helen Epstein, "Lead Poisoning: The Ignored Scandal," *New York Review of Books*, Vol. XL (March 21, 2013), pp. 30–32. This is a review of Gerald Markowitz and David Rosner, *Lead Wars: The Politics of Science and the Fate of America's Children* (Berkeley, CA: University of California Press/Milbank Memorial Fund, 2013).

67. Quoted in Richard E. Neustadt, *Presidential Power* (New York: Wiley, 1960), p. 102.

68. Francis E. Rourke and Paul R. Schulman, "Adhocracy in Policy Development." Unpublished paper presented at the Annual Meeting of the American Political Science Association (September 1988).

69. *Congressional Quarterly Weekly Report*, Vol. 46 (February 6, 1988), pp. 243–245.

70. Emmette S. Redford and Richard T. McCulley *White House Operations: The Johnson Presidency* (Austin, TX: University of Texas Press, 1986), Chap. 5.

71. Richard E. Cohen, *Washington at Work: Backrooms and Clean Air*, 2nd ed. (Boston, MA: Allyn and Bacon, 1995), Chap. 11.

72. Robert Pear, "It Should Be Called the Grossman Health Care Bill," *The New York Times*, November 26, 1993, p. A20; and Cohen, op. cit.

73. Gilbert Y. Steiner and Samuel K. Gove, *Legislative Politics in Illinois* (Urbana, IL: University of Illinois Press, 1960), p. 52. Also Diane Blair, *Arkansas Politics and Government* (Lincoln, NE: University of Nebraska Press, 1988), Chap. 9.

74. Quoted in *The New York Times*, November 18, 1991, p. C10.

75. Note, "Why Learned Hand Would Never Consult Legislative History Today," *Harvard Law Review*, CV (April 1992), p. 1005.

76. Robert A. Katzman, *Courts and Congress* (Washington, DC: Brookings Institution, 1997), p. 57.

77. This case study draws mostly on *CQ Almanac 2010* (Washington, DC: CQ-Roll Call, 2011); Lawrence R. Jacobs and Theda Skocpol, *Health Care Reform and American Politics*, rev. ed. (New York: Oxford University Press, 2012); and Paul Starr, *Remedy and Reaction* (New Haven, CT: Yale University Press, 2011).

78. T. R. Reid, *The Healing of America* (New York: Penguin Press, 2009).

79. Starr, op. cit., p. 123.

80. Jacobs and Skocpol, op. cit., p. 88.

81. CQ Almanac, op. cit., pp. 9-6–9-13.

82. *National Federation of Independent Business v. Sebelius* (U.S. Supreme Court) 2012.

83. Schattschneider, op. cit., p. 68. See also Sarah B. Pralle, *Branching Qut. Digging In: Environmental Advocacy and Agenda Setting* (Washington, DC: Georgetown University Press, 2006).

84. Charles O. Jones, *An Introduction to the Study of Public Policy* (Belmont, CA: Wadsworth, 1970), p. 53.

4

Policy Adoption

A policy decision involves action by some official person or body to adopt, modify, or reject a preferred policy alternative. In positive fashion, it takes such forms as the enactment of legislation or the issuance of an executive order. It is helpful to recall the distinction made in the chapter titled "The Study of Public Policy" between policy decisions, which significantly affect the content of public policy, and routine decisions, which involve the day-to-day application of policy. Furthermore, a policy decision is usually the culmination of many decisions, some routine and some not so routine, made during the operation of the policy process.

What is typically involved at the policy-adoption stage is not selection from among a number of full-blown policy alternatives but rather action on a preferred policy alternative for which the proponents of action think they can win approval, even though it does not provide all they might like. As the formulation process moves toward the decision stage, some provisions will be rejected, others accepted, and still others modified; differences will be narrowed; bargains will be struck, until ultimately, in some instances, the final policy decision will be only a formality. In other instances, the question may be in doubt until the votes are counted or the decision is announced.

Although private individuals and organizations also participate in making policy decisions, the formal authority to decide rests with public officials: legislators, executives, administrators, and judges. Through the adoption process policies acquire the "weight of public authority." In democracies, the task of making policy decisions is most closely identified with the legislature, which is designed to represent the interests of the populace. One frequently hears that a majority of the legislature represents a majority of the people. Whatever its accuracy in describing reality, such a contention does accord with our notion that in a democracy the people should rule, at least through their representatives. Policy decisions made by the legislature are usually accepted as legitimate, as being made in the proper way and hence binding on all. Generally, decisions made by public officials are regarded as legitimate if the officials have legal authority to act and if they meet accepted procedural and substantive standards in taking action.

Legitimacy is a difficult concept to define. It is not the same as legality although legality can contribute to belief in legitimacy which focuses people's attention on the rightness or appropriateness of government and its actions. For policymaking, legitimacy is affected both by how something is done (i.e., whether proper procedures are used) and by what is being done. Some actions of government, even when within the legal or constitutional authority of officials, may not be regarded as legitimate because they depart too far from prevailing notions of what is acceptable. Thus, many Americans never accepted the legitimacy of the Vietnam War. Other people do not accept the legitimacy of a constitutional right to privacy as a barrier to some governmental actions, such as the prohibition of abortions. On the other hand, even though the legislative veto was held unconstitutional in 1983 by the Supreme Court, it continues to be regarded as a necessary and appropriate—that is, legitimate— arrangement by Congress and the executive. Legislative veto arrangements have been incorporated into legislation hundreds of times since 1983.[1]

Constitutionality is not always a *sine qua non* for legitimacy. Legitimacy is an important factor in developing public support and acceptance for both government and the policies that it adopts. Public officials must be cognizant of this importance. When legitimacy erodes, governments and their policies diminish in effectiveness.

Political and social scientists have produced a large body of theoretical and empirical literature on political decision-making. In this literature, the reader will discover there are many disagreements and divergences over such matters as how best to study decision-making, how decisions are actually made, and even over what constitutes a decision. No attempt is made here to resolve any of these controversies. Rather, some topics are discussed that should assist the reader in getting a handle on political decision-making. These include some decision-making theories, criteria, and styles; the process of majority building (or decision-making) in Congress; and presidential decision-making.

As the discussion indicates, many forces, pressures, and constraints may play upon political decision-makers. They will likely try to cope by developing routines or procedures that simplify the making of choices. Incrementalism and decision rules are two illustrations of such behavior. In many instances, however, there are no easy routes to a good decision.

Theories of Decision-Making

Decision-making, as stated in the chapter "The Study of Public Policy," involves making a choice from among alternatives. Many highly formal, quantitative models of decision-making exist, including linear programming, game theory, and the Monte Carlo method. These are often grouped under the rubric "decision sciences." Some very informal and nonrational ways to make decisions include palmistry, dart throwing, coin flipping, and reflection on one's belly button. None of these genres is reviewed here.

People also make decisions on the basis of intuition.[2] President George W. Bush said he made some decisions on "gut instinct." A nonrational process, intuition relies on "hunches," a "feel for the situation," and other improvised premises. Lower-level administrative officials, for example, often need to act at least partly on the basis of intuition because of the lack of firm standards or rules. The judgments or decisions yielded by intuition are sometimes right, sometimes wrong, and sometimes even egregious. This, of course, is also true for other, more formalized modes of decision-making.

Three theories of decision-making that emphasize the procedure and intellectual activities involved in making a decision are presented here: the rational-comprehensive theory, the incremental theory, and mixed scanning theory. To the extent that these theories may describe how decisions are actually made by individuals and groups, they are empirical. Viewed as statements of how decisions *should* be made, they become normative. It is not always easy to separate these two qualities in decision-making theories and studies, as we will discover.

The Rational-Comprehensive Theory

Perhaps the best-known theory of decision-making is the rational-comprehensive theory. It draws considerably from the economist's view of how a rational person would make decisions as well as from theories of rational decision-making developed by mathematicians, psychologists, and other social scientists. It should not be confused with rational-choice theory. Whereas rational-choice theory is used for developing deductive models of self-interested decision-makers, the rational-comprehensive theory specifies the procedures involved in making well-considered rational decisions that maximize the attainment of goals, whether personal or organizational.

The rational-comprehensive theory usually includes these elements:

1. The decision-maker is confronted with a problem that can be separated from other problems or at least considered meaningfully in comparison with them.

2. The goals, values, or objectives that guide the decision-maker are known and can be clarified and ranked according to their importance.

3. The various alternatives for dealing with the problem are examined.

4. The consequences (costs and benefits, advantages and disadvantages) that would follow from selecting each alternative are investigated.

5. Each alternative, and its attendant consequences, is then compared with the other alternatives.

6. The decision-maker will choose the alternative, and its consequences, that maximizes attainment of his or her goals, values, or objectives.

The result of this procedure is a rational decision—that is, one that most effectively achieves a given end. In short, it optimizes; it is the best possible decision. Rational decisions may make either large and basic or limited changes in public policies.

The rational-comprehensive theory has received substantial criticism. Professor Charles Lindblom contends that decision-makers usually are not faced with concrete, clearly defined problems. Rather, he says that they first have to identify and formulate the problems on which they make decisions. For example, when prices are rising rapidly and people are saying, "We must do something about the problem of inflation," what is the problem? Excessive demand? Inadequate production of goods and services? Administered prices controlled by powerful corporations and unions? Inflationary psychology? Some combination of these? One does not, willy-nilly, attack inflation. Instead, the causes of inflation must be dealt with, and these may be difficult to determine. Defining the problem is, in short, often a challenging task for the decision-maker.

A second criticism holds that rational-comprehensive theory is unrealistic in the intellectual demands it makes on the decision-maker. It assumes that he or she will have enough information on the alternatives for dealing with a problem, will be able to predict their consequences with some accuracy, and will be capable of making correct cost–benefit comparisons of the alternatives.

A moment's reflection on the informational and intellectual resources needed for acting rationally on the problem of inflation indicates the barriers to rational action implied in these assumptions: lack of time, difficulty in collecting information and predicting the future, and complexity of calculations. Even use of that modern miracle, the computer, and sophisticated economic models replete with equations cannot fully alleviate these problems, as economists continually demonstrate. There is no need to overload the arguments, as some do, by talking of the need to consider all possible alternatives. Even a rational-comprehensive decision-maker should be permitted to ignore the absurd and the far-fetched.

The value aspect of the rational-comprehensive theory also draws some criticism. It is contended that in actuality the public decision-maker is usually confronted with a situation of value conflict rather than value agreement, and that the conflicting values do not permit easy comparison or weighing. Moreover, the decision-maker might confuse personal values with those of the public. In addition, the rationalistic assumption that facts and values can be readily separated does not hold up in practice. Some may support a dam on a stream as demonstrably necessary to control flooding, and others may oppose it, preferring a free-flowing stream for aesthetic and ecological reasons. Recourse to the "facts," even lots of them, will not resolve such controversies.

Yet another problem is that of "sunk costs." Previous decisions and commitments, investments in existing policies and programs, may foreclose or severely complicate the consideration of many alternatives. The Clinton administration's formulation of a national health-care program was restricted by the nation's extensive reliance upon employer-sponsored health insurance. So too was that of the Obama administration. An airport, once constructed, cannot be easily moved to the other side of town. Even if a project is only partially constructed, pressure will be strong to complete the project rather than "waste" the money already invested by relocating the airport.

Finally, the rational-comprehensive model assumes the existence of a unitary decision-maker. This condition cannot be met by legislative bodies, plural-headed agencies, multiple-member courts, or nation-states in international relations.

The Incremental Theory   The incremental theory of decision-making is presented as a decision theory that avoids many of the pitfalls of the rational-comprehensive theory and, at the same time, is more descriptive of the way in which public officials actually make decisions.[3] Certainly there is little evidence to indicate that the members of Congress utilize anything akin to the rational-comprehensive model in enacting legislation. Incremental decisions involve limited changes or additions to existing policies, such as a small-percentage increase in an agency's budget or a modest tightening of eligibility requirements for student loans. Incrementalism (Lindblom refers to it as "disjointed incrementalism") can be summarized in the following manner:

1. The selection of goals or objectives and the empirical analysis of the action needed to attain them are closely intertwined with, rather than distinct from, one another.

2. The decision-maker considers only a few of the alternatives for dealing with a problem, which will differ only incrementally (i.e., marginally) from existing policies.

3. For each alternative, only a limited number of "important" consequences are evaluated.

4. The problem confronting the decision-maker is continually modified. Incrementalism allows for countless ends-means and means-ends adjustments that help make the problem more manageable.

5. There is no single decision or "right" solution for a problem. The test of a good decision is that various analysts find themselves agreeing on it, without agreeing that the decision is the most appropriate or optimum means to an agreed objective.

6. Incremental decision-making is essentially remedial and is geared more to ameliorating present, concrete social imperfections than to promoting major future social goals.[4]

Lindblom contends that incrementalism is the typical decision-making procedure in pluralist societies such as the United States. Decisions and policies are the product of give and take and mutual consent among numerous participants ("partisans") in the decision process. Incrementalism is politically expedient because it is easier to reach agreement when the matters in dispute among various groups are only limited modifications of existing programs rather than policy issues of great magnitude or of an "all-or-nothing" character.

Because decision-makers operate under conditions of uncertainty about the future consequences of their actions, incremental decisions reduce the risks and costs of uncertainty.

Incrementalism is seen as realistic because it recognizes that decision-makers lack the time, intelligence, and other resources needed to engage in comprehensive analysis of all alternative solutions to existing problems. Moreover, people are essentially pragmatic, seeking not always the single best way to deal with a problem but, more modestly, "something that will work." Incrementalism, in short, utilizes limited analysis to yield limited, practical, and acceptable decisions. A sequence of incremental decisions, however, may produce a fundamental change in public policy. Myriad incremental decisions have made Social Security a vastly different program from the one Congress first authorized in 1935.

Various criticisms have been directed at incrementalism. One is that it is too conservative, too focused on the current order; hence, it is a barrier to innovation, which is often necessary for effective public policies. Another is that in crisis situations (such as the American invasion of Iraq) or when major changes are made in policy (for instance, the 2001 tax cut), incrementalism provides no guidelines for handling the tasks of decision. Third, geared as it is to past actions and existing programs, and to limited changes in them, incrementalism may discourage the search for or use of other readily available alternatives. Fourth, incrementalism does not eliminate the need for theory in decision-making, as some of its more enthusiastic advocates contend. Unless changes in policy (increments) are to be made simply at random or arbitrarily, some theory (of causation, relationships, etc.) is needed to guide the action and to indicate the relevance and likely effects of proposed changes.[5]

Notwithstanding reservations of these sorts, incrementalism has become a form of conventional wisdom. Statements to the effect that policymaking in the United States is incremental are common. National budgeting during the three decades following World War II epitomized incrementalism. (See the "Budgeting and Public Policy" chapter.)

Analytical techniques such as cost–benefit analysis (see the chapter titled "Policy Impact, Evaluation, and Change"), risk analysis, and the planning-programming-budgeting system (PPBS), which was in vogue during the Johnson administration, are intended to move decision-making away from incrementalism and toward the rational-comprehensive model. The impact of these techniques will depend upon whether the information they produce is sound and impartial and on the disposition of decision-makers to rely upon them.

Mixed Scanning   Sociologist Amitai Etzioni believes that both the rational-comprehensive theory and incremental theory have shortcomings. For instance, he says that decisions made by incrementalists will reflect the interests of the most powerful and organized groups in society while neglecting the interests of the underprivileged and politically unorganized. Great or fundamental decisions, a declaration of war, for example, do not come within the ambit of incrementalism. Although limited in number, these fundamental decisions are highly significant and often provide the context for numerous incremental decisions.[6]

Etzioni presents mixed scanning as an approach to decision-making that draws on both fundamental and incremental decisions and provides for "high-order, fundamental policy-making processes which set basic directions and . . . incremental processes which prepare for fundamental decisions and work them out after they have been reached." He offers the following illustration:

> Assume we are about to set up a worldwide weather observation system using weather satellites. The rationalistic approach would seek an exhaustive survey of weather conditions by using cameras capable of detailed observations and by scheduling reviews of the entire sky as often as possible. This would yield an avalanche of details, costly to analyze and likely to overwhelm our action capacities (e.g., "seeding" cloud formations that could develop into hurricanes or bring rain to arid areas). Incrementalism would focus on those areas in which similar patterns developed in the recent past and, perhaps, on a few nearby regions; it would thus ignore all formations which might deserve attention if they arose in unexpected areas.
>
> A mixed-scanning strategy would include elements of both approaches by employing two cameras: a broad-angle camera that would cover all parts of the sky but not in great detail, and a second one which would zero in on those areas revealed by the first camera to require a more in-depth examination. While mixed-scanning might miss areas in which only a detailed camera could reveal trouble, it is less likely than incrementalism to miss obvious trouble spots in unfamiliar areas.[7]

Mixed scanning enables decision-makers to utilize both the rational-comprehensive and incremental theories, but in different situations. In some instances, incrementalism will be adequate; in others, a more thorough approach along rational-comprehensive lines will be needed. Mixed scanning also takes into account differing capacities of decision-makers. The greater their capacity to mobilize power to implement their decisions, the more scanning they can realistically engage in; the more encompassing the scanning, the more effective the decision-making.

Professors David Rosenbloom and Robert Kravchuk state that something akin to mixed scanning is used by the national government from time to time. The Council of Economic Advisers (CEA) analyzes the national economy; alerts the president to failures, threats of failure, or problems; and recommends policies for economic growth and stability. The CEA thus looks at both the overall operation of the economic and particular trouble spots. Again, agencies make five- or ten-year budget projections when attempting to realistically appraise where they are heading. These projections can serve as a check on administrative "drift" because of incremental budgeting.[8] Mixed scanning is thus an attempt to combine the use of incrementalism and rationalism, drawing upon strengths while avoiding shortcomings.

Decision Criteria

Decision-making can be studied as either an individual or a collective process. In the first instance, the focus is on the criteria individual's use in making choices. In the latter, the focus is the processes by which majorities are built, or by which approval is otherwise gained, for specific decisions. Individual choices, of course, are usually made with some reference to how others involved in the decisional situation are likely to respond.

An individual may be subject to various influencing factors when deciding how to vote on or resolve a policy question. Which of these concerns is most crucial to the choice is often hard to specify. Public officials frequently make statements explaining their decisions in the *Congressional Record*, constituency newsletters, speeches, press conferences, court opinions, memoirs, and elsewhere. The reasons they give for their decisions may be those that were actually controlling, or they may be those that are thought to be acceptable to the public at large or to important constituents while their actual bases for choice go unstated. Nonetheless, it is often possible, by careful observation and analysis, to determine which factors were operating in a situation, if not necessarily to assign them specific weights. A number of criteria that may influence policy choice are discussed here. They include values, party affiliation, constituency interests, public opinion, deference, and decision rules. The concept of the public interest is scrutinized in the following section.

Values   In considering the broader social and political forces that impinge on decision-makers, we tend to neglect their own values (or standards or preferences), which help them decide what is good or bad, desirable or undesirable. Often these may be difficult to determine and impossible to isolate. Decision-making persons, however, are not simply pieces of clay to be molded by others. Rather, their values or ideas may be important or even determinative in shaping their behavior. Some decision-makers may come under criticism if they insist too strenuously on the primacy of what they personally value. Here I comment on five categories of values that may guide the behavior of decision-makers: organizational, professional, personal, policy, and ideological.

ORGANIZATIONAL VALUES Decision-makers, especially bureaucrats, may be influenced by organizational values. Those who work for any agency for any extended period of time, whether the Tennessee Valley Authority, the Social Security Administration, or the Federal Trade Commission, are likely to become firm believers in the importance of the agency's goals and programs. Moreover, organizations may utilize rewards and sanctions to induce their members to accept and act in accordance with organizationally determined values.[9] Consequently, agency officials' decisions may reflect such considerations as a desire to see the agency survive, to increase its budget, to enhance or expand its programs, or to maintain its power and prerogatives against external assaults. Career officials in the Environmental Protection Agency (EPA), successfully resisted the Reagan administration's attempt to blunt the enforcement of agency programs.

Organizational values sometimes lead to conflict among agencies with competing or overlapping jurisdictions. The Army Corps of Engineers, the Bureau of Reclamation, and the Natural Resources Conservation Service (formerly the Soil Conservation Service) have differed over water-resource policies and projects.[10] "Turf" battles of this sort are an understandable, if not laudable, manifestation of differing organizational values.

PROFESSIONAL VALUES   The professional values of agency personnel may be important. Professions tend to form distinctive preferences as to how problems should be handled. Professionally trained people carry these preferences or values with them into organizations, some of which become dominated by particular professions; two such examples are the prevalence of engineers in the National Highway Traffic Safety Administration (NHTSA) and industrial hygienists in the Occupational Safety and Health Administration (OSHA). OSHA's industrial health and safety rules reflect the industrial hygienist's preference for engineering or design standards over performance standards. Design standards specify the use of particular equipment, ventilating systems, and safety devices and are intended to eliminate hazards. Performance standards, in contrast, set health or safety goals but leave the methods for attaining these goals to the company's discretion.

Economists, preferring market solutions and efficiency, have held sway in the Federal Trade Commission since the 1980s. Their influence is manifested in the agency's disinclination to challenge many large corporate mergers and unfair trade practices on the grounds that mergers contribute to efficiency and that the latter were simply forms of intense competition.[11]

PERSONAL VALUES   Decision-makers may also be guided by their personal values, or by the urge to protect or promote their own physical or financial well-being, reputation, or historical position. The politician who accepts a bribe to make a decision, such as the award of a license or contract, obviously has personal benefit in mind. On a different plane, the president who says he is not going to be "the first president to lose a war" and then acts accordingly is also manifesting the influence of personal values, such as concern for his place in history.

Personal values are important, but the rational-choice theorists go much too far when they try to explain officials' behavior as totally driven by self-interest. The location of public buildings is probably better explained by self-interest than is the adoption of civil-rights policies.

POLICY VALUES   Policy values, which also can be called *public ideas*, are frequently underestimated in their importance.[12] Neither the discussion of values thus far nor cynicism should lead us to assume that decision-makers are driven only by personal, professional, or organizational considerations. Decision-makers may well act on the basis of their perceptions of the public interest; of what is necessary, proper, or morally correct public policy; or, simply put, of what is the "right thing" to do. As Professor Gary Orren has remarked: "Evidence has steadily accumulated that ideas and values are autonomous and do not merely rationalize action in accordance with self-interest. Often values arise quite independently of an individual's life experiences and exert an independent influence on political behavior."[13]

Legislators may vote for civil-rights legislation because they believe that it is morally correct and that equality of opportunity is a desirable policy goal, even though their votes might entail some political risk. Studies of the Supreme Court indicate that in deciding cases the justices are influenced by policy values.[14] Of course, citizens and officials will differ over what constitutes good public policy on abortion, immigration, care of the mentally disturbed, and other topics.

IDEOLOGICAL VALUES   Finally, we come to ideological values. Ideologies are sets of coherent or logically related values and beliefs that present simplified pictures of the world and serve as guides to action for believers. For Communists, Marxist–Leninist ideology has served at least partly as a set of prescriptions for social and economic change. Although the Soviets sometimes deviated from this body of beliefs, as in their use of economic incentives to increase production toward the end of the regime, Marxist–Leninist ideology still served the regime as a means for rationalizing and legitimizing policy actions. In the twentieth and twenty-first centuries, *nationalism*—the desire of a nation or people for autonomy and the deep regard for their own characteristics, needs, and problems—has been a major factor shaping the actions of many nations, especially developing countries in Asia, Africa, and the Middle East.

During the Reagan years, conservative ideology, and notably its intense variant known as "movement conservatism," influenced the actions of many Reagan administration members. Devout believers in individualism, minimal government, and the free market, they strongly supported deregulation, privatization, and reduced governmental spending. For movement conservatives, that ideology was both their beacon and their shepherd. For some, it was more important to be right—to be true to their ideology—than to win on some legislative issue by compromising their principles. To them, "pragmatist" was a pejorative label, the American cultural preference for practicality notwithstanding. Quite a few members of the Republican House members reside in this category.

Arrayed against conservatives are modern liberals (or progressives). Their ideology calls for vigorous use of the government's powers to serve the interests of the poor, working people, minorities, and the disadvantaged generally.[15] They are defenders of civil rights and liberties, protectors of the environment, and proponents of consumer interests. "The regulatory state and the welfare state are two pillars of modern liberal ideology." On the other hand, they are skeptical about the maintenance of a large defense establishment in the post–Cold War era. Although liberals are less sure of their policy preferences than they once were, on the whole they are optimistic concerning their ability to use government to improve the human condition and promote an egalitarian society.

Very few people, we should note, consistently or rigidly conform to the precepts of a particular ideology. Thus, conservatives, though they generally favor minimal government, often support regulation of personal behavior.

Political-Party Affiliation   Party loyalty is an important decision-making criterion for most members of Congress, even though it is difficult to separate that loyalty from such other influences as party leadership pressures, ideological commitments, and constituency interests. Party affiliation is the best single predictor as to how members of Congress will vote on legislative issues. If one knows a member's party affiliation and the party's position on issues, and then uses party affiliation as the basis for predicting votes, he or she will probably be correct more often than when using any other indicator. In recent years, the average legislator has voted with the majority of his or her party about three-fourths of the time.[16] Party-unity (or party-line) voting, in which a majority of one party opposes a majority of the other party, has also been increasing. In the 1990s, party-unity votes occurred on over half of the roll-call votes in both the House and the Senate[17] (See Figure 4.1).

Contributing to an increase in voting along party lines has been a decrease in the appearance of the conservative coalition, an alliance between Republicans and conservative southern Democrats that formed on social welfare, labor, and some other issues. Electoral changes in the South have led to the replacement of most conservative Democrats by Republicans. The remaining southern Democrats, being mostly black, vote with their other Democratic colleagues. There are a number of "Blue Dog" or "moderate" Democrats in both houses

FIGURE 4.1

Party-Line Votes in Congress

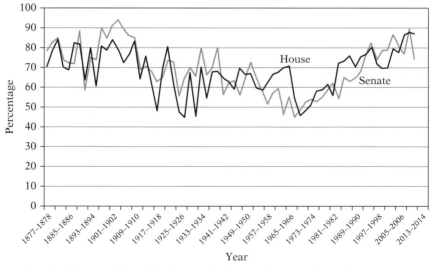

Source: From Jon R. Bond and Kevin B. Smith, *Analyzing American Democracy* (New York: Routledge, 2013), p. 260.

of congress. In Republican ranks, the number of "liberals" and moderates has essentially vanished.[18] The inclination of the parties in Congress to engage in party-based conflict has also increased as they have become more polarized. This has been highly evident in the House in recent years.

Strong-party voting, in which 90 percent or more of one party is aligned against 90 percent or more of the other party, customarily occurs on only a small percentage of roll-call votes in either the House or the Senate. This type of party voting reached a peak in the nineteenth century during the McKinley era, when approximately 50 percent of the House votes met this standard.[19] The strong-party leadership and control that yielded such voting proved to be unacceptable to both members of Congress and the public, however, and were eliminated by congressional reforms early in the twentieth century.

In parliamentary systems, such as the British House of Commons, voting along strict party lines is the order of the day. In Commons most votes meet the "90 percent versus 90 percent" strong-party vote criterion. On many government proposals, formal votes (divisions) are not taken because they are unnecessary. Although dissenting votes to party positions have increased in recent years, they usually involve only a handful of a party's members and customarily do not occur on crucial issues.[20]

Party loyalties or attachments in Congress have varied in importance among issue areas. Party conflict has arisen most consistently on such topics as business regulation, labor–management relations, social welfare, taxation, and agricultural income supports. Democrats have been more inclined, for example, to support new welfare programs—such as family leave and child care—and expansion of or increased funding for existing ones—such as Medicare and food stamps—than have Republicans. Again, Democrats have been stronger supporters of air and water pollution-control regulations than have Republicans. Tax cuts, balanced budgets, military spending, and something called "small government" are strong Republican preferences.

In some issue areas, however, it is difficult to delineate distinct and persistent party differences. Public works, veterans' benefits, medical research, and international trade are illustrative. Members of both parties, until recently, have displayed a proclivity for securing pork-barrel projects (research facilities, public buildings, dams, highway "demonstration" projects), that is, those that are of particular benefit to their states and districts.

Party affiliation also influences the decisions of federal judges. Republican presidents typically appoint conservative Republicans to judgeships; Democratic presidents manifest a preference for moderate to liberal Democrats. Once appointed, federal judges do not entirely shed their partisan raiment. Based on their examination of tens of thousands of federal district court opinions issued by more than 1,500 judges between 1933 and 1987, Professors Robert A. Carp and Claude K. Rowland found that 48 percent of the decisions of Democratic judges were liberal compared with 39 percent of Republican jurists' decisions. In cases involving civil rights and liberties, labor relations, and economic regulation, Democratic judges were more likely to take liberal positions, such as making pro-labor decisions.[21]

Constituency Interests   A bit of conventional wisdom in Congress holds that when party interests and state or district constituency interests conflict on some issue, members should "vote their constituency." It is, after all, the voters at home who hold the ultimate power to hire and fire. In looking after the interests of constituents, the representative may act as either a delegate, carrying out their actual or perceived instructions, or a trustee, exercising his or her best judgment in their behalf, when voting on policy questions.[22] Of course, the representative may try to combine these two styles, acting as a delegate on some issues and as a trustee on others, thus becoming a "politico."

In some instances, constituents' interests will be rather clear and strongly held, and representatives will act contrary to them at their own peril. In the past, southern members of Congress were well aware of the strong opposition among their white constituents to civil-rights legislation and voted accordingly. A legislator from a strong labor district will likewise probably have little doubt about the constituents' interests on minimum-wage and right-to-work legislation.

On a great many issues, however, representatives will be hard put to determine what their constituents want. Large portions of the electorate have little knowledge of most issues. How do representatives measure which way the wind is blowing from their districts if no air currents are moving? Legislators must then make a decision drawing on their own values or other criteria, such as recommendations from party leaders or the chief executive. They may also solicit opinions from some of their constituents or listen to the interested few.

Nonelected public officials, such as administrators, may also act as representatives. Agencies often have well-developed relationships with interest groups and strive to represent their interests in forming and administering policy. The Department of Agriculture is especially responsive to the interests of commercial farmers, and the Federal Maritime Commission has viewed itself as the representative of international shipping interests in the national administrative system. The two agencies' decisions and actions have reflected the interests of their clientele. Some commentators have contended that administrative agencies may in fact be more representative of particular interests in society than are elected officials.[23] Whatever the validity of this contention, it is clear that legislators are not the only officials influenced by the need or desire to act representatively in making decisions.

Public Opinion   Public opinion can be defined operationally as those public perspectives or viewpoints on policy issues that public officials consider or take into account in making decisions. Public opinion may be expressed in many ways—letters to the editor and to public officials, meetings, public demonstrations, editorials, election results, legislators meeting with constituents, plebiscites, and radio talk shows. Most commonly, however, public opinion is identified with the findings of opinion surveys that poll a representative sample of the population on political issues. Despite their increasing numbers and sophistication, opinion surveys have various limitations. Notably, they do not provide much insight into either the depth or intensity of people's opinions. Small focus groups are sometimes used to gauge the depth or intensity of feelings on some issues.

Moreover, although most people are quite willing to express their opinions to pollsters, typically it is unclear how much information or understanding underlies their perspectives. Consider this example. In 1995, a University of Maryland research organization released an opinion survey that found that 75 percent of the respondents thought the national government spent too much money on foreign-aid programs. Asked how much of the national budget went for foreign aid, the median response was 15 percent, and the average response was 18 percent. In actuality, foreign aid accounted for less than 1 percent of the budget (about $14 billion). To questions about how much foreign spending would be "appropriate" and how much would be "too little," the median responses were 5 percent and 3 percent, respectively.[24] The lack of respondent information indicated by this poll suggests that the "don't know" should have been the standard response. Overestimation of foreign aid spending continues to prevail.

Economist Alan Blinder contends that the Troubled Assets Relief Program (TARP), enacted by Congress in 2008, "may be among the most successful— but least understood—economic policy innovations in our nation's history." A Pew poll in early 2012 found that only 39 percent of those polled agreed that the loan program to prevent a financial crisis was the right thing for government to do. Fifty-two percent disagreed. Asked then how much of the money had been paid back, only 15 percent gave the right answer—either "all of it" or "most of it." Seventy-two percent said "only some of it" or "none of it." TARP continues to be negatively viewed. A great many people continue to believe the money was *given* to the banks.[25]

Public opinion is also subject to manipulation by public officials, as through the management of the news—that is, the careful control of information provided to media representatives. Reagan administration officials, for instance, used a "theme of the day" format to influence the view of the president and his policies presented through the media to the public. Moreover, "the historical record indicates that government officials often mislead and sometimes lie, particularly in foreign affairs, where government control of information is great. . . . This tendency is not unique to the United States."[26]

Notwithstanding their limitations, opinion surveys draw much attention because of their frequency, regularity, and accessibility, and the seeming precision of the numbers they yield. Political scientists devote much time and effort to studying the formation, content, and change of public opinion on political issues. The more philosophically inclined consider the role of public opinion in the governmental process. Our subject is the effect of public opinion on the actions of policy-makers. Are the policy-makers' choices shaped or determined by public opinion? Does public opinion serve as a criterion for decision? It is advisable to proceed tentatively in answering such questions, bearing in mind Professor V. O. Key's comment that "to speak with precision of public opinion is a task not unlike coming to grips with the Holy Ghost."[27]

A useful way to approach the problem of how public opinion influences policymaking is to distinguish between decisions that shape the broad direction of policy and the day-to-day, often routine decisions on specific aspects of policy. Public opinion is probably not a significant criterion for decisions in the second category. Drawing on Key again, "Many, if not most, policy decisions by legislatures and by other authorities exercising broad discretion are made under circumstances in which extremely small proportions of the general public have any awareness of the particular issue, much less any understanding of the consequences of the decision."[28] The legislator deciding how to vote on a specific tax amendment or a public-works bill will probably be unaffected by public opinion in any direct sense. Of course, he or she may try to anticipate the public's reaction to such votes, but this tactic will leave substantial latitude to the legislator because of the shortage of public awareness previously mentioned.

Nonetheless, the general boundaries and direction of public policy may be shaped by public opinion. Given public attitudes, such actions as nationalizing the airline industry, repealing the Clean Air Act, or making a major cutback in the Social Security program appear highly unlikely. Conversely, officials may come to believe that public opinion demands some kind of policy action, as with education reform in 2001 and gun control in 2013. These were generalized rather than specific demands, which left to Congress much discretion on details.

In foreign policy, public opinion appears to accord wide latitude to executive officials, as the conduct of American intervention in Vietnam during the 1960s clearly indicates. Ultimately, however, growing public opposition to the Vietnam War apparently contributed to President Johnson's decision not to run for reelection in 1968 and to begin to "wind down the war and withdraw."[29]Conversely, public opinion was strongly supportive of the George Bush administration's campaign to drive the Iraqis out of Kuwait.[30]

Public opinion sometimes has a permissive quality in that action on some topic is favored but not required. For years, public-opinion polls have indicated that a strong majority of the American population supports stronger gun-control legislation, such as requiring a police permit for the purchase of a handgun.[31] However, restrictive legislation has been scarce because of the strong, well-financed opposition of the National Rifle Association. In instances like this, an intense minority may prevail over a much larger but less committed majority. This is one of the dilemmas of democracy.

To conclude, policy-makers do not seem to be unaffected in making decisions by public opinion, especially if it trends strongly on some matter. The relationship between public opinion and the actions of elected officials is neither as simple nor as direct as posited by democratic theory. As Professor Larry Bartels remarks: "In practice . . . elected officials have a great deal of political leeway. This fact is strikingly illustrated by the behavior of Democratic and Republican Senators from the same state, who routinely pursue vastly different policies while 'representing' precisely the same constituents."[32] This is not to say, however, that elected officials can totally ignore public opinion, but it is not the compelling influence that public opinion studies sometimes appear to indicate.

Deference   Officials confronted with the task of making a decision may decide how to act by deferring to the judgment of others. The "others" to whom deference is given may or may not be hierarchic superiors. Administrative officials often do make decisions in accordance with directives from department heads or chief executives. That is how we expect them to act, especially when the directives of superiors are clear in meaning, which, it must be added, they sometimes are not. Administrators may also defer to the suggestions or judgments of members of Congress, as Department of Agriculture officials did when receiving advice from Congressman Jamie Whitten (D, Mississippi). Whitten chaired the House Agricultural Appropriations Subcommittee from 1949 to 1992 (except for 1953 to 1954, when the Republicans controlled the House) and later the full Appropriations Committee. Because of his position and strong influence on the actions of the Department of Agriculture, Whitten was sometimes referred to as the "permanent Secretary of Agriculture."[33] This is a classic example.

Members of Congress often have to vote on issues that are of little interest to them, such as those that do not affect the members' constituents, those on which they have little information, or those that are highly complex. On such issues they may decide how to vote by seeking the advice of other legislators whose judgment they trust, whether party leaders, committee chairs, or policy experts. Staff members are also influential here. When members are unable to decide how to vote from their own analysis of an issue, deference to someone whose judgment they trust is a reasonably rational, low-information strategy for making decisions. Political scientist Donald R. Matthews argues that because of the widespread practice of deference to policy experts, "few institutions provide more power to the exceptionally competent member than does the House of Representatives."[34]

Judges, too, make decisions that reflect deference. When they interpret a statute, in either applying it to a case or determining its constitutionality, they may defer to the intent of the legislature.[35] Statutory language is often ambiguous and unclear. In trying to determine what the legislature intends by phrases such as "restraint of trade" or "all lawful means," they may make use of the legislative histories of statutes. One tenet in the theory of "judicial self-restraint" holds that judges "are not free to invoke their own personal notions of right and wrong or of good and bad public policy when they examine the constitutionality of legislation."[36] To the extent that judges act accordingly in deciding cases, this course involves some deference to the judgment of legislatures.

Decision Rules   Those confronted with the task of making many decisions often devise rules of thumb, or guidelines, to focus on facts and relationships and thereby both simplify and regularize decision-making. No set of decision rules is common to all decision-makers, although some may be widely utilized. Which guidelines apply in a situation is a matter to be determined by empirical investigation. Some examples are presented here to illustrate the concept.

The rule of *stare decisis* (in effect, "let the precedents stand") is often used by the judiciary in deciding cases. According to this decision rule or principle, current cases should be decided in the same way as similar cases were decided in the past. Using precedents to guide decision-making is by no means limited to the judiciary. Executives, administrators, and legislators also frequently make decisions on the basis of precedents. They are often urged to do so by those who would be affected by their actions, particularly if this act will help maintain a desired status quo. Those adversely affected by precedents are likely to find them lacking in virtue and utility, or hopelessly out-of-date.

In the antitrust area, some *per se* rules have been developed to ease enforcement. Certain economic actions, such as price fixing and market allocation, have been held to be *per se* (in effect, "as such") violations of the Sherman Act. If the prohibited action is found to exist, this finding is sufficient to prove violation, and no effort is made to inquire into the reasonableness of the prices fixed or other possible justifications for the action in question. *Per se* rules thus add simplicity and certainty to antitrust decision-making.

Professor Richard F. Fenno Jr., in his study of a number of congressional committees, finds that each committee has some rules for decision (strategic premises) that help shape its decision-making activities. Thus, the House Appropriations Committee, seeking to maintain its independence from the executive, has a "rule" that it should reduce executive budget requests, and in fact many requests are reduced. The Education and Labor Committee has a rule for decision, in Fenno's words, "to prosecute policy partisanship." That is, strong ideological conflict between its Republican and Democratic contingents is the expected style of committee behavior.[37] Fenno points out that every committee has decision rules, although some are easier to discover than others, and they will change over time.

Science

Science has become an important consideration in policy-making on environmental, public health, and workplace health and safety matters. The EPA makes extensive use of scientific information, much of it from academic sources, in developing air and water quality standards.[38] The United States Fish and Wildlife Service, in making decisions on the listing of endangered species, is directed by the Endangered Species Act (1973) to act on the basis of "the best scientific and commercial data available."

A leading environmental historian, Samuel P. Hays, a couple of decades ago, wrote: "The customary image of the role of science in public affairs was that as disinterested and objective investigators, scientists would gather knowledge that then could be applied by others for the public benefit."[39] In practice, of course, there is disagreement among scientists on many policy issues. Because of differences in training, institutional affiliations, and personal values, scientists can reach different conclusions on the same body of data. Policy-makers may choose sides, opting to act on the basis of a particular scientific viewpoint because it accords with their policy preferences than because they find the science *per se* compelling.

Uncertainty is endemic in most policymaking. Good science—that using appropriate methodology and fairly and objectively conducted—can reduce uncertainty. There is, however, often a shortage of good data or information on which to base decisions. What then is the decision-maker to do? A standard ploy is to call for more research, which is what the Reagan administration did on the problem of acid rain. Those whose economic interests would be adversely affected by a health standard might contend that action should be taken only on the basis of conclusive or "iron-clad" evidence.

Reliance could be placed upon the precautionary principle as a guide to action. This holds that where there are threats of serious or irreversible harm to human health or the environment, a "lack of full scientific certainty should not be used as reason for postponing" remedial measures.[40] The precautionary principle does not eliminate the need for policy judgments, but it does increase the likelihood of positive action. European policy-makers have been more inclined to utilize it than have their American counterparts on matters such as genetically modified foods.

Most elected and politically appointed public officials are neither scientists nor possessed of a high degree of scientific literacy—an understanding of science, of scientific research methodology, or how science contributes to knowledge. When decision-making calls for an appraisal of scientific information or data, how do they do it? How do they distinguish "good science" from "junk science"? How do they weigh scientific evidence? Conflicting scientific arguments? There seems to be no easy answer.[41]

The Public Interest

The task of government, it is often proclaimed, is to serve or promote the public interest. Statutes sometimes include the public interest as a guide for agency action, as when the Federal Communications Commission is directed to license broadcasters for the "public interest, convenience, and necessity." In this section, this rather elusive normative concept and its usefulness as a criterion for decision-making will be discussed.

Most people, if asked whether public policy should be in accord with the public interest or with private interests, would opt for the former. As Professor Charles Anderson remarks: "One cannot justify a policy recommendation on the grounds that 'it would make me and my friends richer.' However refreshing the candor of such an argument might be, it does not and cannot stand as legitimate warrant for a public action."[42]

Difficulty arises, however, when one is asked to define *the public interest.* Is it the interest of the majority? If so, how do we determine what policy the majority really wants? Is it the interest of consumers, who are a rather large group? Is it what people would want if they "thought clearly and acted rationally"? How does one define *the public interest*?

Many people, including most political scientists, would say that it is not possible to provide a universally accepted or objective definition of the concept, especially in substantive terms. Some would contend that whatever results from the political struggle over policy issues is the public interest. If all groups and persons had an equal chance to engage in that struggle, which in fact they do not, this notion of the public interest might be more appealing. An individual may not care to define a multitude of tax loopholes or inaction that permits the wanton destruction of natural resources as in the public interest. (That statement, of course, indicates a normative bias, which will be disturbing to those who hold rather simplistically that "one person's opinion is as good as another's.")

Sometimes the public interest is depicted as a myth by which policy, however particularistic, can be rationalized as in the general interest and hence made more publicly acceptable. This stratagem is attempted or performed with regularity (just as scoundrels sometimes wrap themselves in the flag or cite Scripture to justify their predations). Beyond that, however, the concept can be given enough content to render it useful as a general standard for decision-making on public policy. When evaluating policy, we need to be able to state not only whether the policy is accomplishing its asserted objectives but also whether the objectives are worthy of accomplishment. For the latter question, a standard of more noble quality than "it is (or is not) in my interest" seems needed.

The question now arises about how to determine what constitutes the public interest. Professor Emmette S. Redford suggests three approaches to this task.[43] One is to look at policy areas rich in conflict among group interests, as in agriculture, labor relations, energy, and transportation. In some instances, the direct interests of one group or another may prevail and become accepted as the public interest. There is no reason to assume that private interests and the public interest must always be antithetical. If it is in the private interest of medical doctors to prevent the practice of medicine by various quacks because this would give the medical profession a bad reputation, so, too, it is in the public interest not to have unqualified people or charlatans practicing medicine. (It would seem difficult to argue the contrary position reasonably.)

In the struggle among private group interests, however, it may become apparent that others are indirectly involved and have interests that should be considered in policymaking. These public interests, though not represented by organized groups, may be responded to by decision-makers, perhaps positively, and thus influence the outcome.

In the conflict between labor and management over terms and conditions of employment, it becomes apparent that the public has an interest in maintaining industrial peace and preventing disruptions in the flow of vital goods and services. The result has been the adoption of several procedures for settling labor disputes. In a dispute such as one involving the railroad industry, a public interest may become clear along with those of the railroad companies and labor unions.

A second approach is to search for widely and continuously shared interests that, because of these characteristics, can be called public interests. Illustrative are the interests of people in such matters as world peace, better education, clean air, avoidance of severe inflation, and an adequate traffic-control system. Here the public interest appears as public needs. Especially in large cities there is a clear public interest in having a traffic-control system to facilitate safe, orderly, and convenient movement of pedestrians and vehicles. That various alternatives are available for meeting this need can be taken to mean that more than one way can be found to meet the public interest, that availability does not negate its existence. Nor does the concept, to be meaningful, need to be so precise as to indicate whether the traffic flow on a certain street should be one-way or two-way. A concept to be useful need not always yield answers to the most minute questions.

There is nothing very mystical in talking about the public interest as a widely shared interest. We speak, for example, of wheat farmers' shared interest in higher wheat prices or that of sport fishermen in an adequate fish-stocking program, and attribute much reality to such interests. The public interest differs only in its wider scope. There is no way to determine precisely at what point the interest is widely enough shared as to become a public interest. Few interests, indeed, would be shared by everyone. The survival of the nation-state may be opposed by the advocate of world government; even at old-time western rustler lynchings at least one dissenter might be heard. Qualitative judgments are obviously called for in determining the existence of a public interest, as in many areas of political life and academic activity. They should be made with as much care and rigor as possible.[44]

A third approach to determining the public interest is to look at the need for organization and procedures to represent and balance interests, to resolve issues, to effect compromise in policy formation, and to carry public policy into effect. There is, in short, a public interest in fair, orderly, and effective government. The focus here is on process rather than policy content. The noted columnist Walter Lippmann many years ago wrote,

> The public is interested in law, not in the laws; in the method of law, not in the substance; in the sanctity of contract, not in a particular contract; in understanding based on custom, not in this custom or that. It is concerned in these things to the end that men in their active affairs shall find a modus vivendi; its interest is in the workable rule which will define and predict the behavior of men so that they can make their adjustments.[45]

Although the public is obviously interested in individual laws as well as in the law, Lippmann states well the desire for adequate process. How things are done, moreover, often affects the public's attitude toward their legitimacy.

The public interest is thus diverse and somewhat fugitive, and must be searched for in various ways. Although it probably cannot be converted into a precise set of guidelines to inform the action of decision-makers, neither can it fairly be described as merely a myth. It directs attention beyond narrow or specific interests and the more immediate toward broader, more universal interests. It also directs attention toward unorganized and unarticulated interests that otherwise may be ignored in both the development and evaluation of policy. Moreover, it is an ideal, like justice and equality of opportunity, to which all can aspire.

Styles of Decision-Making

Most policy decisions of any magnitude are made by coalitions, which frequently take the form of numerical majorities, whether one's attention is on Congress, the Michigan State Legislature, the Oakland City Council, or the Danish Folketing. Even when a single political party has a majority in a legislative body, factions within the party may require attention to coalition building.

Much executive decision-making does not require numerical majorities. However, the support (or consent, which is much the same) of others is often needed to ensure that the decision is implemented and compliance is achieved. President Lyndon Johnson was famous for seeking consensus on actions; in many instances he could have acted unilaterally but chose not to. The noted presidential scholar Richard E. Neustadt remarks, "Underneath our images of Presidents-in-boots, astride decisions, are the half-observed realities of Presidents-in-sneakers, stirrups in hand, trying to induce particular department heads, or Congressmen or Senators, to climb aboard."[46] President John F. Kennedy sometimes told friends who offered policy suggestions or criticism, "Well I agree with you, but I'm not sure the government will."[47] These comments emphasize the coalitional form of much presidential decision-making and the president's need to induce others to go along if he or she is to be successful.

Although coalition building is necessary in all democratic legislative bodies, it is especially notable in multiparty legislatures. This requirement is well illustrated by the Danish Folketing, whose 179 seats are divided among 9 or 10 parties, none of which holds close to a majority of seats. To take office, a Danish prime minister must draw on several parties to put together a majority coalition, which takes considerable negotiation and bargaining. Once in office, the prime minister, in taking policy actions, must always be alert to the need to hold the coalition together, lest he lose his majority and thus the power to govern.

In the January 2013 Israeli national elections, fourteen political parties participated, and all but one won seats in the 120-member Knesset (the parliament). The two biggest winners—Likud-Beiteinu and Yesh Atid—won 31 and 19 seats, respectively.[48] Benjamin Netanyahu, the Likud leader and current prime minister, was asked to put together a governing coalition. After several weeks of struggle, Netanyahu was able to fashion a 68-member coalition. Twenty-two of its members were made cabinet ministers. Ultra-Orthodox parties were excluded from the coalition, much to their displeasure. It was thought the new coalition would make significant changes in domestic policies while faltering on the Mideast peace process.[49] Holding the coalition together will be challenging.

In this section, the focus shifts from individual decision-making to decision-making as a social or collective process. We examine three styles of collective decision-making: bargaining, persuasion, and command. Each entails action to reach agreement and induce others to comply. Practitioners of these styles of decision-making will be motivated by the decision criteria examined in the preceding section.

Bargaining   The most common style of decision-making in the American political system is bargaining. *Bargaining* can be defined as a process in which two or more persons in positions of power or authority adjust their at least partially inconsistent goals in order to formulate a course of action that is acceptable but not necessarily ideal for all the participants. In short, bargaining involves negotiation, give and take, and compromise to reach a mutually acceptable position. In the private realm, it is epitomized in collective bargaining over the terms of work by union leaders and management officials, or by the haggling that takes place at flea markets. For bargaining to occur, the bargainers must be willing to negotiate, they must have something to negotiate about, and each must have something (i.e., resources) that others want or need.

Two factors seem especially important in making bargaining the dominant mode of decision-making in our society. One is social pluralism, or the presence of a multitude of partially autonomous groups such as labor unions, business organizations, professional associations, farm organizations, environmental groups, sportsmen's clubs, and civil-rights groups. Although partially autonomous, these groups are also interdependent and "must bargain with one another for protection and advantage."[50] The second factor is the existence of such constitutional practices as federalism, separation of powers, bicameral legislatures, and legislative committees, which fragment and disperse political power among many public officials and decision points. Major policy decisions at the national level often require approval by all branches of government plus acceptance by state or local governments and affected private groups. This is the case with many current federal policies on aid to public education and environmental-pollution control.

Bargaining may be either explicit or implicit. When it is explicit, the bargainers (group leaders, party officials, committee chairs, department heads, executives, etc.) state their agreements (bargains) clearly to minimize the likelihood of misunderstanding. The U.S. Constitution was a product of explicit bargaining between large and small states, North and South, and other interests at the Philadelphia convention in 1787. An explicit bargain was struck by President George Bush and the Democratic congressional leadership in 1990 when the president agreed to tax increases in return for the Democratic agreement to expenditure reductions in order to reduce the budget deficit. In international politics, treaties exemplify explicit bargains. Bargaining is widely practiced in the international arena because the idea of national interests is well accepted. In domestic politics, bargaining, however necessary and prevalent, is often looked upon as incompatible with a quest for the "public interest" or, in more crude language, as a sellout.

More frequently, however, bargaining is probably implicit. In implicit bargaining, the terms of agreement among the bargainers are frequently vague or ambiguous and may be expressed in such phrases as "future support" or "favorable disposition." Such bargaining frequently occurs in Congress, where one member will agree to support another on a bill in return for "future cooperation." Understandings or "gentlemen's agreements" may be negotiated by administrators in agencies with overlapping responsibilities for administering programs so as to reduce or eliminate conflict among themselves. Sometimes implicit bargaining is so nebulous that it is unclear whether an agreement actually has been reached. In Congress, bargaining frequently occurs on procedural actions intended either to slow down or to accelerate the handling of legislation as well as on the content of legislation.

Three common forms of bargaining are logrolling, side payments, and compromise. Logrolling, a way of gaining support from those who are indifferent to or have little interest in a matter, usually encompasses a straightforward mutual exchange of support on two different topics. This is a common form of bargaining because every item on an agenda is not of interest to all decision-makers. The classic example of logrolling is an appropriations bill for rivers-and-harbors legislation, which funds various river, harbor, and flood-control projects. Members of Congress care mainly about the projects in their own districts; consequently, those who want a project in their district essentially agree to support the projects for all the other members' districts. Logrolling is usually implicit.[51]

Side payments are rewards offered to prospective supporters or coalition members who are not directly related to the decision at hand, or at least to its main provisions, but are valued by them for other reasons. Legislative leaders may use committee assignments, allocation of office space, campaign assistance, and support for members' "pet" bills as means of securing their support for legislation.

During consideration of the 1986 tax-reform legislation, the chairman of the House Ways and Means Committee, Dan Rostenkowski (D, Illinois), used "transition rules" to gain support for it.[52] Supposedly, these rules ease the transition between current tax law and a new tax law for various taxpayers. However, transition rules also become legislative favors that can be doled out to win or confirm votes. Because they provide millions of dollars in tax benefits to companies and others in legislators' home states or districts, they are highly valued. The chairman of the Senate Finance Committee also used this form of bargaining to elicit support for the tax-reform proposal. In all, about 340 transition rules were included in the Tax Reform Act at an estimated total cost in lost revenue of $10.6 billion over five years.[53]

Compromise typically involves explicit bargaining, is normally centered on a single issue, and involves questions of more or less of something. Here the bargainers regard half a loaf as better than none and consequently adjust their differences, each giving up something so as to come into agreement. This tactic contrasts with logrolling, which requires no change in the bargainers' original positions. A fine historical example is the Missouri Compromise of 1820, which temporarily settled the conflict between North and South over extending slavery into the Louisiana Territory. The North wanted slavery excluded from the territory, and the South wanted no such prohibition. It was finally agreed that slavery would be prohibited in the territory except in Missouri, north of latitude 36° 30'.

The Civil Rights Act of 1964 also involved many compromises between those favoring stronger legislation and those wanting weaker or no legislation, especially on the provisions pertaining to public accommodations, equal employment opportunity, and judicial enforcement. On equal employment opportunity it was provided that the federal Equal Employment Opportunity Commission (EEOC) could handle discrimination cases only after existing state equal-opportunity agencies had a chance to act, and even then the EEOC could use only voluntary means to reach settlements. This limited enforcement authority was agreed to in an attempt to reduce conservative opposition to the legislation. Issues involving money, such as budgets, are probably the easiest matters on which to compromise because they are readily amenable to the splitting of differences.

Persuasion   Persuasion involves the marshaling of facts, data, and information; the skillful construction of arguments; and the use of reason and logic to convince another person of the wisdom or correctness of one's own position.[54] Unlike bargainers, persuaders seek to build support for what they favor without having to modify their own positions. This task may involve striving to convince others of the merits or soundness of one's position, or the benefits that will accrue to them or their constituents if they accept it, or some combination of the two. In short, persuaders seek to induce others to go along or do it their way. Accurate information, reason and logic, and effective argument are the instruments of persuasion; manipulation, deception, and bullying and hectoring are beyond its bounds. They are compelling, not persuasive; but they are sometimes used to gain what one wants.

President Harry S. Truman once remarked, "I sit here all day trying to persuade people to do things that they ought to have sense enough to do without my persuading them. . . . That's all the powers of the President amount to."[55] Presidential meetings with congressional leaders, for example, are often sessions in which presidential programs and priorities are explained, their likely benefits for members of Congress and their constituents are outlined, and appeals are made for congressional leaders' support. Meetings with administrative officials are used to explain presidential preferences and to win their allegiance. "A President is most persuasive when he or she makes his pitch personally in direct conversation with those involved."[56] Presidents, of course, also have extensive capacity to bargain and command.

The use of persuasion is widespread in the governmental process. Attorneys who argue cases before the Supreme Court not only present their side of the issue through written briefs and oral arguments but also seek to convince a majority of the justices of the correctness of their position. In this process, the justices are more than inert sponges absorbing the advocacy directed at them. Their questions and comments provide positive or negative responses and guidance to the opposing attorneys.

Within Congress, appeals by party leaders to the rank-and-file members to the effect that "your party needs your support on this issue; can't you go along?" are essentially persuasive in style and content. In these and many other instances, decision-makers or those wishing to influence their decisions, as the case may be, either lack the capacity to command or know that bargaining is inappropriate or of limited utility. Persuasion is then the alternative on which they must rely.

Command   Bargaining involves interaction among peers; command involves hierarchic relationships among superordinates and subordinates. Command is the ability of those in superior positions to make decisions that are binding upon those who come within their jurisdiction. They may use sanctions in the form of either rewards or penalties, although usually sanctions are thought of as penalties, to reinforce their decisions. Thus, the subordinate who faithfully accepts and carries out a superior's decision may be rewarded with favorable recognition or a promotion, and the one who refuses to comply may be fired or demoted. President Clinton's decision to issue an executive order replacing the Reagan–Bush regulatory review program with one of his own devising was essentially an act of command.

The Office of Management and Budget engages in command behavior when it approves, rejects, or modifies agency requests for appropriations and proposals for legislation prior to their transmittal to Congress. On the whole, however, command is more characteristic of decision processes in dictatorial rather than democratic societies and in military rather than civilian organizations because of their greater hierarchic qualities. Command is the primary style of decision-making in many developing countries in Africa and Southeast Asia.

In practice, bargaining, persuasion, and command often run together in decisional situations. The president, although he or she has authority to make many decisions unilaterally, may nonetheless also implicitly bargain with subordinates, modifying his or her position somewhat and accepting some of their suggestions, in order to gain more ready and enthusiastic support.[57]

Within agencies, subordinates often seek to convert command relationships into bargaining relationships. A bureau that gains considerable congressional support may thus put itself into position to bargain with, rather than simply be commanded by, the department head. A pollution-control agency may have the statutory authority to set and enforce pollutant-emission standards. In the course of setting the standards, it may, however, bargain with those potentially affected, hoping to gain easier and greater compliance with the standards set. Presidential and gubernatorial efforts to win support for legislative proposals also typically combine persuasion and bargaining.

In summary, bargaining is the most common form of decision-making in the American policy process. Persuasion and command are supplementary, being "better suited to a society marked by more universal agreements on values and a more tightly integrated system of authority."[58] Nowhere has the bargaining process been better illustrated than in Congress, to which we now turn.

Majority Building in Congress   The enactment of major legislation by Congress requires development of a numerical majority or, more likely, a series of numerical majorities, which are most commonly created by bargaining. Even if a majority in Congress agrees on the need for action on an issue such as labor-union reform, they may not agree on the form it should take, thereby making bargaining essential.

A highly important characteristic of Congress that has much importance for policy formation is its decentralization of political power. Three factors contribute to this condition. First, the political parties in Congress are weak in that party leaders have only limited power to control and discipline party members. In contrast with the strong-party leaders in the British House of Commons, who have a variety of means for ensuring support of party policy proposals by party members, congressional leaders, such as the floor leaders, have few sanctions with which to discipline or punish recalcitrant party members. The party leadership possess only "bits and fragments" of power, such as desired committee assignments, office space, use of the rules, and ability to persuade, with which to influence the rank and file. The member who chooses to defy party leadership can sometimes do so with impunity, and, indeed, not a few people will probably applaud such independence.

Second, the system of geographic representation and decentralized elections contributes to the decentralization of power in Congress. Members of the House and Senate are nominated and elected by the voters in their constituencies and owe little or nothing for their election to the national party organizations or congressional leaders. It is their constituencies that ultimately wield the power to hire and fire them, and it is therefore to their constituencies that they must be responsive, at least on some crucial matters, if they wish to remain in Congress. From time to time, important constituent interests in a district may be adversely affected by party programs. Conventional congressional wisdom holds that when party and constituency interests conflict, members should vote their constituency, as their reelection may depend upon it.

A third factor contributing to the decentralization of power in Congress is the committee system. The House has twenty standing committees and the Senate sixteen, with jurisdiction over legislation in such areas as agriculture, appropriations, energy and natural resources, international relations, and human resources. Traditionally, these committees have done most of the legislative work in Congress. Nearly all bills are referred to the appropriate standing committees for consideration before being brought to the floor of the House or Senate for debate and decision. The standing committees possess vast power to kill, alter, or report unchanged the bills sent to them; most bills sent to committees are never heard from again.

Until the 1970s, the committee chairs, who gained their positions by seniority, had much power over the operation of their committees. Often referred to as "barons," they selected the committee staff, scheduled and presided over meetings, set the agenda, scheduled hearings and chose witnesses, and decided when votes would be taken. Through long experience, they were often highly knowledgeable on the policy matters within their committees' jurisdiction. Because of the fairly large number of interests that came within their jurisdiction, the chairs could act as brokers to build compromises among conflicting or differing interests.

Reforms in the 1970s reduced the power of committee chairs and altered the organization and operation of the committee. Most committees divided their jurisdiction among a number of subcommittees. In the House, a subcommittee "Bill of Rights" provided substantial independence for subcommittees from their parent committees. This significantly decentralized and fragmented legislative work and power, and produced what some called "subcommittee government." Changes made by the House Republicans after they gained the majority in 1995 restored some of the power of committee chairs and reduced the independence of subcommittees. On the other hand, seniority is now often bypassed in the selection of House committee chairs. The Senate Democrats, however, do continue to stress seniority in selecting committee chairs.

Currently, the number of subcommittees totals eighty-eight in the House and sixty-eight in the Senate. They do much of the legislative work for most committees and give members, if they so choose, additional opportunities to specialize and develop policy expertise.

Committees in the House and Senate generally act as gatekeepers, controlling the flow of legislation to the floors. "The bills they report largely determine what each chamber will debate and in what form."[59] The committee system also increases the points of access for interest groups, administrative officials, and others wanting to get involved in the legislative process.

Decentralization of power in Congress, together with the complexities of its legislative procedures, usually requires the cobbling together of a series of majorities to enact important legislation. A bill must pass through a number of decision stages (they have also been called obstacles) in becoming a law.[60] Briefly, in the House, these are subcommittee, committee, Rules Committee, and finally, floor action; and in the Senate, subcommittee, committee, and floor action. Assuming that the bill is passed in different versions by the two houses, a conference committee must agree on a compromise version, which then must be approved by the two houses. (In recent years, however, other alternatives have often been used to gain agreement between the two houses.) If the president approves it, the bill becomes law; if he vetoes it, however, the bill becomes law only if it is passed again by a two-thirds majority in each house. Thus, at ten or twelve stages, a bill requires approval by some kind of majority. If it fails to win majority approval at any one of these stages, it is probably dead. Should it win approval, its enactment is not ensured; rather, its supporters face the task of building a majority at the next stage.

Extraordinary majorities are constitutionally required for some matters. Two-thirds majorities are required for Senate approval of treaties and in both houses to propose constitutional amendments. I earlier referred to the two-thirds majorities required to override presidential vetoes. From 1789 to 2012, of the 2,567 bills vetoed by the presidents, only 109 were subsequently enacted into law. Congress overrode one of George Bush's forty-six vetoes, two of Bill Clinton's, four of George W. Bush's, and neither of Barack Obama's two. Bills that are vetoed usually stay vetoed.

Debate on a bill in the Senate usually can be ended only by a unanimous-consent agreement (which lets a single senator obstruct action) or by imposing cloture.[61] The cloture rule now provides that debate (or what passes for it) can be halted by a motion signed by sixteen senators and approved by three-fifths of the entire Senate (sixty senators). Because one senator who opposes a bill can prevent the closing of debate by a unanimous-consent agreement, cloture is the only alternative for shutting down a filibuster, other than giving up the bill.

As Congress became more sharply polarized in the last decade, filibustering in the Senate skyrocketed; there were 112 cloture motions or votes in the 110th Congress (2007–2008), 137 cloture votes in the 111th Congress (2009–2010), and 115 in the 112th Congress (2011–2012). Nothing of importance escaped the threat of a filibuster. Sixty votes became necessary to pass important bills. Majority rule gave way to minority rule in the Senate.[62]

Some Democrats became restive and called for reform. One proposal said the filibuster should be banned. Another said those involved in a filibuster should be required to be present on the Senate floor and speak to impede action on a bill. (This was not required, nor did they have to show they actually had forty-one votes.)

In January 2013, Senate leaders, responding to criticism and pressure for change, negotiated a modest compromise. A motion to proceed and begin debate on a bill could not be filibustered if the Republicans were permitted to offer two amendments. (This held only for 2013–2014.) Other changes were intended to quicken legislative action *after* a cloture vote succeeded, as was action of the approval of federal district judges and lower-level executive appointments. Filibusters continued to be in order on the enactment of legislation and the approval of appointments. In short, the filibuster was still alive and well; the minority continued to be able to prevail.[63]

Indeed, for controversial legislation, the multiplicity of stages, or decision points, in the congressional legislative process provides access for many groups and interests. Those who lack access or influence at one stage may secure it at another. It thus becomes quite unlikely that one group or interest will dominate the process. The complexity of the legislative process, however, has a conservative effect in that it gives an advantage to those seeking to block the enactment of legislation. And it is well to remember that many groups are more interested in preventing than securing enactment of legislation, or in holding change to a minimum when the adoption of legislation is inevitable. All they have to do to achieve their preference is to win support by a majority, or perhaps only a dominant legislator, at one stage in the process. Here is support for the familiar generalization that procedure is not neutral in its effects.

Much bargaining is usually necessary for the enactment of major legislation by Congress, even within the Democratic Party when it is in the majority. Those who control the various decision points, or whose votes are needed to construct a majority may require the modification of a bill as a condition for their approval, or they may exact future support for some item of interest to themselves. Bargaining is facilitated not only by the many decision points but also because legislators are not intensely interested in many matters on which they must decide. It is no doubt easier for them to bargain on such issues than on issues on which they have strong feelings. It seems unnecessary to elaborate further here upon the ubiquity of bargaining in Congress.

Presidential Decision-Making

Apart from playing an integral role in the legislative process, the president can also be viewed as a policy adopter in his own right. In foreign affairs, much policy is a product of presidential actions and decisions, based on the president's constitutional authority and/or on broad congressional delegations of power. Decisions to recognize foreign governments and to establish formal diplomatic relations with them, as the Nixon and Carter administrations did with the People's Republic of China, are in the president's domain. Treaties with other nations are made and entered into on behalf of the United States by the president, subject to approval by the Senate. One can cavil on whether the president is the true decision-maker here.

In the instance of executive agreements, which have the same legal force as treaties, and which are used much more frequently than treaties in foreign relations, there can be no doubt: the president makes the decisions. Executive agreements have been used to end wars, establish or expand military bases in other countries, and limit possession of offensive weapons by the United States and foreign nations. They are also often used for more routine purposes such as tariff reductions and customs enforcement.[64]

For more than a half-century, international trade policies have been primarily a construct of presidential action, albeit based on congressional authorizations because the Constitution delegates to Congress control of "commerce with foreign nations." Through the time of the 1930 Smoot–Hawley Tariff, by which Congress in a frenzy of logrolling elevated tariffs to an all-time high, this issue area had been dominated by Congress. Change began with the New Deal and enactment of the Reciprocal Trade Agreements Act of 1934.[65] This statute authorized the president to enter into agreements with other nations to lower tariffs and other trade barriers (e.g., import quotas). Since then, under the guidance of presidential leadership and decisions, the United States has continually advocated and moved toward free trade. All presidents since the Great Depression have been advocates of the reduction of trade barriers. U.S. tariffs now average less than 5 percent of the value of imported products.

In domestic matters, Congress often delegates discretionary authority to the president or to agencies under his direction and control. Executive orders, which are not mentioned in the Constitution, but which have become an accepted presidential prerogative, are also used by presidents for making domestic policies.[66] Executive orders have been promulgated to desegregate the armed services, establish loyalty-security programs, require affirmative action by government contractors, classify and withhold government documents from the public, and provide for presidential supervision of agency rule-making. Presidents Johnson and Carter used executive orders to establish systems of voluntary wage and price controls to combat inflation. Nothing in the Constitution or laws specifically authorized them to so act. On the other hand, nothing prohibited them from so doing. Operating with a broad view of presidential power under the Constitution, they responded to necessity as they saw it.

By considering some of the factors that shape and limit presidential decision-making, we not only can gain useful insight into presidential decision-making but also discover another perspective from which to view decision-making in general. Before proceeding further, it must be stressed that presidential decision-making is an institutional process. Many executive staff agencies, White House aides, and other advisers (both official and unofficial) assist the president in the discharge of his or her responsibilities. But whether he or she simply approves a recommendation from below or makes his or her own independent choice, the president alone has the ultimate formal responsibility for the decision.

Several factors help shape and limit presidential decision-making.[67] One is permissibility, an aspect of which is legality. The president is expected to act in conformity with the Constitution, statutes, and court decisions. The lack of a clear constitutional or legal basis certainly contributed to congressional criticism of the Nixon administration's Cambodian bombing policy in the summer of 1973 and to an agreement by the administration to cease bombing after August 15, 1973, in the absence of congressional authorization. The George W. Bush administration developed a theory of the "unitary executive," which stretched presidential power beyond normal bounds in an attempt to validate its actions. In the view of many, it was highly dubious.

Another aspect of permissibility is acceptability. Foreign-policy decisions often depend for their effectiveness upon acceptance by other nations, and domestic-policy decisions, such as that by President Reagan to recommend elimination of the Department of Energy, may depend upon their acceptance by Congress, executive-branch officials and agencies, or the public.

A second factor is available resources. The president does not have the resources to do everything he or she might want to do, whether by *resources* one means money, personnel, patronage, time, or credibility. Funds allocated to defense are not available for education or medical research. Only a limited number of appeals to the public for support for his or her actions can be made without the possibility of diminishing returns. Time devoted to foreign-policy problems is time not available for domestic matters. Although the president has considerable control over the use of his or her time—over whether devoting more time to foreign than to domestic affairs, for instance—he or she does not have time to get involved with everything that he or she might wish.[68] Lack of credibility (or the existence of a "credibility gap") may also limit the president, as the experiences of Presidents Johnson and Nixon attest.

A third factor is available time, in the sense of timing and the need to act. A foreign-policy crisis may require a quick response, as in the historic Cuban missile crisis of 1962, or the Iraqi invasion of Kuwait in 1990, or the September 11, 2001, terrorist attack, without all the time for deliberation and fact-gathering one might prefer.[69] Domestic-policy decisions may be "forced," as by the need to submit the annual budget to Congress in February or the constitutional requirement to act on a bill passed by Congress within ten days if the president wishes to veto it, barring the possibility of a pocket veto. (If a bill reaches the president during the last ten days of a session, or after the Congress has adjourned, and the president does not sign it, it is automatically vetoed.) Former White House aide Theodore C. Sorensen states,

> There is a time to act and a time to wait. By not acting too soon, the President may find that the problem dissolves or resolves itself, that the facts are different from what he thought, or that the state of the nation has changed. By not waiting too long, he may make the most of the mood of the moment, or retain that element of surprise which is so often essential to military and other maneuvers.[70]

President Reagan demonstrated the importance of timing when he moved quickly and decisively in the first months of his term to secure adoption of his economic program of tax cuts and reductions in domestic expenditures. By so doing, he was able to capitalize on the euphoria and political support that usually attend the early days of a new administration. As time goes on, these conditions decline, and the president's political life becomes more difficult.

Professor Paul Light states that presidents are confronted with cycles of increasing effectiveness and decreasing influence. Presidents become more effective over the course of their terms as their information and expertness expand and as their staffs become more knowledgeable and skilled in handling their duties. In short, learning occurs. At the same time, however, presidential influence diminishes. Presidents customarily suffer a midterm loss of party seats in Congress, and their standing in public-opinion polls declines as more people find fault with their performance. Also, time becomes too short to launch major initiatives, and staff energy and creative stamina lessen. The two cycles create a presidential dilemma. The cycle of decreasing influence encourages a president to move quickly on his agenda; the cycle of increasing effectiveness suggests restraint. "If there is any point in the presidential term when the cycles are at the best blend," Light says, "it is in the first moments of the second term."[71] But that depends on the president's being lucky enough to have a second term.

Previous commitments are a fourth factor that may shape presidential decisions. These commitments may be personal, taking the form, for instance, of campaign promises or earlier decisions. Although too much emphasis can be placed on the need for consistency, the president must avoid the appearance of deception or vacillation if he or she is to retain credibility and political support. Jimmy Carter suffered from a reputation (not fully deserved) for indecisiveness, as when in 1977 he proposed a tax rebate to stimulate the economy and then reversed himself a few months later because of economic conditions. Campaigning for the presidency in 1980, Ronald Reagan pledged to eliminate the Department of Education. He neither made good on the pledge nor suffered much in reputation as a consequence. People were often more attentive to and influenced by the president's words than by his actions. But woe may befall the reneger. When George Bush violated his ill-advised 1988 campaign pledge of "Read my lips. No new taxes" by supporting a tax increase in 1990, this greatly angered many of his more conservative supporters and caused him much political discomfort.

Commitments may also take the form of traditions and principles, such as those holding that the United States meets its treaty obligations and engages in military action only if attacked. During the Cuban missile crisis, an air strike without warning on the Soviet missile sites was rejected by the Kennedy administration as a "Pearl Harbor in reverse"; a naval blockade of Cuba was chosen instead. A "first-strike" strategy generally has been excluded from American foreign policy. A major exception was the George W. Bush administration's decision to wage "preemptive " war against Iraq.

Finally, available information can be an important influence on presidential decisions. Many sources of information—official and unofficial, overt and covert—are available to the president. At times, particularly on domestic-policy issues, he may be subject to inundation in a torrent of words, paper, and conflicting recommendations. Still, the president at times may be confronted by a shortage of reliable information, especially in foreign affairs, even though he or she likely has the best information that is available. Reliable information on possible national and international reactions to the possible bombing of Serbian forces in Kosovo, the resumption of nuclear testing, or a Strategic Defense Initiative ("Star Wars") may be scarce because of the need to predict what will happen in the future. The George W. Bush administration went to war in Iraq on the basis of faulty information, of which they were likely aware. Predicting the future is an uncertain task, except perhaps for a few who claim a sixth sense or a clear crystal ball.

Domestic-policy decisions also often involve some uncertainty. This may become quite obvious when economic-stability policy is under consideration. Will a reduction in income taxes encourage higher levels of investment and economic growth? How much restraint must be imposed on the economy to break the back of the inflationary psychology contributing to inflation? When all the advice is in, the president has to make a choice—a calculated one based on limited information—that the alternative chosen will produce the desired result. Uncertainty may contribute to delay and lack of action on some matters. Amid doubts as to what needs to be done, or what effect an action may have, the decision may be to hold off, to see whether things will work themselves out or to let the situation "clarify itself" (i.e., to give oneself more time to gather information on conditions and alternatives). Sometimes doing nothing can be a good policy. On the other hand, the economic situation may be so bad that as in 2008–2009, inaction is simply unacceptable to most informed people.

As a leader in policy formation, the president is subject to numerous political pressures and constraints, however great his or her legal powers may appear to be. Legal authority by itself often does not convey the capacity to act effectively. Thus, presidents may have to persuade because they cannot command; they may have to bargain because they cannot compel action. On many issues, once they have made a decision, they must seek the support of an often fickle public or a skeptical Washington community. "The struggling facilitator, not the dominating director, is the description that generally matches the process of presidential decision-making."[72]

| CASE STUDY | *Policy Adoption: Consumer Bankruptcy* |

This case illustrates some of the difficulties involved in getting policy adopted, even when the votes are apparently there. Subsidiary issues, largely symbolic in nature, can and do complicate the process.

The Constitution delegates authority to Congress "to establish . . . uniform laws on the subject of bankruptcies throughout the United States." Congress did not accomplish this until 1898, when it adopted the National Bankruptcy Act. Periodically this law has been altered in response to pro-creditor or pro-debtor forces. In 1978, the policy pendulum swung in a pro-debtor direction. The Bankruptcy Reform Act of 1994 made a variety of changes in the bankruptcy code and provided for the appointment of a National Bankruptcy Review Commission, whose mandate was to determine whether yet more changes were needed.

People filing for personal bankruptcy, which is the subject of this case study, may do so under either Chapter 7 or Chapter 13 of the bankruptcy code, subject to the approval of a bankruptcy judge. Under Chapter 7, a person is required to sell all of his or her eligible assets (work tools and home furnishings are exempted). The proceeds are then allocated among those owed unsecured credit, such as credit card companies and hospitals. Secured credit—as for cars and houses—is handled separately. In contrast, under the more stringent Chapter 13, the debtor is required to restructure her debt and work out a plan to repay as much of her debt as possible over a three- to five-year period. Assuming that the debtor can do this, creditors will recover more of their money under Chapter 13 proceedings.

Since the early 1980s, personal bankruptcy filings, which constitute more than 95 percent of total filings, have greatly increased (see Table 4.1). Solid evidence on how to explain the increase is lacking. It is indisputable that buying on credit has become part of the American way of life and that the use of credit cards has increased exponentially. A Federal Reserve Board study found that only 15 percent of Americans possessed credit cards like Visa and MasterCard in 1970. In 1983, 43 percent did; in 1998, 68 percent carried cards.[73] As one would expect, consumer debt skyrocketed.

Many argue that personal crises—divorce, job loss, and major illness among them—have caused many people to be unable to pay their debts and consequently to choose to file for bankruptcy. Other proffered explanations include the consequences of legalized gambling; the increased social

TABLE 4.1
Personal Bankruptcy Filings, 1980–2012

Year	Filings
1980	287,570
1985	341,233
1990	718,107
1995	874,107
1996	1,125,006
1997	1,260,118
1998	1,398,182
1999	1,281,581
2000	1,217,972
2001	1,452,030
2002	1,539,111
2003	1,625,208
2004	1,563,145
2005	2,039,214
2006	597,265
2007	822,590
2008	1,064,927
2009	1,412,838
2010	1,536,799
2011	1,362,847
2012 (est.)	1,300,000

Source: American Bankruptcy Institute.

acceptability (or decreased social stigma) of bankruptcy; a large number of small, independent-business failures; and aggressive advertising by bankruptcy attorneys seeking clients. Many place some of the blame on creditors themselves and their profligate distribution of credit cards, even to unemployed college students with no credit history.

In its 1999 final report, the National Bankruptcy Review Commission said that the rise in consumer bankruptcies was probably "more a function of a changing debt structure [on the part of consumers] than a sudden willingness to take advantage of the bankruptcy system." The commission noted that between 1977 and 1997, consumer debt had increased by nearly 700 percent. It recommended many limited changes in the bankruptcy code to block both creditor and debtor abuses.[74]

Undeterred by the commission's report, creditor groups launched an intense campaign to get Congress to make major changes in the bankruptcy code.[75] They most strongly wanted provisions for "means testing" that would herd many people into filing under Chapter 13 rather than Chapter 7. Banks, credit card companies, retailers, and other lenders, many allied in the National Consumer Bankruptcy Coalition, vigorously lobbied members of Congress. Campaign contributions flowed in generous quantities to both parties, amounting to hundreds of millions of dollars over a six-year period.[76] Opinion polls showing public support for bankruptcy reform were commissioned, as were studies on the costs of bankruptcy. Newspaper advertising trumpeted dubious claims like "Today's record number of personal bankruptcies costs every American family $400 a year." As a likely consequence of all of this, bankruptcy reform became a top item on the congressional agenda. Its strong bipartisan support includes practically all Republicans and a substantial contingent of Democrats.

The legislative struggle over consumer bankruptcy got underway in 1997. Legislation was sponsored in the House by Representative George Gekas (R, Pennsylvania) and in the Senate by Charles Grassley (R, Iowa) and Richard Durbin (D, Illinois). Both bills were intended to make it more difficult for people to file for bankruptcy under Chapter 7, although the "means test" used for this purpose was more stringent in the House bill. The Senate bill provided more protection for consumers, as in a provision requiring credit card companies to tell a borrower in every monthly statement how long it would take to pay off the balance if only the minimum payment was made each month.[77]

The House acted first, passing its bill in June 1998 by a vote of 306 to118. No Republicans voted against the bill whereas eighty-four Democrats voted in favor. The Senate followed in September, passing its bill by a 97-to-1 vote. Many Democrats supported it because of its consumer-protection provisions. The conference committee that met to resolve differences in the two bills was dominated by the Republicans, who stripped many of the consumer-protection provisions from the compromise version, even though the Clinton administration threatened a veto if the bill was too hard on borrowers. Because of the conference committee action, Senator Durbin now opposed the bill.

The House adopted the conference committee report, 300 to 125. Because of Democratic opposition and end-of-the-sessions pressures, the Senate never voted on the conference report. The Republicans proposed that the measure be included in an omnibus appropriations bill that was moving through Congress. This ploy failed because the Clinton administration insisted on changes in the means test that creditors would not accept.[78]

The consumer bankruptcy struggle was renewed during the 106th Congress (1999–2000). The House Judiciary Committee quickly reported a bankruptcy bill similar to the previous bill. On May 5, 1999, the bill passed the House, 331 to 108, after some consumer-friendly amendments to it were adopted. For example, credit card companies were required to state when initial low "teaser" interest rates would expire and what higher rate of interest would then apply.

The Senate Judiciary Committee reported a bankruptcy bill on April 14 by a 14-to-4 vote. Bipartisan support was achieved by leaving some issues, such as information disclosure by credit card companies, unresolved. The bill encountered major difficulty when it was targeted by proponents of several nongermane amendments, including an increase in the minimum wage. Not until February 2000 was the Senate able to act on the bankruptcy bill, which it then easily passed, 83 to 14. However, the bill included controversial provisions raising the minimum wage to $6.15 an hour over three years and providing $18.4 billion in tax cuts, mostly for small businesses. These were opposed by the White House.[79] The Senate bill imposed fewer restrictions on bankruptcy filers than did the House bill.

In time, Senate leaders were able to disentangle the minimum-wage and tax provisions from the bankruptcy bill. Then they confronted the task of reaching agreement with the House. Two issues—the Schumer Amendment and the homestead exemption—were major sticking points.

An amendment to the Senate bill proposed by Senator Charles Schumer (D, New York) barred protestors at abortion clinics from declaring bankruptcy to avoid paying fines or other financial judgments imposed on them. Republicans argued that it was unfair to single out abortion protestors. Representative Henry Hyde (R, Illinois) sponsored an amendment that provides that any individual convicted of "willful and malicious" acts of violence in any venue should be unable to use bankruptcy to discharge debts resulting from those actions. This was acceptable to Republican leaders but not to many Democrats, who argued that it would be too difficult to enforce. It was also opposed by President Bill Clinton.

The homestead exemption in the bankruptcy code permits many debtors to protect home equity from creditors. The limits are set by the states and in most range from $40,000 down to zero. However, in five states—Florida, Iowa, Kansas, South Dakota, and Texas—there is no limit. As a consequence, Texas and Florida have developed reputations as havens for wealthy bankruptcy filers. (There has been no great urge to relocate to the other three states). An example is the often-cited case of movie actor Burt Reynolds, who used a bankruptcy proceeding to shed $8 million of debt while retaining title to his $2.5 million Florida mansion. The conference committee set the cap on the homestead exemption at $100,000, but only for homes bought within two years of a bankruptcy filing. Many, including the president, saw this as a loop-hole and favored a limit with no conditions.

The House approved the conference committee report by a voice vote on October 12. Because of delaying tactics by the conference report's opponents, the Senate Republican leaders were not able to get a vote on it until near the session's end on December 7. It was approved, 70 to 28. Called the Bankruptcy Reform Act of 2000, it was pocket-vetoed by President Clinton after Congress adjourned. In addition to the absence of the Schumer Amendment and the nature of the homestead exemption, Clinton objected to the bill because it would put too much pressure on low-income families.

Round three of the consumer bankruptcy struggle began in January 2001. The situation looked favorable to the proponents of bankruptcy overhaul because President George W. Bush pledged to sign the bill when it reached him. Bills similar to the one vetoed by President Clinton were introduced in the House and Senate. The "means test" included in them provided that persons filing for bankruptcy would have to use Chapter 13 if they had incomes sufficient to repay 25 percent of their debt or $10,000, whichever was less, over five years. However, debtors who earned less than the state median income would be exempt and could file under Chapter 7.

The House Judiciary Committee, after acting to block amendments to the bill, approved it by a 19-to-8 vote. On March 1, following rejection of a Democratic substitute more friendly to debtors, the House passed the bill, 306 to 108. In the Senate Judiciary Committee, the Republicans sought to speed up floor action by cutting deals with the Democrats. A compromise was reached on the Schumer Amendment. Now, rather than specifically mention-ing abortion protestors, it referred to the 1994 Freedom of Access to Clinics Act, which made obstructing access to abortion clinics a federal crime.

The bankruptcy bill reached the Senate floor early in March. Republican leaders were able to defeat almost all amendments to the bill, which passed by an 83 to 15 margin after the Senate had voted, 80 to 19, to close debate. Republican leaders in the two houses had hoped to be able to avoid a conference committee. House Republican leaders, however, indicated that the Schumer Amendment was objectionable to them. House Republicans opposed to abortion rights were expected to try to remove the provision in the conference committee. That, however, would increase Democratic objections to the entire bill. Another sticking point was an amendment to the Senate bill putting a $125,000 limit on a house, whenever purchased, that could be shielded from bankruptcy. This was strongly opposed by Florida and Texas legislators.[80] No surprise here.

Moving the bankruptcy bill to conference was delayed by a Senate dis-agreement because of its membership. The Senate was evenly split, 50–50, between the parties; the Democrats insisted on an even split of all seats on conference committees; the Republicans said they were entitled to at least a one-seat edge over the Democrats. This logjam was finally broken in June, when the Democrats took over the Senate, following Senator James Jeffords's (I, Vermont) departure from the Republican Party. Democratic leader Senator Tom Daschle (D, South Dakota), a supporter of the bankruptcy bill, pledged to get the bill passed.

The conference committee was scheduled to meet on September 12. That meeting was put off, however, because of the September 11 terrorist attacks. Then, as the economy lapsed into recession, some members of Congress, notably Democrats, lost some of their enthusiasm for cracking down on debtors.[81] Consequently, not until November 14 did the conference committee meet, and then no real bargaining was done. Staff members of the House and Senate Judiciary Committees then began working to resolve differences between the houses. Neither side was willing to give much ground on the homestead exemption, in which the House favored a two-year time limit, and the Schumer Amendment.

In April 2002, House and Senate negotiators were finally able to resolve the homestead exemption issue. It was agreed that no more than $125,000 in home equity could be shielded from creditors when the home had been bought less than forty months prior to the bankruptcy filing. Prompted by the collapse of the Enron Corporation, the time limit was denied to persons convicted of felonies and securities fraud.

The abortion issue was not resolved, however, because of the intransigence of Senator Schumer and Representative Hyde, who were backed by the Senate Democrats and House Republicans, respectively. Each "offered compromise versions of the abortion provision that would narrow it to cover only certain intentional criminal acts against abortion clinics. But they disagree[d] on the wording and the crimes that would be covered."[82] A meeting of the conference committee in late May adjourned without being able to settle the issue. Despite renewed pressure from the financial interests, who feared their hopes would be again dashed, the stalemate persisted on into the summer.

Finally, in late July, Schumer and Hyde were able to reach agreement. The wording of the bill was tweaked by removing "reproductive health services" and substituting general language ensuring that abortion clinic protesters could not hide behind the bankruptcy laws. The way now appeared clear for enactment of the bankruptcy-reform bill.

The compromise provision on abortion clinic protesters was not acceptable to a bloc of eighty-seven antiabortion House Republicans, however. They joined with House Democrats who opposed the bill as being anticonsumer to reject it by a 243-to-172 vote. The Senate Democratic leadership refused to consider a bill not including the abortion-protestor provision.[83] Once more bankruptcy overhaul failed to win adoption because of an extraneous issue.

Round four of the bankruptcy struggle took place during the 108th Congress (2003–2004). Early in 2003, by a 315-to-113 margin, the House passed a bankruptcy-reform bill without the abortion-protestor provision. Senator Schumer announced that he would try to attach this provision to the Senate bill. Supporters of bankruptcy reform were hopeful that with the Republicans in control of the Senate this action could be blocked.[84] They were unsuccessful.

In January 2004, in an attempt to spur Senate action, the House attached the personal bankruptcy-reform bill to a Senate-passed bill renewing bankruptcy protection only for farmers and requested a conference.[85] This ploy failed, and the bankruptcy bill remained bottled up in the Senate Judiciary Committee. Thus, the 108th Congress adjourned without passage of the bankruptcy bill, again to the dismay of business and financial groups.

The fifth round of the bankruptcy battle got underway quickly in the 109th Congress (2005–2006). Prospects for the legislation were enhanced by the fifty-five-member Republican Senate majority resulting from the 2004 congressional elections. The Senate Judiciary Committee reported the bankruptcy bill, now titled the Bankruptcy Abuse Prevention and Consumer Protection Act, in February; it was considered on the Senate floor in March. Democratic amendments to ease the bill's impact on senior citizens and on persons with catastrophic medical expenses were rejected, as was the Schumer Amendment on abortion protestors, the latter by a near-party-line vote of 46 to 53. The Senate then voted, 69 to 31, to invoke cloture, which guaranteed passage of the bill.[86] The vote on final passage was 74 to 25.

In the House, the Republican leadership's strategy was to pass the Senate bill without amendments, thereby obviating the need for a conference committee.[87] Consequently, the bill was reported out of the Judiciary Committee without change and debated on the House floor under a closed rule, much to the ire of some Democrats. The bill passed by a vote of 302 to 126; no Republican voted nay. President George W. Bush signed it into law in mid-April, saying it would "make our financial system stronger and better."

The Bankruptcy Abuse Prevention and Consumer Protection Act includes a "means test" providing that bankruptcy filers who earn more than their state's median income, and who can pay back at least $6,000 over five years after allowable expenses—for food, clothing, and other necessary matters—are deducted, must file under Chapter 13 rather than Chapter 7.[88] The homestead exemption is limited to $125,000 for homes purchased within forty months of filing. Beyond this limit, wealthy filers can buy large estates in Texas and Florida to protect assets. Another loophole, which also benefits the wealthy, permits people to set up "asset protection trusts," which are exempt from bankruptcy proceedings.

Other provisions make some debts—for alimony, child support, and student loans—nondischargeable; require most persons to receive credit counseling prior to filing; seek to prevent repeat bankruptcy filings; raise filing fees and paperwork requirements; and require credit card companies to provide more information on repayment practices.

After nine years of struggle, corporate financial interests finally prevailed over consumer interests. The profits of money lenders will rise; life becomes harder for debtors.[89]

Personal bankruptcy filings increased sharply in 2005 as those in financial difficulty rushed to gain relief before the new law became effective (See Table 4.1). Filings then declined only to surge beginning in 2008 because of the burst of the housing bubble and the onset of the Great Recession. Still, those who had supported the new law benefited because they fared better than they would have earlier. Corporations, of course, were better treated under other parts of the bankruptcy law. ■

CASE STUDY	*Policy Adoption: The Family Smoking Prevention and Tobacco Control Act*

Tobacco has been cultivated in the southeastern United States since early in the seventeenth century. The modern tobacco industry, featuring mass production and mass marketing of tobacco products, especially the increasingly popular cigarettes, developed in the latter part of the nineteenth century. It became vital to the economic well-being of the tobacco states.[90]

Tobacco has no value as food or fiber. It is an addictive product whose use is harmful and causes serious illness. But it was widely used for recreational purposes. As an old rhyme stated: "Some it chew, and some it smoke, and some it up their nose do poke." It was, however, an important source of income to tobacco farmers and a highly profitable product for tobacco companies.

In the twentieth century, medical research began to establish a positive link between smoking and illness.[91] The tobacco companies and their supporters, who dominated the political subsystem governing tobacco policy, fended off regulatory efforts. They were joined by tobacco growers who benefited from a price-support program put in place by Congress in 1933.

In 1964, however, an event occurred which would produce major change in tobacco politics. In January, 1964, the Surgeon General of the United States released the report of his expert Advisory Committee on Smoking and Health. In a nutshell, the Advisory Committee found a strong tie between smoking and cancer and other illnesses.

The report of the Surgeon General's Committee launched a campaign against the tobacco industry that is ongoing.[92] In 1965, Congress adopted the Cigarette Labeling and Advertising Act, which required health warnings on cigarette packages. It banned other regulation of the industry for four years. Then in 1970, legislation banned cigarette advertising on radio and television. More restrictions began to be imposed on tobacco. Smoking bans on commercial air flights, in public places, in schools, and elsewhere were instituted.

In 1994, Commissioner David Kessler of the Food and Drug Administration (FDA) announced an intention to regulate cigarettes because of their addictive character from nicotine. Two years later, the FDA issued its regulations, which prohibited the sale of cigarettes to persons under eighteen and banned various forms of advertising, labeling, promotion, and event sponsorship. The FDA's regulations were immediately challenged in the federal courts by Big Tobacco. The U.S. Supreme Court in 2000 ruled that the FDA lacked authority under the Food, Drug, and Cosmetic Act to do this.[93]

The campaign against tobacco by public health advocates and anti-tobacco activists in time bore fruit. The number of smokers declined and the demand for tobacco fell accordingly. Tobacco farmers became worried about their economic future. Tobacco opponents saw an opportunity to pry the farmers away from the tobacco companies. A deal was put together. A buyout to end the tobacco price support program was combined with a smoking regulatory program run by the FDA. The Senate, in July 2004, added a buyout and regulatory program to a tax relief bill, which passed by a vote of 78 to 15. The House Republicans, always concerned with the well-being of corporate interests, refused to go along. The regulatory program was excised from the bill; the buyout took effect. A consequence was a substantial reduction in the ranks of tobacco farmers and a lessening of their political influence.

A few years passed. The Democrats regained control of the House in 2007 and renewed their push for the regulation of tobacco. Although few would now argue that tobacco was not a dangerous product or publicly defend the tobacco business, there were those (mostly Republicans) willing to defend the companies' interests. A regulatory bill cleared the House Committee on Energy and Commerce and passed in the House in July, 2008 by a 362-to-102 vote. In the Senate, it received approval of the Health, Education, Labor, and Pensions (HELP) Committee but was never brought to the floor before Congress adjourned in late 2008. The Bush administration had threatened a veto, but tobacco companies with the exception of Phillip Morris (the largest company) were stoutly opposed, and opposition led by "Tobacco Road" Senator Richard Burr (R, North Carolina) produced inaction.[94]

When 2009 dawned, the Democrats controlled both houses of Congress and the Presidency. Early in the year, the House Committees on Energy and Commerce and Oversight and Government Reform approved a bill empowering the FDA to regulate tobacco marketing and advertising, to regulate or reduce nicotine levels but not to outlaw nicotine, and to require tobacco companies to reduce the harmful effects of their products. Most of the cost of the program would be covered by user fees on tobacco products.[95]

In April, the House passed the bill by a vote of 298 to 112. A Republican alternative was rejected by 142 to 284. It would have lodged authority to regulate tobacco in a "Tobacco Harm Reduction Center" in the Department of Health and Human Services rather than the FDA. Also, rather than restricting advertising, it would have provided for studying the issue. Other amendments were also defeated.[96]

Action now shifted to the Senate HELP committee, where an amended tobacco control bill was approved 15 to 8. A major substitute amendment had fallen by 9 to 13. Supported by Senator Burr, who continued to fight control, it would have created a Federal Tobacco Regulatory Authority as an independent agency. Also, it would have permitted easier market access for reduced-risk products such as "smokeless tobacco." On the other hand, it would have allowed marketing and advertising restrictions and required disclosure of tobacco product ingredients.[97] Even tobacco's supporters now acknowledged the need for some regulation.

Two weeks were spent debating the bill on the Senate floor because its opponents did not give up readily. Various weakening amendments, such as one to create an independent "tobacco harm reeducation center," were proposed and defeated. Senate Majority Leader Harry Reid (D, Nevada) had to use three cloture votes—to bring the bill to the floor, to limit debate on an amendment, and on the bill itself—to get the bill passed. The final vote was 79 to 17.[98] The next day (June 12), the House agreed to the Senate bill, 307 to 97. President Obama, a sometime smoker, signed it into law, ending two decades of legislative struggle between tobacco forces and anti-smoking activists.

We turn now to a short summary of the Family Smoking Prevention and Tobacco Control Act. It creates a Center for Tobacco Products within the FDA to handle implementation. Authority is bestowed on the FDA to regulate the sale, distribution, advertising, production, and use of tobacco products to protect the public health. The FDA can regulate nicotine levels and set product standards to eliminate harmful ingredients. It cannot, however, totally ban either nicotine or tobacco products. Warning labels are required on tobacco packages and advertisements. Moreover, terms such as "light," "mild," or "low tar" can no longer appear on labels or in ads. Tobacco products can no longer contain flavorings like chocolate, grape, orange, or cherry, which were thought to make cigarettes more enticing to young people. At the insistence of the Congressional Black Caucus, menthol was accepted, however. A substantial portion of black smokers apparently prefer menthol cigarettes. Much of the funding to implement FSPTCA is provided by user fees levied on the producers and importers of tobacco products.[99]

Having just lost in the legislative arena, the tobacco companies (other than Phillip Morris) shifted to the judicial arena, which, given the American policy process and our litigious political culture, should not startle anyone. The requirement of sharp and graphic warnings on cigarette packages was attacked as a violation of commercial freedom of speech protected by the First Amendment. This contention was upheld by the Court of Appeals for the D.C. Circuit in November 2011. Earlier, another court of appeals had upheld the constitutionality of FSPTCA. This makes it likely that the U.S. Supreme Court will decide the issue.[100] Those who benefit from profitable activities do not give up easily. ■

For Further Exploration

▌ *http://www.gallup.com*

The Gallup Organization's website contains public-opinion survey results on many issues, such as presidential approval, the state of the economy, and various policy issues currently affecting the country.

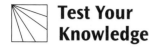

Test Your Knowledge

Log on to the student companion website at

login.cengage.com

to access tutorial quizzes, chapter outlines, crossword puzzles, and glossary flashcards that review chapter concepts and terminology.

Suggested Readings

Barbara Sinclair, *Unorthodox Lawmaking: New Legislative Processes in the U.S. Congress*, 2nd ed. (Washington, DC: CQ Press, 2000). General analysis and case studies are used in this book to demonstrate that the legislative process often departs from the textbook model.

Deborah Stone, *Policy Paradox: The Art of Political Decision Making* (New York: Norton, 1998). Readable, insightful, theoretical, and stimulating, this book looks at goals, problems, and solutions in the policy process.

Diana Evans, *Greasing the Wheels* (New York: Cambridge University Press, 2004). Evans provides a savvy analysis of the use of pork barrel projects to build congressional coalitions.

Graham T. Allison and Philip Zelikow, *Essence of Decision: Explaining the Cuban Missile Crisis*, 2nd ed. (New York: Longman, 1999). This edition, which draws on recently available evidence, examines decision-making from the rational actor, organizational process, and governmental politics perspectives.

Michael T. Hayes, *Incrementalism and Public Policy* (New York: Longman, 1992). Several major policymaking models are examined here as the sources of incrementalism. Nonincremental policy change is also treated.

Notes

1. Louis Fisher, *Constitutional Conflicts Between Congress and the President*, 4th ed., revised (Lawrence, KS: University Press of Kansas, 1997), pp. 152–159.
2. David H. Rosenblum and James D. Carroll, eds., *Toward Constitutional Competence: A Casebook for Administrators* (Englewood Cliffs, NJ: Prentice-Hall, 1990), pp. 54–56.
3. The leading proponent of incrementalism undoubtedly is Charles Lindblom. See his "The Science of Muddling Through," *Public Administration Review*, XIX (1959), pp. 79–88; *The Intelligence of Democracy* (New York: Macmillan, 1964); *The Policy-Making Process* (Englewood Cliffs, NJ: Prentice-Hall, 1964); and, with David Braybrook, *The Strategy of Decision* (New York: Free Press, 1963).

4. This summary draws primarily on Lindblom's "The Science of Muddling Through," op. cit, and *The Intelligence of Democracy*, op. cit., pp. 144–148. See also Charles E. Lindblom, "Still Muddling, Not Yet Through," *Public Administration Review*, XLIX (November–December 1979), pp. 517–526.

5. Michael T. Hayes, *Incrementalism and Public Policy* (New York: Longman, 1992), Chap. 2.

6. Amitai Etzioni, "Mixed Scanning: A 'Third' Approach to Decision-Making," *Public Administration Review*, XXVII (December 1967), pp. 385–392.

7. Ibid., p. 389.

8. This paragraph relies on David S. Rosenbloom and Robert S. Kravchuk, *Public Administration*, 5th ed. (New York: McGraw-Hill, 2002), p. 369.

9. A classic study is Herbert Kaufman, *The Forest Ranger: A Study in Administrative Behavior* (Baltimore, MD: Johns Hopkins University Press, 1960).

10. Daniel McCool, *Command of the Waters* (Berkeley, CA: University of California Press, 1987).

11. Marc Allen Eisner, Jeff Worsham, and Evan J. Ringquist, *Contemporary Regulatory Policy* (Boulder, CO: Lynne Rienner Publishers, 2000), Chap. 4.

12. Robert B. Reich, ed., *The Power of Public Ideas* (Cambridge, MA: Ballinger, 1988).

13. Gary R. Orren, "Beyond Self-Interest," ibid., p. 24.

14. Lee Epstein and Jack Knight, *The Choices Justices Make* (Washington, DC: CQ Press, 1998).

15. This paragraph draws on Charles Funderburk and Robert G. Thobaben, *Political Ideologies: Left, Center, Right*, 2nd ed. (New York: HarperCollins, 1994), Chap. 5. The quotation is on p. 113.

16. Roger H. Davidson and Walter J. Oleszek, *Congress and Its Member*, 8th ed. (Washington, DC: CQ Press, 2002), pp. 274–277.

17. Harold W. Stanley and Richard G. Niemi, *Vital Statistics on American Politics, 1999–2000* (Washington, DC: CQ Press, 2000), p. 211.

18. Davidson and Oleszek, op. cit., pp. 275–276.

19. David W. Brady, "Congressional Leadership and Party Voting in the McKinley Era: A Comparison to the Modern House," *Midwest Journal of Political Science*, XVI (August 1972), pp. 439–441.

20. Richard Rose, *Do Parties Make a Difference?* 2nd ed. (Chatham, NJ: Chatham House, 1984), pp. 74–91; and Edward Crowe, "Consensus and Structure in Legislative Norms: Party Discipline in the House of Commons," *Journal of Politics*, XLV (August 1983), pp. 907–931.

21. C. K. Rowland and Robert A. Carp, *Politics and Judgment in Federal Courts* (Lawrence, KS: University Press of Kansas, 1996), Chap. 2.

22. Discussions of the concept of representation can be found in John C. Wahlke et al., *The Legislative System* (New York: Wiley, 1962), Chap. 12; and Leroy N. Reiselbach, *Congressional Politics*, 2nd ed. (Boulder, CO: Westview Press, 1995), Chap. 17.

23. See, for example, Peter Woll, *American Bureaucracy*, 2nd ed. (New York: Norton, 1977).

24. Michael Kinsley, "The Intellectual Free Lunch," *The New Yorker*, Vol. 71 (February 6, 1995), p. 4. See also Richard Morin, "Tuned Out, Turned Off: Millions of Americans Know Little About How Their Government Works," *Washington Post Weekly Edition*, February 5–11, 1996, pp. 6–7.

25. Alan S. Blinder, *After the Music Stopped: The Financial Crisis, the Response, and the Work Ahead* (New York: Penguin Press, 2013), pp. 128 and Chap. 7. Blinder was a former vice chairman of the Federal Reserve Board.

26. Benjamin I. Page and Robert Y. Shapiro, *The Rational Public: Fifty Years of Trends in Americans' Policy Preference* (Chicago, IL: University of Chicago Press, 1992), p. 394.
27. V. O. Key Jr., *Public Opinion and American Democracy* (New York: Knopf, 1961), p. 14.
28. Ibid., pp. 81–90.
29. Cf. John E. Mueller, "Trends in Popular Support for the Wars in Korea and Vietnam," *American Political Science Review*, LXV (June 1971), pp. 358–375.
30. Thomas Patterson, *The American Democracy*, 3rd ed. (New York: McGraw-Hill, 1996), pp. 147–148.
31. Cf. Robert J. Spitzer, *The Politics of Gun Control* (Chatham, NJ: Chatham House, 1995), p. 118.
32. Larry M. Bartels, *Unequal Democracy* (Princeton, NJ: Princeton University Press, 2008), p. 3.
33. Nick Kotz, *Let Them Eat Promises: The Politics of Hunger in America* (Englewood Cliffs, NJ: Prentice-Hall, 1969).
34. Donald R. Matthews and James A. Stimson, "The Decision-Making Approach to the Study of Legislative Behavior." Unpublished paper presented at the annual meeting of the American Political Science Association (September 1969), p. 19.
35. Robert H. Salisbury, *Governing America: Public Choice and Political Action* (New York: Appleton-Century-Crofts, 1973), p. 237. Chapter 13 includes a very useful treatment of decision-making.
36. Robert A. Carp and Ronald Stidham, *The Federal Courts* (Washington, DC: Congressional Quarterly Press, 1985), p. 57.
37. Richard F. Fenno Jr., *Congressmen in Committees* (Boston, MA: Little, Brown, 1973), pp. 48–75.
38. Mark R. Powell, *Science at EPA: Information in the Regulatory Process* (Washington, DC: Resources for the Future, 1999), Chap. 2.
39. Samuel P. Hays, *Beauty, Health, and Permanence* (New York: Cambridge University Press, 1987), p. 331.
40. Robert F. Durant, Daniel J. Fiorino, and Rosemary O'Leary eds., *Environmental Governance Reconsidered* (Cambridge, MA: MIT Press, 2004), Chap. 3.
41. See Michelle Morone and Timothy W. Lohner, *Sound Science, Junk Science: Environmental and Health Science and the Decisionmaking Process* (Westport, CT: Greenwood Publishing Group, 2002). See also Chris Mooney, *The Republican War on Science* (New York: Basic Books, 2005).
42. Charles W Anderson, "The Place of Principles in Policy Analysis," *American Political Science Review*, LXXIII (September 1979), p. 718.
43. Emmette S. Redford, *Ideal and Practice in Public Administration* (Tuscaloosa, AL: University of Alabama Press, 1957), Chap. 5.
44. Cf. Robert E. Goodin, "Institutionalizing the Public Interest: The Defense of Deadlock and Beyond," *American Political Science Review*, XC (June 1996), pp. 331–343. See also Clarke E. Cochran, "Political Science and the Public Interest," *Journal of Politics*, XXXVI (May 1974), pp. 327–355.
45. Walter Lippmann, *The Phantom Public* (New York: Harcourt, Brace, 1925), p. 105. Cf. Frank J. Sorauf, "The Public Interest Reconsidered," *Journal of Politics*, XIX (November 1957), pp. 616–639.
46. Richard E. Neustadt, "White House and Whitehall," *The Public Interest* (Winter 1966), pp. 55–69.
47. As quoted in Roger Hilsman, *The Politics of Policy Making in Defense and Foreign Affairs* (New York: Harper & Row, 1971), p. 1.

48. *The Economist*, January 26, 2013, pp. 43–44.
49. *The New York Times*, March 15, 2013, p. A9.
50. Robert A. Dahl and Charles E. Lindblom, *Politics, Economics, and Welfare* (New York: Harper & Row, 1953), p. 328. Chapters 12 and 13 present a thorough and insightful discussion of bargaining in American politics.
51. Lewis A. Froman Jr., *People and Politics* (Englewood Cliffs, NJ: Prentice-Hall, 1962), pp. 56–57.
52. Jeffrey H. Birnbaum and Alan S. Murray, *Showdown at Gucci Gulch* (New York: Random House, 1987), pp. 146, 240–243.
53. *The New York Times*, September 20, 1986, p. 24.
54. Peter Burnell and Andrew Reeve, "Persuasion as a Political Concept," *British Journal of Political Studies*, XIV (October 1984), pp. 393–410.
55. Quoted in Richard E. Neustadt, *Presidential Power* (New York: Wiley, 1960), pp. 9–10.
56. Morton H. Halperin, *Bureaucratic Politics and Foreign Policy* (Washington, DC: Brookings Institution, 1974), p. 282.
57. Neustadt, op. cit., Chap. 3.
58. Dan Nimmo and Thomas D. Ungs, *American Political Patterns*, 2nd ed. (Boston, MA: Little, Brown, 1969), p. 367.
59. Davidson and Oleszek, op. cit., p. 228.
60. A good discussion of congressional procedures can be found in Walter J. Oleszak, *Congressional Procedures and the Policy Process*, 5th ed. (Washington, DC: Brookings Institution, 2001), Chaps. 5–8.
61. See Sarah A. Binder and Steven S. Smith, *Politics or Principle: Filibustering in the United States Senate* (Washington, DC: Brookings Institution Press, 1997) and Gregory Koger, *Filibustering: A Political History of Obstruction in the House and Senate* (Chicago, IL: University of Chicago Press, 2010).
62. Thomas E. Mann and Norman J. Ornstein, *It's Even Worse than It Looks* (New York: Basic Books, 2012), pp. 84–98.
63. Ezra Klein, "Let's Talk," *The New Yorker*, January 28, 2013, pp. 24 ff; *The New York Times*, January 24, 2013, p. 16A; and January 25, 2013, p. 18A.
64. Norman C. Thomas, Joseph A. Pika, and Richard A. Watson, *The Politics of the Presidency*, 3rd ed. (Washington, DC: CQ Press, 1993), pp. 258–262. See also General Accounting Office, *National Security: The Use of Presidential Directives to Make and Implement U.S. Policy* (Washington, DC: USGAO, December 1988).
65. Douglas Irwin, *From Smoot-Hawley to Reciprocal Trade Agreements*.
66. Kenneth R. Meyer, *With the Stroke of a Pen, Executive Orders and Presidential Power* (Princeton, NJ: Princeton University Press, 2001). Cf. Ruth P. Morgan, *The President and Civil Rights: Policy-Making by Executive Order* (New York: St. Martin's, 1970).
67. In this discussion, I draw on an insightful little book by Theodore C. Sorensen, *Decision-Making in the White House* (New York: Columbia University Press, 1963). Sorensen served as Special Counsel to President John F. Kennedy.
68. Cf. George Reedy, *The Twilight of the Presidency*, 2nd ed. (New York: New American Library, 1987).
69. See Graham Allisons classic study, *The Essence of Decision: Explaining the Cuban Missile Crisis* (Boston, MA: Little, Brown, 1971).
70. Sorensen, op. cit., p. 29.
71. Paul C. Light, *The President's Agenda*, 3rd ed. (Baltimore, MD: Johns Hopkins University Press, 1999), pp. 36–38, 60.

72. George C. Edwards III and Stephen J. Wayne, *Presidential Leadership: Politics and Policy-Making*, 5th ed. (New York: St. Martin's, 1999), p. 246.
73. *Wall Street Journal*, May 22, 2001, p. 1.
74. *Final Report*, National Bankruptcy Review Commission (Washington, DC: October 20, 1997), Chap. 1.
75. *Wall Street Journal*, June 17, 1998, pp. 1, 9; Donald L. Bartlett and James B. Steele, "Soaked by Congress," *Time*, May 15, 2000, pp. 64–75.
76. *Wall Street Journal*, May 8, 2002, p. A4.
77. *Congressional Quarterly Weekly Report*, Vol. 58 (October 10, 1998), p. 2746.
78. *Congressional Quarterly Weekly Report*, Vol. 58 (November 14, 1998), p. 3099.
79. *Congressional Quarterly Weekly Report*, Vol. 60 (February 5, 2000), p. 243.
80. *Wall Street Journal*, March 16, 2001, p. A3.
81. *Congressional Quarterly Weekly Report*, Vol. 61 (November 17, 2001), p. 2743.
82. *Congressional Quarterly Weekly Report*, Vol. 60 (May 18, 2002), p. 1310.
83. *Wall Street Journal*, November 15, 2002, p. 1.
84. *The New York Times*, March 20, 2003, p. A24.
85. *CQ Weekly*, Vol. 62 (January 31, 2004), p. 297.
86. *The New York Times*, March 9, 2005, p. 1, and *Wall Street Journal*, March 8, 2005, p. 2.
87. *The New York Times*, April 15, 2005, p. 14; *Wall Street Journal*, April 5, 2005, p. 4.
88. Michael R. Crittenden, "Bankruptcy Bill Leaves Senate, Unscathed," *CQ Weekly*, Vol. 63 (March 14, 2005), pp. 652–653.
89. *Wall Street Journal*, April 4, 2005, p. 1. And also Paul Krugman, "The Debt-Peonage Society," *The New York Times*, March 8, 2005, p. A23.
90. *The Oxford Companion to United States History*, ed. Paul S. Boyer (New York: Oxford University Press, 2001), pp. 779–780.
91. A. Lee Fritschler and Catherine E. Rudder, *Smoking and Politics*, 6th ed. (Upper Saddle River, NJ: Prentice-Hall, 2011), Chap. 2.
92. Martha A. Derthick, *Up in Smoke*, 3rd ed. (Washington, DC: CQ Press, 2012).
93. *Food and Drug Administration v. Brown S. Williamson Tobacco Corp.*, 529 U.S. 120 (2000).
94. *CQ Weekly*, Vol. 66 (April 7, 2008), pp. 886–887.
95. *CQ Weekly*, Vol. 67 (March 23, 2009), p. 678.
96. *CQ Weekly*, Vol. 67 (April 6, 2009), p. 780.
97. *CQ Weekly*, Vol. 67 (June 15, 2009), pp. 1378–1379.
98. *CQ Almanac 2009* (Washington, DC: *CQ Roll Call Group*, 2010), pp. 174–176.
99. Ibid. Also Roseann B. Termini, "The Family Smoking Prevention and Tobacco Control Act and Public Health," *Pennsylvania Bar Association Quarterly* (October 2010), pp. 147–162.
100. http://en.wikipedia.org/wiki/Family_Smoking_Prevention_and_Tobacco_Control_Act.

5

Budgeting and Public Policy

U ntil the 1920s, national budgeting in the United States was a disjointed activity lacking central direction. On their own initiative, departments and agencies prepared their annual budget requests. These requests were then assembled by the Department of the Treasury, without alteration, in a book of estimates and transmitted to Congress for its consideration and enactment. The president typically had little to do with agency budget requests, either prior to or after their enactment. This haphazard and fragmented budgetary process was satisfactory because ample funds were available to finance the national government's limited array of agencies and programs. Indeed, in the later decades of the nineteenth century, the major financial problem confronting the government was how to spend all of the revenues produced by high protective tariffs so as to provide for their continued justification.

This rather idyllic situation evanesced after the turn of the century. The expansion of the national government's activities during the Progressive Era created strong pressures on the national revenue system. The level of government expenditures soared upward during World War I, and following the Armistice, remained above pre-war levels. These changed conditions generated pressure for budget reform. The executive budget, whereby the chief executive in a government has responsibility for budget formulation, was identified as an appropriate corrective measure.

After several years of study, reports, deliberation, and political struggle, Congress enacted legislation creating an executive budget, only to have it vetoed by President Woodrow Wilson. The next year it was again adopted and signed into law by President Warren G. Harding, as the Budget and Accounting Act of 1921. The executive budget came into being. Support for it emanated from two disparate sources. Conservatives and businessmen (obviously there was much overlap) supported it as a means of retrenchment, or reducing governmental spending. Democrats, liberals, and reformers viewed the executive budget as a way of achieving more with a given level of expenditures, as a way of increasing government effectiveness.

180

The Budget and Accounting Act delegated authority to the president to annually prepare a budget and submit it for Congress's approval. Agencies were prohibited from submitting funding requests directly to Congress unless specifically requested to do so. (In the 1970s, displeased with the Nixon administration, Congress adopted legislation directing several agencies to submit their budget requests concurrently to itself and the executive.)[1] The Bureau of the Budget (BOB) (now the Office of Management and Budget) was created to assist the president in budget preparation, and the General Accounting Office was set up to handle the auditing of expenditures. Finally, each department and agency was directed to appoint a budget officer. Reform also occurred separately in the House of Representatives, where authority over appropriations bills, which previously had been scattered among several committees, was consolidated into a single appropriations committee. That had long been the practice in the Senate. Collectively, these reforms were designed to produce a more centralized budgeting system.

The discussion in this chapter has three purposes. First, how the budget and budget decisions affect public policies is discussed. Budgeting is a means, and a source of opportunities, for shaping the direction, intensity, and impact of public policies. Agency budgets may be expanded, cut back, or even "zeroed out." Many policy issues are examined and worked over in the budgetary process. Second, the structure and operation of the national budgetary process—its participants, procedures, and practices—are examined. This will cast light on how budgetary decisions are made and what influences them. Third, we discuss the political struggle to control the budget deficit and balance the national budget, which had temporary success in the period 1998 to 2001. Also of concern here is the national debt. Some call this *macrobudgeting*. In recent years, this has become intensely political and a major policy issue, partly symbolic, but of much importance for the operation of the economy.

The Budget and Public Policy

Once a policy or program has been legislatively authorized, its supporters cannot relax and rest content. Now they must strive to ensure that it is funded, and continues to be funded, at levels sufficient to guarantee satisfactory attainment of its goals. Conversely, opponents of the policy have annual opportunities to modify, cripple, or perhaps kill it by getting its funding reduced or eliminated. Consequently, once substantive legislation is enacted, the political struggle over a policy may be renewed in another arena during the appropriations process. Policy supporters must be vigilant, lest they be sandbagged in this arena.

Rare is the public policy that can be implemented without the expenditure of money. At a minimum, funding will be required for personnel, office space, equipment, travel, and other operating expenses. The rigor or effectiveness of antitrust, consumer product safety, banking regulations, industrial safety, and other regulatory programs depends on their levels of funding. Law Professor Thomas McGarity comments, "The business community discovered a long time ago that the best way to achieve regulatory relief is to starve the agencies' budgets while maintaining the appearance of a protective regime."

The control of illegal immigration, the maintenance of national parks, the conducting of medical research, national defense, and the collection of taxes by the Internal Revenue Service (IRS) are some activities that are significantly affected by funding levels. Increases in funding for the IRS, for instance, would enable it to collect hundreds of billions of dollars in taxes that are legally owed but go unpaid. Why not better funding for the IRS as a budget deficit reduction measure?

A stark example involves the Occupational Safety and Health Administration (OSHA), which has a legislative mandate to ensure that workplaces, which number in the hundreds of thousands, are safe and healthful. It has funding, however, only to hire enough inspectors to permit inspection of workplaces on the average of once in every ten years, at best. Twenty-five workers were killed in 1991 by a fire in a North Carolina food-processing plant. The building had no sprinklers, and the fire doors could not be opened from the inside. It had never been inspected by OSHA. In April 2013, the explosion of a chemical plant in the town of West, Texas, killed at least fourteen people and injured many more. It had not been inspected by OSHA since 1985.

Many important programs, such as Social Security, Medicare, Medicaid, and unemployment compensation primarily entail transfer payments— moving large sums of money from taxpayers to government and then to eligible beneficiaries, who spend it on goods and services in the private economy. Money is also central to the farm income-support, highway, AMTRAK, public-housing, medical-research, and Pell Grant programs. The proportion of low-income people who can receive housing assistance, for instance, depends on the amount of money made available for this purpose.

An example of how unfavorable budgetary action can cripple a policy involves noise control. In 1972, Congress passed the Noise Control Act in response to complaints about "noise pollution." The law authorized the Environmental Protection Agency (EPA) to issue and enforce standards reducing the noise coming from industrial and commercial vehicles and products (e.g., air compressors and jackhammers) when these adversely affected human health.[2] An Office of Noise Abatement and Control (ONAC) was set up in the EPA to implement the act. During the next several years, ONAC issued standards, coordinated noise research, and disseminated information. However, late in the 1970s, its efforts to reduce noise emanating from garbage trucks caused a major political stink and focused adverse attention on it.

The Reagan administration in 1981 decided to terminate funding specifically for ONAC, a decision acquiesced to by the EPA leadership and, in turn, by Congress. The ONAC, which lacked strong political allies, expired. Since then, next to nothing has been done by the EPA to carry out the Noise Control Act because the agency is strapped for resources to enforce its many other programs.[3] America continues to be a noisy society, though local governments sometimes act on the problem.

At the extreme, policies without funding become nullities. Thus, Congress killed the Cold War Subversive Activities Control Program, which was an expression of the anti-communism phobia of the time, not by repealing the legislation upon which it was based but rather by ceasing to appropriate funds for its operation. Although the Subversive Activities Control Board, which administered the program, had never succeeded in registering any subversive persons or organizations (e.g., the Communist Party), the program was a source of symbolic comfort for some conservatives and a source of employment for a few others for more than two decades.

Farm groups in 2002 finally secured the enactment of country of origin labeling (COOL) for meat products; fruits, vegetables, and nuts; and seafood. Intended to promote the sale of American products rather than protect consumers, it rested on the policy notion that, if informed, consumers would often choose domestic products over foreign products. Opponents were able to block its implementation until 2009 through riders in appropriations legislation.[4]

Here is another example. There has long been controversy over the slaughter of horses, whether for human food, pet food, or other purposes. Some Europeans have a taste for horse meat, but to Americans, horses are pets, not food. In 2007, a rider in an Agricultural Appropriations Act provided that funds could not be spent on the United States Department of Agriculture (USDA) inspection of plants slaughtering horses. Without inspection the plants could not operate. Seemingly, the protectors of horses had prevailed. In 2011, however, the rider mysteriously disappeared. The controversy over horse slaughter has resumed, albeit beyond the visibility of most people.

Money is not always trump, however. Some public policies entail little or no expenditure of money, or may even prohibit its expenditure. What can be called prohibitory policies—those which impose bans on such actions as fetal-tissue research, human cloning, prayer in the public schools, and the taking of some migratory birds—have sometimes produced major political controversies. Money is not really the issue here, nor is money involved in the Defense of Marriage Act (1996), in which Congress declared that a state does not legally have to recognize a same-sex marriage performed in another state.

Some of the policies discussed in this book—the War Powers Resolution, family and medical leaves, and personal bankruptcy—are little affected by budgetary action. These policies, and others similar to them, are unlikely to receive much attention in the budgetary process. They will usually be dealt with in other policy arenas.

The national budget has grown greatly in size and complexity in recent decades. In 1960, federal expenditures totaled $92.2 billion. When Lyndon Johnson became president in late 1964, he strove to keep the budget below the $100 billion milestone. By 2012 it had soared to over $3 trillion. Even when inflation is taken into account, the budget has more than quadrupled. New policies and programs have been added and existing programs expanded during these decades. In 1960, for example, Medicare and Medicaid did not exist; and Social Security outlays were quite modest, since many people died before reaching retirement age, especially those in the working class.

Much of the growth in expenditures is accounted for by a few policy areas—national defense, social and income security, medical care, and interest on the national debt. Table 5.1 portrays expenditure patterns for several functional (or policy) areas from 1950 to 2010. It deserves a close look. In addition to providing details on major areas of spending and growth, the table indicates how spending patterns vary with changing policy preferences. The jump in natural-resource spending in the 1970s reflects the politics of environmental concern and the proliferation of environmental-protection policies. Also in the 1970s, the energy crises triggered greater spending on energy-development programs. Then, as worries about energy supplies, especially oil, faded in the 1980s, and the Reagan administration put more reliance on the private market, energy spending diminished markedly. Spending for Medicare, which went into effect in 1966, has soared because of strong support for the program, an increasing number of eligible persons, and rapidly rising medical costs.

Table 5.1 also indicates that a small set of government activities—national defense, income security, Social Security, Medicare, and the payment of interest on the national debt—account for three-fourths of total national spending. Most of these activities involve direct spending (see the following discussion) and have a lot of political support or, in the case of interest payments on the national debt, cannot be avoided. This structural feature of the national budget looms as a major obstacle to those wanting to reduce government spending.

Until the 1960s, most governmental expenditures paid the direct costs of operating government agencies and programs. Taxpayer dollars were used mostly to pay the salaries of government employees, buy vehicles and equipment, cover rent and building-maintenance costs, and the like. Consequently, most people were at best indirectly affected by budget decisions. Whether appropriations were increased for the Department of Commerce or sharply cut for the foreign-aid program had little bearing on the lives of people in Des Moines, Detroit, Dayton, or Dixon. No longer does government spending have this distant or abstract quality. Now, much of the budget goes directly to provide income support for retired persons, veterans, farmers, the needy, bondholders, and other claimants. Also, many corporations and communities have come to rely upon defense spending (or contracting) for their continued prosperity. Projected and actual cutbacks in defense spending for a few years after the end of the Cold War caused consternation in many corporate boardrooms and communities around the nation. They continue to do so.

TABLE 5.1

National Government Expenditures for Selected Functions and Selected Years, 1950–2010, in Billions of Current Dollars

	1950	1960	1970	1975	1980	1985	1990	1995	2000	2005	2010*
National Defense	13.7	48.1	81.7	86.5	134.0	252.8	299.3	272.1	294.4	495.3	693.5
Income Security†	4.1	7.4	15.7	51.2	32.1	129.0	147.3	223.8	253.7	345.9	622.2
Social Security	0.8	11.6	30.3	64.7	118.6	188.6	248.6	335.9	409.4	523.3	683.4
Medicare	—	—	5.9	12.9	23.1	65.8	98.1	159.9	197.1	298.6	369.1
Agriculture	2.1	2.6	5.2	3.1	8.9	25.6	12.0	9.7	36.5	26.6	17.8
Natural Resources	1.3	1.6	3.1	7.4	13.9	13.6	17.1	21.9	25.0	28.0	41.6
Energy	0.3	0.5	1.0	2.9	10.2	5.6	2.4	4.9	-0.8	0.4	14.9
Veterans' Benefits	8.8	5.4	8.7	16.6	21.2	26.3	29.1	37.9	47.1	70.2	108.4
Net Interest on Debt	4.8	7.0	14.4	23.3	52.6	129.5	184.2	232.1	222.9	183.9	220.4
All Others‡	9.7	8.0	29.7	64.7	176.3	109.6	213.7	217.8	303.9	500.0	685.8
Total	45.6	92.2	195.7	332.3	590.9	946.4	1,251.8	1,515.9	1,789.2	2,472.2	3,457.1

*Estimated.

†Income security includes public assistance, food stamps, railroad and federal employee retirement benefits, and unemployment compensation.

‡"All Others" includes international affairs, science, space, transportation, education, commerce, community development, justice, health, and general government.

Source: Budget of the United States Government, Fiscal Year 2014, Historical Tables (Washington, DC: Government Printing Office, 2008), Table 3.2.

These changes in the composition of the budget reflect changes in national policy priorities. They also have important consequences for the politics of the budgetary process. Persons directly affected by governmental programs have organized to defend and increase their benefits and have become major participants in the budgetary process. This development has made budget decision-making both more political and more difficult. AARP (formerly the American Association of Retired Persons), for instance, with its many millions of members and hundreds of staff people, strongly opposes efforts to cut back Social Security and Medicare benefits. Even in an age of trillion-dollar budgets, there is not enough money to meet all demands. As elsewhere in the political process, those who are of higher socioeconomic status and are organized tend to fare better than the poor or unorganized.

The budget conveys a good overview of the government's total set of policies for the fiscal year it covers. In the budget, one can find or extract answers to such policy issues as the balance between private and governmental (national) spending, the balance between civilian and military spending, whether medical research (including AIDS research) will be accelerated or slowed, whether welfare spending in general as well as spending for specific welfare programs will be expanded or contracted, whether more or less regulation is planned for surface or strip-mining, and whether more or less emphasis will be given to environmental protection. This happens because the budgetary process, within the framework of substantive law, is a means for making choices among competing social values and allocating resources for their attainment. The budget is not simply a financial statement; it is also a statement of policy. Conflicts over money are usually conflicts over policy.

The budgetary process also provides the president and Congress with an opportunity to review periodically the various policies and programs of the government, to assess their effectiveness, and to inquire into the manner of their administration. Not every policy and program will be examined in detail every year, but over a few years most, if not all, will come under scrutiny. Thus, the budgetary process provides a continuing opportunity for exerting presidential and congressional influence and control over implementation of policies. Favored agencies and programs are likely to prosper; those under attack, whether for wasting money, harassing citizens, or misconstruing policies, may suffer cutbacks and restraints.

Consider the plight of the National Endowment for the Arts (NEA). Many conservatives, inside and outside of Congress, had never been enamored with the NEA, believing that support of the arts was not an appropriate or necessary national activity. In 1989, congressional conservatives were galvanized because two art exhibits that they considered pornographic were sponsored by an organization partly funded by the NEA. (Good art, as is known, is not easily specified.) They called for "zeroing out" NEAs appropriation. With the help of the Clinton administration and congressional supporters, the NEA was able to survive, but at the cost of a severe cutback in its appropriation. For several years the NEA's funding remained flat, hovering around $100 million annually.

Only recently did the NEA's funding begin to rebound. The conservative assault had important consequences for the agency.

Although most of the budget decisions made during a given year are incremental, involving marginal increases or decreases in agency funds, this constraint does not diminish their importance. At a minimum, they mean that an agency or program will continue to operate. Beyond that, incremental expansion of an agency's funding, compounded over a number of years, can significantly enlarge its budget.

Fiscal Policy

In addition to being used to finance the government's activities and policies, the budget can also be used as an instrument to stabilize the economy, to help prevent inflation or recession.[5] Fiscal policy involves the deliberate use of the government's taxing and spending powers to stimulate or restrain the economy by incurring budget deficits or surpluses, respectively. Briefly stated, according to Keynesian economic theory, a budget deficit, or a larger budget deficit, by putting more money into the hands of people and businesses, adds to the total demand for goods and services in the economy, thereby stimulating the economy. Conversely, a budget surplus, or a smaller budget deficit, will extract money from the economy and reduce the total demand for goods and services, thereby imposing restraint on the economy.

Major reliance was placed on fiscal policy in the 1960s and 1970s by presidential administrations trying to stabilize the economy. However, the large budget deficits annually incurred by the government in the 1980s and 1990s, along with the existence of strong antitax attitudes, "neutralized" fiscal policy by foreclosing most major changes in taxing and spending rates.[6] Some argued, however, that the deficits provided continuing stimulus to the economy. Regardless of which interpretation is more accurate, the budgetary situation shifted the task of economic stabilization to the Federal Reserve Board (FRB) and monetary policy, which relies on manipulating the interest rate and money supply to influence operation of the economy. The FRB has been especially concerned with combating inflation. Conservatives favor monetary policy because they view it as less intrusive and less likely to contribute to "big government."

Discretionary fiscal policy came back into play to combat the major recession that began in December 2007. Monetary policy under control of the FRB had proven insufficient though interest rates had been greatly lowered. Congressional leaders from both parties and Bush administration officials, in a spasm of bipartisanship, quickly put together and adopted the Economic Stimulus Act in February 2008. Intended to "jump-start" the economy, it provided for $180 billion in one-time lump-sum tax rebates to lower- and middle-income persons and business tax breaks to encourage investment. Most of the money went for tax rebates.[7] Senate Democrats had favored a more expansive bill, including funding for unemployment benefits and incentives for renewable energy initiatives. These were abandoned in the interest of speedy action and because of Republican opposition.

As it turned out, the stimulus plan did not have the intended effect. Surveys revealed that much of the rebate money either was saved or used to pay down existing debts.[8] By the time the Obama administration took office on January 20, 2009, the recession had worsened. The economy was now mired in the sharpest downturn since the Great Depression. Unemployment was rising, reaching 8.5 percent in March, 9.8 percent in September, and finally reaching 10 percent.

Responding to President Barack Obama's call for quick action on major economic stimulus legislation, in a few weeks, the Democratic-controlled Congress passed the American Recovery and Reinvestment Act (ARRA). (Work had started on the legislation weeks before the inauguration.) Although the president made appeals for bipartisan support, the act received only three Republican votes in the Senate and none in the House, despite the president's appeals.

A massive, complex piece of legislation, the ARRA provided for $575 billion in increased expenditures and $212 billion in tax cuts and rebates.[9] Some Democrats and liberals said that a considerably larger amount was needed to provide adequate stimulus to the sagging economy. Republicans contended it was too large, full of pork, wasteful, even "socialistic." They succeeded in time in making "stimulus" an "eight-letter" word.

Expenditure programs in ARRA included infrastructure, public education, transportation, public housing, unemployment benefits, energy efficiency and research, and financial aid to the states. Emphasis was on activities that could quickly get underway (or "shovel ready," as it was sometimes put), although these were in limited supply. Most of the tax benefits went to individuals, although some tax breaks were awarded to businesses to placate Republicans.[10]

Controversy persists concerning the effects of ARRA. It is difficult to assess or measure. However, Republican claims that it "did not create a single job" are obviously sheer hyperbole. Jobs were created. The Great Recession would have been worse had there been no ARRA.[11]

The National Budgetary Process

The national budgetary process, as well as state and local budgetary processes, can be divided into four fairly distinct stages: preparation, authorization, execution, and audit. Auditing, which involves checking on expenditures for evidence of illegality, waste, or abuse, is handled by the Government Accountability Office and the Offices of Inspector General located in many departments and agencies and will not be discussed here.

The president's budget, which is supposed to be sent to Congress in February (in 2013 it did not arrive until early April), covers a single fiscal year. The budget year that extends from October 1, 2013, through September 30, 2014 is designated fiscal year (FY) 2014, taking its name from the calendar year in which it ends. Table 5.2 outlines the national budgetary process and indicates the time sequences

TABLE 5.2

Major Steps in the National Budget Process

Formulation of the president's budget for FY 2014	Agencies develop requests for funds and submit them to OMB. The president makes the final decisions on what goes into the budget.	February–December 2012
Budget preparation and transmittal	The budget documents are prepared and sent to Congress.	December 2012–February 2013
Congressional action on the budget	Congress reviews the president's budget, develops its budget resolution, and approves spending and revenue bills.	March–September 2013
Fiscal year begins		October 1, 2013
Budget execution	Agency officials execute the budget as enacted into law.	October 1, 2013–September 30, 2014
Audit		Before or after the end of the fiscal year

Source: Office of Management and Budget.

involved (ideally) for FY 2014. It should be noted that from the initiation of budget preparation through the close of the fiscal year some thirty months elapse. This contributes to uncertainty in fiscal planning and decision-making.

The budget also covers the nine years following the fiscal year (say 2014) for which it is intended. These are called the "out years." This practice is intended to convey information on the longer term effects of budget decisions. The further into the future, the spongier these projections are likely to be. A broad look at the FY 2014 budget is provided in Figure 5.1.

Executive Preparation

The executive budget system set in place by the Budget and Accounting Act of 1921 required agencies (Congress and the Supreme Court are exempted) to transmit their budget requests to the president for approval before they were sent to Congress in a single, comprehensive budget document. The BOB was delegated authority to "assemble, correlate, revise, reduce, or increase the estimates." In its early years, BOB acted on the assumption that its major task was to hold down agency spending and ensure efficiency and economy in the operation of the government. This orientation continues to motivate the Office of Management and Budget (OMB).

Preparation of the national budget within the executive branch begins nine months or so before it is sent to Congress in February. Most of the day-to-day work in developing the budget is handled by the OMB and the executive departments and agencies. Acting on the basis of presidential directives, the OMB provides

FIGURE 5.1

Budget for Fiscal Year 2014

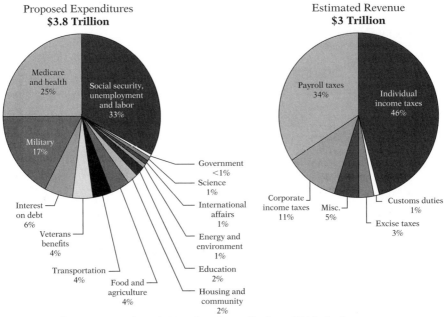

Proposed Expenditures
$3.8 Trillion

Estimated Revenue
$3 Trillion

Source: nationalpriorities.org/analysis/2013/president-obamas-fiscal-year-2014-budget/

instructions, policy guidance, and tentative budget ceilings to help the departments and agencies assemble their budget requests. The latter, which are directly and specifically affected by budget decisions, and which are normally believers in the value and necessity of their programs, are expected to act as the advocates of increased spending (appropriations). What they request is subject to review and revision, upward or downward, by OMB in accordance with the policies and programs of the president.

Because the "policies and programs" of the president are not subject to precise definition, OMB has latitude in determining what is consistent with them. Agencies sufficiently aggrieved by OMB decisions may try to appeal them to the president, who more often than not will uphold the OMB. Some presidents (Richard M. Nixon, for one) have discouraged the appeal of OMB decisions, however, thereby letting OMB make the final decisions on agency appropriations requests.

Presidents typically do not become much engaged with budgetary details. An exception was President Bill Clinton. As budget expert Allen Schick states:

> Each budget bore Clinton's imprint: he actively participated in making budget policy was well informed on matters in dispute, and was familiar with salient details of federal programs.... He made decisions concerning the size and direction of government, the composition of tax legislation, and the

shape of policy initiatives. He invested time in mastering the details of the budget, meeting with department heads to discuss their budgets and to resolve issues that remained after OMB completed its review.[12]

During the early years of the Reagan administration, a "top-down" budgetary process overlaid the traditional ("bottom-up") budgetary pattern, except for the Department of Defense. Basic budget decisions were made at the presidential level by the OMB director and others and, in effect, imposed on the departments and agencies. This sequence meant that departments and agencies had less budgetary influence and discretion than under the former bottom-up procedure. As time went on, however, the centralization of executive authority and ideological unity necessary to make top-down budgeting workable and acceptable waned within the administration. The budgetary process then inched back toward the traditional bottom-up pattern, in which the agencies have more influences on the size and content of their budget requests. Whether a subsequent presidential administration will be able to duplicate the early Reagan administration's budgetary control is problematical.[13]

The budget sent to Congress reflects presidential decisions and priorities on such matters as its overall size, its possible effects on the economy, its major directions in public policy, and its allocation of funds among the major agencies and programs. Lyndon Johnson in 1967 wanted both "guns and butter"— increased spending for both the Vietnam War and the social-welfare programs for his Great Society. Ronald Reagan in the 1980s, on the other hand, wanted less spending for various welfare and domestic programs and more spending for national defense. President George Bush's budget priorities in his first year in office were unclear. Campaigning for the presidency, he had advocated a "flexible freeze" on spending, no new taxes, and a reduction in the budget deficit. Although these goals were perhaps sufficient for campaign purposes, they did not amount to a real set of priorities. Once in office, he did little to clarify them.

Unlike his father, President George W. Bush never wavered on taxes—he was always in favor of tax cuts. However, he was not much concerned with spending and signed into law several bills providing for substantially more expenditures than he had recommended. Toward the end of his second term he took a stronger stance against spending increases; details, however, were beyond his purview.[14]

Presidential and congressional discretion in making budget decisions is constrained by the fact that two-thirds of national expenditures are direct or mandatory in nature and do not depend upon annual appropriations. Most direct spending is accounted for by entitlement programs such as Social Security, Medicare, Medicaid, food stamps, federal retirement benefits, veterans' pensions, Guaranteed Student Loans, agricultural income-support payments, and many grant-in-aid payments to the states. Interest payments on the national debt, while technically not an entitlement, are clearly mandatory. Entitlement programs are so called because everyone meeting the eligibility standards is legally entitled to benefit payments on the basis of a formula spelled out in law. Direct expenditures, whether entitlements or otherwise, represent continuing obligations and commitments that can be modified or eliminated only if the statutes authorizing them are amended.

Entitlement programs are typically funded by permanent, open-ended appropriations—that is, the payment of benefits is authorized to all who are eligible and apply, whatever the ultimate total may amount to. Surprisingly, for instance, some people eligible for Medicaid benefits do not request them.

Many of the entitlement programs are indexed to the consumer price index in order to maintain the real purchasing power of recipients. Consequently, expenditures for these programs automatically rise during inflationary periods. Much of the indexing was put in place during the early 1970s, when inflation was low, and consequently, automatic increases were low. As inflation became stronger, the increases became larger and contributed to rising entitlement expenditure levels. Sometimes referred to as "automatic government," at the time it was instituted, indexation was a technique that policy-makers also could use to avoid being blamed for potentially unpopular decisions.[15] Entitlement-program beneficiaries have been able to mobilize strong political support for the retention of indexation. Thus, indexation stands as another practice that inhibits the ability of the president and Congress to control expenditures or to alter budget priorities.

Much of the one-third of national spending classified as discretionary falls within the national security area and, as a political matter, even with the demise of the Soviet Union and the end of the Cold War, is not subject to extensive alteration.[16] Department of Defense officials and their congressional and corporate allies successfully argued that reductions in military personnel and weapons procurement would weaken military preparedness and the capacity of the armed forces to simultaneously conduct two major military operations, should such be necessary. There was also concern that military cutbacks would adversely affect the economic well-being of localities that are home to defense contractors and military installations. After limited success in reducing defense expenditures in its first term, the Clinton administration shifted ground and sought increased military spending in its second term. The September 11 terrorist attack produced pressure for a major increase in defense spending (see Table 5.1). The decisions to go to war in Afghanistan and Iraq further led to increased defense spending.

All of this means that when pressures develop to cut government spending, the primary target is likely to be domestic discretionary spending, which accounts for only about one-sixth of total spending. This money goes to support a broad array of law-enforcement, education, regulatory, welfare, housing, natural-resource, agricultural, and other programs—in short, much of what government does. Spending in these areas was strongly squeezed since the 1990s because of pressure to reduce government spending in the name of deficit reduction.

A point needs to be made explicitly here before we move on. With few exceptions (the food stamp program is one), only discretionary spending programs go through the appropriations process sketched out in this section. Unless the laws on which they are based are changed, funding is automatically provided for mandatory or entitlement programs, sufficient to meet all obligations.

Congressional Authorization   The Constitution provides in Article I that "no money shall be drawn from the treasury, but in consequence of appropriations made by law," which means appropriations legislation enacted by Congress. To begin, two distinct steps are usually involved in the funding of public policies and programs. First, substantive legislation has to be enacted establishing a policy or program (e.g., the Clean Water Act) and authorizing the expenditure of money in its support. Second, money actually has to be made available for the policy or program by the adoption of appropriations legislation. The House has had a rule since 1833 stating that "no appropriation shall be reported in any general appropriations bill, or be in order as an amendment thereto, for any expenditure not previously authorized by law." (This rule, like other congressional rules, is sometimes waived.)

Authorization legislation is handled by the substantive or legislative committees (such as Agriculture, Commerce, and Armed Services), and appropriations legislation is the domain of the House and Senate Appropriations Committees. Programs for which funding is authorized sometimes either go unfunded or are funded at levels lower than those authorized. The foreign-aid program has frequently been funded below its authorized level. Different committees, members, and processes in Congress can produce different policy results.

The legislative committees have sometimes circumvented the appropriations committees and the obstacles they represent by resorting to "backdoor spending," which takes a number of forms. Backdoor spending may involve authorizing an agency to borrow money from the Treasury, which the agency can then spend. Or it may involve authorizing an agency to contract for purchasing goods and services. Subsequently, funds will have to be appropriated to cover the borrowing or contracts. The alternative would be for the government to renege on its commitments, which is highly unlikely. Entitlement spending also falls within the backdoor category. The House Appropriations Committee has been especially opposed to backdoor practices because they effectively diminish the committee's authority over agency spending.

For purposes of legislative enactment, the president's budget, which comes to Congress as a document of several hundred pages, is divided into twelve appropriations bills (e.g., for defense, energy and water development, interior and related agencies, and foreign operations; see Table 5.3). These are then referred to the House Appropriations Committee, which by long custom acts first on the budget. Its twelve subcommittees hold hearings, at which agency officials and others testify in explanation and defense of their budget requests, and otherwise do most of the detailed legislative work on the budget. In reviewing agencies and their programs, the members of Congress may seek information on topics such as these[17]:

1. Existence. Is the agency or the program necessary? Should it be modified or retained? Abstractly, it is easy to state that ineffective agencies or programs should be "zeroed out." It is the rare agency or program, however, that does not have some supporters who are intensely committed to it and may also directly benefit from it.

TABLE 5.3

Annual Appropriations Bills

Agriculture
Commerce–Justice–Science
Energy–Water
Financial Services
Homeland Security
Interior–Environment
Labor–Health and Human Services–Education
Legislative Branch
Military Construction–Veterans Administration
National Defense
State Department–Foreign Operations
Transportation–Housing and Urban Development

© Cengage learning

2. Objectives. What are the goals of an agency or a program? Are they the correct ones? Are they appropriate for government? What does one decide when goals are multiple and conflicting? Or unclear?

3. Results. What is the program accomplishing? What societal changes (outcomes), intended or unintended, flow from it? Can the agency demonstrate results, as required by the Government Performance and Results Act? (See the chapter titled "Policy Impact, Evaluation, and Change.") Are there complaints about agency or program operations?

4. Line-item changes. Why does the agency want more money for personnel, equipment, or other matters? Why does it cost so much to administer a program, such as predator control or airline security? What will be the costs of a proposed new program? What will be accomplished by an agency or program with increased funding?

Hearings often focus on the fourth item, which involves changes in the level of an agency's program funding. This is both easier and more determinate than is deciding whether a program is necessary or what a program has accomplished or might accomplish. Members appear more comfortable in dealing with the financial aspects of agency operations. They are also much interested in how an agency's activities and expenditures will affect their constituents.

The subcommittees' recommendations are usually accepted with only minimal change by the full Appropriations Committee. In turn, its recommendations are customarily approved by the House with few changes. As a consequence of this pattern, detailed decision-making on appropriations is handled by small groups of House members with a strong interest in the programs with which they deal.

The Senate Appropriations Committee, to which appropriations bills passed by the House are sent, does not examine budget requests as intensively as does the House. Rather, the Senate Appropriations Committee tends to focus on "items in dispute," and serves as an appellate body to which agencies that have had their budget requests reduced in the House can appeal for restoration of at least a portion of the cuts. The Senate frequently responds positively to such pleas.

Conference committees drawn from the members of the relevant subcommittees are used to resolve the differences between the House and Senate versions of appropriations bills. Conflict resolution here often involves "splitting the difference" between the two bills. Compromises are considerably easier to reach on money matters than on social issues such as abortion, school prayer, or gun control. The latter involve "moral" choices on which it is hard to compromise or divide up the difference. Because its members are more specialized and better informed, and have more time and determination, the House usually does better than the Senate in appropriations conferences.[18]

The budgetary process also provides legislators with opportunities to pass legislation that would likely not be enacted on its own by inserting it into appropriations bills. For instance, in 2000 a lobbyist persuaded Representative Jo Ann Emerson (R, Missouri) to insert a couple of paragraphs in a 712-page appropriations bill providing for the Data Quality Act. Almost no one else understood what was involved.[19] The Data Quality Act has been used mostly to complicate and obstruct regulatory rulemaking, as intended. Policymaking is sometimes done by stealth.

BUDGETARY DECISION-MAKING The 1950s and 1960s were the heyday of budgetary incrementalism.[20] Economic growth made more revenue available to the government each year; consequently, most agencies requested, and the president typically recommended, increased funding for their programs for the next year. In incremental budgeting, an agency's budget for the current year became its "base"; the additional funds sought for the next year were an "increment," which was to be used to improve or expand its activities and which represented its "fair share" of the government's additional revenues. Congressional examination of agency budget requests centered on the increments; the frequent result was a congressional decision to provide an agency with more funds than it had in the current year but less than the president's recommendation for the next. This permitted members of Congress to claim that they were holding down or cutting spending at the same time that they were increasing funding for public programs.

Incremental budgeting was depicted by its proponents as a good budgeting process because it lessened conflict over budgetary issues, simplified budgetary decision-making by reducing the need for information and planning, and contributed to stability and predictability in budgeting. Critics contended that incrementalism was a barrier to rational decision-making and change that it assumed a situation involving only public officials, and that it did not adequately acknowledge differences among budgetary actors in power and influence.[21]

Incrementalism continues to substantially characterize budgetary decision-making, although its scope has been restricted by the growth of entitlements, and for a time the reality of budget cutbacks altered the nature of the action.

Budgeting for agency and program reductions, or what budget expert Allen Schick calls *decrementalism*, produced conflict because of its redistributive effects.[22] More for one agency frequently meant less for another. Agency officials were often pleased to be able to hold cutbacks to modest proportions. In 1995, the House Republican majority sought to make large reductions in some agency budgets, or to eliminate entire agencies in their quest for a smaller national government. Many of these actions were fended off or mitigated by agency supporters in the House, Senate, or executive branch.

Most budget changes, whether incremental or decremental, continue to be limited or marginal in size. Agencies and programs with strong political support still fare best in the appropriations process. Budgetary decision-making can still be well-described as based on limited analysis rather than on systematic or comprehensive analysis. Incrementalism, in short, remains alive and doing well.

Baseline budgeting, though by no means comparable to incrementalism, has become an important aspect of budgetary decision-making. Essentially, baseline budgeting involves the estimation of the future budget implications of current policies, taking into account inflation and uncontrollable changes such as population growth, unemployment rates, and the extent to which people eligible for program benefits will seek them.[23] Changes in expenditures caused by new legislation or presidential actions are omitted from baseline projections. What the baseline projection does, in short, is project, on the basis of a number of assumptions, such as the expected inflation rate and growth in target populations, the real future costs of current policies. This can be done for next year, the next five years, or some other time period. It yields what are essentially imaginary numbers.

Baseline budgeting also involves making estimates of the future revenues that will be generated by existing tax programs. These estimates will depend upon the assumptions made about the rate of economic growth, employment levels, and other economic variables. As with spending projections, revenue projections will be as sound and accurate as the assumptions on which they are based. By manipulating assumptions, officials can increase or decrease projected future revenue and spending levels.

Although appropriate as a way for policy-makers to estimate future revenue and spending levels and the impact that policy changes will have on them, baseline budgeting also can be used for less laudable purposes. It can be used, for instance, to make a particular budget decision appear as a reduction or an increase, depending on one's preference. Take the case of the Reagan administration's famous fiscal 1982 baseline budget reduction of $35 billion in domestic spending. On a current law projection, which does not figure in inflation, the amount was estimated at $10 billion, a less impressive sum. Allen Schick provides an explanation for the choice of the larger figure:

> Why did the Republicans, who only a few years earlier lambasted the current policy [baseline] concept as biased and expansionary, embrace it in 1981, and why did the congressional Democrats go along with this method of measuring cutbacks? The simple but sufficient answer is that the Republicans wanted to

magnify the reported savings, and the Democrats wanted the actual cuts to be less than they appeared to be. The ... baseline allowed the Republicans to claim more savings and the Democrats to save more programs, a happy combination for politicians facing difficult choices.[24]

Gimmickry and symbolic action are regular components of the budgetary process.

PRESIDENTIAL ACTION   Following the completion of congressional action, appropriations bills are transmitted to the president for approval. Although these bills were once described as "veto-proof" because the continued operation of the government depends on the spending they authorize, recent presidents have invalidated this bit of conventional wisdom. A number of appropriations bills viewed as budget-busting or inflationary, or including funding for purposes not favored, have been turned down by the executive. Congress must then either rework the appropriations bill to meet presidential objections or seek to override the veto.

Presidents may also use their veto power more positively by threatening to wield it on an appropriations bill under congressional consideration. This threat may induce Congress to tailor the bill to fit presidential objectives and avoid the veto, especially if congressional leaders think the votes are not available for an override. This is really a form of strategic bargaining, in which the possibility of future action is used in an effort to influence current action.

Most of the nation's governors long have had item-veto authority, which enables them to reject, or perhaps reduce, particular items in a spending bill while approving most of the bill. This enhances their power vis-à-vis the legislature on appropriations. In comparison, the president has had to accept or reject a budget bill in its entirety. Consequently, provisions for pork-barrel projects or other matters objectionable to the president could get past him or her if incorporated in general appropriations bills that he or she felt compelled to approve.

Many presidents recommended that they be given the item veto. President Ronald Reagan, for example, frequently asserted that he would balance the budget if Congress gave him the item veto, ostensibly by rejecting wasteful pork-barrel projects. The Democratic majorities in Congress displayed scant interest in this proposal. Historically, Congress has jealously guarded its power of the purse; potentially, the item veto could produce a major shift in budgetary power from Congress to the executive.

In 1996, however, the Republican majorities in Congress, joined by many Democrats, passed the Line-Item Veto Act. They apparently saw this as a means of helping to bring government spending under control and balance the budget, matters that drew much public support.[25] It was provided that the law would not take effect until 1997, by which time many Republicans thought that President Bill Clinton would be out of office. Bad guess.

The Line-Item Veto Act authorized presidential cancellation of particular discretionary spending items, including items in lump-sum appropriations that were described in the committee reports or manager's statements accompanying spending bills; authorization of new or expanded entitlement programs; and tax provisions affecting 100 or fewer beneficiaries. After signing the bill into law, the president had five days in which to cancel specific items. Such items, enumerated by the president in a special message to Congress, were automatically vetoed unless Congress passed a "disapproval bill" reversing the president's cancellations. This bill was subject to a presidential veto, which in turn could be overridden by a two-thirds vote of each house. This convoluted procedure was sometimes called *enhanced rescission.*

Opponents of the item veto feared that it might be used extensively as a pork-slashing tool or as a means of putting presidential pressure on legislators to support his programs or face rejection of desired projects.[26] As it turned out, President Clinton made limited use of the item veto. When he did veto items, members of both parties in Congress howled. In 1997, his vetoes of thirty-eight projects in a military construction bill were overridden.

The constitutionality of the item veto was quickly challenged by some adversely affected parties. Reaching the U.S. Supreme Court under expedited procedure, it was struck down by a 6-to-3 vote in June 1998.[27] "If the Line-Item Veto Act were valid, it would authorize the president to create a different law— one whose text was not voted on by either House of Congress or presented to the president for signature," said Justice John Paul Stevens for the Court. "If there is to be a new procedure in which the president will play a different role in determining the final text of what may 'become a law,' such change must come not by legislation but through the amendment procedures set forth in ... the Constitution."

In its short life span, the item veto had little impact on government spending. Efforts to overcome the Court's decision have gone nowhere.

The total amount of funds appropriated by Congress for a fiscal year does not deviate much from the president's recommendation. A change of 3 or 4 percent, up or down, would be exceptional. For FY 1995, for example, President Clinton sought $1,537 billion in new spending authority; Congress appropriated $1,540.7 billion. For some agencies and programs, however, congressional action may differ substantially from the president's requests, reflecting differences in policy priorities. In 2002, for example, the Bush administration requested a supplemental appropriation of $20 billion for antiterrorism programs. Of this sum, $7.4 billion was allocated for defense programs, $7.1 billion for disaster recovery in New York and other states, and $5.5 billion for homeland security. Unsuccessful in their efforts to appropriate a larger amount, the Senate Democrats altered the Bush request. As enacted, the appropriation provided $3.5 for defense, $8.2 for disaster recovery, and $8.3 billion for homeland security.

Action on all the appropriations bills, including presidential approval, is supposed to be completed before the beginning of the fiscal year on October 1. It is quite common, however, for some or all of the bills to be pending on that date. Only three of the appropriations bills for FY 2009 had been adopted when it began on October 1, 2008. In 2012, Congress "worsted" this performance by enactment of none of the appropriations bills by the start of FY 2013.

When this sort of inaction occurs, a continuing resolution (CR) will be needed to preclude shutdown of the unfunded agencies and programs. Continuing rules have been used for many decades. A CR may cover a few agencies or programs or it may take omnibus proportions and cover several or all of the appropriations bills. Under House rules, CRs are not considered to be regular appropriations bills. Consequently, just about anything can be stuck in them—unauthorized appropriations, substantive legislation, pork-barrel projects—without being subject to points of order and removed. Spending authorized by a CR for agencies and programs is usually the lower of either the previous fiscal year level or the president's budget recommendation.

More often than not, Congress has not enacted all of the appropriations bills before the beginning of the fiscal year. These unpassed bills may then be combined in a large omnibus bill. Thus, nine of the appropriations bills for FY 2009 were joined in a 1,100-page omnibus bill and enacted in March 2009, some five months after the inception of the fiscal year. This practice departs from the standard that appropriations bills should be separately enacted. It also makes it more likely that many members will be poorly informed about what they are voting on. Omnibus bills often serve as the vehicles for legislation (riders) that could not move independently through the legislative process. And they were sometimes loaded down with earmarks; there were more than 8,000 in the 2009 omnibus bill. Since then, Congress has mended its ways.

Some technical aspects of budgeting now need to be confronted. An appropriations act creates budget authority (BA), which permits agencies to obligate (or commit) themselves for the expenditure or lending of money. When the money is actually paid out or expended, it is called an outlay. An agency must have budget authority before it can make outlays. When Congress considers and acts on presidential budget requests, the focus is on BA (a.k.a., appropriations). Discussion of budget deficits and surpluses, however, are concerned with outlays (or money that is actually paid out). The money that an agency obligates itself to pay out in a given fiscal year, however, may not actually go to the recipient until the next year or later. Many Department of Defense purchases of complex weapons systems may be paid to contractors over the course of several years. Many appropriations are for the current budget year only. If the money is not obligated, the agency loses it. Hence, "September buying" occurs. Also, budget authority may be good for a multiyear or indefinite period of time (a "no-year" appropriation). Thus, outlays or expenditures for a given fiscal year cannot be precisely known until after the year is over.

The relationship between appropriations and outlays is illustrated in Figure 5.2. In a given year, FY 2014, for instance, the money spent (outlays) will come from both that year's budget and previous budgets (in the form of unspent authority). Also, some of the funds appropriated for FY 2014 will actually be paid out in later years. Once money gets into the pipeline—that is, once expenditures are authorized—tremendous pressure grows to

FIGURE 5.2

Relationship of Budget Authority to Outlays for 2014 (billions of dollars)

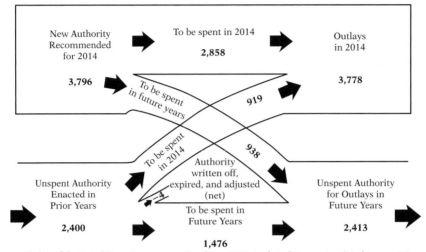

Source: *Budget of the United States Government, Fiscal Year 2014, Analytical Perspectives* (Washington, DC: Government Printing Office, 2013), p. 130.

spend the money. If one wants to choke off government spending, the best time to act is at the appropriations (or authorization) stage in the budgetary process, before money enters the spending pipeline, but even then it is politically difficult.

THE CONGRESSIONAL BUDGET PROCESS In the decades immediately after World War II, the budgetary process had again become somewhat disjointed and chaotic. Appropriations and revenues were considered separately by different committees and processes. The budget surplus or deficit for a fiscal year was an "accidental figure," determined only when all the appropriations bills, considered separately, were enacted, totaled, and compared with available revenue. Dissatisfaction with this situation, concern about the rapid growth of governmental spending and continued budget deficits, and a desire for greater congressional attention to the fiscal-policy implications of the budget contributed to adoption of the Congressional Budget and Impoundment Control Act of 1974.[28]

The budgetary reform provisions of the act provide for a congressional budget process to coordinate the decentralized process by which budget decisions in Congress had been made. This procedure involves setting overall levels of revenues and expenditures and establishing priorities (and spending limits) among functional areas (such as agriculture, international relations, and transportation) included in the budget. New budget committees were created in the House and Senate to handle these tasks, subject to approval by the full houses. To assist the budget committees in their work, and to provide Congress with its own source of budgeting data and studies, a Congressional Budget Office (CBO) was established. The CBO has typically been more accurate than the OMB in making budgetary estimations and economic forecasts.

Based on their review of the president's budget proposal, and on information from CBO and other congressional committees, the budget committees produce a concurrent budget resolution that sets overall levels of budget authority, outlays, revenues, and the budget surplus or deficit.[29] The budget resolution also specifies spending ceilings for each of the functional areas. It is supposed to be passed by April 15, although this is rarely achieved, and it does not require presidential approval. The appropriations committees are then expected to perform their scrutiny and evaluation of agency budget requests within the policy framework provided by the budget resolution. (See Table 5.4.) In some years, Congress has been unable to pass budget resolutions because of House–Senate, Democratic-Republican differences.

Reconciliation legislation is subsequently adopted in most years to ensure that the revenue goals and spending limits in the budget resolution are actually met. In the reconciliation process, the taxation and the legislative committees propose changes in *existing* tax laws and entitlement programs (usually to increase revenues or cut spending by specified amounts). These proposed changes are packaged by the budget committees into a single omnibus reconciliation bill, which must be adopted by both houses and, unlike the budget resolution, signed into law by the president. Reconciliation, which makes permanent changes in the affected policies and programs, has been used to cut entitlement spending, increase taxes, modify discretionary programs, and sell government assets.[30]

Reconciliation was first used in 1980 under the Carter administration to make a modest reduction in the budget deficit for FY 1981. The next year the Reagan administration and the Republican leadership in Congress employed

TABLE 5.4
The Congressional Budget Process

February	Presidential budget is sent to Congress on the first Monday of the month.
March 15	Standing committees send their budget estimates to the House and Senate budget committees.
April 1	Budget committees report budget resolutions to the House and the Senate.
April 15	Congress adopts a concurrent resolution setting targets for revenues, budget authorities, and outlays.
May–July	House completes action on appropriations bills.
July–September	Senate acts on appropriations bills; conference committees resolve differences; appropriations are enacted.
September	Reconciliation legislation enacted if needed.
October 1	Fiscal year begins; continuing resolutions are passed if all appropriations have not been enacted.

© Cengage learning

reconciliation to impose a $35 billion cutback in baseline spending. This constitutes the most sweeping use of reconciliation to the present time.

Observers seem to agree that the new budgetary process has improved the quality of congressional decision-making on the budget. More and better budgetary information is available to Congress. Budget decisions are more fully considered and debated, and members of Congress are compelled to address the overall dimensions of the budget. The budget decision-making process has been made more complex by the new procedures and participation by the budget committees. Conflict sometimes occurs between the budget committees and the appropriations and tax committees. The House Appropriations Committee, once famed for its role as "guardian of the Treasury," and its subcommittees have consequently become more protective of their members' favorite agencies and programs. This change in committee behavior illustrates one of the propositions of systems theory, namely, that change in one part of a system will produce changes elsewhere in the system.

Budget
Execution

The obligation and actual expenditure (or outlay) of funds, once appropriated, rest with the various departments and agencies. To begin spending, however, they must first secure an *apportionment* from the OMB, which is authorized by the Antideficiency Act of 1905, as amended. An apportionment distributes "appropriations and other budgetary resources" (e.g., the authority to borrow money) to an agency "by time periods [usually quarterly] and by activities in order to ensure the effective use of available resources and to preclude the need for additional appropriations."[31] The OMB may also direct agencies to set aside funds for contingencies or not to spend funds when greater efficiency in operations or altered needs permit savings to be achieved without restricting accomplishment of agency goals.

The discretion that officials have in spending funds and achieving objectives is significantly affected by the language included in appropriations laws. Executive officials prefer to have broad discretion to decide whether to spend funds or to shift funds among programs (reprogramming). Congress does sometimes provide agencies with "lump-sum" or very broad appropriations that confer much spending leeway, albeit within boundaries set by the substantive legislation governing agency action.

Figure 5.3 is the section of the 2010 Agriculture Appropriation Act pertaining to the Animal and Plant Health Inspection Service (APHIS). The amounts of money that can be expended on various programs are specified, some limitations and conditions are imposed, and some transfer of funds from other Department of Agriculture programs is permitted. Some of the money is available to the agency until expended. This is a "no-year" appropriation. The agency is also authorized to collect fees for some of its services and retain them until expended. The president's budget contains more information about the programs and activities of APHIS.

FIGURE 5.3

Appropriation for the Animal and Plant Health Inspection Service, Fiscal Year 2010

PUBLIC LAW 111–80—OCT. 21, 2009   123 STAT. 2097

ANIMAL AND PLANT HEALTH INSPECTION SERVICE

SALARIES AND EXPENSES

(INCLUDING TRANSFERS OF FUNDS)

For necessary expenses of the Animal and Plant Health Inspection Service, including up to $30,000 for representation allowances and for expenses pursuant to the Foreign Service Act of 1980 (22 U.S.C. 4085), $904,953,000, of which $24,410,000 shall be for the purposes, and in the amounts, specified in the table titled "Congressionally Designated Projects" in the statement of managers to accompany this Act, of which $2,058,000 shall be available for the control of outbreaks of insects, plant diseases, animal diseases and for control of pest animals and birds to the extent necessary to meet emergency conditions; of which $23,390,000 shall be used for the cotton pests program for cost share purposes or for debt retirement for active eradication zones; of which $5,300,000 shall be for a National Animal Identification program; of which $60,243,000 shall be used to prevent and control avian influenza and shall remain available until expended: *Provided*, That funds provided for the contingency fund to meet emergency conditions, information technology infrastructure, fruit fly program, emerging plant pests, cotton pests program, grasshopper and mormon cricket program, the plum pox program, the National Veterinary Stockpile, the National Animal Identification System, up to $1,500,000 in the scrapie program for indemnities, up to $1,000,000 for wildlife services methods development, up to $1,500,000 of the wildlife services operations program for aviation safety, and up to 25 percent of the screwworm program shall remain available until expended: *Provided further*, That no funds shall be used to formulate or administer a brucellosis eradication program for the current fiscal year that does not require minimum matching by the States of at least 40 percent: *Provided further*, That this appropriation shall be available for the operation and maintenance of aircraft and the purchase of not to exceed four, of which two shall be for replacement only: *Provided further*, That, in addition, in emergencies which threaten any segment of the agricultural production industry of this country, the Secretary may transfer from other appropriations or funds available to the agencies or corporations of the Department such sums as may be deemed necessary, to be available only in such emergencies for the arrest and eradication of contagious or infectious disease or pests of animals, poultry, or plants, and for expenses in accordance with sections 10411 and 10417 of the Animal Health Protection Act (7 U.S.C. 8310 and

8316) and sections 431 and 442 of the Plant Protection Act (7 U.S.C. 7751 and 7772), and any unexpended balances of funds transferred for such emergency purposes in the preceding fiscal year shall be merged with such transferred amounts: *Provided further*, That appropriations hereunder shall be available pursuant to law (7 U.S.C. 2250) for the repair and alteration of leased buildings and improvements, but unless otherwise provided the cost of altering any one building during the fiscal year shall not exceed 10 percent of the current replacement value of the building.

In fiscal year 2010, the agency is authorized to collect fees to cover the total costs of providing technical assistance, goods, or services requested by States, other political subdivisions, domestic and international organizations, foreign governments, or individuals, provided that such fees are structured such that any entity's liability for such fees is reasonably based on the technical assistance, goods, or services provided to the entity by the agency, and such fees shall be credited to this account, to remain available until expended, without further appropriation, for providing such assistance, goods, or services.

In recent years the Congress, under Republican leadership, has frequently included, or tried to include, specific restrictions in appropriations laws. Such provisions are negatively phrased, that is, "None of the funds provided in this Act shall be used for [a specified purpose]." These provisions, in effect, make policy in the guise of spending limitations. A classic example of a limitation provision is the Hyde amendment (named for former Representative Henry Hyde, R, Illinois), which provides: "None of the funds appropriated under this act shall be expended for any abortion except when it is made known to the federal entity or official … that such procedure is necessary to save the life of the mother, or that the pregnancy is the result of an act of rape or incest." This provision has been included in several appropriations laws.[32]

The committee and subcommittee reports accompanying appropriations bills are commonly used to specify how members of Congress think funds should be spent and to help shape policy. The following example comes from the House Appropriations Committee's report on the annual appropriation for the Food Safety and Inspection Service (FSIS), located in the Department of Agriculture. FSIS has responsibility for regulating the meat and poultry industries to ensure that meat and poultry products are safe, wholesome, and accurately labeled.

> The Committee believes a HACCP regulatory reform process is needed to maintain the production of a clean, safe, quality meat product that ensures consumer confidence. The Committee believes its objective of timely implementation of regulations that make the strongest practicable improvement in food safety is dependent upon the development of workable, scientifically sound rules. Therefore, the Committee has included language directing the Department to convert the rulemaking on Pathogen Reduction, Hazard Analysis and Critical Control Point (HACCP) Systems, the so-called "Mega-Reg," to a negotiated rulemaking procedure. The Committee expects that the Department will be able to develop more effective food safety rules due to the quality of input this procedure will permit regarding issues addressed in this rulemaking and related regulatory requirements. Further, the Committee directs the Department to proceed expeditiously with this rulemaking to avoid significant delay in the promulgation of modernized meat and poultry regulations. Specifically, the Department is expected to act promptly to initiate a negotiated rulemaking and to require a report from the negotiated rulemaking committee within nine months of its establishment.[33]

The negotiated rule-making specified by the committee in its convoluted language is authorized by the Negotiated Rulemaking Act (1990). Here, it was intended to provide meat-industry groups with greater opportunity to intervene and soften the content of new meat and poultry regulations. Designed to reduce bacterial contamination, the new rules did not bear down as hard on the meat-packing industry as consumer groups had hoped, though they were better than the "poke and sniff" method. Also, the new rules could be enforced more stoutly.

The funding of pork-barrel projects that benefit particular localities or groups—such as a railroad museum, a blueberry research program, research on reduction of hog manure odor, or a highway interchange—was also frequently provided in committee reports. There it may be stated that the committee hopes, expects, or directs that funding will be used for specified purposes. Although committee and subcommittee reports are not legally binding on agencies, it is impolitic for officials to ignore them. Members of Congress may subsequently call to account those who disregard committee instructions.

The practice of presidential impoundment of funds has frequently stirred controversy with Congress.[34] The first impoundment on record was made by President Thomas Jefferson, who withheld funds for a couple of gunboats to operate on the Mississippi River. With the Louisiana Purchase in 1803 and the departure of the French from the New World, there was no longer need for them. Since then, presidents have claimed and exercised authority to prevent expenditure of funds for purposes they disagreed with on budgetary or policy grounds. Presidents Truman and Eisenhower refused to spend funds for military programs that they had not requested. President Lyndon Johnson impounded billions of dollars to combat inflation, although much of what he held back was subsequently released. Until the 1970s, impoundment was usually done on a selective and limited basis, and although some dissatisfaction was created and voiced in Congress, major confrontations were avoided.

President Nixon, however, precipitated an intense political conflict over impoundment that made it a high-priority item on the national policy agenda. Following his reelection in 1972, he decided to use an administrative strategy to "take on the bureaucracy and take over the government." One facet of this strategy entailed extensive impoundment of appropriations for water-pollution controls, mass transit, food stamps, medical research, urban renewal, agricultural programs, and highway construction. These impoundments "were unprecedented in their scope and severity."[35] Numerous rationales were provided, including the need to prevent the inflationary effects of "reckless" spending and the existence of inherent and implied executive power under the Constitution to take such action. In various instances, however, it was apparent that presidential impoundment was simply being used to reduce or eliminate congressionally authorized programs of which the administration disapproved. Nearly all the impoundments were challenged by adversely affected parties and were held to be illegal by the federal courts.[36]

Congress was provoked into action by the Nixon impoundments and included some controls on impoundment in the 1974 budget law. Under the act, a deferral of expenditures, in which the executive seeks to delay or stretch out spending until a time in the fiscal year when it is needed, could be done unless or until either house of Congress voted to disapprove. In contrast, an executive rescission of funds, which cancels budget authority and thus stops the expenditure of funds, becomes effective only if, within forty-five days of notification, both houses pass a rescission bill. In actuality it is not always easy to distinguish deferrals from rescissions. Overall, the new impoundment procedures gave Congress more (and the executive less) authority over spending and made appropriations legislation more of a mandate for agencies to spend allocated funds.

In *Immigration and Naturalization Service* v. *Chadha* of 1983,[37] a case involving a minor immigration matter, the Supreme Court declared unconstitutional the use of the legislative veto. The legislative veto was held to permit Congress or its committee to disapprove rules or actions of executive agencies and officials, such as deferral of spending, in violation of the Constitution's presentment clause, which requires that bills must be presented to the president for approval or veto before they become law. Did this ruling mean, then, that the president could still engage in deferral of spending although Congress, if it so desired, could not veto the actions? This issue came to a head when President Reagan moved to defer expenditure of $5.1 billion for housing and related aid to low-income people. This action was quickly contested in the courts. In May 1986, a federal district court, later upheld by an appeals court, ruled that the president no longer had deferral authority under the 1974 budget law. Both courts took the view that Congress would not have given deferral authority to the president without retaining a legislative veto for itself. Hence, when the legislative veto perished, deferral authority for the president, based on policy or programmatic premises, also bit the dust. Deferrals based on the Antideficiency Act are still permitted. These provide for contingencies or take into account savings made possible through changes in requirements or efficiencies in operations.[38]

The problem pointed up in the controversy over deferral applies to the budgetary process generally: What is the appropriate balance between presidential discretion and congressional control in spending? In cases of conflict, whose judgment should prevail? It would be much easier to answer these questions if only managerial matters were at stake. As we have seen, though, the budget is a policy document that reflects major policy values and priorities, a characteristic that makes budgetary decision-making much more contentious.

Among others, economists disagree about the importance of budget deficits and their impact on the economy. Historically, however, popular belief in the desirability of a balanced federal budget has persisted. A balanced budget has been seen as emblematic of "prudent management," as a source of restraint on government, and as necessary to prevent shifting the costs of government to future generations. The notion that government, like a family, cannot live forever beyond its means is conventional wisdom. Almost all the American states constitutionally require an annually balanced budget. Most public officials have thought it wise to pay homage to the goal, sooner or later, of a balanced budget. Balancing the budget has often become a political issue, with the "out" party criticizing the party in the White House for its failure to balance the budget.

CASE STUDY	*The Struggle to Balance the Budget*

The national debt of the United States is a cumulation of annual budget deficits minus budget surpluses (which have been uncommon in the last half century). Except for a brief period in the mid-1830s, the nation has always had a national debt.[39] In the 1960s and 1970s, budget deficits were usually in the single-digit range, and thus did not add much to the national debt.

Change came in the 1980s with the Reagan administration. Government revenues declined because of a recession early in the administration and large tax cuts, in line with supply-side economics, which Reagan embraced. According to supply-side economics theory, tax cuts would encourage people to work, save, and invest, and the lower tax rates would "pay for themselves." It did not work out that way. Spending for national defense and entitlement programs increased. Revenues declined. The result: budgets of more than $200 billion annually. Many considered this alarming; some said the budget was "hemorrhaging." The national budget was raised a record eighteen times during Reagan's administration (see Table 5.5).

In this section, some efforts to devise and implement policies to bring the deficit, and the national debt, under control will be surveyed. It is a complex story, but then, life is often not simple—except, perhaps, for the simple-minded.

Congress adopted the Balanced Budget and Emergency Deficit Control Act (better known as the Gramm-Rudman-Hollings Act) in December 1985. Public and congressional concern over the large budget deficits in the early 1980s provided the context and motivation for its enactment. Efforts to reduce the deficit by conventional budgetary procedures had been unsuccessful because of strong partisan differences between members of Congress (especially the Democrats) and the Reagan administration on military and social-welfare spending as well as tax increases.

The Gramm-Rudman-Hollings (GRH) proposal was introduced in the Senate in late September 1985 as an amendment to a bill authorizing an increase in the national debt, which was required to enable the government to continue borrowing money to meet its spending obligations. The amendment never received committee hearings or consideration in either house, however, although these are customary for legislation of such importance. The proposal required the president and Congress to eliminate the budget deficit within five years, either by regular budget procedures or, if these were unavailing, with automatic, uniform, across-the-board budget cuts implemented by the CBO and the OMB. Described by Senator Warren Rudman (R, New Hampshire) as "a bad idea whose time had come," within a couple of weeks the Republican-led Senate had passed the measure by a 75-to-24 vote. This indicates how strongly the Senate felt compelled to do something about the deficit, even if its action was only symbolic.

TABLE 5.5

Budget Receipts, Outlays, Surplus or Deficit, and Gross National Debt, Selected Years from 1940 to 2013, in Billions of Current Dollars

Year	Receipts	Outlays	Surplus or Deficit	National Debt
1940	6.5	9.5	−2.9	50.7
1945	45.2	92.7	−47.6	260.1
1950	39.4	42.6	−3.1	256.7
1955	65.5	68.4	−4.1	274.4
1960	92.5	92.3	0.3	290.5
1965	116.8	118.2	−1.4	322.3
1970	186.9	183.6	3.2	380.9
1975	279.1	332.3	−2.8	541.9
1980	517.1	590.9	−53.2	909.1
1985	734.1	946.3	−212.3	1,817.5
1990	1,032.0	1,253.2	−221.2	3,026.6
1995	1,351.8	1,515.8	−164.0	4,921.0
1996	1,453.1	1,560.6	−107.5	5,181.9
1997	1,579.3	1,601.3	−22.0	5,369.7
1998	1,721.8	1,652.6	69.2	5,478.7
1999	1,827.5	1,701.9	125.5	5,606.1
2000	2,025.2	1,788.6	236.4	5,629.0
2001	1,991.0	1,863.9	127.4	5,770.3
2002	1,853.2	2,011.0	−157.8	6,198.4
2003	1,782.3	2,157.6	−375.3	6,760.0
2004	1,880.0	2,290.0	−412.0	7,355.0
2005	2,153.9	2,472.2	−318.3	7,905.3
2006	2,407.3	2,655.4	−248.2	8,451.4
2007	2,568.2	2,730.2	−162.0	8,950.7
2008	2,524.0	2,983.0	−459.0	9,986.0
2009	2,105.0	3,517.7	−1,412.7	11,857.9
2010	2,162.7	3,457.1	−1,294.1	13,528.8
2011	2,303.5	3,603.1	−1,299.6	14,764.4
2012*	2,441.9	3,652.6	−1,201.7	16,207.0
2013*	2,763.6	3,754.2	−990.6	17,482.7

*Estimated
Sources: *Economic Report of the President*, 2013 (Washington, DC: Government Printing Office, 2013), p. 421, Table B-78.

After much to-ing and fro-ing by the House and Senate on the bill, negotiations were entered into by a small group of congressional leaders. Meeting in private sessions, they were able to hammer out an agreement; it was passed by both houses and signed into law by the president in mid-December 1985.

As adopted, the GRH required that the national budget deficit be reduced to $171.9 billion in FY 1987 and then be lowered annually by $36 billion until it reached zero in 1991. (In 1987, the zero date was reset to 1993 because the original targets were too difficult to reach.) At the insistence of the Democrats, a number of social-welfare programs and interest on the national debt were exempted from the automatic budget cuts, and only limited cuts were permitted for some health programs, including Medicare. These limitations indicated congressional priorities on spending.

If regular budget and appropriations action failed to reach the deficit target for a year, then uniform, across-the-board reductions, divided equally between defense programs and non-exempted domestic programs would be imposed. Because a large portion of the budget was exempted from these automatic reductions, the cutbacks would hit hard on non-exempt programs. This process was called *sequestration*.

The GRH sequestration process did not work well. By setting a deficit target to be reached at the beginning of a fiscal year, GRH encouraged short-term calculations and reliance on budgetary tricks. Costs could be shifted from the current year to an earlier or later one to improve budget figures. Budget projections (the "rosy scenario") could be used that met deficit targets at the beginning of the fiscal year, however, far off the mark that they might later prove to be. As a member of Congress remarked: "The President submits a budget that relies on very optimistic technical and economic assumptions and questionable savings proposals to meet the Gramm-Rudman deficit target. Congress attacks the assumptions and proposals as phony, but uses them in the budget resolution anyway." Congress did not want to take the political "heat" by using more accurate figures that would make it look like a big spender.[40] The Gramm-Rudman-Hollings Act became a policy failure.

Another chapter was added to the saga of budget-deficit reduction in 1990. By the time President Bush sent his proposed budget to Congress for FY 1991, it appeared that the budget deficit would be at least $150 billion.[41] As the months passed, the budgetary situation worsened, partly fueled by the recession afflicting the economy. By September the situation had become ominous; deficit predictions for the FY 1991 reached $170 billion. (The actual deficit turned out to be $269 billion.)

During spring and summer, desultory budget negotiations between the White House and Congress had been unproductive. President Bush continued for a time to stick with his ill-advised 1988 campaign pledge of "Read my lips. No new taxes." In June, under pressure from Democratic congressional leaders, he backed away from his "no new taxes" position: everything was put on the table. As the beginning of the 1991 fiscal year neared, bargaining became more intense, and finally, agreement on a package of tax increases and spending cutbacks was reached at the end of September. Dissatisfaction about this agreement was rife, and it was rejected in the House by an "unholy" alliance of liberal Democrats and conservative Republicans. The latter, led by Representative Newt Gingrich (R, Georgia), were outraged by the president's violation of his "no new taxes" vow.

Negotiations between the White House and Congress resumed in the context of recriminations from both sides. At the end of October, agreement finally was reached on a new combination of tax increases, spending reductions, and budget procedures. With approval by both houses of Congress and the president, it became law as part of the Omnibus Budget Reconciliation Act (OBRA). Called the Budget Enforcement Act, its provisions are summarized here.

For 1991 to 1993, the Budget Enforcement Act (BEA) established separate limits for discretionary spending: domestic, international, and defense. If spending exceeded the limits in an area, automatic cutbacks would be levied on all programs in that area. For 1994 and 1995, the BEA provided only a total discretionary-spending cap. In the mandatory spending area, a pay-as-you-go rule (PAYGO) applied; spending increases or tax decreases were permitted but only if offset by other spending decreases or tax increases. These BEA rules were later extended through FY 2002. Second, the act provided for various tax increases, including five cents a gallon on gasoline and a new 31 percent income-tax bracket. Third, new budget-deficit targets were specified, which could be adjusted (in all likelihood, upward) when economic conditions changed. The president and Congress could also designate "emergency spending" that was exempt from spending limitations. In all, it was predicted that the budget agreement would reduce projected budget deficits by $496 billion over the 1991 to 1995 period.

The budget deficit and what to do about it were major issues in the 1992 presidential campaign. Billionaire and independent candidate Ross Perot constantly harped about the need to eliminate the deficit. Democratic candidate Bill Clinton pledged to cut the deficit in half by the end of his first term. Once in office, however, he found this to be a daunting task. Not only did he want to increase government spending ("investment") for several purposes, but he also found that the budget deficit was larger than anticipated.

Early in 1993, the Clinton administration devised a budget plan combining tax increases (for instance, an energy tax based on the heat content of fuels and hikes in personal and corporate income taxes) and spending cutbacks in both discretionary and entitlement programs. The administration estimated that this plan would reduce the deficit by a total of $447 billion over a five-year period, thereby lowering the deficit in 1997 to around $200 billion. Democrats in Congress were generally supportive of the proposal, but Republicans sharply criticized it for including too many tax increases and insufficient spending decreases, and for not reducing the deficit enough.

Over the next several months, a titanic partisan political struggle took place in Congress, first over the adoption of a congressional budget resolution in line with the president's proposal and then over the enactment of reconciliation legislation to implement the budget resolution. The budget resolution passed by partisan votes of 240 to 184 in the House and 55 to 45 in the Senate. No Republicans voted in favor of the resolution, and only a few conservative Democrats voted against it. The budget resolution called for $246 billion in tax increases, mostly on higher-income groups, and $247 billion in spending cutbacks. The amount of spending cutbacks had been enlarged in the House to mollify conservative Democrats.[42]

Reconciliation legislation was required to implement the tax increases and entitlement spending reductions (about two-thirds of the $493 billion total). The remainder of the spending cutbacks (those in discretionary spending) was left to the appropriations committees. Partisan and interest-group conflict intensified over reconciliation because of its binding character. Clinton administration officials, including the president and vice president, had to do much persuading and bargaining in order to secure Democratic majorities sufficient for its enactment, there being little hope of picking up Republican votes.

The Omnibus Budget Reconciliation Act of 1993 was adopted by votes of 218 to 216 in the House and 51 to 50 in the Senate. Forty-one conservative House Democrats voted against it. In the Senate, Vice President Al Gore cast the tie-breaking vote as five Democratic senators joined the opposition. In addition to the gasoline tax, the reconciliation act increased corporate income taxes; added personal income-tax brackets of 36 percent and 39.6 percent, which hit higher-income individuals; and raised many user fees. Cuts were made in many spending programs, most notably defense and Medicare. In all, the act made several hundreds of changes in existing laws and programs.[43]

Although Republicans and conservative Democrats in 1994 called for additional spending cutbacks, the Clinton administration, preoccupied with such matters as reform of the nation's medical system that year, chose not to renew the deficit-reduction struggle.

The Republican majorities swept into Congress by the 1994 congressional elections made not merely deficit reduction but also balancing the budget top agenda items. They launched a two-pronged attack on the deficit. First, they sought to propose a constitutional amendment requiring an annually balanced budget, as was called for by the House Republicans' "Contract with America." Readily winning approval in the House, the amendment fell one vote short of the two-thirds approval needed in the Senate. Proponents of the amendment contended that it was needed to provide officials with sufficient motivation (or backbone) to balance the budget. Opponents questioned whether this would happen. Further, they argued that the annually balanced budget requirement would handcuff the government in dealing with economic fluctuations, especially recessions.

Dismayed, but undaunted by the failure to pass the balanced-budget amendment, the Republicans now trained their guns directly on the budget. In June 1995, once again sharply split along party lines, Congress passed a budget resolution calling for a balanced budget by the year 2002. To achieve this goal, over a seven-year period, spending was to be reduced by a total of $984 billion while taxes were to be cut by $245 billion. This arrangement represented a compromise between the tax-cutting and deficit-hawk segments of the congressional Republicans.[44] (The Clinton administration's proposed budget was ignored.)

The Republicans' attention then turned to the complex task of drafting reconciliation legislation to put their plan into law. Work on the reconciliation bill was not completed until late in November 1995. In final form, it specified, over a seven-year span, a reduction of $270 billion in

Medicare, $163 billion in Medicaid, $114 billion in entitlement programs for the poor, and a multitude of other cutbacks. The $245 billion in tax cuts included a $500-per-child tax credit for families with incomes under $110,000 and reductions in the capital-gains tax and various business taxes.[45] When the reconciliation bill reached President Clinton, it received the expected veto. Denouncing the bill as extreme and wrongheaded, the president said he would present a more acceptable proposal for balancing the budget by 2002. Indeed, negotiations on an alternative had been underway prior to his veto.[46]

To back up for a bit, when FY 1996 got underway on October 1, none of the appropriations bills had been enacted into law. Consequently, a continuing resolution providing for partial and temporary funding was enacted to permit the government to continue operating. When that resolution expired in November, a partial, four-day shutdown of the government occurred. In the parlance of budgetary negotiations, this was a "train wreck." Subsequently, another continuing resolution was passed to permit the government to resume full operations. Also, by this time (late November) a half-dozen appropriations bills had been enacted into law.

Following President Clinton's veto of the reconciliation bill, protracted negotiations over balancing the budget occurred between executive officials, including the president, and congressional leaders from both parties; these negotiations were not concluded until near the end of April 1996. During this time span the president vetoed three appropriations bills, another partial government shutdown lasting twenty-one days occurred, and a dozen temporary continuing resolutions were adopted. Much acrimony, wheeling and dealing, dissembling, and bargaining accompanied the negotiations.[47]

In April, with half of the 1996 fiscal year gone, five appropriations bills not enacted, and the likelihood of an agreement on a balanced budget a poor bet, the White House and the Republicans reached agreement on an omnibus appropriations bill to fund much of the government for the remainder of the fiscal year.[48] Both sides could claim some success. The Republicans succeeded in reducing discretionary spending by $20 billion below its 1995 level, in the process cutting funding for many agencies and programs and eliminating a substantial number of small programs. They also got President Clinton to agree to their goal of a balanced budget in 2002 and to using the more cautious CBO figures in making budget estimates.

For his part, President Clinton had been able to protect his priorities on education, job training, and the environment. For example, the EPA's budget was cut by about 10 percent, but that was less than half of the cut that was initially sought by the House Republicans. Also, almost all of the restrictive riders added by House Republicans to reorient regulatory policies were deleted. Except for agriculture, where the Federal Agricultural Improvement and Reform (FAIR) Act removed production controls as a condition for receiving income supports for most farmers, no major changes were made in entitlement programs.

When President Clinton sent his proposed budget for FY 1997 to Congress, he called for the national budget to be balanced by 2002. Because neither side wanted to renew the intense political struggle that had revolved around the 1996 budget, however, the action to achieve balance was restrained. For example, the Republicans decided to try to hold discretionary spending at its 1996 level rather than work for another round of substantial reductions, and plans for major changes in entitlement spending and for tax reductions were deferred until after the 1996 elections.

The 1996 elections resulted in the return of Clinton to the White House and reduced Republican majorities in Congress. This, plus continued public support for a balanced budget, convinced both sides that they needed to deal with one another.[49] The strong economy also made reaching a budget agreement easier because it produced more revenue. Serious negotiations ensued between Clinton administration officials and the Republican leadership. Although they were consulted, to their dismay, Democratic congressional leaders were not direct participants.

In the budget agreement concluded in May 1997, each side got some of what it wanted. The Republicans, for instance, got larger tax cuts than Clinton preferred, whereas Medicare reductions, which were less than the Republicans wanted, were more to his liking. He also got tax credits for education and additional discretionary funding. Further, it was agreed that the budget should be balanced by FY 2002. The spending caps initiated in 1990 were continued until then.[50]

The May agreement provided only the outlines of a deal; it became necessary to incorporate it in specific legislation. This task was complicated by disputes over what actually had been agreed upon (apparently there was no note-taker present). Also, most House Democrats were opposed to the agreement. The final terms of the agreement were incorporated in two reconciliation bills, which became law in August 1997. It was estimated that the Balanced Budget Act, for spending, and the Taxpayer Relief Act, for tax changes, together would reduce budget deficits by $204 billion over a five-year period.

The balanced budget arrived sooner than expected. The budget for FY 1998 produced a $69 billion surplus; surpluses followed for the next three fiscal years (see Table 5.5). Predictions of budget surpluses for the next decade and beyond replaced pessimism about the effects of budget-deficit reduction efforts and predictions of budget deficits for years to come. The CBO, which has a better record on these matters than the OMB, in early 1999 forecast that budget surpluses for the 2000–2010 period would cumulate to $2.6 trillion dollars. The future looked even better early in 2001 when OMB and CBO both forecast a cumulative surplus of $5.6 trillion for the next decade. (Almost as far "as the eye could see.")

This reversal in budgetary fortunes was the product of several factors. First was the cumulative impact of the 1990 budget agreement, the Clinton administration's 1993 budget-deficit reduction plan, and the 1997 Clinton-Republican agreement. All together, these actions provided for considerably more than a trillion dollars in budget-deficit reduction.[51] Second, there was substantial growth in government revenues because of the robust economy and the higher tax rates imposed on upper-income receivers by the 1990 and 1993 actions. Third, the strong economy operated to hold down some entitlement spending.[52]

Although the estimated budget projects were only projections, and projections have a way of missing the mark, many Washington officials chose to reify them. Consequently, the problem of what to do *about* the budget deficit was replaced on the policy agenda by the problem of what to do *with* the budget surpluses.[53] Alternative proposals quickly emerged. The Clinton administration advocated using the surpluses primarily to strengthen Social Security and pay down the national debt. Many Republicans advocated converting the surpluses into tax cuts, both to benefit taxpayers at all income levels and to ward off new spending programs. Liberal Democrats wanted to use some of the surpluses for new or expanded governmental programs, especially for low-income groups. Nor were all Republicans opposed to more spending if it went for purposes like highways and military programs.

Spending increased, exceeding the BEA caps. This was justified by designating various expenditures, even those for the 2000 decennial census, which is called for by the Constitution, as "emergency" spending.

Campaigning for the presidency in 2000, George W. Bush called for a massive tax cut to return some of the "people's money" to them. Once in office, he made tax cuts his top priority. When it became apparent that the economy was slipping into recession in early 2001, the tax cut was declared necessary to stimulate the economy, even though most of the proposed tax reductions were slated to take effect several years into the future and were for upper-income people.[54] Drawing support from Republicans and moderate Democrats, the complex measure was enacted in June 2001, amid estimates that it would reduce taxes by $1.35 trillion over a ten-year time span. Income-tax rates were lowered, especially for wealthier people, the estate tax was phased out, child and family tax credits were increased, and tax exemptions for retirement plans were increased. The law also contained a provision stating that it would be repealed in its entirety at the end of 2010; that is, all taxes would then revert to their 2001 levels. This was a gimmick used to hold down its estimated cost and to avoid Senate budget rules.[55]

The September 11 terrorist attacks on the World Trade Center towers and the Pentagon exacerbated concerns about the state of the economy and created demands for increased spending for national defense, homeland security, and recovery from the attacks. On September 15, Congress unanimously enacted a $40 billion emergency appropriation for response and recovery. This was followed in a few days by a $15 billion aid package for the beleaguered airline industry. Increased spending for antiterrorism activity and national defense soon followed.

The CBO and OMB projections of a $5.6 trillion ten-year budget surplus had rested on the assumptions, among others, that there would be neither a recession nor major changes in taxing and spending policies. Always questionable, the unrealistic character of these assumptions was revealed by the recession, the huge tax cut, and soaring spending. Budget deficits reappeared.[56] The Bush administration said that the budget deficit for FY 2002 (October 1, 2001, to September 30, 2002) would exceed $100 billion, to be followed by smaller deficits in the next two years, after which it optimistically foresaw the return of surpluses. For its part, the CBO in January 2002 estimated that the cumulative budget surplus for the decade running through 2011 would be $1.6 trillion, down $4 trillion from its forecast of a year earlier. Moreover, according to CBO, most of this surplus would occur in the final two years of the decade, when time makes such lengthy projections most dubious.[57] All of this proved false, not surprisingly.

The budget deficit reached a then-record level (in current dollars) of $412 billion in FY 2004. Early in 2005, President Bush pledged to cut the budget deficit in half within five years, mostly by reductions in spending, including for popular entitlement programs.[58] Tax increases of course were out of the question. Budget deficits did shrink for three years (see Table 5.5), more because of increased revenues generated by the improving economy than because of spending cutbacks. Revenue growth tailed off, however, because of the Great Recession that began in late 2007, the Bush administration's tax cuts, spending increases, and the rebates enacted to stimulate the economy. The FY 2008 budget deficit soared to a new record high of $459 billion. But, worse was soon to come.

Democrats chose to assign major responsibility for the return of budget deficits to the Bush tax cuts. Republicans pointed their fingers at increased government spending, especially for domestic programs, and the recessions. Although the Congressional Republicans had been highly vocal on the need for balanced budgets during the Clinton years, they now muted their concerns. Vice-President Richard Cheney asserted that "Ronald Reagan proved that deficits don't matter." Members of both parties supported more spending for politically popular and preferred programs. The Republicans also continued to call for more tax cuts and, indeed, in 2003 Congress had passed another big tax cut, this one for $350 billion.[59]

As 2008 wore on, the economic situation became graver. The bursting of the housing bubble that had developed in the early 2000s, which had been fueled by reckless lending and the notion that housing prices would forever rise, and bad investment practices combined to produce a financial crisis in American and global credit markets. Bush administration officials urged Congress to authorize the U.S. Treasury to spend $700 billion to stabilize (or "bail out") American banks. After some balkiness, Congress yielded and passed the Emergency Economic Stabilization Act in early October 2008.

Money was poured into banks in an effort to get the financial system on its feet and lending again. Many billions were also committed to the ailing American automobile industry. There was hope that in time some of the government's money would be paid back.[60] The short run effect was to further inflate the national budget deficit. More bailout spending in the future was a possibility.

The return of budget deficits has brought back another policy problem— the need to raise the legal limit on the national debt from time to time to enable the government to borrow money to meet its obligations. President George W. Bush got Congress to raise the debt limit several times during his tenure. Republicans are loathe to vote for debt increases, if at all, but prefer to attach them to other legislation where they are less obvious. Democrats have customarily supported debt increases, perhaps after engaging in some "political theater." Early in 2009 the debt limit was elevated to $12.104 trillion (an interesting bit of precision!). More increases in the debt limit will be required as deficits continue. There really is no viable alternative. Fortunately, Americans and foreigners continue to be willing to lend money to the government at low interest rates.

Mid-January 2009, when the Obama administration took office, was clearly not the best of times. If not the worst of times, it was moving in that direction. The initial year of the administration was taken up by stimulus legislation, financial regulation, health-care reform, and more. Unemployment was rapidly rising (and in time would reach 10 percent), entitlement spending was growing, and revenue was declining. The Great Recession was in full force. When FY 2009 ended that fall, the budget deficit was $1.4 trillion, and all-time record. It was to be followed by three more trillion dollar plus deficits (see Table 5.5). It is now in order to look at some of the Obama administration deficit reduction efforts and woes.

Pressure developed in 2009 for some kind of action to deal with the budget deficit, Senators Kent Conrad (D, South Dakota) and Judd (R, New Hampshire), a pair of deficit hawks, advocated the creation of a bipartisan commission to develop a plan to reduce annual deficits. In time, President Obama gave it his support but conservatives were wary, thinking the commission might lead to tax increases. When the conrad–Gregg proposal was voted on in January 2010, it was rejected 53 to 46, 60 votes being needed to move it to the Senate floor. Several Republicans, who had previously been supporters of the bipartisan commission, now voted no.

President Obama then decided to act issuing an executive order establishing a National Commission on Fiscal Responsibility and Reform. It had six members each from the House and Senate, divided equally between Democrats and Republicans, and six civilian members. The cochairs were Alan Simpson, the Republican Senator from Wyoming, and Erskine Bowles, who had served for a time as chief of staff in the Clinton administration. They were another pair of deficit hawks. The Simpson–Bowles Commission, as it came to be known, was to report its handiwork in December 2010.

When the commission reported, it called for deficit reduction of $3.9 trillion over a ten-year period.[61] This would be generated by cuts in discretionary and mandatory spending, revenue increases (mostly by eliminating some tax expenditures), and net savings in interest. Only eleven of the eighteen members gave the report their approval. The executive order specified that fourteen favorable votes were needed for the report to be "officially" submitted to Congress. Hence, the Simpson–Bowles report went nowhere. Simpson and Bowles later tried to revive it. That did not take wing, either.

In May 2011, the government reached the current national debt limit. The Treasury Department estimated that it could use extraordinary measures to meet the government's financial obligations until August. Many Republicans saw this as an opportunity to pressure the administration for budget reductions in return for raising the debt limit. As the August deadline drew closer, the President, Congressional leaders, and Treasury officials were able to reach agreement on a debt limit deal and stave off sovereign default. The Budget Control Act, as the resulting legislation was known, passed by a vote of 269 to 11 in the House and 76 to 24 in the Senate.

The Budget Control Act provided for several actions.[62] First, the national debt limit was immediately increased by $400 billion. Additional increases of up to $1.7 billion were authorized as they became necessary. In all, this provided for a national debt of $16.4 trillion, enough to eliminate the need for further increases until early 2013.

Second, it imposed statutory limits on discretionary spending totaling $917 billion for fiscal years 2012–2021. Automatic spending cuts would be imposed whenever annual appropriations limits were exceeded. Some emergency spending, as for the war on terror, was exempt from the limits.

Third, the act required additional deficit reductions of no less than $1.2 trillion over the 2012–2021 periods. A twelve-member Joint Select Committee on Deficit Reduction was created to write legislation to accomplish these reductions. Quickly dubbed the "super committee," it had twelve members, three from each party in each house, selection by party leaders. There were no restrictions on what the super committee could recommend, but it was to report toward the end of November 2011. Close to the deadline, it reported that it was hopelessly deadlocked. Republican members blamed the Democrats for refusing to make changes in entitlements; Democrats said the fault was with the Republicans who would not consider tax increases.

Fourth, the act provided that if the super committee failed to propose legislation, automatic deficit reductions totaling $1.2 trillion for 2013–2021 would go into effect. The act specified that it would include $216 billion in debt interest savings and $984 billion in spending cutbacks divided equally between defense and domestic discretionary spending. (In Congressional parlance, these automatic reductions were called sequestration.) Most entitlement programs were exempt. It was thought, at least by some, that the threat of this drastic action would spur Congress to enact alternative legislation.

Fifth, the Budget Control Act called for the House and Senate to vote on a balanced budget amendment to the Constitution by the end of 2011. Conservative Republicans, especially in the House, had insisted on this. When the votes were taken, almost all of the House Republicans voted for the amendment. It was well short of the two-thirds majority needed in both houses, however.

Following the November 2012 elections, in which Barack Obama decisively won a second term, an observer, perhaps from another planet, might have thought that the Republicans would be more willing to bargain and compromise. That was not the case. Partisan conflict now developed over what to do about the "fiscal cliff."[63]

The fiscal cliff was the combination of circumstances that included the expiration of the Bush-era tax cuts, the end of a two percentage point reduction in payroll taxes to stimulate the economy, the termination of extended unemployment benefits, and the inception of budget sequestration, all of which would occur on January 1, 2013. This, it was thought, would be an economic catastrophe, though some of its impact would not be experienced immediately.

Negotiations between Senate leaders and Obama administration officials got underway, but progress was at first slow. Finally, at almost the final hour, an agreement was reached. Much credit was accorded talks between Vice President Joseph Biden and Republican Senate leader Mitch McConnell (R, Kentucky), who had served together in the Senate for many years and who trusted one another. On New Year's Day, 2013, Congress passed the American Taxpayer Relief Act by votes of 89 to 8 in the Senate and 257 to 167 in the House. A majority of the House Republicans opposed it. The president signed it the next day.

The American Taxpayer Relief Act made all of the Bush-era tax cuts permanent with one exception. For persons with taxable income above $400,000 ($450,000 for couples) the marginal rate was set at 39.6 percent, which it had been during the Clinton administration. Other provisions included setting the estate tax at 40 percent of the value above $5 million; extension of several corporate tax breaks; extension of some tax credits for lower-income families, such as the Earned Income Tax Credit; and a phase-out of tax credits and deductions for higher-income persons. The two-year-old cut in payroll tax was ended and the onset of budget sequestration was delayed until March 1. The latter action ostensibly was to give Congress an opportunity to enact an alternative. Nothing was accomplished in that matter.

On March 1, budget sequestration for FY 2013 went into effect.[64] The target figure for the remainder of the year was $85 billion, to be divided equally between military and domestic discretionary spending. Cutbacks were required in agency activities and services. Tens of thousands of children were not able to enter Head Start programs, for example. Because a large portion of many agencies' budgets go for personnel expenses, agencies initiated such practices as furloughing (and not paying) many employees for a day every two weeks.

A vignette. For the Federal Aviation Administration, sequestration meant, inter alia, reducing the availability of air traffic controllers, which caused airport delays.[65] Complaints from irritated travelers poured in. Congress scurried to alleviate this situation and passed (by large bipartisan majorities) legislation permitting the FAA to use funds from other accounts to restore the air traffic control system to full strength. As someone said, all members of Congress fly. No other agencies were authorized to take similar action.

Early on it is difficult to assess the impact of sequestration on agency programs or on local communities where there are significant numbers of government employees. One prediction was that sequestration would cause the economy to "start moving more slowly."[66]

On May 19, the national debt limit, which had been temporarily suspended by congressional action in February, went back in force.[67] The $16.4 trillion limit had already been exceeded. The Treasury Department estimated it could use various stratagems to meet the government's obligations until sometime in the fall of 2013.[68] Some Republicans indicated that they would use this as another opportunity to seek reductions in government spending and the deficit.

After thirty years of conflict and struggle, the budget deficit is still a major public issue. Its resolution does not seem near. A "Grand Bargain" seems not very likely.[69]

When the policy goal of a budget surplus and national debt reduction was realized for a few years during the Clinton administration, the surpluses were the product of tax increases, spending cutbacks, and a strong economy. Taxing and spending changes were not easy to obtain. Partly this was because of partisan political differences, although the parties were not as polarized as they now are. Partly, too, it was because the public, while unhappy with budget deficits, likes neither tax increases nor reductions in favored programs. The George W. Bush and Clinton administrations paid a heavy political price for their tax increases. As has been said, "No good deed goes unpunished."

Budget deficits were annual events from 1970 to 1998 (see Figure 5.4). In a sense, people learned to live with deficits (if they were aware of them), if not necessarily to approve of them. (After all, there is something immoral about debt.) The nation now confronts another extended period of budget deficits and expanded national debt. (If it is any comfort, total private debt in the United States now stands at $25 trillion.) What are the real (not alleged) policy consequences of deficits and debts? Is there a point at which the national debt becomes "unsustainable" or "catastrophic"? How can this be objectively determined? If there were no national debt, in what ways would life in America be better?—Policy riddles about which to think.

Postscript: The CBO, in May 2013, projected that the baseline budget deficit for FY 2013 would be around $642 billion, much less than previous estimates.

FIGURE 5.4

Budget Deficits or Surpluses

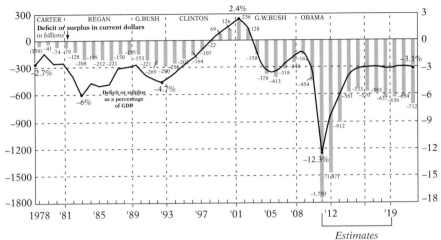

Source: *CQ Weekly, Vol 67* (March 2, 2009), p. 473.

Further, they project the deficits will continue to decline for the next three years. Then, barring policy changes, the budget deficits would resume their annual increases.[70] ■

For Further Exploration

■ *http://www.cbo.gov/*
> The Congressional Budget Office (CBO) website contains reports assessing various proposed congressional policies involving the use of appropriations. This site also provides documents such as cost-estimate reports on all congressional bills and official letters sent to individual representatives and senators by the CBO.

■ *http://www.publicdebt.treas.gov/*
> The Bureau of the Public Debt's website provides a useful link to statistical information regarding the current status of the national debt.

■ *http://www.taxfoundation.org/*
> Maintained by the Tax Foundation, which is a nonpartisan organization devoted to providing information on tax policies at the federal, state, and local levels, this site contains information on recent tax laws passed by Congress and provides discussions and statistical data on fiscal issues.

▌*http://www.whitehouse.gov/omb*
>   The homepage of the Office of Management and Budget provides access to numerous budget-related documents, including testimony of OMB officials before congressional committees, OMB circulars and press releases, the current federal budget, and the *Economic Report of the President.*

Test Your Knowledge

Log on to the student companion website at

login.cengage.com

to access tutorial quizzes, chapter outlines, crossword puzzles, and glossary flashcards that review chapter concepts and terminology.

Suggested Readings

Aaron Wildavsky and Naomi Caiden, *The New Politics of the Budgetary Process*, 4th ed. (New York: Longman, 2001). The political and institutional aspects of national budgeting in the United States are woven together in this classic work.

Allen Schick, *The Federal Budget: Politics, Policy, Process*, 3rd. ed. (Washington, DC: Brookings Institution, 2007). The leading student of the federal budget process here describes and analyzes its operation and the consequences of budget rules for policy decisions.

Daniel J. Palazzolo, *Done Deal? The Politics of the 1997 Budget Agreement* (New York: Chatham House, 1999). A well-constructed case study of the Clinton-Republican agreement to balance the budget.

Dennis S. Ippolito, *Deficits, Debt, and the New Politics of Tax Politics* (New York: Cambridge University Press, 2012). This book provides a compact and insightful historical analysis of fiscal policy under the Constitution, concluding with the early years of the Obama administration.

Irene S. Rubin, *Balancing the Federal Budget* (New York: Chatham House, 2002). Rubin looks at efforts by Congress and the administration to balance the budget and their sometimes-damaging consequences to agencies.

Irene S. Rubin, *The Politics of Public Budgeting*, 5th ed. (Washington, DC: CQ Press, 2006). Budgeting at the national, state, and local levels is examined in this information-packed book.

James D. Savage, *Balanced Budgets and American Politics* (Ithaca, NY: Cornell University Press, 1988). This is a strong historical account of the budget-balancing issue as a perennial source of conflict in American politics.

Notes

1. Louis Fisher, *The Politics of Shared Power: Congress and the Executive*, 3rd ed. (Washington, DC: CQ Press, 1993), p. 133.
2. Gordon McKay Stevenson Jr., *The Politics of Airport Noise* (Belmont, CA: Duxbury Press, 1972).
3. Sidney A. Shapiro, "Lessons from a Public Policy Failure: EPA and Noise Abatement," *Ecology Law Quarterly*, Vol. 19, no. 1 (1992), p. 1062.
4. *Illinois Agri-News*, January 23, 2009, p. C2. The final rule is in *Federal Register*, Vol. 74 (January 15, 2009), pp. 2658ff.
5. G. Calvin Mackenzie and Saranna Thornton, *Bucking the Deficit: Economic Policymaking in America* (Boulder, CO: Westview Press, 1996), Chap. 3.
6. Herbert Stein, *Presidential Economics* (Washington, DC: American Enterprise Institute Press, 1994), Chap. x.
7. Richard Rubin, "Expanded Stimulus Bill Clears," *CQ Weekly*, Vol. 66 (February 11, 2008), pp. 390–391.
8. *The New York Times*, January 10, 2009, p. 11.
9. Michael Grunwald, *The New New Deal* (New York: Simon and Schuster, 2012). This is a thorough look at its adoption and implementation.
10. CQ Almanac 2009 (Washington, DC: CQ-Roll Call Group, 2010), Vol. 65, pp. 7-3–7-10.
11. Alan Blinder, *After the Music Stopped* (New York: Penguin Press, 2013), Chap. 8; Congressional Budget Office, "Estimates of ARRA's Economic Impact," http://www.cbo.gov/publication/43014; and Mark Zandi, *Paying the Price* (Upper Saddle River, NJ: FT Press, 2013), Chap. 5.
12. Allen Schick, *The Federal Budget: Politics, Policy, Process*, 3rd ed. (Washington, DC: Brookings Institution Press, 2007), p. 88.
13. Hugh Heclo, "Executive Budget Making," in Gregory B. Mills and John L. Palmer, eds., *Federal Budget Policy in the 1980s* (Washington, DC: Urban Institute Press, 1984), pp. 255–291.
14. Schick, op. cit., pp. 116–117.
15. R. Kent Weaver, *Automatic Government: The Politics of Indexation* (Washington, DC: Brookings Institution, 1988).
16. Cf. James L. True, "Is the National Budget Controllable?" *Public Budgeting and Finance*, Vol. 15 (Summer 1995), pp. 18–32.
17. Lance L. LeLoup, *Budgetary Politics*, 2nd ed. (Brunswick, OH: King's Court Communications, 1980), p. 200.
18. Howard E. Shuman, *Politics and the Budget*, 2nd ed. (Englewood Cliffs, NJ: Prentice-Hall, 1988), p. 79.
19. Ken Godwin, Scott H. Ainsworth, and Erik Godwin, *Lobbying and Policymaking* (Los Angeles: Sage, 2013), pp. 63–65, 84–87; and Chris Mooney, *The Republican War on Science* (New York: Basic Books, 2005), Chap. 8.
20. The classic statement of incremental budgeting is Aaron Wildavsky, *The Politics of the Budgetary Process* (Boston, MA: Little, Brown, 1964).
21. Irene S. Rubin, *The Politics of Public Budgeting*, 4th ed. (Chatham, NJ: Chatham House, 2000), pp. 127–128.
22. Allen Schick, "Incremental Budgeting in a Decremental Age," in Albert C. Hyde, ed., *Government Budgeting: Theory, Process, Politics* (Pacific Grove, CA: Brooks/Cole, 1992), pp. 410–425.

23. This discussion draws on Schick, *The Federal Budget*, op. cit., pp. 66–70.
24. Allen Schick, *The Capacity to Budget* (Washington, DC: Urban Institute Press, 1990), p. 99.
25. Andrew Taylor, "Congress Hands President a Budgetary Scalpel," *Congressional Quarterly Weekly Report*, Vol. 56 (March 30, 1996), pp. 864–867.
26. R. W Apple Jr., "Line-Item Veto Is a Great Unknown," *The New York Times*, March 27, 1996, p. 1.
27. *Clinton v. City of New York*, No. 97–1374, June 1998. See also Andrew Taylor, "Few in Congress Grieve as Justices Give Line-Item Veto the Ax," *Congressional Quarterly Weekly Report*, Vol. 56 (June 27, 1998), pp. 1747–1749.
28. John W. Ellwood and James A. Thurber, "The Politics of the Congressional Budget Process Re-Examined," in Lawrence C. Dodd and Bruce I. Oppenheimer, eds., *Congress Reconsidered*, 2nd ed. (Washington, DC: Congressional Quarterly Press, 1981), pp. 247–251.
29. John Cranford, *Budgeting for America*, 2nd ed. (Washington, DC: Congressional Quarterly Press, 1989), pp. 197–198.
30. Ibid., p. 200.
31. *Budget of the United States Government, Fiscal Year 1989* (Washington, DC: U.S. Government Printing Office, 1988), p. 6e.
32. Walter J. Oleszek, *Congressional Procedures and the Policy Process*, 5th ed. (Washington, DC: CQ Press, 2001), p. 54.
33. Committee on Appropriations, "Agriculture, Rural Development, Food and Drug Administration, and Related Agencies Appropriations Bill, 1996," House Report 172, 104th Cong., 1st Sess., 1995, p. 39.
34. For fuller discussions, see Louis Fisher, *Presidential Spending Power* (Princeton, NJ: Princeton University Press, 1975), Chaps. 7–8; and James P. Pfiffner, *The President, the Budget, and Congress: Impoundment and the 1974 Budget Act* (Boulder, CO: Westview Press, 1979).
35. Fisher, op. cit., p. 176.
36. Louis Fisher, *Constitutional Conflicts Between Congress and the President*, 4th ed., rev. (Lawrence, KS: University Press of Kansas, 1997), pp. 204–206.
37. *Immigration and Naturalization Service v. Chadha*, 462 U.S. 919 (1983).
38. Schick, *The Federal Budget*, op. cit., p. 286.
39. James D. Savage, *Balanced Budgets and American Politics* (Ithaca, NY: Cornell University Press, 1988).
40. Louis Fisher, *The Politics of Shared Power*, 4th ed. (College Station: Texas A&M University Press, 1998), pp. 238–239. The quotation is on p. 239.
41. The following account draws on Daniel P. Franklin, *Making Ends Meet: Congressional Budgeting in the Age of Deficits* (Washington, DC: Congressional Quarterly Press, 1993); and *Congressional Quarterly Almanac 1990* (Washington, DC: Congressional Quarterly Press, 1991), Vol. 46, pp. 111–178.
42. *Congressional Quarterly Weekly Report*, Vol. 51 (February 20, 1993), pp. 355–359.
43. *Congressional Quarterly Almanac, 1993* (Washington, DC: Congressional Quarterly Press, 1994), Vol. 49, pp. 107–124.
44. *Congressional Quarterly Weekly Report*, June 24, 1995, p. 1814.
45. *The New York Times*, November 17, 1995, p. A14.
46. *The New York Times*, December 7, 1995, pp. 1, A14.

47. For accounts of some of the negotiations, see Elizabeth Drew, *Showdown: The Struggle Between the Gingrich Congress and the Clinton White House* (New York: Simon & Schuster, 1996), Chaps. 16–24; and Michael Weisskopf and David Maraniss, "Behind the Stage: Common Problems," *Washington Post National Weekly Edition*, February 5–11, 1996, pp. 9–13.

48. *Congressional Quarterly Weekly Report*, Vol. 54 (April 27, 1996), pp. 1155–1162.

49. This discussion draws on Lance T. LeLoup, Carolyn N. Long, and James N. Giodano, "President Clinton's Fiscal 1998 Budget: Political and Constitutional Paths to Balance," *Public Budgeting and Finance*, Vol. 18 (Spring 1998), pp. 3–32. See also George Hager, "Clinton, GOP Congress Strike Historic Path to Agreement," *Congressional Quarterly Weekly Report*, Vol. 55 (May 3, 1997), pp. 993–999.

50. Ronald Elving and Andrew Taylor, "A Balanced-Budget Deal Won, A Defining Issue Lost," *Congressional Quarterly Weekly Report*, Vol. 55 (August 2, 1997), pp. 1831–1836.

51. George Hager and Alissa J. Rubin, "Both Sides Give Some, Get Some as House Panel Oks Resolution," *Congressional Quarterly Weekly Report*, Vol. 55 (May 17, 1997), pp. 1117–1119.

52. Allen Schick, "A Surplus, If We Can Keep It," *Brookings Review*, Vol. 18 (Winter 2000), pp. 36–39.

53. Alexis Simendinger and David Baumann, "Let the Good Times Roll," *National Journal*, Vol. 31 (January 30, 1999), pp. 248–253. See also Greg Hitt, "Rift Develops in GOP Over Tax Cuts," *Wall Street Journal*, February 12, 1999, p. 2A.

54. Jonathan Chait, *The Big Con* (Boston, MA: Houghton Mifflin, 2007).

55. *Congressional Quarterly Weekly Report*, Vol. 59 (June 9, 2001), pp. 1364, 1390–1394.

56. Irene Rubin, "The Great Unraveling: Federal Budgeting, 1998–2006," *Public Administration Review*, Vol. 67 (June 2007), pp. 608–617.

57. *Analysis of the Congressional Budget Office's Budget and Economic Outlook: Fiscal Years 2003–2012* (Washington, DC: The Concord Coalition, January 24, 2002), p. 2.

58. Joseph J. Schatz and Andrew Taylor, "A Thousand Pages of Political Pain," *Congressional Quarterly Weekly Report*, Vol. 63 (February 14, 2005), pp. 366–373.

59. Bryan D. Jones and Walter Williams, *The Politics of Bad Ideas* (New York: Pearson Longman, 2008), have much to say about the Bush administrations fiscal policies.

60. See "Sorting Out the Bailouts," *CO Weekly*, Vol. 67 (February 23, 2009), pp. 394–409, for a readable discussion of this complex matter.

61. *National Commission on Fiscal Responsibility and Reform* (Washington, DC: The White House, December 2010).

62. Here I draw on Dennis S. Ippolito, *Deficits, Debt, and the New Policy of Tax Politics* (New York: Cambridge University Press, 2012), pp. 239–243.

63. "United States Fiscal Cliff," https://en.wikipedia.org/wiki/United_States_fiscal_cliff.

64. "Budged Sequestration in 2013," https://en.wikipedia.org/wiki/2013_sequestration.

65. *The New York Times*, April 27, 2013, p. A-1.

66. Nancy Cook, "Manifest Destiny," *National Journal*, Vol. 45 (March 2, 2013), p. 30.

67. *The New York Times*, January 16, 2012, P. A-1.

68. D. Andrew Austin and Mindy R. Levit, *The Debt Limit: History and Recent Increases* (Washington, DC: Congressional Research Service, April 10, 2013).

69. David Kanim, "The Congress-Does-Nothing Deficit Reduction Plan," *Washington Monthly*, Vol. 45 (March/April, 2013), pp. 10–11.

70. Congressional Budget Office "Updated Budget Projections: Fiscal Years 2013 to 2023" (Washington, DC: Government Printing Office, May 2013).

6

Policy Implementation

When the adoption phase of the policy process has been completed and, for instance, a bill has been enacted into law by a legislature, we can begin to refer to something called *public policy*. Policymaking is not concluded, however, once a policy decision has been expressed in statutory or other official form. The policies that are embodied in statutes, for example, often are rudimentary and require much additional development. Thus, the Americans with Disabilities Act, which prohibited discrimination against the 43 million Americans with disabilities, has required extensive rule-making to spell out its requirements by the Equal Employment Opportunity Commission (EEOC), the Department of Transportation, the Department of Education, the Federal Communications Commission, and other agencies. Subsequently, they produced hundreds of pages of detailed rules in the *Federal Register*.[1]

With this qualification in mind, we turn to the policy implementation stage of the policy process. Implementation (or administration) has been referred to as "what happens after a bill becomes law." More precisely, implementation encompasses whatever is done to carry a law into effect, to apply it to the target population (e.g., small businesses or motorcycle operators), and to achieve its goals. The study of policy implementation is concerned with the agencies and officials involved, the procedures they follow, the techniques (or tools) they employ, and the political support and opposition that they encounter.[2] In so doing, it focuses attention on the day-to-day operation of government.

There is often considerable uncertainty about what a policy will accomplish, how effective in terms of its goals it will be, or the consequences that it will have for society. It is this uncertainty that makes the study of policy implementation interesting and worthwhile. Policy implementation often is neither a routine nor a very predictable process. Why some policies succeed and others fail remains a challenging puzzle.

In actuality, it is frequently difficult, sometimes impossible, to neatly separate a policy's adoption from its implementation. Here again, we may find that the line between functional activities is smudgy. Statutes sometimes do not do much

225

beyond setting some policy goals and creating a framework of guidelines and restrictions for their realization. Congress usually does not attempt to define fully the intended impact of a law nor try to anticipate all of the problems and situations that may be encountered in its implementation.[3] Even the goals of a statute may not be clearly or consistently specified.

Administrative agencies are often delegated discretion or latitude to issue rules and directives that will fill in the details of policy and make it more specific. The Occupational Safety and Health Act of 1970 exemplifies this pattern. Although the right of workers to a safe and healthful workplace is generally guaranteed, the statute itself does not contain substantive health and safety standards. Rather, the Occupational Safety and Health Administration (OSHA), a bureau in the Department of Labor, is authorized to promulgate rules creating specific health and safety standards. Only as this occurs do we have meaningful and enforceable standards that can be applied to protect workers' health and safety. In effect, within the framework provided by Congress, OSHA both makes and implements policy on industrial health and safety. Different units within OSHA handle the tasks of rule-making and enforcement.

Much of what agencies do during the implementation of policies may appear to be routine, mundane, or tedious—processing requests or applications, inspecting records, collecting information, writing reports, and so forth. Most people may have little or no awareness of what agencies are doing unless they are directly affected. Nonetheless, the consequences of implementation for the content or substance of policy, and for its impact and degree of success, are every bit as important as what transpires during the formulation and adoption stages. Indeed, if implementation fails, then all that preceded was of no avail.

Vigorous and sometimes bitter political struggles attend the implementation of policies, such as those pertaining to environmental-pollution control, affirmative action, and the practice of abortion. Groups that suffer losses in the legislative arena may seek to recoup some of their losses by influencing or disrupting the administration of a policy. Thus, the automobile companies for decades were able to delay the National Highway Traffic Safety Administration's air-bag requirement. The coal-mine industry has persistently worked to lessen the effectiveness of both surface mining and mine-safety regulation.

A few policy decisions are essentially self-executing, such as the national government's refusal to extend formal recognition to the government of a foreign country, presidential decisions to veto legislation passed by Congress (especially when it involves a pocket veto), and the National Park Service's decision in the early 1970s not to fight fires caused by lightning in the national parks. Such decisions, entailing clear-cut, one-time actions, are relatively few, however. Those who study public policy, consequently, can ill afford to neglect the implementation stage of the policy process.

Until the great expansion of social-welfare programs during the Johnson years focused their attention on *implementation* (the term began to gain currency in the 1960s), it had not been of much interest to most political and social scientists.[4] The study of implementation was made salient for political scientists by Professors

Jeffrey L. Pressman and Aaron Wildavsky's *Implementation*, a case study of the failure in the early 1970s of a federal jobs-creation project undertaken by the Economic Development Administration in Oakland, California.[5] Since that seminal event, political scientists have been actively researching the implementation of public policies, debating whether policies can be successfully implemented (or administered), and, finally, striving to build systematic theories that will rigorously explain why some policies are likely to be more successfully implemented than others. They have yet to strike theoretical pay dirt, such as identifying the specific variables critical to successful implementation. Their labors, however, have produced a mound of implementation literature and increased our understanding of the implementation process.[6]

Most of the implementation studies take either a "top-down" or "bottom-up" approach. Top-downers focus on the actions of top-level officials, the factors affecting their behavior, whether policy goals are attained, and whether policy was reformulated on the basis of experience. Bottom-uppers contend that this approach gives too much attention to top-level officials and either ignores or underestimates the efforts of lower-level (or "street-level") officials to either avoid policy or divert it to their own purposes. Implementation studies, they argue, should focus on lower-level officials and how they interact with their clients. State and local economic conditions, the attitudes of local officials, and the actions of clients are among the factors affecting implementation. As one would expect, there have also been efforts to combine these two approaches.[7] Agreement has not been reached, however, on what is the best way to study implementation.

Although drawing on this implementation literature, this chapter takes a more traditional approach to policy implementation and opens with a survey of some of the players in policy implementation. It then narrows its focus to administrative agencies. Administrative organization, the political context, policymaking patterns, and implementation techniques are taken up in order. Along with financial resources (dealt with in Chapter 5, "Budgeting and Public Policy"), these can be viewed as independent variables that affect policy outcomes and implementation success. The concluding section on compliance with policy looks at the responses of those benefited or regulated. The goal of this chapter is to provide readers with a working knowledge of the politics and processes of policy implementation and to furnish some tools for their analysis. Figure 6.1 provides a simplified look at the implementation process.

Federalism and Implementation

Federalism frequently complicates the implementation of national policies. Although various policies—Social Security, commercial airline safety, bank-deposit insurance—are handled solely by national officials, many national policies depend significantly upon state and local governments for grass-roots or street-level support and implementation. This holds true for many national policies on education (both lower and higher), environmental

FIGURE 6.1

The Implementation Process

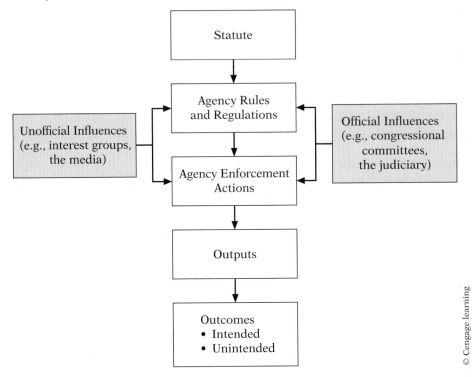

protection, highways, social welfare, and law enforcement.[8] In such areas, Congress has been either reluctant or unable (as in the instance of public education) to bypass the states when it makes policy. Moreover, Congress has found that it can shift many of the costs of national programs to states and localities.

Cost shifting often occurred as the national government, by direction or indirection, imposed program costs on state and local governments. As one might guess, this brought complaints from their officials. In 1995, not long after the Republicans gained control of Congress, the Unfunded Mandates Reform Act passed with large bipartisan majorities. The act was intended to ensure that the costs of mandates enacted by Congress were apparent and to cause Congress to provide financing when intergovernmental mandates were made law. A procedural point of order required Congress to acknowledge it was imposing a mandate. It did not prohibit them.

This has not done much to alter Congressional behavior. Following the adoption of UMRA, Congress has imposed scores of mandates. Many were beyond the scope of the act, which contained several loopholes, such as legislation included in appropriations bills. As Congress responds to pressure to decrease budget deficits, unfunded mandates will help the national government lower its spending while meeting demands for action.

National legislation and agencies may provide policy goals, performance standards, technical assistance, financial support, and more, but much of the day-to-day administrative action necessary to apply policies to the target populations must come from the states. In most states, for example, the Environmental Protection Agency (EPA) has delegated enforcement of its air- and water-quality standards to state environmental agencies. This creates a bilevel implementation situation: macro-implementation and micro-implementation.[9] At the macro level, national officials must act to secure effective action by state officials. Then, at the micro level, state officials must gain compliance from the target populations. Macro–micro implementation increases the likelihood of slippage.

The Clinton administration devised the National Environmental Performance Partnership System (NEPPS) to give the states more flexibility in managing federal environmental programs if they show innovation and better performance in improving environmental quality. Unfortunately, the implementation of NEPPS fell short of expectations. EPA officials often were reluctant to modify existing practices. The states, in turn, proved to be less open to innovation than had been hoped. "They tended to balk at any possibility that the federal government would establish—and publicize—serious performance measures that would evaluate their effectiveness and determine their ability to deviate from federal controls."[10] Administrations since 2000 have displayed minimal interest in promoting NEPPS.

CASE STUDY   *The Elementary and Secondary Education Act*

The Elementary and Secondary Education Act (ESEA) of 1965 was part of the Johnson administration's War on Poverty. Its Title I provided federal financial aid to the states to support better education for disadvantaged children in poor urban and rural areas. It provides a good example of federalism and policy administration.

The social-reform advocates among its supporters thought that this policy was intended to reduce poverty by improving the educational facilities and opportunities that state and local governments made available to the educationally disadvantaged children of low-income families. As initially administered by the Office of Education (now the Department of Education), however, it was unclear to what extent the funds were actually expended on poor children, and whether they bought services beyond the level of those provided for other children in the districts aided. Many cases of the misdirection of funds were reported.[11]

A number of things contributed to this situation. Although the ESEA clearly specified that disadvantaged children were its target population, its legislative history provided "the semblance if not the reality of general aid." This ambiguity, together with the reality that reformers supporting the legislation did not themselves get much involved in implementation, meant that officials in the then-Office of Education were given leeway to interpret the legislation in accord with accepted modes of operation.

The traditional task of the Office of Education had long been to provide assistance and advice to state and local school agencies. It was not inclined to regulate or police their activities and consequently acted with little vigor to ensure that Title I funds were expended as intended. Further, as noted earlier in the chapter, state and local agencies had historically dominated public education, and they enjoyed strong political support for their hegemony. This meant that it would have been difficult for national officials, even if they were so inclined, to impose directives that did not mesh with local priorities.

By the end of the 1970s, however, the administration of the ESEA's Title I had changed markedly. New staff members in the Office of Education had succeeded in securing much tighter supervision of spending under the program. Interest groups, such as the National Welfare Rights Organization and the National Advisory Council for Education of Disadvantaged Children, helped keep the program centered on the disadvantaged. Offices dealing with compensatory education were established in most state departments of education, and they developed a stake in ensuring that funds were used for the disadvantaged. These developments made the effort to target Title I funds on the disadvantaged much more successful. Studies indicated that Title I funds had strengthened the educational performance of the students affected.

This change in the way the Title I program was administered aligned it more closely with the intention of its original supporters. It was retained as a separate program in 1981 when many other education programs were combined into an education block grant by the Education Consolidation and Improvement Act, a Reagan administration initiative.

During the Clinton administration, funding for the Title I program continued to expand. However, efforts to direct more money to districts with large numbers of low-income pupils, and to increase accountability for the use of federal funds, did not succeed.

The No Child Left Behind Act (NCLBA) of 2001, a complicated, lengthy, and bipartisan statute that reauthorized for six years the ESEA is a major expansion of federal involvement and control in public education. Promoted by the George W. Bush administration, it was adopted by strong bipartisan congressional majorities.[12] It was the administration's signature domestic policy achievement other than tax cuts.

The No Child Left Behind Act requires the states, as a condition for receiving federal education funding, to test students annually in grades three through eight, and in one year of high school, on reading and mathematics. Science tests are required for one grade each in elementary, middle, and high schools. This testing is intended to ensure that by 2014 all students reach a level of "academic proficiency" set by their state, including those students with learning disabilities and those for whom English is a second language. The states are responsible for designing and administering their tests under the supervision of the U.S. Department of Education.

Schools that do not make "adequate yearly progress" toward meeting the proficiency goal for two consecutive years are deemed "in need of improvement." They must take such prescribed actions as permitting students to transfer to other public schools or providing supplemental services such as tutoring. Ultimately, a school failing to make adequate progress could be "reconstituted"—that is, turned over to state control or converted into a charter school.

The basic intent of NCLBA is to pressure the states and their more than 95,000 public schools to improve the quality of public education by increasing their "accountability" for the use of federal funds by requiring an extensive testing program. It builds on an effort initiated by the 1994 reauthorization of the ESEA which was only partially successful, during the Clinton administration.

Implementation of NCLBA has been a contentious matter.[13] State and local officials complain that they were largely ignored by the Department of Education when it drafted implementing regulations, that they have been accorded insufficient flexibility in meeting federal mandates, and that insufficient federal funds have been provided to cover the costs of expanded testing. The Department of Education has responded to some complaints, such as by making it easier for rural schools to meet the requirement that all teachers be "highly certified."

Of course, the states and their school districts continue to have responsibility for the day-to-day operation of the public schools and to provide most of their funding. Currently, the federal government provides about 8 percent of the total funding for public schools. To some, the impact of federal intervention and NCLBA is out of proportion to this amount. State officials could reject federal funding and free themselves from controls, as some state legislatures have threatened to do.[14] In actuality, however, federal money is rarely turned down. State and local governments are often strapped for resources and want to claim their share of federal dollars. In the education area, moreover, some states and school districts are more heavily dependent on federal funds than are others.

Although NCLBA has led to much testing, and preparation for testing, in public school students, and pressures for improvement, it is unclear what impact if any this has had on the quality of education.[15] Though the act was slated to be reauthorized in 2006, this has yet to occur. Sharp disagreement continues over what should be done to change the act; and some would prefer it be abandoned. In the early months of 2009, NCLBA was crowded off of the agenda by the recession and the financial and energy crisis. Moreover, it was viewed as a "political hot potato" to be avoided. It has not since been high on the agenda, partly because of disagreement on the form change should take.

For many national policies, such as NCLBA, successful implementation requires coordination and cooperation among a web of national, state, and local governments and agencies. To achieve this end, national policies may have to be tempered to better accord with state and local interests and perspectives. Command must often yield to persuasion and bargaining. ■

Who Implements Policy?

In the United States, as in other modern political systems, policy implementation is formally the province of a complex array of administrative agencies, now often referred to as *bureaucracies*, a term that carries both descriptive and pejorative connotations.[16] Administrative agencies collect taxes; operate the postal system, prisons, and schools; regulate banks, utility companies, and agricultural production; construct and maintain streets and highways; inspect food, meat, water, and drugs to ensure their safety; provide medical benefits and services; and perform many other tasks of modern governments.

Although there are myriad complaints about agencies and bureaucrats, their bungling and lethargy, the fact is that administration is the central process in governance—it provides action, continuity, and stability. Someone who wants to more fully understand the nature, use, and impact of political power cannot afford to ignore administrative processes, notably policy implementation. It has much consequence for who actually gets "what, when, and how."[17]

Because they perform most of the day-to-day work of government, their actions affect citizens more regularly and directly than those of other governmental bodies. Nevertheless, policy students would not need to spend much time fretting about implementation except that agencies usually have much discretion (i.e., leeway or the opportunity to choose among alternatives) in carrying out policies under their jurisdiction. Although at one time it was widely believed that agencies automatically applied policies adopted by legislatures and executives, this is not generally the case except in such matters as the sale of postage stamps and the printing of currency.

A classic feature of the traditional literature of public administration was the notion that politics and administration were separate and distinct spheres of activity. Politics, wrote Professor Frank Goodnow in 1900, dealt with formulating the will of the state, with making value judgments, and with determining what government should or should not do, in short, with making policy. It was to be handled by the "political" branches of government—that is, the legislature and the executive.[18] Administration, on the other hand, was concerned with implementing the "will of the state," with carrying into effect the decisions of the political branches. Administration dealt with questions of fact, with what is rather than what should be, and consequently could focus on identifying the most efficient means (or "one best way") of implementing policy. Were this viewpoint indeed accurate, policy analysts could end their inquiry with the adoption of policy.

Administrative agencies often are provided with broad and ambiguous statutory mandates that leave them with much room for choice in deciding what should or should not be done on some matter. Thus, the National Labor Relations Board (NLRB) is directed to ensure that labor and management bargain in "good faith"; the Federal Communications Commission to license television broadcasters for the "public interest, convenience and necessity"; the Forest

Service to follow a "multiple-use" policy in managing the national forests that balances the interests of lumber companies, sportsmen and sportswomen, livestock grazers, and other users; the Consumer Product Safety Commission to ban products that present an "unreasonable hazard"; and the EPA to ensure that the "best available technology economically achievable" is used to control water pollution. Such statutory mandates are essentially directives to agencies to go out and make some policy. Moreover, because they possess discretion, they become the political targets of pressure groups and others seeking to influence the content of their decisions. Consequently, agencies become embroiled in policy politics.

Frequently those who participate in the legislative process are unable or unwilling to arrive at precise settlements among the conflicting interests on many issues. Only by leaving some matters nebulous and unsettled can agreement on legislation be reached. Lack of time, interest, information, and expertise as well as the need for flexibility in implementation may also help explain the delegation of broad authority to agencies. The product of these factors is a statute couched in general language, such as that mentioned above, which shifts to agencies the tasks of filling in the details, making policy more precise and concrete, and trying to make more definitive adjustments among conflicting interests. Under these conditions, the administrative process becomes an extension of the legislative process.

Although legislatures have delegated much policymaking authority to administrative agencies, it should not be assumed that legislatures cannot act with specificity. An illustration is Social Security legislation, which sets forth in explicit terms the standards for eligibility, the levels of benefits, the amount of additional earnings permitted, and other considerations for old-age and survivors' benefits. Most administrative decisions on application for these benefits simply involve applying the legislatively set standards to the facts of the case at hand and deciding whether an applicant is entitled to retirement benefits and, if so, what the level of benefits should be. Under such circumstances, administrative decision-making becomes mostly routine and is therefore unlikely to produce controversy.

In comparison, the disability standard under the Social Security program has produced considerable controversy. *Disability* is loosely defined as the inability to engage in any substantial gainful activity by reason of a medically determinable physical or mental impairment expected to result in death or to last at least twelve months. This definition leaves much room for interpretation, conjecture, and disagreement.[19] Thousands of cases involving the denial of disability benefits are litigated in the federal courts.

Although administrative agencies are the primary implementers of public policy, many other players may also be involved and contribute in various ways to the execution of policies. Those examined here include the legislature, the courts, pressure groups, and community organizations. These may be directly involved in policy implementation or act to influence administrative agencies, or both. By no means are agencies fully in control of the implementation process. Here again, we find competition for power in the American political system.

The President   Article II of the Constitution states that "the executive Power shall be vested in a President...." No explanation is provided of what this entails. Further on, Article II says that "he shall take Care that the Laws be faithfully executed." This would appear to empower and obligate the president to be involved in policy implementation.

The president, however, has a wide range of duties and obligations. These include foreign affairs, economic policy and the wellbeing of the economy, policy development, and ceremonial activities as chief of state, as well as policy implementation. As Professors George Edwards and Stephen Wayne state, "Policy implementation has had a low priority in most [recent] administrations." They explain, "Presidents know they will receive little credit if policies are managed well because it is very difficult to attribute effective implementation to them personally."[20]

Lyndon B. Johnson was the last president to become fairly extensively involved in policy implementation.[21] He received regular reports on agency officials, questioned officials about their programs, made recommendations for action, and more. He had a remarkable capacity to participate without getting bogged down in details. As an example, wage-price guideposts were used to combat inflation. Johnson "met with business groups and labor leaders ..., made appeals in person and by telephone and telegram, suggested 'levers' that could be used to help induce compliance, and encouraged and pressured his subordinates to act. No major wage-price actions were taken without his approval." Johnson was the quintessential activist president.

Occasionally a president and some of his advisers may decide that a law on the statute book is unconstitutional. What then should the president do? Should he direct that the law not be enforced? Or should it be enforced until the courts have rendered a definitive verdict? Recently President Obama faced this dilemma with respect to the Defense of Marriage Act (DOMA).[22] He decided the law was unconstitutional and that his administration would no longer defend it in court. Together with his attorney general and some (but not all) of his advisers, he concluded it should be carried out. Other presidents have acted similarly. In June 2013, the U.S. Supreme Court, in a 5 to 4 decision, declared DOMA to be unconstitutional.

Presidents now rarely participate in the details of policy implementation. The best means that a president has for exercising control and direction over the executive branch, for getting officials and agencies generally to act as he wishes, is the power of appointment and removal. The president makes many hundreds of appointments to top-level positions in the departments and agencies. The president will be careful to select persons who share his political philosophy or policy orientations. George W. Bush's conservative appointments to regulatory agencies and commissions (e.g., the EPA, Antitrust Division, and Securities and Exchange) were not vigorous regulators. They did not ignore the laws under their jurisdictions, but they did ease up on enforcement. In contrast, Obama's appointments to these and many other agencies were much more activist. Thus, for instance, the EPA bore down much harder on air and water pollution regulations.

Presidents do not often remove officials from office. It is messy and unpleasant, and seldom done. Presidential appointees generally regard following presidential leadership as one of the rules of the game. If you can't do what the president wants, then you ought to get out, as a former Johnson administration official told me.

The Legislature   Some members of legislative bodies display much interest in the implementation of policies. Indeed, Professor Theodore Lowi holds that "the major problem and major focus of Congress is no longer simply that of prescribing the behavior of citizens but more often that of affecting the behavior of administrators."[23] Some of the techniques used by Congress and its members to influence administrative action and hold agencies accountable for what they do are examined here.

Committee hearings and investigations are used to gather information, review the implementation of policies, publicize agency actions, put pressure on agency officials, and enhance the political reputations of members of Congress. (Technically, hearings focus on proposed legislation, whereas investigations deal with problems. They are lumped together here.) In 1997, the Senate Finance Committee held hearings on the Internal Revenue Service (IRS) at which taxpayers told "horror" stories about the IRS. Their sensational quality attracted much media attention and helped build bipartisan political support for the IRS Restructuring and Reform Act of 1998.[24] This law created an independent board to supervise the IRS, called for the agency's reorganization, provided for disciplining agency employees who abused their authority, and expanded protection for taxpayer rights. Generally, it was intended to make the IRS a less adversarial and more taxpayer-friendly agency. Interestingly, it was later found that many of the horror stories related at the Senate hearings were unfounded or exaggerated.[25]

Another control device is the specificity of legislation. The more detail in the legislation that Congress passes, the less discretion agencies usually will have. Specific limitations on the use of funds may be written into statutes, or deadlines may be specified for some actions, as has been done in some environmental-protection laws; "hammers," or stringent rules or requirements, may be incorporated in a law, to go into effect if an agency does not act with alacrity or effectiveness; or specific standards may be set, as in minimum-wage legislation. The committee reports that accompany many bills often include suggestions or statements explaining how legislation should be implemented or specifying projects that money should go for. These reports do not have the force of law but are ignored by administrators only at their own peril.

Senatorial approval, which is required for many top-level executive appointments, provides senators with a lever that can be used to influence policy. Commitments on policy matters may be extracted by senators from nominees during hearings on their appointment. Or a nominee for a position may be rejected because some senators find objectionable his or her policy views or actions. This happened to two persons nominated by President Bill Clinton to head the Civil Rights Division of the Department of Justice. Conservative senators considered them to be "too liberal," that is, they were supporters of civil rights.

The legislative veto is an arrangement whereby either congressional approval has to be secured before an administrative action can be taken or a specific action can be subsequently rejected by Congress or its committees; the veto originated in 1932. President Herbert Hoover wanted authority to reorganize the national administrative system, but Congress was reluctant to grant it. A deal was made. The president was authorized to reorganize the system, but Congress gave itself the right to disapprove his actions if it deemed them objectionable. The legislative veto gives administrative agencies flexibility in the implementation of legislation while permitting Congress, if it so chooses, to exercise control over what is done. It also enables Congress to become involved in the details of administration.[26]

As reported in Chapter 5, "Budgeting and Public Policy," the Supreme Court in 1983 declared the legislative veto unconstitutional. Nonetheless, since then some 400 legislative veto provisions have been included in laws passed by Congress. Others have been put in place by informal agreements between Congress and the executive. During the George Bush administration, for example, the secretary of state agreed to give four congressional committees a veto over the expenditure of funds appropriate to support the Contras (rebels) in Nicaragua. Had this not been done, Congress might not have enacted legislation creating the aid program, which was strongly desired by the Bush administration.[27] The legislative veto persists because the legislative and executive branches view it as a practical way to handle some of their differing interests.

Finally, much of the time of many members of Congress and their staffs, and some of the time of all members, is devoted to "casework."[28] Typically, casework involves handling problems that constituents have with administrative agencies such as delayed Social Security or veterans' benefits, difficulty in getting action on a license application, or uncertainty about how to apply for a grant. The constituents, of course, want their representatives to secure favorable action for them. Members of Congress engage in casework because it is thought helpful to their chances of reelection and because it contributes to their oversight of agencies. Beyond that, the practice helps "humanize" administration by making it more responsive to individual needs and problems. As for agency officials, responsiveness to congressional inquiries is seen both as appropriate and as a means of building or maintaining political support.

The Courts   Some legislation is enforced primarily through judicial action. Laws dealing with crimes are the most obvious example. Some economic regulatory statutes, such as the Sherman Act, are enforced by lawsuits brought in the federal district courts, some of which are eventually appealed to the Supreme Court. Because of this tactic and the act's general language, the meaning of antitrust policy depends greatly upon judicial interpretation and application of the statute. In the nineteenth century, it was quite common for legislatures to enact laws requiring or prohibiting some action and then to leave it to the citizens to protect their rights under the law through proceedings brought in the courts. Generally, administrative regulation, in which primary responsibility is assigned to an agency for the enforcement of a statute, is now much more common than judicial regulation in the American political system. It is also more effective.

In some instances, the courts may be directly involved in the administration of policy. Naturalization proceedings for aliens are really administrative in form, but they are handled by the federal district courts. Bankruptcy proceedings are another illustration. A complex system of trustees, receivers, appraisers, accountants, auctioneers, and others is supervised by federal bankruptcy courts. In all, it is "a large scale example of routine administrative machinery."[29] A national bankruptcy agency could handle much of this activity. Many divorce and domestic-relations cases handled by state courts also appear essentially administrative, involving matters of guidance and management rather than disputed law or facts. There is no reason to assume that persons appointed or elected to judgeships are distinctly qualified to act in these matters.

The courts' most important influence on administration, however, flows from their interpretation of statutes and administrative rules and regulations, and their review of administrative decisions in cases brought before them. Courts can facilitate, hinder, or largely nullify implementation of a policy through their decisions. The story of how the Supreme Court destroyed the effectiveness of early national railroad regulation under the Interstate Commerce Act of 1887 by unfavorable rulings on the Interstate Commerce Commission's (ICC) authority to regulate rates is well-recorded history.

In recent years, the Supreme Court's rulings have complicated and restricted the enforcement of equal-opportunity and affirmative-action programs. For instance, the Court has ruled that to be constitutional, an affirmative-action program has to be "narrowly tailored" to meet "a compelling government interest." A Colorado program providing for the award of a portion of highway construction projects to minority contractors was struck down because it failed to square with this standard.[30]

Pressure Groups   Because of the discretion often vested in agencies by legislation, once an act is adopted, the group struggle shifts from the legislative to the administrative arena. A group that can successfully influence agency action may have a substantial effect on the course and impact of public policies. Sometimes relationships between a group and an agency may become so close as to lead to the allegation that the group has "captured" the agency. In the past it was frequently stated that the ICC was the captive of the railroads,[31] and it is not uncommon now to hear comments to the effect that the Federal Maritime Commission is unduly influenced by the shipping companies and that the Forest Service is too responsive to the interests of commercial timber companies. Also, groups may complain to Congress or the executive if they believe a statute is not being implemented in accordance with the intent of Congress (as they interpret it).

Groups also directly participate in administration, as when the representation of particular interests is specified for the boards of plural-headed agencies. A common illustration is state occupational licensing boards, whose governing statutes frequently provide that some or all of the board members must come from the licensed profession. Occupational licensing (and regulatory) programs are usually controlled by the dominant elements within the licensed groups. Consequently, such programs may do more to protect the interests of the licensed group than those of the general public.

Advisory bodies, such as the Advisory Committee on Vocational Education, the Advisory Committee on Hog Cholera Eradication, and the Advisory Committee on Reactor Safeguards, are another means by which groups may become participants in policy administration. Currently, around a thousand advisory groups serve national administrative agencies.[32] Some simply provide needed advice to agencies and their officials, as their name implies; others become more directly involved in program administration. Membership in advisory bodies may give group representatives privileged or special access to governmental agencies. Thus, many large defense contractors are represented on advisory committees for the Department of Defense. When advisory groups have a role in agency decision-making, they can add legitimacy to the policies that they have helped to develop.[33]

Some advisory committees may have direct control over program administration. Each of the nineteen institutes within the National Institutes of Health (NIH) has an advisory council whose members must be leaders in science, medicine, and public affairs, including some who are specialists in the field covered by a particular institute (e.g., cancer, aging, or allergy and infectious diseases). Research grants to medical schools, universities, and others, which total more than $30 billion annually, can be made only after review and approval by each institute's advisory council. This is intended to ensure that grants meet both scientific norms and public-policy criteria.[34]

Community Organizations   At the local level, community and other organizations occasionally have been used in the administration of national policies. Examples include farmer committees under the income-support and soil-conservation programs of the Department of Agriculture, resource advisory councils for the Bureau of Land Management, and representatives of the poor for Community Action agencies. Participatory democracy of this sort may give those involved considerable influence over the application of programs at the grass-roots level and also build program support. Local draft boards ("little groups of neighbors," as they were sometimes called) had a vital role during the Vietnam War years in determining, when only a portion of eligible males were required to meet military needs, who got drafted and who did not.[35] Many of those drafted were sent to Vietnam. The compulsory draft and draft boards were later eliminated, although eligible males are still required to register with the Selective Service System.

Very early on in his administration, President George W. Bush created a White House Office of Faith-Based and Community Initiatives. Subsequently, several of the executive departments established similar offices. All of this was in accord with the President's claims about "compassionate conservatism" during the 2000 campaign. The notion was that federal funds for social services should be funneled through local organizations, of which there were a vast number and variety in American society, because they would be more effective than governmental organizations.[36] During the course of the Bush administration, many billions of dollars were channeled through these organizations. It was a controversial initiative because many observers thought that it violated (or could) the constitutional separation of church and state. President Barack Obama has continued a version of this program.

Concluding Comments

In summary, a variety of entities may play a role in implementing a policy of any complexity. In addition to those discussed here, the communications media (by reporting and criticizing an agency's operations), other agencies with competing or overlapping jurisdictions, presidential staff agencies, and the judiciary, when used to challenge agency actions, may also get involved. These amalgams of participants are now often called "networks."

As an example, there is the Office of Management and Budget (OMB), whose interests reach beyond the funding of agencies. OMB is concerned with whether agency actions are in accord with the "policies and programs" of the president. Moreover, since 1981, the Office of Information and Regulatory Affairs (OIRA), an OMB unit, has been authorized by executive orders to oversee the issuance of rules and regulations by executive branch agencies. (More is said on this topic in Chapter 7, "Policy Impact, Evaluation, and Change.")

The number and variety of participants in the implementation process will differ among policy arenas, depending upon policy salience, target populations, and the costs and impact of policies. The operations of the Railroad Retirement Board, which is located in Chicago rather than Washington, DC, draws little attention. In comparison, the Securities and Exchange Commission is a political magnet, attracting much attention and many interested parties.

Administrative Organization

One could say that one administrative agency looks pretty much like another, or if you have seen one agency, you have seen them all. Such a notion, however, is erroneous. Agencies in fact do vary greatly in structure, operating style, political support, expertness, and policy orientation. Those who want to influence the nature of public policy often are very interested in which agency or type of agency will administer a policy. Conflict over questions of administrative organization can be every bit as sharp as conflict over substantive policies. Forming administrative organizations is a political as well as a technical task. As a longtime observer of administration has remarked:

> Organizational arrangements are not neutral. We do not organize in a vacuum. Organization is one way of expressing national commitments, influencing program direction, and ordering priorities. Organizational arrangements tend to give some interests and perspectives more effective access to those with decision-making authority, whether they be in the Congress or in the executive branch.[37]

The national executive branch comprises approximately seventy-five separate administrative entities and 2.8 million civilian employees (this includes the U.S. Postal Service), most of whom are covered by merit systems. Basically, there are four kinds of agencies: executive departments, independent regulatory commissions, government corporations, and independent agencies. They are listed in the historical order in which they appeared in the national administrative system.

The fifteen executive departments—State, Defense, Commerce, Health and Human Services, to name a few—constitute the core of the executive branch. At the helm of an executive department is a presidentially appointed secretary who has cabinet rank and who is assisted in running it by various under-, deputy, and assistant secretaries. These are all political appointees, whose number has greatly expanded in recent decades.[38]

Most of the work of the departments in implementing programs and policies is handled by major administrative units that can generically be designated as "bureaus." Thus, in the Department of Justice, one finds bureaus such as the Federal Bureau of Investigation, the Bureau of Prisons, the Drug Enforcement Administration, the Civil Rights Division, the Antitrust Division, and the U.S. Marshals Service. Because of their typically short tenure in office and lack of technical knowledge, the political appointees at the top levels of a department are often hard-pressed to exercise effective control and direction of its bureaus.

Independent regulatory commissions are plural-headed agencies that engage in the regulation of private economic activities, such as stock markets, banks, or labor-management relations (see Figure 6.2). Appointed by the president for fixed, staggered terms of office, only a majority of a commission's members can come from the same political party. Unlike department secretaries, who serve for "the time being" and can be fired by the president whenever he or she chooses, regulatory commissioners can be removed only for such specified causes as malfeasance, inefficiency, and neglect of duties. None has been. Some have been pressured or urged to resign.

Thus, as a practical matter, the independent regulatory commissions, which handle a significant share of the government's regulatory programs, are somewhat free from presidential control and direction. This is one reason why Congress has created them. On the other hand, the president can try to bring the commissions under his sway by appointing commissioners who share his

FIGURE 6.2

Independent Regulatory Commissions

Federal Reserve Board (1913)

Federal Trade Commission (1914)

Securities and Exchange Commission (1934)

Federal Communications Commission (1934)

National Labor Relations Board (1935)

Federal Maritime Commission (1961)

Consumer Product Safety Commission (1972)

Nuclear Regulatory Commission (1974)

Commodity Futures Trading Commission (1975)

Federal Energy Regulatory Commission (1977)

© Cengage learning

policy preferences. The George W. Bush administration did this with the SEC. The results were not good for the performance of the economy.

Government corporations, which first became a part of the executive branch during the World War I era, are sometimes set up to handle businesslike or commercial activities for the government. Prominent examples are the U.S. Postal Service, the Tennessee Valley Authority, and the Federal Deposit Insurance Corporation. Wholly owned by the government, they look pretty much like other government agencies, but they have greater operating flexibility in financial and personnel matters. Typically, they impose fees or charges for the goods or services that they provide and can reinvest earnings.

Independent agencies number close to forty and, like independent and regulatory commissions and government corporations, are located outside of the executive departments. Some are large, well-known, and important, such as the National Aeronautics and Space Administration (NASA), the EPA, and the Central Intelligence Agency; others are smaller and somewhat obscure, such as the National Mediation and Conciliation Service, the Railroad Retirement Board, and the National Credit Union Administration. A variety of factors has contributed to their establishment. Some would not fit well into the executive departments (such as NASA and the EPA), others have watchdog or review duties (such as the Occupational Safety and Health Review Commission), still others provide services to a variety of agencies (such as the Office of Personnel Management), and some provide special notice for programs (such as the Peace Corps and the Commission on Civil Rights). Although all are subject to presidential control, much of what many of them do is not of presidential interest.

The Dodd-Frank Act (2010) provided for stronger protection of consumers by regulating financial products and services (e.g., payday loans and home mortgages) to ensure fairness and understanding of their terms. Implementation was assigned to a new Consumer Financial Protection Bureau, located in but independent of the Federal Reserve System (although it is funded by the

FRS). Its director is presidentially appointed with Senate approval for a five-year term. Harvard law professor Elizabeth Warren (now a U.S. Senator) was instrumental in the bureau's creation by her strong and persuasive advocacy.

Responsibility for implementing a new public policy usually is assigned to an existing agency. Occasionally, however, a new agency is created for this purpose, usually by legislative action. Thus, in 2001, Congress established the Transportation Security Administration in the Department of Transportation to handle airport security. (It has been moved to the Department of Homeland Security.) In other instances, new agencies were set up by the executive using administrative reorganization authority (now lapsed), which permitted the president to propose reorganization plans that went into effect automatically unless disapproved by either house of Congress. The EPA, established by a Nixon administration 1970 reorganization plan, administers environmental-protection programs formerly scattered among several agencies. A few other agencies—such as the Department of Agriculture's Farm Service Agency, which administers income- and price-support programs, and the Centers for Medicare and Medicaid Services in the Department of Health and Human Services—have been created under broad statutory authority delegated by Congress to executive officials.

When a new policy or program is developed, the contending parties often seek to have its implementation awarded to an agency that they think will act favorably toward their interests. The case of occupational health and safety legislation is one in point. When it became evident in 1970 that legislation would be enacted, attention focused on how it would be implemented.[39] Business groups, along with the Nixon administration, did not want the Department of Labor, which they viewed as pro-labor, to set health and safety standards. Nor did they want standard-setting and enforcement to be lodged in the same agency. Their preference was to have an independent board to set standards, Labor to inspect workplaces, and either the courts or another agency to impose penalties and hear appeals. Organized labor, spearheaded by the United Steel Workers, and liberal Democrats wanted all standard-setting and enforcement authority located in Labor.

The result was a compromise. The Department of Labor was awarded authority to set health and safety standards, enforce them, and impose penalties for their violation. Within the department these tasks were assigned to OSHA. An independent, quasi-judicial agency, the Occupational Safety and Health Review Commission, was created to hear appeals of OSHA enforcement action. The National Institute for Occupational Safety and Health within the Department of Health and Human Services (formerly the Department of Health, Education, and Welfare) was authorized to conduct research and to develop and recommend health and safety standards. Moreover, enforcement authority could be delegated to state governments with acceptable programs. This fragmented organizational structure has complicated and softened implementation of the occupational safety and health program. For example, enforcement and penalty decisions made by OSHA have frequently been modified or overturned by the review commission.

Viewed as a course of action, the content and impact of policy is affected by how it is implemented. How it is implemented, in turn, will be shaped in part by which agency implements it. Organization matters. Consequently, deciding which agency should implement the program, or where it should be located, is more than a technical task; it is also a political issue. All administrative agencies have some sort of political life, a topic to which we now turn.

Administrative Politics

A statute only gives an agency the legal authority to take action to implement policy on some topic. How effectively the agency carries out its legal mandate and what it actually does or does not accomplish will be substantially affected by the amount of cooperation and political support it gets and, conversely, the political opposition it runs into. To put it differently, an agency dwells and acts in a political milieu that affects how it exercises power and carries out its programs.

The environments of some agencies are more political, more volatile, and more tumultuous than those of others. The Bureau of Engraving and Printing and the U.S. Geological Survey lead much more serene political lives than do the EPA and the Federal Communications Commission. But whatever the conditions, the environment in which an agency exists may contain many forces that may, at one time or another, impinge on it and help give direction to its actions in multitudinous ways.[40] These forces may arise out of the following sources.

THE "BASIC RULES OF THE GAME"   Included here are the relevant laws, rules, and regulations, accepted modes of procedure, and concepts of fair play that help form and guide official behavior and to which officials are expected to conform. Public opinion and group pressures may focus adversely on officials who violate the rules of the game, as by appearing or proposing not to enforce a statutory provision or by enticing persons to violate a law so that they can be prosecuted. Officials who are overly zealous in enforcing laws, who cite companies for too many minor violations of health or safety standards, may be seen as unreasonable zealots. Adverse executive or legislative action may stem from such criticism.

THE CHIEF EXECUTIVE   Most administrative agencies are located within the presidential chain of command or are otherwise subject to presidential control and direction in such matters as top-level personnel appointments, budget recommendations, expenditure controls, and policy directives. The presidential chain of command includes agencies and officials in the Executive Office of the President and top-level political appointees (e.g., secretaries and assistant secretaries) in the departments and agencies. Control and direction are much more likely to emanate from those who work for the president than from the president himself. Those who act for the president may or may not always act according to his or her preferences. There is sometimes suspicion, for example, that White House aides "go into business for themselves." Presidents in recent decades seem not to have spent much time mulling over the operations of administrative agencies. Perhaps they should have.

THE CONGRESSIONAL SYSTEM OF OVERSIGHT   This supervisory system includes the standing committees and subcommittees, their chairs, committee staffs, and influential members of Congress. Congressional concern and influence is fragmented and sporadic rather than monolithic and continuous. It flows from parts of Congress, rarely from Congress as a whole, and focuses mostly on specific issues or controversies. Professional staff members handle much of the day-to-day congressional communication with agencies and may develop close working relationships with agency officials.

THE COURTS   Agencies may be strongly affected by the judiciary's use of its powers of judicial review and statutory interpretation. Agencies may have their statutory authority expanded or shorn by judicial interpretation, or their decisions may be overruled because improper procedures were employed in making them. OSHA and the Federal Trade Commission (FTC) have often had their actions challenged in the courts. Other agencies, such as the Federal Reserve Board (FRB) and the Bureau of the Mint, have little contact with the courts because their operations do not give rise to issues of the sort normally handled by the judiciary. The greater the likelihood of challenges in the courts of agency actions, the more influence lawyers have in shaping agency actions.

OTHER ADMINISTRATIVE AGENCIES   Agencies with competing or overlapping jurisdictions may affect one another's operations. In drug-law enforcement, the Drug Enforcement Administration, the U.S. Coast Guard, the Customs Service, and other agencies have engaged in turf battles and competed for recognition and credit in making drug busts, sometimes appearing to lose sight of their main task.[41] Water agencies such as the Army Corps of Engineers and the Bureau of Reclamation (BOR) have also been rivals for the right to control and construct water projects. Occasionally, an agency may aspire to take over a program of another agency, and may succeed. Thus, the Department of Labor acquired the Job Corps program, which was initially run by the Office of Economic Opportunity. Agency imperialism, however, is not as rampant as some commentators imply.[42] Agencies sometimes do not want to take on new programs, especially if they are likely to be difficult to administer.

Moreover, agencies need to be cautious about intruding on the "organizational heartland" of other agencies—the programs or responsibilities they view as essential to their missions and well-being.[43] The U.S. Fish and Wildlife Service risks doing this when enforcing the Endangered Species Act to prevent habitat destruction threatening the survival of species by actions of the Corps of Engineers or the Forest Service.

Some agencies may form cooperative relationships, as have the FTC and the Antitrust Division of the Department of Justice in antitrust enforcement. An agency may even refuse to take a program from another agency. Stuart Udall, secretary of the interior during the Johnson administration, relates that he offered to give the Bureau of Indian Affairs Indian-education program to the Department of Health, Education, and Welfare so that its secretary, John Gardner, would have his own school system to run. Gardner refused the offer.[44]

OTHER GOVERNMENTS   State, municipal, and county governments, school districts, and associations of state and local officials (such as the National League of Cities) may attempt to influence a national agency's decisions. Associations of state highway officials are much interested in the activities of the Federal Highway Administration. The EPA encounters quite a lot of pressure, criticism, and resistance from state and local governments and their environmental agencies in developing and implementing standards for pollution control. The effectiveness of many national programs depends upon how they are implemented by state and local agencies, which provide such governments with some leverage over their conduct. The No Child Left Behind Act is a case in point.

INTEREST GROUPS   The group context differs considerably from one agency to another. Some agencies—the Forest Service and the Food and Drug Administration (FDA) are examples—attract the attention of many groups, some supportive and others hostile. Buffeted by opposition, such agencies may move more cautiously than others that deal primarily with one group, such as the Department of Veterans Affairs. No matter what the FDA's decision is on an important issue, some groups probably will be sufficiently offended as to launch a judicial or legislative challenge. Other agencies—for instance, the Inter-American Foundation and the Railroad Retirement Board—experience few group pressures.

Agencies often actively seek group support (or consent) to increase the size, ease, or effectiveness of their operations. Advisory groups may be created, presentations made at group meetings by agency officials, and program modifications initiated in the quest for support.

POLITICAL PARTIES   The role of the party organizations has declined in recent decades with the extension of merit systems of hiring to most agency personnel. Appointments to top-level agency positions, however, still may be influenced by considerations of party welfare and policy orientation. Because only a majority of the members of an independent regulatory commission can belong to the same political party, party affiliation is an explicit consideration in these appointments. Some agency actions may be influenced by an urge to enhance party success at the polls, as when the Reagan administration expanded the availability of agricultural loans in the months prior to the 1986 congressional elections.

COMMUNICATIONS MEDIA   Beyond their use as forums for pressure groups, political parties, and others trying to influence an agency's action, the mass-communications media have an independent role. The media may play an important part in shaping public opinion toward an agency by revealing and publicizing its actions, favorably or unfavorably. For decades, the Federal Bureau of Investigation was quite well treated by the press, although its problems in recent years have caused a decline in its support. In contrast, the political lives of the IRS and the Bureau of Alcohol, Tobacco, Firearms, and Explosives have been made more difficult by the battering they have received in the media. Also, it should be noted that agencies scrutinize the media in order to acquire information about the public and its preferences.

Specialized media, too, mostly journals, newspapers, newsletters, and websites, inform their clients and other interested persons about the operations of agencies or programs. These are increasingly more important for many agencies than are the more general media. This would be true of the Agricultural Marketing Service and the U.S. Fish and Wildlife Service. *Field and Stream* and *Outdoor Life* provide their readers with a particular slant on the U.S. Fish and Wildlife Service. So do local outdoors editors.

Each of the forces sketched here is multiple rather than monolithic. Conflicting viewpoints may be held by members in the same category as well as by those in different ones. Thus, a number of political forces may impinge on an agency, pushing and pulling against each other with varying intensity, and growing and ebbing. Agencies, of course, are not simply sitting ducks but rather will try to shape, influence, and mollify the forces in their environment. Pressure relationships between an agency and those who seek to influence it are therefore usually reciprocal.

The field of forces surrounding an agency (as shown in Figure 6.3) will be drawn from the preceding categories and will form the constituency of the agency, that is, "any group, body, or interest to which [an administrator] looks for aid or guidance, or which seeks to establish itself as so important [in his or her judgment] that he [or she] 'had better' take account of its preferences even if he [or she] is averse to those preferences."[45] The concept of constituency is broader than that of clientele, which comprises the reasonably distinct set of individuals and groups directly served or regulated by an agency. Thus, savings and loan associations were the clientele of the Office of Thrift Supervision; its constituency comprised a broader set of forces or stakeholders concerned with its operations. The OTC was abolished in 2010 for being too "chummy" with savings and loan associations.

The constituency of an agency is dynamic rather than static. Some constituents will be concerned with the agency only as certain issues arise or are settled; others will be more or less continually involved and will compose the stable core of the agency's constituency. The stable core of the Food Safety and Inspection Service (FSIS) in the Department of Agriculture includes commercial meat- and poultry-processing companies, the congressional Agriculture Committees, and the relevant appropriations subcommittees. The chief

FIGURE 6.3

The Political Environment of an Agency

Note: The two-headed arrows indicate that influence relationships may run in both directions.

executive, the FDA, the communications media, and consumer groups are intermittently involved with the FSIS. All other things being equal, the constituents who continually interact with an agency are likely to have the most success in influencing the agency's action.

The character of an agency's constituency will affect its power relations and capacity to make policy decisions and carry those decisions into effect. The relationship of an agency to one part of its constituency will partially depend on the kinds of relationships it has with other parts. For example, an agency with strong presidential support can afford to be less responsive to pressure groups than an agency without such support. On the other hand, strong congressional and group support may lessen presidential influence, as with the Army Corps of Engineers.[46] An agency encountering criticism from state and local government officials may find that its congressional support also wanes as a consequence. As a general rule, an agency's policymaking and implementation activities will reflect the interests supported by the dominant elements within its constituency, whether they are hostile or supportive.

An agency's clientele is an important component of its constituency. Some agencies benefit from large, active clienteles. This is true for the Social Security Administration, the Small Business Administration, and some units within the Department of Agriculture. But size alone is not enough. Consumers are a vast group, but because they tend to be poorly organized and lack self-consciousness as a group, they provide little support to consumer agencies such as the FDA and the Consumer Product Safety Commission. If the FDA has been unduly responsive to food and drug manufacturers, as some allege, it is partly because it lacks consumer support and partly because the agency both needs the manufacturers' cooperation in the administration of its programs and encounters organized pressure from them.

Some agencies have underprivileged or disadvantaged clientele; the Legal Services Corporation, the Federal Bureau of Prisons, and most welfare agencies fit in here. These clienteles will not be able to provide much help politically. Thus the Office of Economic Opportunity was hampered in administering poverty programs because its clientele, the poor and especially the black poor, were not a strong source of political support. An agency with a two-party clientele, such as the NLRB, whose clientele includes labor union and management groups, may be able to maintain some independence by playing one off against the other.

Agencies implementing distributive programs that provide services usually elicit more support from their clientele than do regulatory agencies. Most people obviously prefer receiving benefits to being restricted or controlled. An agency with a foreign clientele (the Agency for International Development is an example) can draw little usable political support from its clientele. The lack of a domestic clientele has clearly been disadvantageous for the foreign-aid program. It has been a prime target for budget reductions.

Examining an agency's constituency and clientele can provide insight into, and explanation of, why an agency acts as it does. It should not, however, be assumed that an agency is an inert force at the mercy of its constituency or the dominant elements therein. Because of their expertise, organizational spirit, or administrative statecraft, agencies can exert some independent control over events and help determine the scope of their power.[47]

Any bureaucratic agency has some expertise in the performance of its assigned tasks, whether these entail garbage collection, killing predators, regulating banks, or the conduct of diplomatic relations. All bureaucratic skills, however, do not receive equal deference from society. Agencies whose expertise derives from the natural and physical ("hard") sciences will receive more deference than those drawing from the social sciences, which are less highly regarded in society. Compare, for example, the situations of NASA and the National Cancer Institute with the Census Bureau and the Economic Research Service (U.S. Department of Agriculture). Considerable deference is shown to the military as "specialists in violence," and Congress often defers to the judgment of the Department of Defense and the Joint Chiefs of Staff in military and defense policy. Professional diplomats ("cookie pushers in striped pants"), on the other hand, no longer receive the deference in foreign policy that they once did. Power based on expertise may fluctuate as conditions and attitudes change.

Some agencies are more capable than others of generating interest in, and enthusiasm and commitment for, their programs from both their own members and the public. This condition is designated organizational esprit. It depends upon an agency's capacity to develop "an appropriate ideology or sense of mission, both as a method of binding outsiders to the agency and as a technique for intensifying its employees' loyalty to its purposes."[48] The Marine Corps, Peace Corps, Forest Service, and EPA are served with considerable fervor and commitment by their members. Other agencies have displayed much zeal in their early years, only to ease into bureaucratic routines and stodginess as the years slip by. This decline has weakened some of the national independent regulatory commissions.

Leadership, or the ability Professor Francis E. Rourke calls "administrative statecraft,"[49] can also enhance an agency's power and effectiveness. A government agency's leadership, like that in all organizations, is situational, being shaped significantly by factors in the environment other than the leaders themselves. Nevertheless, leadership can still significantly influence the agency's operation and success. Some agency leaders are more effective than others in dealing with outside interest groups, cultivating congressional committees, opening the organization to new ideas, and communicating a sense of purpose to its personnel. The mid-1980s revitalization of the EPA following its decline in the early years of the Reagan administration was aided by the able leadership of William Ruckelshaus and Lee Thomas as successive administrators.

Under the leadership of Paul Volcker, Alan Greenspan, and Ben Bernanke, the FRB carried the major burden in stabilizing the economy for more than two decades. In the early 2000s, however, Greenspan kept interest rates low and believed financial institutions would regulate themselves (which they did not). This contributed to the nation's financial crisis. Greenspan later acknowledged that he had been wrong about self-regulation.

Administrative Policymaking

As we saw in Chapter 3, "Policy Formation: Problems, Agendas, and Formulation," administrative agencies frequently participate in policymaking at the legislative stage. Here our analytical lens shifts to the administrative arena, where administrative officials have the capacity to make decisions that shape policy and are subject to influences radiating from their clientele and constituencies. Something of a role reversal occurs for legislators, who now act not as decision-makers but as potential influencers of decisions. Agency policymakers—political appointees and upper-level civil servants—occupy positions that convey discretion to them in the direction of the agency and its programs.

Tension often exists between the civil servants—possessed of long service and experience in agency affairs—and political appointees who represent the victorious political party and sometimes manifest a desire to make substantial alterations in agency activities, but who lack knowledge about the agency and its policies. Both differ greatly from the lower-level agency personnel a citizen is most likely to encounter—those selling stamps, guiding tours at national parks, handling customs matters at international airports, or processing Social Security documents. For these lower-level personnel, the line between politics and administration remains fairly distinct.

In this section, two aspects of agency policymaking are examined: the characteristics of agency decision-making and the processes by which an agency can develop policy. It is well to keep in mind here the distinction between a decision and a policy.

DECISION-MAKING   Hierarchy is of central importance in agency decision-making. Although in legislatures each member has an equal vote, if not equal influence, within agencies those at upper levels have more authority over final decisions than the occupants of lower levels. To be sure, factors such as decentralization of authority, responsiveness of subunits to outside forces (such as pressure groups), and participation by professionals in administrative activity may work against hierarchical authority, but hierarchy should nonetheless not be underestimated. Complexity, size, and the desire for economical operation and more control over the bureaucratic apparatus all contribute to the development of hierarchical authority. Also, compliance with hierarchical authority is one of the rules of the game that organization members generally accept.

As for its consequences for decision-making, hierarchy provides a means by which discrete decisions can be coordinated and conflicts among officials at lower levels in the agency can be resolved. Hierarchy also means that those at upper levels have a larger voice in agency decisions because of their higher status and authority, even though lower-level officials may have more substantive qualifications and information. A separation of power and knowledge may thus threaten the rationality of administrative decisions.[50] Hierarchy can also adversely affect the free flow of ideas and information in an organization; subordinates may hesitate to advance proposals they think might run counter to "official" policy or antagonize their superiors. Few want to carry the message that causes the messenger to be shot.

Low visibility is another important feature of administrative decision-making. Compared with that of legislatures, administrative decision-making is a relatively invisible part of government. Agencies may hold public hearings, issue press releases, and the like, but they exercise much control over the information that becomes available about their internal deliberations and decisions. Much of what they do is little noticed by the public or reported by the media. This invisibility can contribute to the effectiveness of decisions by providing a congenial environment for presenting and discussing policy proposals that might otherwise be avoided as publicly unpopular.

Deliberations by Kennedy administration officials during the Cuban missile crisis were more effective because they were private, or closed.[51] Additionally, low visibility may facilitate the bargaining and compromise often necessary to reach decisions and take action because officials find it easier to move away from privately stated than from publicly stated positions. On the other hand, privacy in administrative deliberation could mean that some pertinent facts are not considered and that significant interests are not consulted. Though secrecy contributed to the effectiveness of the Cuban missile crisis decisions, it had the opposite effect with regard to the Bay of Pigs invasion debacle in the previous year.

Low visibility is, on the whole, more a part of administrative deliberations in foreign and defense policy than in domestic matters.[52] In the latter area, confidentiality has been reduced by legislation designed to open the administrative process to greater public participation and scrutiny. The Freedom of Information Act provides a procedure for extracting documents and records from agencies, and the Government in the Sunshine Act requires most plural-headed agencies to open their decision-making sessions to the public.

Administrative agencies constitute "a governmental habitat in which expertise finds a wealth of opportunity to exert itself and to influence policy."[53] Agencies clearly are affected by political considerations, including the wish to protect their own power, in making decisions. Thus, the Department of Commerce is unlikely to make policy decisions that sharply conflict with important business interests. Nor is the Tennessee Valley Authority inclined to ignore major economic interests in its region. Agencies nonetheless do provide a context within which experts and professionals, official and private, can work on policy problems.

Scientific and technical considerations and professional advice are important factors in most administrative decision-making. Whether it is the Federal Aviation Agency considering the adoption of a rule on aircraft safety, the FDA acting on the safety of implanted medical devices, or the secretary of labor confronting a major choice on job-training programs, each needs good information on the technical feasibility of proposed alternatives. Decisions that are made without adequate consideration of their technical aspects or that conflict with strong professional advice may turn out to be faulty on both technical and political grounds.

Professional and scientific advice is not always sound, however. In 1976, following the identification of a few cases of influenza at Fort Dix, New Jersey, public-health officials decided that the nation was confronted with the possibility of a swine-flu epidemic similar to one that had killed 500,000 people in the United States in 1918. Acting on their advice, the Ford administration decided to initiate a costly nationwide immunization campaign. The flu epidemic never came, however, and the entire venture became a policy fiasco.[54]

Finally, administrative decision-making is very frequently characterized by bargaining. Experts and facts are important in administrative decision-making, but so also are accommodation and compromise. Some agencies may be less apt to engage in bargaining than others. Decisions from the National Institute of Standards and Technology and the Patent and Trademark Office are primarily expert findings based on factual records. Economic regulatory agencies, such as the Securities and Exchange Commission and the EPA, often find it necessary to bargain with those whom they regulate. In setting emission standards, the EPA has had to bargain with both polluters and state and local officials to reach tolerable decisions and help secure compliance. Another notable example of bargaining involves the consent decrees used by the Antitrust Division of the Department of Justice to close most civil antitrust cases. Negotiated beyond public view by representatives of the division and the alleged offender, the consent decree states that the division will drop its formal proceedings in turn for the alleged offender's agreement to stop practices such as price-fixing or acquisition of a competitor. Negotiations with other countries for tariff reductions also illustrate bargaining, in this instance with foreign officials.[55]

Patterns of Policymaking   Administrative agencies engage in a wide range of activities and make multitudes of decisions as they administer the laws within their jurisdiction. (Some of these activities or techniques are discussed in the next section.) Out of this welter of activity, four patterns can be identified and designated as policymaking because of the ways in which they help define the content and thrust of public policies. These patterns are rule-making, adjudication, law-enforcement practices, and program operations.

RULE-MAKING   The Administrative Procedure Act defines a *rule* as "an agency statement of general or particular applicability and future effect designed to implement, interpret, or prescribe law or policy or describing the organization, procedure, or practice requirements of an agency." Substantive rules fill in the details of general statutory provisions and have the force and effect of law. Interpretive rules indicate how an agency views or interprets the laws that it enforces and the meaning it gives to statutory terms such as *discriminate*, *small business*, or *an appropriate education*. Procedural rules describe an agency's organization and how it will conduct its various activities. In practice, it is not always easy to distinguish these types of rules, or to separate them from informal statements of agency policy or practice.[56]

Congress has delegated rule-making authority to a large number of administrative agencies. Thus, the Securities and Exchange Commission is authorized to make rules governing the stock exchanges "as it deems necessary in the public interest or for the protection of investors." OSHA is empowered to make rules setting health and safety standards for workplaces. In the case of toxic substances, OSHA is directed to set the standard "which most adequately assures, to the extent feasible, on the basis of the best available evidence, that no worker suffers material impairment of health," even when exposed to a toxic substance over the course of a working career. The conditions embedded in this delegation reflect compromises made during the legislative process. They leave the meaning of the law vague and the agency uncertain as to what is required to meet the standard.

Rule-making, which is one of the primary instruments of government in the United States, is the part of the administrative process that most resembles the legislative process.[57] Most frequently it takes the form of informal, or notice and comment, rule-making. The procedural requirements governing informal rule-making are set forth by the Administrative Procedure Act (Section 553):

1. A notice of proposed rule-making (NPRM) must be published in the *Federal Register* that specifies the legal authority for the rule, the terms or substance of the proposed rule, and the time, place, and nature of the public rule-making proceeding.

2. An opportunity must be provided for interested persons to participate in the rule-making, through either oral or written comments. For controversial rules, agencies will often choose to hold hearings. Although

a hearing rarely changes anyone's mind on a proposed rule, it serves to educate the public and permits a more extensive record of public participation to be compiled. This can help the agency if the rule is challenged in the courts.[58]

3. A concise statement of the rule's "basis and purpose" must be included with the final rule. In the preamble to a rule, the agency indicates the information, data, and analyses that it relied on in developing the rule. Also, the number and nature of public comments, the issues that they raised, and actions taken (or not taken) by the agency in response may be detailed. The preambles to rules often exceed the actual rules in length.[59]

4. The final rule must be published at least thirty days before it becomes effective.

These requirements are intended to provide for fairness in rule-making, which includes furnishing those interested in or affected by a rule with an opportunity to participate in its development and perhaps influence its content. (In actuality, most final rules differ little from their proposed form.)

In some instances, agencies are required by statutes to follow more detailed and stringent procedures in rule-making actions (see Figure 6.4). Thus, if a statute specifies that rules must be based on a formal record, then an agency, in making a rule, must hold a trial-type hearing, follow rigorous procedures, allow legal representation and cross examination of witnesses, and base its rule on "substantial evidence in the record." The comparable standard for rules emanating from informal proceedings is that they must not constitute an "arbitrary or capricious abuse of discretion." This is yet another of the mushy standards that one encounters in the policy world.

In addition to the Administrative Procedure Act, some other statutes impose procedural requirements on rule-making agencies. If a rule has a significant impact on the environment, the National Environmental Policy Act requires the agency to prepare an environmental impact statement. Should small businesses be disproportionately affected, the Regulatory Flexibility Act requires the agency to take steps to reduce a rule's impact on them. If a rule necessitates the collection of information from the public, then the Paperwork Reduction Act applies. OMB approval is needed to ensure that the information collection does not impose an unnecessary burden on the public. These various requirements complicate and slow the rule-making process. And, as law-school dean Cornelius Kerwin notes:

> Our legislators enact programs of regulation or social welfare but then encumber them with procedural requirements that will almost certainly stall their implementation. This simply confirms that political decision making is multidimensional. The combination of an aggressive and ambitious substantive mission combined with a cautious and painstaking process of implementation can satisfy different sets of constituents.[60]

FIGURE 6.4

The Federal Rule-Making Process

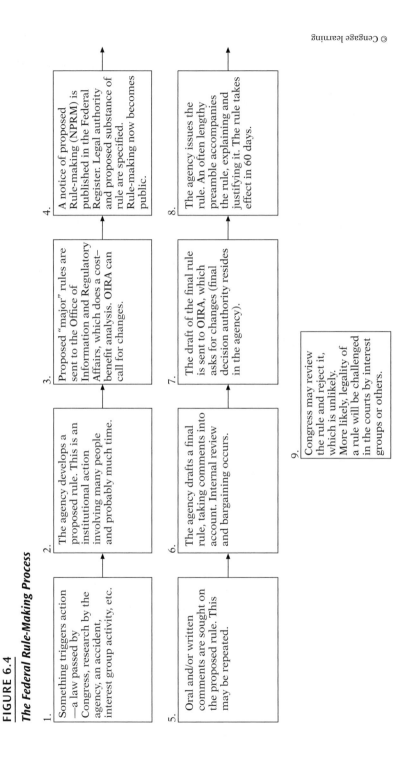

1. Something triggers action —a law passed by Congress, research by the agency, an accident, interest group activity, etc.

2. The agency develops a proposed rule. This is an institutional action involving many people and probably much time.

3. Proposed "major" rules are sent to the Office of Information and Regulatory Affairs, which does a cost–benefit analysis. OIRA can call for changes.

4. A notice of proposed Rule-making (NPRM) is published in the Federal Register: Legal authority and proposed substance of rule are specified. Rule-making now becomes public.

5. Oral and/or written comments are sought on the proposed rule. This may be repeated.

6. The agency drafts a final rule, taking comments into account. Internal review and bargaining occurs.

7. The draft of the final rule is sent to OIRA, which asks for changes (final decision authority resides in the agency).

8. The agency issues the rule. An often lengthy preamble accompanies the rule, explaining and justifying it. The rule takes effect in 60 days.

9. Congress may review the rule and reject it, which is unlikely. More likely, legality of a rule will be challenged in the courts by interest groups or others.

In addition to legislative requirements, beginning in the early 1980s, presidential executive orders have required agencies (other than independent regulatory commissions) to submit proposed rules rated as significant or major to the Office of Information and Regulatory Affairs (OIRA) for cost–benefit analysis. OIRA gets a few "whacks" at such rules and can delay their issuance if it decides they do not pass cost–benefit muster. (See the discussion of CBA in Chapter 7, "Policy Impact, Evaluation, and Change.")

A variety of factors may initiate the agency rule-making process. A few are noted here. The Dodd-Frank Act directed the Bureau of Consumer Financial Protection, the Commodity Future Trading Commission, and other agencies to make hundreds of rules spelling out the law's provisions. Pressure groups may lobby for agency action and, moreover, use litigation to back up their demands. Legal action by the Center for Biological Diversity has caused the U.S. Fish and Wildlife Service to list scores of species as endangered. Agency research and enforcement experience may identify problems to be dealt with by rules. During the George W. Bush administration, the OIRA occasionally issued "prompt letters" to encourage rule-making on some topic or to give it higher priority. Some sort of crisis or accident also may generate rule-making. Presidential directives and recommendations from Congressional committees or federal advisory committees are other possibilities.

Notwithstanding the procedural and other obstacles that they encounter, national administrative agencies issue thousands of rules annually. These range from those that are of small moment and short duration—such as some Agricultural Marketing Service rules on the quality of fruits and vegetables— to those that impose major costs and affect large numbers of people—such as EPA rules on air quality and hazardous-waste disposal. Collectively, these rules, which daily are reported in the *Federal Register*, are much larger in volume than the legislation enacted by Congress. Agency rules are codified in the *Code of Federal Regulations*.

ADJUDICATION   Agencies can make policy when they apply existing laws or rules to particular situations by case-to-case decision-making. In so doing, they act in much the same manner as courts, just as they act in legislative fashion when engaged in rule-making. In the past, the FTC made policy by applying the legislative prohibition of unfair methods of competition to specific cases. These cases gradually marked out public policy and by induction indicated the kinds of practices banned by the general prohibition.

An agency also may make policy when it gives an interpretation to a statutory provision in applying it in a case. The NLRB, which administers labor-management relations legislation, makes and announces statutory interpretations in deciding unfair-practice cases, which then inform its action in future cases. NLRB opinions on such matters as what constitutes "good faith" in collective bargaining become policy statements of importance to union and company officials.

Agencies frequently choose to make policy by adjudication, even though they have rule-making authority. This is true for the NLRB, for instance. (They may be authorized, but not required, to engage in rule-making.) An agency may find it no easier than a legislature to reach a decision on the content of general policy, especially in a novel or highly controversial situation. Consequently, it can choose to proceed in a more piecemeal or incremental manner. Those affected by agency action, however, may be left in the dark as to what policy is supposed to be when it is made case by case. And indeed, agencies have been criticized for relying too much on adjudication and too little on rule-making as they develop policy.[61]

Much of the adjudication that administrative agencies engage in is informal or routine, such as the hundreds of thousands of decisions made annually by the Department of Veterans Affairs and the Social Security Administration on applications for benefits. Still, within the framework of statutory language, seemingly routine decisions may shift the direction or skew the effect of policy.

LAW ENFORCEMENT   Agencies may also mold policy through their various law-enforcement actions. A statute may be enforced vigorously or even rigidly, in a lax manner, or not at all; it may be applied in some situations and not in others, or to some persons or companies and not to others. Everyone is familiar with the discretion exercised by the police officer on the beat or, what is more likely, in the patrol car. A ticket may be given to a speeder, or only a warning may be issued. If no drivers are ticketed unless they exceed posted speed limits by a specific rate, this choice amounts to an amendment of public policy. Even when statutory provisions are quite precise, thus seeming to eliminate discretion in their interpretation, enforcement officers still have some discretion with respect to the manner in which they will be enforced.

Policy may be shaped by administrative inaction or apathy as well as by an agency's positive action and zeal. Inaction often adversely affects only the inarticulate or inattentive general public and consequently may pass unnoticed. In 1936, Congress enacted the Robinson-Patman Act to protect small retailers against price discrimination by large competitors such as chain stores and discount houses. Economists have long criticized the law as a barrier to price competition. During the past decade or two, both the FTC and the Antitrust Division of the Department of Justice, under whose jurisdiction the Robinson-Patman Act falls, have ceased to enforce it. Some question exists as to whether agencies should be able to ignore a law in this manner.

A second example involves the Reclamation Act of 1902, which authorized a massive irrigation program to encourage agricultural development in the western states. The land that a farmer could irrigate with low-cost water from federally constructed reservoirs was limited to 160 acres, or 320 acres for a farmer and spouse. Further, they were required to live on or near their land. For many decades these restrictions, which were clearly spelled out in the law, were not enforced by the BOR. As a consequence, much of the below-market-cost water from federal reclamation projects was provided to large farms, often owned by corporations, encompassing thousands of acres. Many were (and are) located in California's Central Valley. These large landholders were strong supporters of BOR's reinterpretation of the law.[62]

Pressure by environmentalists and organizations representing small farmers finally induced Congress in 1982 to pass the Reclamation Reform Act. The irrigation limit was increased to 960 acres and the residency requirement was repealed. Large landholders then created "farming trusts" to manage supposedly separate units not subject to the 960 acre cap. Collectively they far exceed it. Still intransigent, the BOR has continued to acquiesce in this subterfuge.[63] In this instance, as well as that of the Robinson-Patman Act, one encounters agency nullification of legislative policy. What becomes of the rule of law?

In addition to the attitudes and motives of its officials, external pressures, and financial resources, an agency's capacity to carry out policies will be significantly affected by the enforcement authority and techniques available to it. Opponents unable to block legislative enactment of a law may seek to blunt its impact by handicapping its enforcement. Take the equal employment opportunity provisions in Title 7 of the Civil Rights Act of 1964, which prohibit firms or unions representing fifteen or more employees from discriminating against individuals because of their race, color, religion, national origin, or sex. Along with the other titles in the act, these provisions were adopted over strong conservative opposition.

The EEOC was authorized to enforce the law through investigations, conferences, and conciliation, which means essentially voluntary action. If these methods failed, the EEOC could recommend civil action in the federal courts, which required cooperation by the Department of Justice to prosecute cases. Moreover, the law provided that the EEOC could not act on complaints from states that had an antidiscrimination law and an agency to enforce it, unless the state agency was unable to complete action within sixty days. Complaints had to be filed "in writing under oath," which is an unusual requirement for a law-violation complaint. This stipulation undoubtedly had a chilling effect on many southern blacks and others. Whatever the intent behind these provisions, they clearly limited the law's effectiveness by making the successful completion of cases a slow, tedious process.

After 1964, the EEOC and many supporters of stronger enforcement advocated giving the agency authority to issue cease-and-desist orders[64] in discrimination cases and then to seek, on its own initiative, their enforcement in the federal courts. Opposition to this proposed change was particularly strong from conservatives and southerners. The EEOC was eventually empowered to bring court action on its own initiative but not to issue cease-and-desist orders when the conciliation of complaints was not successful. Though perhaps not as much as hoped, this new authority did help strengthen the enforcement and effectiveness of the anti-job-discrimination policy.

PROGRAM OPERATIONS Many agencies administer loan, grant, benefit, insurance, and service policies and programs, or engage in the management of public properties such as forests, parks, and hydroelectric plants. Although these activities are not usually thought of as law enforcement because they are not designed directly to regulate or shape people's behavior, they are often of much importance to many people. How such programs are implemented helps determine policy both directly and indirectly. Some examples will provide clarification.

CASE STUDY   *The Nuclear Waste Disposal Act*

A problem resulting from the development of the commercial nuclear power industry was how to handle the disposal of high-level radioactive nuclear waste, which remains highly dangerous for many thousands of years. Public officials and Congress fretted about this matter for several years. Then, in 1982, Congress enacted the Nuclear Waste Policy Act in an effort to provide a "permanent" solution.

The Nuclear Waste Policy Act assigned the Department of Energy the task of picking two storage sites—one east and one west of the Mississippi River. Following the procedures specified in the act, in 1985 DOE designated three western sites—Deaf Smith County, Texas; Yucca Mountain, Nevada; and Hanford Nuclear Reservation, Washington. All fought against being selected as the final disposal site. Then in 1987, rather than follow the specified procedures, Congress summarily passed legislation making Yucca Mountain the waste disposal site. Nevadans were outraged by this action.

Many years and much money ($10 billion as of 2008) have been spent doing research on the safety and viability of the Yucca Mountain site. Nevadans, Democrats and Republicans, officials and citizens remained steadfast in their opposition, using political and public relations tactics, initiating lawsuits, and disputing scientific findings. They have drawn support from the ranks of environmental and consumer groups and nuclear power opponents. The nuclear power industry and various business groups, such as the U.S. Chamber of Commerce, have favored completion of the project.

Finally, in February 2002 President George W. Bush, who favored expansion of the nuclear power industry, gave his approval to the Yucca Mountain site. Under the 1987 statute which designated it, Nevada was entitled to exercise a veto, which it quickly did. Congress, however, adopted a resolution which overrode the veto. Then in July 2002, President Bush signed legislation making Yucca Mountain the nation's high-level radio-active waste depository. This cleared the way for the Department of Energy to seek a license for the project from the Nuclear Regulatory Commission.[65] This was expected to take several years. If all went well, officials expected to begin moving nuclear waste in the repository by 2010. This proved to be wrong.

President Barack Obama, who had been critical of nuclear power during the 2008 presidential campaign, moved the following March to eliminate most of the funding for the Yucca Mountain site.[66] After decades of struggle and the expenditure of many billions of dollars, the nation remains without a permanent solution to its nuclear waste disposal problem. There is no Plan B. High-level waste remains "temporarily" stored at 121 sites scattered around 39 states, who had hoped to rid themselves of it. This is not an acceptable solution.

The nuclear disaster in April 2011 at Japan's Fukushima Daiichi nuclear power plant, caused by an earthquake and tsunami, stimulated efforts to develop a new solution. Waste disposal experts urged that nuclear wastes be moved to a "halfway house" for at least a century until a new burial site could be built. Bipartisan interest in something along these lines developed in Congress. Whether it will result in action is anyone's guess. The intractability of the nuclear waste disposal problem remains high. ■

CASE STUDY   *The Total Maximum Daily Load Program*

The Clean Water Act (1972) mandated technological standards to reduce water pollution coming from stationary sources—factories and municipal sewage treatment plants. Because these standards did not apply to all sources of water pollution, it was not likely that the goals of the act would be achieved by the technological standards alone. As a backup, the Clean Water Act in Section 303 created the Total Maximum Daily Load (TMDL) program, a complex matter.[67]

Under the TMDL program, states were directed to establish ambient water quality standards for water bodies (rivers, streams, lakes). These standards were to comprise the designated use or uses of a water body (e.g., public water supply, industrial water supply, recreation) and to estimate the total maximum daily amount of various pollutants that a water body could receive and still meet appropriate water quality standards with a margin of safety. If a state failed to take this action, then the EPA was directed to develop a list of water bodies for a state and to set the TMDLs.

To implement a TMDL and achieve the water quality standard it sets, a state can consider all water pollution sources—point sources, such as municipal sewage facilities or industrial plants; and nonpoint sources, such as livestock feeding operations and forests (the EPA cannot deal directly with nonpoint sources).

For two decades, the TMDL program was essentially dormant. National and state attention centered on the development and implementation of the technological standards. Then in 1992, recognizing that more controls on pollution were needed to attain water quality standards, the EPA issued a regulation directing states to list water bodies every two years that did not meet water quality standards and to develop TMDLs to achieve these standards.

Dissatisfied with inaction, environmental groups filed dozens of lawsuits to compel action. They believed that implementation of the TMDL program would help achieve the goals of the Clean Water Act and also pressure the EPA and the states to control nonpoint source pollution. Nonpoint sources had become the major cause of impairment for many water bodies. Many of the lawsuits culminated with court orders mandating expeditious development of TMDLs by the states or the EPA.[68]

The lawsuits helped goad the EPA into action, and in 1997, it called on the states to formulate long-term plans for implementing TMDLs. As a consequence, action in some of the states began to intensify.

Then in August 1999, the EPA proposed a rule to clarify, strengthen, and accelerate the TMDL program. Changes included requirements for more comprehensive listing of polluted water bodies; more specification of the content of TMDLs; a requirement that an implementation plan be included in TMDLs; and provision of greater opportunity for public participation. The proposed new rule attracted much opposition. States complained about the burdens the new rule would impose on them. Farm groups, the forestry industry, and other nonpoint dischargers questioned the EPA's authority to include nonpoint source pollution in the TMDL program. Municipal and industry groups worried that their burden under the technological standards might be further increased. Environmental groups, which favored a stronger TMDL program, fretted about possible delays in cleaning up impaired water bodies.

The final EPA rule was issued in July 2000. Although some provisions were dropped, including several affecting agriculture and forestry, in all, the new rule put more backbone in the TMDL program. However, the controversy over the rule had attracted unfavorable congressional attention. A rider was added to an appropriations act that prohibited the expenditure of any funds to implement the new rule until after the end of fiscal year 2001 (October 31).

The Bush administration now came to the aid of the rule's opponents, stating that it would delay its effective date until May 2003. The administration said it needed time to review the rule and to consider alterations. In March 2003 it withdrew the rule, stating that it was not workable without major changes.[69] A new weaker rule was given some consideration, but the ultimate decision was to do nothing. Thus, the TMDL program continues to be administered under the 1992 rule.

In recent years, the rule-making failure aside, activity under the TMDL programs has gained momentum. By 2008, some 34,000 TMDLs had been developed by the states and the EPA. How effectively they are being implemented is another matter. Good information on this is hard to acquire.

There appear to be two major obstacles to a fully effective TMDL program.[70] One is that good data on water quality are scarce and costly. Moreover, it is highly difficult to calculate the maximum amount of each pollutant that can be permitted in each water body during a twenty-four hour period.[71] Second, there is the matter of political will or commitment. To accomplish its goals, the TMDL program needs political support and adequate resources at both state and national levels. People and public officials must want clean water and be willing to support its attainment. Some states, such as California and New Jersey, have shown more commitment to pollution control than have others, such as Texas and Kansas.[72] ■

Techniques of Control

Whether labeled promotional, regulatory, prohibitive, redistributive, or whatever, almost all policies incorporate an element of control. That is, by one means or another, overtly or subtly, they are designed to cause people to do things, refrain from doing things, or continue doing things that they otherwise would not do. This holds true whether reference is to tax provisions intended to encourage industrial-plant modernization or charitable giving, the provision of information and financial assistance to expand international trade, or a prohibition of an activity such as price-fixing with penalties for violators. Even Smokey Bear's admonition that "only you can prevent forest fires" embodies a control element.[73]

The control techniques authorized for their implementation are an important component of public policies. Decisions on these matters, like those on the substance of policy itself, can be highly productive of controversy during the policy-adoption process. The control techniques that an agency is permitted to use may in practice have important consequences for the content and impact of policy, for policy as an "operational reality" that affects human behavior. Those who oppose a policy, for example, may attempt to lessen or even negate its effects by restricting the administering agency's powers of enforcement or implementation. Two examples illustrate this point. In 1912, Massachusetts became the first state to enact a minimum-wage law. While strongly supported by organized labor, it met with vigorous opposition from manufacturers. The result was compromise legislation that provided for enforcement only by the publication in newspapers of the names of companies not complying with the wage standard. As one might guess, the Massachusetts law was not effective.

In the 1970s, a wave of corporate mergers led to efforts to strengthen antimerger law. After much struggle, including a Senate filibuster by opponents, legislation was enacted providing that the Antitrust Division of the Department of Justice had to be given advance notice of proposed large corporate mergers. Proponents believed that this requirement would increase the effectiveness of antitrust enforcement by enabling the government to block mergers before they were completed and the companies involved lost their separate identities. Opponents, notably investment bankers, who put together mergers, and others in conservative and business ranks, apparently shared this view. Otherwise, there would have been no controversy.

Control techniques may rely on a number of behavioral assumptions.[74] Economic incentives such as subsidies, tax credits, and loans are based on the assumption that people are utility maximizers. Incentives to act in their own interest will cause them to comply with policies. Capacity-enhancing techniques, such as job training, information, and counseling programs, rely on the notion that people have the desire or motivation to do what is required but lack the capacity to act accordingly.

Hortatory techniques—declarations of policy, appeals for voluntary cooperation, admonitions against littering or drunk driving—assume that people act on the basis of their beliefs or values, that they will do what is right if informed ·about what is right. If one looks along roadways, however, it is quite apparent that appeals not to be a litterbug often miss the mark. Also, let it be noted that hortatory appeals may often be a substitute for more compelling action.

Authoritative techniques rest on the premise that requirements and restrictions, backed up by sanctions, are necessary to prevent people from engaging in undesirable, evil, immoral, or unfair behavior. Many government agencies, consequently, have authority to set and enforce standards on environmental pollution, consumer safety, financial transactions, and other topics.

In sum, for a policy to be effective, more is needed than substantive authority and sufficient funding to cover the financial costs for implementation. Adequate and suitable techniques of control and implementation must be authorized for the responsible agency. In this section a variety of control techniques are examined, but the list is not exhaustive.

Noncoercive Forms of Action   Many of the methods used to implement policies to bring about compliance are noncoercive. Here, *noncoercive* means that they do not involve the imposition of legal sanctions or penalties, rewards, or deprivations. The effectiveness of these forms depends mostly upon voluntary collaboration or acceptance by the affected parties, although social and economic pressures arising out of society may lend them an element of compulsion. The following are examples of noncoercive forms of action.

Declarations of policy by themselves may cause many people to comply, "to go along." This result seems reasonable, especially if the declarations are made by respected or high-status officials. Presidential appeals to labor and management to avoid making inflationary wage contracts or price increases, for example, may themselves have a restraining effect, as may mayoral appeals to citizens to conserve water by not watering their lawns during periods of drought.

In a book entitled *Nudge*, Professors Richard Thaler and Cass Sunstein argue for what they call "libertarian paternalism."[75] Drawing on behavioral economics and psychology, they propose structuring choice situations to encourage but not compel decisions that will make people's lives longer, healthier, and better. For example, a nudge would involve arranging foods in a school cafeteria to make choosing healthy foods easier than choosing junk foods. As a second example, Thaler and Sunstein cite the Texas Department of Transportation's effort to reduce littering by posting signs along highways proclaiming "Don't Mess with Texas." This they label a "stunning success." (They apparently have not spent much time traveling in Texas.)

Voluntary standards may be established by official action. The National Institute of Standards and Technology has developed commercial standards, such as uniform weights, measures, and grades of products and materials, which are not mandatory. They are widely adhered to because their use facilitates or promotes business and economic activity. While the use of most of the standard grades—such as prime, choice, and select for beef—established by the U.S. Department of Agriculture for agricultural commodities is permissive (some are mandatory for interstate commerce), they are widely followed in practice because they facilitate trade.

Mediation and conciliation are noncoercive measures often used in efforts to settle labor-management disputes, as by the Federal Mediation and Conciliation Service. The mediator works to bring the parties together, to clarify the facts in the disputes and the points at issue, and to offer advice and suggestions to promote settlement. The mediator, however, has no formal powers of decision or sanction. Many labor-management disputes are successfully resolved by these procedures.

The use of publicity to bring the social and economic effects of adverse public opinion to bear on violators may induce compliance with policy. Much stress was placed on "pitiless publicity" during the Progressive Era as a way of preventing monopoly. Although labor and business organizations today exhibit much awareness about their public image, it is impossible to measure how effective publicity is as a control device. Still, the revelation of "poor" working conditions or "undesirable" business practices by congressional or agency investigations may produce some correction or improvement.

Educational and demonstration programs are widely used by agencies in securing compliance with policy. Much effort is expended to inform people about their rights under Social Security and veterans' benefits programs, for example. Employers are informed through publications and conferences about the meaning and requirements of wage and hours legislation. The demonstration technique is especially used in agriculture. Preferred practices in soil conservation and crop production are shown and explained to farmers with the hope that their demonstrated superiority will lead to widespread acceptance and use.

Inspection   Inspection is the examination of some matter (such as premises, products, or records) to determine whether it conforms to officially prescribed standards. The inspection may be either continuous, as in the inspection of meat in packing plants, or periodic, as in the inspection of banks and food-processing establishments. Whichever form it takes, inspection is intended to reveal compliance or noncompliance with rules or standards by those involved in an activity, with the objective of preventing or correcting undesirable or dangerous conditions. Typically, an effort is first made to persuade violators to conform with the law; imposing sanctions or penalties is a last recourse. Indeed, the ultimate purpose of inspection is to help gain the cooperation of the regulated.

Inspection is the most commonly used form of regulatory action. Examples of its use at the national level include the inspection of locomotives and railroad safety devices by the Federal Railroad Administration, sanitary conditions in food- and drug-manufacturing establishments by the FDA, income-tax returns by the IRS, and national banks by the Comptroller of the Currency.

Licensing   *Licensing*, or *enabling action*, as it is sometimes called, involves government authorization to engage in a business or profession or to do something otherwise forbidden. An extensively used form of action, licensing is known by various names. Licenses are required to engage in many professions and occupations and to do such things as operate motor vehicles and radio stations. In addition, the term *certificate of public convenience and necessity* is used in the public-utility field. *Permits* may be necessary to drill oil wells, the *corporate charter* authorizes the use of a form of business organization, and *franchises* are granted to utilities to use city streets for their pipe- and wire lines.

Licensing is a form of advance check in which a person who wishes to engage in a particular activity (such as driving a car) must demonstrate certain qualifications or meet specified standards or requirements. The burden of proof in securing a license rests with the applicant rather than the granting official. The use of licensing ordinarily goes beyond the initial authorization or denial to do something. It may also include "(1) imposition of conditions as part of the authorization; (2) modification of the terms or conditions at the discretion of the granting authority; (3) renewal or denial of the authorization at periodic intervals; (4) revocation of the authorization." When these are included, licensing becomes a form of continuing control.[76] Radio and television broadcasters, for example, must periodically renew their licenses with the FCC and may have them revoked under specified circumstances. Only rarely, however, is an applicant's request for a broadcast license renewal denied.[77]

Loans, Subsidies,   Loans, subsidies, and benefits are means by which public
and Benefits   purposes are advanced through aid, in the form of money
                     or other resources, to companies, farmers, students, home
buyers, and others. Under the Essential Air Service Program, cash operating subsidies are granted to some commuter airlines to maintain an adequate system of air transport. Operating subsidies are used to promote the American merchant marine. It also benefits from the Jones Act, which provides that ocean commerce among U.S. ports can be carried only in ships built and registered in the United States. Commodity loans and payments are made to farmers to support farm prices and income. Small businesses are assisted by loans from the Small Business Administration. Also related is the guarantee of loans by the government to expand the volume of private lending, as with the guarantee of home mortgages by the Federal Housing Administration.

In addition to their broad control quality, loans, subsidies, and benefit programs may include explicit regulatory features. Under the agricultural income-support programs, commodity loans and payments are not available to those who do not comply with various conservation requirements. Farm Service Agency loans for purchasing farms are made under conditions designed to ensure good farm management. In effect, the government is using the loan and benefit operations to purchase consent to policies. The effectiveness of such programs depends considerably upon the need or desire for the assistance offered.

Contracts   Many governmental programs are carried out in substantial part through contracts with private entities. At the national level, the defense, nuclear weapons, and space programs are well-known examples. State and local governments contract with private companies for the construction of highways and streets and, in some instances, the management of public schools and prisons. Many private companies looking for profits want to do business with the government, and some, as in the aerospace industry, depend heavily upon government contracts for their very existence. The power to grant or deny contracts includes an obvious element of control.

Every presidential administration since Dwight Eisenhower's has encouraged agencies to contract out commercial activities. The OMB, pursuant to its Circular A-76, directs them to contract for goods and services when these can be obtained at lower cost from the private sector. Implementation of A-76, however, has varied widely among federal agencies and its cost savings are difficult to measure.[78]

Contracts sometimes serve as the basis for specific economic controls. Under the Walsh-Healey Act, companies wanting to sell goods or services to the national government must pay prevailing wages and comply with other standards on the hours and conditions of work. Executive Order 11246, issued by President Lyndon Johnson, prohibits discrimination in employment by federal contractors. The Office of Federal Contract Compliance programs, which administers the order, requires that contractors also have affirmative-action programs.[79] Violators of these requirements can be denied present or future government contracts.

After its adventure in Iraq began in 2003, the United States made extensive use of contracting. The Congressional Budget Office (CBO) reports that in 2007 at least 160,000 contract personnel worked in Iraq on contracts funded by the United States. (This was about the same as the number of military personnel.) Some of these workers were American citizens, some were Iraqis, and some were third-country nationals. They provided personal protection for American officials, furnished support services for the armed forces, worked on construction and development projects, and much more. In contrast, CBO notes that military personnel outnumbered private contractor personnel by a seven-to-one ratio during World War II.[80] Most of the contract personnel in Iraq have now been let go. Many others remain in Afghanistan.

General   Apart from their use in connection with the loan, sub-
Expenditures   sidy, and benefit operations, governmental expenditures for purchasing goods and services can be used by agency officials to attain various policy goals. Administrative agencies often have considerable discretion in spending funds appropriated by Congress. Expenditures of funds for goods and services can be used to foster favored domestic or local industries, or to increase economic activity in depressed areas. Competition may be promoted by purchasing from smaller rather than larger businesses so as to strengthen their economic position. The rate and timing of expenditures

can be geared to counteract inflationary or recessionary trends in the economy. Thus, in early 2009 the Congress enacted legislation providing for several hundred billion dollars in government spending (plus tax cuts) in an effort to offset the severe recession afflicting the country.

Market and Proprietary Operations   When government enters the market to buy, sell, or provide goods and services, its actions often have control effects. Thus, the purchase and sale of government securities in the market (i.e., open-market operations) is a potent tool used by the FRB to expand or contract the money supply in the economy. When the FRB buys government securities, this increases bank reserves and their lending capacity; the opposite occurs when the FRB sells securities. The prices of some agricultural commodities, such as milk, have been supported by direct Department of Agriculture purchases in the market. The Clinton administration sold petroleum from the Strategic Petroleum Reserve to counter action by the Organization of Petroleum Exporting Countries (OPEC) to raise oil prices. Many observers, however, viewed this as symbolic.

Government enterprises also may have a control effect, as when they compete with private enterprises. Thus, the sale of electric power at "reasonable" rates by the Tennessee Valley Authority led to rate reductions by private companies operating in the region. This is sometimes referred to as "yardstick regulation" in that the reasonableness of private utility rates can be measured by the public rates. Governmental competition has not been used extensively as a control device, although it remains a possibility. Some states use state-owned liquor stores rather than regulation of privately owned stores as a means for controlling liquor traffic.[81]

Taxation   Taxes are important policy instruments "because they not only provide revenue but also serve to sanction or encourage certain types of behavior."[82] The power to tax has occasionally been wielded for regulatory purposes. A 10 percent annual tax on state bank notes levied by Congress in 1865 drove them out of existence. State banks then developed the use of checks to replace their currency. For several decades, high taxes were levied on colored oleomargarine to discourage its use in preference to butter. Uncolored, oleomargarine resembles lard, something that most people do not relish. The Carter administration proposed increasing the federal tax on gasoline as a means of discouraging its consumption and promoting energy conservation. Congress refused to act on the recommendation, however, because of strong public opposition. This is a policy idea that will not die, however. In 1993, a gasoline-tax increase was adopted instead of the Clinton administration's proposal for an energy tax.

The idea of a carbon tax to reduce energy usage, by raising the price of gasoline, and to lessen air pollution, has been with us since the Nixon administration. Many economists are firm proponents of the idea. Although it is good economics and would have positive consequences, in a time when tax increases are anathema to many citizens and officials, it is bad politics. Its near-future prospects are dim.

In recent years, some have advocated more positive use of taxation. Thus, it has been contended that environmental pollution could be better reduced by levying a tax on effluents rather than relying on the system of standard-setting and enforcement.[83] The tax would provide businesses with an economic incentive to reduce discharges while permitting them to determine the most efficient manner to do this. Resistance to the use of taxation in this fashion has been based on various premises: taxes should be used only to raise revenue, the present pattern of regulation is adequate, and the tax device would be difficult to administer in practice. As a consequence, little use has been made of taxation as a more positive regulatory technique.

Tax Expenditures A plethora of deductions, deferrals, credits, exclusions of income, preferential rates, and exemptions enable individuals and corporations who engage in specified activities such as the purchase of homes, the receipt of employer-provided health insurance (which is equal to income), charitable giving, capital investment, the receipt of capital gains, and much more to retain money that otherwise would be paid in taxes. They are frequently called tax expenditures.[84] The effect is the same as if the government had made direct payments to the privileged parties. But, it is less open and obvious, and some beneficiaries may be unaware of their good fortune. For the most part, tax expenditures are meted out through the tax system administered by the IRS and require no special administrative apparatus. Beneficiaries claim their benefits when they file their income-tax forms. A payer simply pays less taxes.[85]

The use of tax expenditures has become widespread. Some were eliminated by the 1986 Tax Reform Act. Since then, however, many more have been added to the U.S. Tax Code. There are hundreds of them. In 2011, they cost the government more than a trillion dollars in lost revenue.[86] The three most costly were dividends and capital gains taxed at lower rates than ordinary income, employer contributions for health insurance, and the home mortgage interest deduction. High-income persons, overall, benefit far more from tax expenditures than do those with lower incomes.

The tax expenditure ploy capitalizes on the general aversion to paying taxes that appears built in to most Americans. It also reduces the visibility of government subsidies.

Directive Power Many agencies have authority, through the use of adjudicatory proceedings, to issue orders or directives that are binding on private parties. (In the preceding section, we discussed the process of administrative adjudication and its use in developing policy.) Agencies may issue orders to settle disputes between private parties, as when a mover claims that a moving company damaged or lost some of his or her furniture; to resolve complaints, as when a company is charged with false or misleading advertising; and to approve or deny applications, as for a license for a nuclear-power project or a Social Security benefit.

Congressional standards governing administrative adjudication are usually more specific for benefit programs, such as Social Security and veterans' benefits, than for regulatory programs, perhaps because political conflict is often less intense over the passage of benefit legislation than regulatory legislation.[87] Consequently, Congress is less inclined to pass the buck to agencies through the guise of general legislation on benefit programs.

Services   Many public policies, mostly of the distributive variety, involve the provision of services such as information, advice, legal counsel, medical treatment, and psychiatric services. Thus, the Small Business Administration, in addition to making loans, administers a variety of informational and technical services for the operators of small businesses. The National Weather Service's forecasts are useful to groups such as farmers, commercial fishermen, and airline companies, as well as to weekend weather watchers generally. The Department of Veterans Affairs provides many medical, psychiatric, and counseling services to veterans, often at no cost.

Service programs variously provide benefits to recipients or users, help enhance the personal or material well-being of many people, and support the more efficient operation of markets (as in job training and the provision of foreign-trade data). Moreover, many services are intended to cause, encourage, or enable recipients to act in preferred ways.

Informal   Much of the work done by agencies in settling questions
Procedures   involving private rights, privileges, and interests is accomplished by informal procedures—that is, without formal action and adversary hearings. Most disputes arising out of income-tax returns are settled by consultation and correspondence between the IRS and the private parties involved. Claims for retirement benefits under the Social Security program are mostly settled by administrative officials using work records, personal interviews, and eligibility rules. A large portion of the complaint cases alleging unfair labor or management practices initiated with the NLRB are also informally disposed of in conferences between agency field examiners and the parties in dispute.

Informal procedures have been referred to as "the lifeblood of the administrative process" because of their contributions to its efficiency and success. Certainly they are an important facet of policy implementation. Many decisions affecting private rights and interests are reached by such means as negotiation, bargaining and compromise, consultation, conference, correspondence, reference to technical data, and examination of material. Extensive use is made of such methods because of the large number of cases coming before agencies, the need or desire for quick action, agencies' wishes to avoid becoming embroiled in formal proceedings, and private parties' desires to avoid the courthouse and unfavorable publicity.

Voluntary
Regulation
Rather than rely on mandatory government controls to protect the public against some evil, voluntary regulation would depend upon companies to regulate themselves, to act with restraint, to reduce pollution emissions, whatever. Thus, George W. Bush, as governor of Texas and then as president, called on public utility companies to voluntarily reduce their emissions of carbon dioxide. In neither case was it effective, although it did create the impression that something was being done.

Trade or industry associations sometimes take responsibility for controlling the behavior of their members. An example is the Responsible Care program of the American chemical industry, whereby industry members agree to comply with a set of ethical and practice guidelines. Another example involves the EPA and the National Pork Producers Council. Under an agreement, the Council funds certification of inspectors who can penalize participating pork producers for Clean Water Act violations.[88] Voluntary regulation can be an appealing notion, but its effectiveness is clearly questionable. It may be only a dodge to avoid positive government action.

Sanctions
Sanctions are the devices, penalties, and rewards that agencies use to encourage or compel compliance.[89] In the form of penalties or deprivations, they put some sting into administrative action. In some instances, sanctions are built into control techniques. Thus, when an agency decides to grant or deny a conditional benefit, the sanction rests in this action. Other sanctions that agencies may be authorized to impose include the threat of prosecution, favorable or unfavorable publicity, modification or revocation of licenses, monetary assessments, product recalls, seizure or destruction of goods, award of damages, and issuance of injunctions or cease-and-desist orders.

Agencies may also seek to impose criminal penalties (fines and jail sentences), but this requires taking action through the courts. On the other hand, agencies may be enabled to assess civil penalties for law violations. A civil penalty looks much like a fine, but it does not entail a finding of criminal guilt. OSHA frequently levies civil penalties for violations of industrial health and safety standards.

Concluding
Comment
There appears to be general agreement that policies should be implemented in such manner as to cause the least possible material and psychological disturbance to the persons affected. (This generalization may not hold for some criminal laws.) Within this constraint, the most technically or economically efficient method of enforcement may not be the most acceptable politically. This consideration will

influence both the legislature in authorizing control techniques for an agency and the agency in using its techniques and sanctions.

Another consideration in choosing control techniques stems from the general objective of public policy, which is to control behavior (or secure compliance) and not to punish violators, except as a last resort. Consequently, the usual preference will be for less harsh or coercive techniques. Some sanctions may be considered so harsh that they are rarely used, as with jail sentences for business executives who violate the antitrust laws. Government tends to follow the rule of parsimony in employing legal restraint and compulsion in policy implementation, except for some types of criminal conduct.

A Controversy: Standards or Incentives?   Traditionally, economic regulatory programs have relied heavily upon such administrative practices as setting standards, inspection to determine compliance, and imposing sanctions upon violators. Following the lead of economist Charles Schultze, however, many now designate and stigmatize this pattern of regulation as "command-and-control" regulation. (In reality, of course, a great deal of education, persuasion, negotiation, bargaining, and compromise goes on in the regulatory process.) Opponents object to use of the "command-and-control" approach because, they say, it dictates behavior, discourages private initiative and innovation in attaining policy goals, and causes waste or misuse of societal resources. In its stead they prefer economic incentives in the form of rewards or penalties, which they see as utilizing individual self-interest to achieve public purposes. The incentive system, it is said, "lets individuals make their own decisions, thus enhancing freedom and voluntarism, and yet (under the right circumstances) achieves desired goals at the lowest possible cost to society."[90]

Let us take the question of how to control environmental pollution as an illustration of the incentive system because it is here that the incentive approach has been most widely proposed. The system apparently would work like this: First, it would be determined how much reduction in a pollutant would be necessary to meet a policy goal. A tax or fee would then be imposed on each unit (perhaps a ton) of the pollutant (perhaps sulfur dioxide) discharged sufficient to achieve the goal. Those discharging the pollutant could then choose to pay the tax or lower their discharges. Ideally, they would choose the latter, reducing their discharges, by whatever means chosen, as much as economically practicable, or to the extent that it costs less to reduce pollution than to pay the tax. Economists Allen Kneese and Charles Schultze explain the consequences of a selected level of taxes:

> Firms with low costs of control would remove a larger percentage [of a pollutant] than would firms with higher costs, precisely the situation needed to achieve a least-cost approach to reducing pollution for the economy as a whole. Firms would tend to choose the least expensive methods of control, whether treatment of wastes, modification in production processes, or substitution of raw materials that had less serious

polluting consequences. Further, the kinds of products whose manufacture entailed a lot of pollution would become more expensive and could carry higher prices than those that generated less, so consumers would be induced to buy more of the latter.[91]

The incentive system, its supporters believe, would be easy to administer. Once the level of taxes appropriate for achieving a policy goal was determined, it would then be a simple matter to monitor discharges and collect the taxes due. Large bureaucracies would be unnecessary, and political struggles would be avoided. Governmental coercion to cause compliance with standards, with all the balkiness that it creates, would give way to choice driven by self-interest.

In practice, however, the incentive system would be unlikely to eliminate either politics or the need for administrative agencies. Determining how much reduction of pollution was necessary (or conversely, how clean the air should be) and what level of taxes would be needed to achieve this goal would be open to much disagreement, conflict, and struggle; in short, such decisions would be highly political. Businesses would want to hold down the taxes, environmentalists would opt for higher taxes, small businesses would seek preferential treatment because it would cost them more to reduce discharges, and so on. Administrative structures would be needed to develop studies and information for making these decisions.

Once goals and taxes were set, an agency would be needed to monitor the discharge of pollutants (unless one was willing to trust polluters to monitor themselves) and to collect the taxes due. The more complex and finely calibrated the structure of pollution taxes, the more complex the monitoring program would have to be. Professor Deborah A. Stone remarks, "Where a standard and penalty system might levy a single fee for all discharges in excess of the standard, an incentive system would vary the taxes according to the amount of the discharges, and thus its information needs are greater than those of a standard system."[92]

Nor would the incentive system eliminate government coercion because it consists of a control system contrived and imposed by government on economic behavior. Companies do have a choice between cleaning up or paying up, or some combination of the two. Their real preference, however, might be to do nothing; they are left to select from among governmentally mandated alternatives.

A couple of other objections to the incentive system should be noted. One is that it leaves decisions on how much to pollute to the judgment of private parties, dictated by self-interest, and fails to stigmatize pollution as "morally wrong."[93] A second objection is based on equity. Because of their stronger economic position, some will be better able to pay the emission taxes and avoid restriction. In other words, the law will bear down more heavily on some than on others.

Emissions trading (or cap and trade) is another alternative to traditional regulation.

CASE STUDY	*The Clean Air Act's Emissions-Trading System*

CASE STUDY An emissions-trading system is authorized by Title IV of the Clean Air Act Amendments (CAAA) of 1990 as part of a strategy to reduce acid rain. A mandatory limit was imposed on nationwide emissions of sulfur dioxide, the primary precursor of acid rain, reducing them by 10 million tons (roughly 50 percent) by the year 2000. Under Phase I, which took effect in 1995, each of 110 electric power plants, located mostly in the Midwest, was issued a specified number of allowables. In Phase II, which got underway in 2000, most electric utilities were brought into the system.

An allowable entitles a utility to discharge a ton of sulfur dioxide annually. Companies reducing their emissions below specified levels, whether by energy conservation programs, conversion to low-sulfur fuels, or the installation of smokestack scrubbers, can sell unneeded allowables or "bank" them for future use. Companies that exceed their specified emission levels and that do not buy additional allowables are subject to heavy fines. Continuous emissions monitoring enables the EPA to keep track of what the companies are doing.

The Chicago Board of Trade (CBOT), a large commodity exchange, was authorized to create a market for the buying and selling of allowables. CBOT's first auction of allowables was held in March 1993. All of the allowables put on the market by the EPA were bought; however, only a few privately offered allowables changed hands. The prices paid were only a fraction of the costs of meeting pollution-reduction requirements by using smokestack scrubbers. Utility companies initially appeared wary of participation in this new market.[94] The volume of allowables traded increased at the 1994 and 1995 CBOT auctions, and prices further declined. An early study reported that "though the auction market has been sluggish and prices have fallen short of expectations, it appears that the intent of CAAA '90 is working."[95] More recently, the market for allowables has become more robust.

The sulfur dioxide emissions-trading system provides an empirical test of the feasibility of using economic incentives to reduce pollution. Preliminary evaluations support the conclusion that it has been fairly successful in reducing the volume of sulfur dioxide emissions. An authority on emissions trading says that "targeted emissions reductions have been achieved and exceeded.... Total abatement costs have been significantly less than what they would have been in the absence of trading provisions."[96] Under the trading system, however, it is possible for emissions to increase in some areas even as they decline overall, thus letting pollution "hot spots" exist.

Data provided by EPA indicate that the Acid Rain Program to reduce sulfur dioxide emissions is accomplishing its goals. Thus, a progress report for 2007 indicates that sulfur dioxide emissions from electric generating units were 43 percent lower than at the program's inception. Estimated public health benefits from ARP reduction exceed program costs by more than a 40:1 ratio. Reduction in nitrogen oxide emissions, another cause of acid rain, and were later included in ARP, also were significantly reduced.[97] These reductions resulted in improved water quality in lakes and streams.

In 2005, the European Union put into place the first emissions trading program to reduce carbon dioxide emissions, a major cause of global warming.[98] It is a large program that now includes twenty-five of the twenty-seven EU members. It got off to a rocky start. Officials initially planned to sell permits but, because of intense industry lobbying, decided to give most permits for free. The system was tightened after a couple of years and fewer permits were issued, and permits gained in value on the trading market. Nonetheless, carbon dioxide emissions rose slightly in 2006 and 2007. Leaders of the EU still hope to reduce emissions by 20 percent by 2020.

American opponents of carbon emissions regulatory program are prone to call the European system a failure. In contrast, a careful study done by two economists holds that the program has worked as intended. A European carbon price has been set, businesses are taking this price into account in making decisions, and a market for trading emissions permits is in place.[99]

Soon after taking office, President Obama proposed an emissions trading system to reduce carbon dioxide and other greenhouse gas emissions. Mandatory limits (caps) would be imposed on emissions and permits for emissions would be auctioned to emitters.[100] He subsequently indicated that he would not oppose the award of some free permits. By a narrow 219 to 212 margin, with no Republican support, the House passed a bill calling for a 17 percent reduction in greenhouse gas emissions from 2005 levels by 2020 and 83 percent by 2050. It also included several energy efficiency measures. The Senate reported a bill from committee but was unable to pass it because the sixty votes needed to block a filibuster could not be rounded up. Global warming dropped off of the Congressional decision agenda for the remainder of Obama's first term. The EPA then began action to use its rule-making authority under the Clean Air Act to restrict greenhouse gas emissions as a threat to the public health.

Should an emissions trading scheme to control greenhouse gas emissions be put in place sometime in the future, most of its cost likely will be passed on to consumers in the form of higher prices. That has been the case with the European trading system. ■

Compliance

All public policies are intended to influence or control human behavior in some way and to induce people to act in accordance with government-prescribed rules or goals, whether reference is to policy on such diverse matters as interest rates, nighttime burglary, patents and copyrights, open housing, agricultural production, or military recruitment. If compliance with policy is not achieved, if people continue to act in undesired ways, if they do not take desired actions, or if they cease doing what is desired, to that extent policy becomes ineffective or, at the extreme, a nullity. (Foreign policy also depends for its effectiveness on compliance by the affected foreign countries and their officials.) To make consideration of this problem more manageable, we focus primarily but not exclusively on compliance with domestic economic policies.

Except perhaps for crime policies, political scientists have not given much attention to the problem of compliance.[101] This neglect may be caused partly by our traditional legalistic approach to government, with the assumption that people have an absolute duty to obey the law. Too, those whose aim is securing governmental action on public problems often lose interest therein or shift their attention elsewhere once they secure the enactment of legislation. Political scientists have certainly been far more interested in the legislative and executive formulation and adoption of policy than in its administration, which is where compliance enters the picture. A complete study of policymaking must cover not only the events leading up to a decision on policy but also what is done to implement it and, ultimately, whether people comply with it.[102]

In this section, we examine some of the conditions affecting compliance and noncompliance with policy, along with the role of administrative agencies in securing compliance.[103] Because empirical data are not plentiful, the discussion must be somewhat tentative.

Causes of Compliance   Respect for authority, including authority as expressed in decisions by governmental agencies, is substantial in our society. Contentions that Americans are a lawless people are exaggerations and should not be permitted to obscure the favorable disposition of most people toward compliance with most public policies. Respect for and deference to authority are built into our psychological makeup by the process of socialization. Most of us are taught from birth to respect the authority of parents, knowledge, status, the law, and governmental officials, especially if these forms of authority are considered reasonable. Consequently, we grow up generally believing it to be morally right and proper to obey the law. Disobeying the law may produce feelings of guilt or shame. Prior conditioning and force of habit thus contribute to policy compliance.

Compliance with policy may also be based on some form of reasoned, conscious acceptance. Even some whose immediate self-interest conflicts with a policy may be convinced that it is reasonable, necessary, or just. Most people undoubtedly would rather not pay taxes, and many do try to avoid or evade their payment. But when people believe that tax laws are reasonable and just, or perhaps that taxation is necessary to provide needed governmental services, such beliefs will in all likelihood contribute to compliance with tax policy. Factors such as this and respect for authority clearly seem to contribute to the high degree of compliance with the national income tax in the United States.

In a study of police–citizen relationships in the Chicago area, Tom Tyler concluded that in complying with the law, people were much influenced by "social values about what is right and proper." He explained:

> People obey the law because they believe that it is proper to do so. They react to their experiences by evaluating their justice or injustice, and in evaluating the justice of their experiences, they consider factors unrelated to outcomes, such as whether they had a chance to state their case and been treated with dignity and respect.[104]

This runs counter to self-interest models of compliance behavior.

Another possible cause of compliance is the belief that a governmental decision or policy should be obeyed because it is legitimate, in the sense that it is constitutional, or was made by officials with proper authority to act, or that correct procedures were followed in its development. People would be less inclined to accept judicial decisions as legitimate if the courts utilized decision-making procedures akin to those of legislatures. Courts gain legitimacy and acceptance for their decisions by acting as courts are supposed to act. Some people in the South were willing to comply with the Supreme Court's 1954 school desegregation decision because they considered it legitimate and within the Court's competence, even though they disagreed with its substance.

Self-interest can be an important consideration in compliance under some circumstances. Individuals and groups may directly benefit from accepting policy norms and standards. Thus, farmers for decades complied with production limitations in the form of acreage allotments, marketing quotas, and set-asides in order to qualify for price supports and deficiency payments. Securities regulation is accepted by responsible members of the securities business as a way of protecting themselves and the reputation of their business against unethical practices by some wayward dealers. Businesses engage in industrial-plant modernization in order to receive investment tax credits. Compliance thus results because private interests and policy prescriptions are harmonious, a fact sometimes ignored. That is, compliance may yield monetary rewards. This arrangement, though, is not likely to occur outside the economic-policy area.

Any legislation, such as a minimum-wage law or an occupational-safety law, has more than simply supporters and opponents. Rather, many points of view will surround it, ranging from strong support through indifference to intense opposition. A sizable proportion of the population will often be indifferent or neutral toward the legislation, if indeed they feel affected by it at all. This group, given the general predisposition toward obedience, would seem especially subject to the authority of the law. Here, in effect, the law becomes a "self-fulfilling prophecy"; by its very existence, it operates to create a climate of opinion conducive to compliance.

The possibility of punishment in the form of fines, jail sentences, and other penalties may also contribute to compliance. "Classical deterrence theory assumes that individuals respond to the severity, certainty, and celerity [speed] of punishment," state political scientists Anne Schneider and Helen Ingram, "and in this respect it implies that individuals are utility maximizers."[105] The threat or imposition of sanctions alone, however, is not always sufficient, even though the likelihood of their use is overestimated. "The strong disposition in this country to believe that any behavior can be controlled by threatening punishment has filled American statute books with hundreds of unenforced and unenforceable laws."[106] Experience with national prohibition, World War II price and rationing controls, many Sunday "blue laws," highway speed limits, and penalties for using marijuana shows that the threat of punishment is not always sufficient to induce general compliance with policies.

Although many people may comply with policies because they fear punishment, the main function of sanctions is to reinforce and supplement other causes of compliance. Policies depend greatly for their effectiveness upon voluntary or noncoerced compliance because those responsible for implementation cannot effectively handle and apply sanctions in large numbers of cases. Moreover, widespread penalization might not be politically acceptable.

The IRS would find itself at an impasse, for example, if several million people decided not to file tax returns because the effectiveness of the income tax depends upon self-administration and voluntary compliance. As it is, the IRS director has estimated that the underreporting of income and the fabrication of deductions cost the Treasury $250 billion annually.[107] Audits of tax returns decreased in recent years because of cuts in the IRS budget and its chariness in enforcement activity resulting from the 1998 reform legislation.[108] An opinion survey found that 76 percent of Americans believed that tax cheating was unacceptable behavior, down from 87 percent in 1999.[109] To counter a feared epidemic in tax cheating, the IRS hired hundreds of tax-collection agents and examiners and stepped up the frequency of taxpayer audits. Shifting course from a few years earlier, when it complained about IRS abuses of taxpayers, the Senate Finance Committee now urged the agency to crack down on tax cheats.[110]

In many instances, sanctions are effective more because people desire to avoid being stigmatized as lawbreakers than because they fear the possible penalties. In criminal proceedings for antitrust violations, the fines levied usually have been quite nominal, considering the violators' economic resources. Not until 1961 did a businessman actually spend time in jail for an antitrust violation, although this punishment had been possible since the Sherman Act was adopted in 1890. The real deterrent in these cases is probably the adverse publicity that flows from the proceedings.

In recent years, Antitrust Division officials have been successfully advocating harsher penalties for antitrust violators, especially jail sentences, to encourage compliance. Legislators and judges, however, remain somewhat reluctant to create or impose jail sentences and other severe penalties on business people because of their social status and because of the often diffuse and complex nature of such law violations as embezzlement and the misuse of "insider information" in stock deals. In other situations, sanctions may be more severe and certain and have a more powerful deterrent effect.

Finally, acceptance of most policies seems to increase with the length of time they are in effect. As time passes (and it always does) a once-controversial policy becomes more familiar, part of the accepted state of things, a condition of doing business. Further, more and more persons come under the policy who have no experience with the prepolicy situation. Because "freedom is (in part) a state of mind, such men feel the restrictions to rest more lightly upon them."[111]

Although at one time business interests found the Wagner Act of 1935 highly objectionable, and the Taft-Hartley Act of 1947 was bitterly opposed by labor unions, today these statutes have lost much of their controversial quality. They have become a fixed part of the environment of labor–management relations, and businesses and labor unions have "learned to live with them." Predictably, environmental pollution-control policies will seem less restrictive or intrusive in a decade or two than they do at present.

Causes of Noncompliance Even to the most casual observer, it is readily apparent that not all persons affected by public policies comply with them. Statistical information on reported violations is readily obtainable, as in the Federal Bureau of Investigation's Uniform Crime Reports. In addition, lots of law violations go undetected or unreported. Why do some people, or in some situations many people, deviate from officially prescribed norms of behavior? As the obverse of compliance, noncompliance may result when laws conflict too sharply with the prevailing values, mores, and beliefs of the people generally or of particular groups. Many of the extensive violations of national prohibition and wartime price and rationing controls can be attributed in considerable measure to this cause, as may much of the noncompliance in the South with the Supreme Court's school desegregation decisions and related policies. In such instances, the general predisposition to obey the law is outweighed by strong attachment to strongly held values and established practices.

It is not very useful, however, to ascribe noncompliance to a broad conflict between law and morality. Those who proclaim that "you can't legislate morality" not only oversimplify the situation but also ignore the fact that morality is frequently legislated with considerable success. (Those who make this contention often cite national prohibition in its support.) Failure to comply results when a law or set of laws conflicts with values or beliefs in a particular time and situation. This law–value conflict must be stated with fair precision if it is to have operational value in explaining noncompliance.

Thus, quite a bit of noncompliance has confronted the Supreme Court's 1962 decision in *Engel* v. *Vitale* that using officially required prayers, even those that were thought nondenominational, in the public schools violated the First and Fourteenth Amendments' prohibition of the establishment of religion.[112] All efforts to legally circumvent this decision have failed.[113] The Supreme Court stirred the fire again in 2000 when, in a Texas case, it upheld an appeals-court ruling that banned religious invocations at public high school football games.[114] In a very different area of human activity, opinion surveys indicate that tax evasion is commonest among persons who do not believe that the federal tax system is fair in its effect.[115]

The concept of selective disobedience of the law is closely related to the law–value conflict.[116] Some laws are thought to be less binding than others on the individual. Those who strongly support and obey the statutes ordinarily labeled criminal laws sometimes have a more relaxed or permissive attitude toward economic regulatory legislation and laws on the conduct of public officials. Here one can aptly reflect on the behavior of Vice President Spiro T. Agnew, a staunch advocate of "law and order," who resigned his position after pleading *nolo contendere* (following plea bargaining) to a charge of federal income-tax evasion. Likewise, many businesspeople apparently believe that laws relating to banking operations, insider stock trading, competitive trade practices, and environmental pollution are not as compelling for individuals as laws prohibiting robbery, burglary, and embezzlement. This attitude may be common partly because legislation controlling economic activity developed later than criminal laws and has yet to gain the same moral force.

Moreover, much economic legislation runs counter to the ideological belief in limited nonintervention by government in the economy held by many people in business. They regard it as "bad law." Also, the same degree of social stigma usually is not attached to violations of economic policies as to criminal law offenses. Sociologist Marshall B. Clinard writes, "This selection of obedience to law rests upon the principle that what the person may be doing is illegal, perhaps even unethical, but certainly not criminal."[117]

One's associates and group memberships may also contribute to noncompliance (or, under other conditions, to compliance). Association with persons who hold ideas disrespectful of law and government, who justify or rationalize violation of the law or who openly violate the law may cause people to acquire deviant norms and values that dispose them to noncompliance.

In a study of labor-relations policy, Professor Robert E. Lane found that the rate of law violations varied with the community in which the firms studied were located. It was "fairly conclusive" that one reason for these patterns of difference was the "difference in attitude toward the law, the government, and the morality of illegality. Plant managers stated that they followed community patterns of behavior in their labor-relations activities."[118]

Similarly, attorneys for some of the defendant executives in the great electrical-industry price-fixing conspiracy late in the 1950s—which involved dozens of companies, including some of the largest in the industry—attempted to explain and justify their actions, hoping to lessen their punishment, as being in accord with the "corporate way of life."[119] The scandals that occurred in the savings and loan business in the 1980s and early 1990s indicate that such attitudes persist.

The desire to make a fast buck, or something akin thereto, is often proposed as a cause of noncompliance. This claim certainly seems applicable to many instances of fraud and misrepresentation, such as short-weighting and passing one product off for another in retail sales, promotion of shady land sales and investment schemes, failure to comply with minimum-wage laws,[120] and price-fixing agreements. (Price-fixing continues to be the most obvious and the commonest violation of the Sherman Act.) It is really not possible, however, to determine how widespread greed is as a motive for noncompliance. By itself it often seems insufficient as an explanation.

If two companies have equal opportunities to profit by violating the law, and one violates the law but the other does not, what is the explanation? One answer may be that companies that are less profitable or in danger of failure are more likely to violate in an effort to survive than are more financially secure firms.[121] One should be careful, however, in attributing noncompliance to pecuniary motives. Many violations of labor–management relations policy stem from a desire to protect management's prerogatives, and noncompliance with some industrial health and safety standards may rest on the conviction that they are unnecessary or unworkable.

Noncompliance may also stem from such factors as ambiguity in the law, lack of clarity, conflicting policy standards, or failure to adequately transmit policies to those affected by them. Income-tax violations often arise from the ambiguity or complexity of provisions of the Internal Revenue Code, which someone once described as a "sustained essay in obscurity." In other instances, persons or companies may believe that a practice is not prohibited by law, only to find upon prosecution that it is. The explanation may be that the frames of reference of businesspeople and public officials are different; thus, each interprets the law differently.

Violations sometimes result from difficulty in complying with the law, even when its meaning is understood. Insufficient time may be allowed for filing complicated forms or for making required changes in patterns of action, as in installing pollution-control devices. Sheer ignorance of laws or rules regulating conduct also cannot be discounted as a cause of noncompliance. Though ignorance of the law may be no excuse, it does account for some violations. In sum, noncompliance may stem from structural defects in the law and its administration, and from ignorance and lack of understanding of the law, as well as from behavior that is more consciously or deliberately deviant.

Administration and Compliance   The burden of securing compliance with public policies rests primarily with administrative agencies; the courts play a lesser role. The broad purpose of many administrative enforcement activities, such as conferences, persuasion, inspection, and prosecution, is to secure compliance with policies rather than merely to punish violators. Conscious human behavior involves making choices among alternatives, deciding to do some things and not others. For purposes of discussion, we can assume that there are essentially three ways in which administrative agencies, or other governmental bodies that engage in implementing public policy, can influence people to act in the desired ways, selecting behavioral alternatives that result in compliance with policy. First, to achieve a desired result, agencies can strive to shape, alter, or utilize the values people employ in making choices. Educational and persuasional activities illustrate this type of activity. Second, agencies can seek to limit the acceptable choices available to people, as by attaching penalties to undesired alternatives and rewards or benefits to desired alternatives. Third, agencies can try to interpret and administer policies in ways designed to facilitate compliance with their requirements. Thus, time limits for compliance were extended to give automobile manufacturers more time to meet tailpipe emission standards. More than one of these alternatives are normally used in seeking compliance with a policy.

Administrative agencies engage in many educational and persuasional activities intended to convince those directly affected, and the public generally, that designated public policies are reasonable, necessary, socially beneficial, or legitimate, in addition to informing them of the existence and meaning of those policies. The effectiveness of public policies depends considerably on the ability of agencies to promote understanding and consent, thereby reducing violations and minimizing use of sanctions. This approach is in keeping with my earlier comment on the importance of voluntary compliance.

When changes are made in the coverage and level of the federal minimum-wage law, the Department of Labor seeks to acquaint the public, and especially employers and employees, about them and their implications by distributing explanatory bulletins, reference guides, and posters; announcements through the news media; meetings with affected groups; appearances at conventions; direct mailings; telephone calls; and the like. After the changes become effective, press releases and mailed materials provide information on enforcement activities and agency interpretations of the law. The Federal Deposit Insurance Corporation likewise relies heavily on advice and warnings to banks, based on inspections, to get them to bring their operations into accord with banking regulations. Formal proceedings are initiated only when persuasion appears ineffective. The Nuclear Regulatory Commission typically compiles a technical-assistance manual to assist the operators of nuclear-power plants in complying with new regulations.[122]

Agencies may also use propaganda appeals in support of compliance. (*Propaganda* is used here not in a pejorative sense but rather to denote efforts to gain acceptance of policies by identifying them with widely held values and beliefs.) Appeals to patriotism were used to win support and acceptance of the military draft. Agricultural programs have been depicted as necessary to ensure equality for agriculture and to help preserve the family farm as a way of life. Antitrust programs have been described as necessary to maintain our system of free competitive enterprise. The Forest Service utilizes Smokey Bear to tell us that "only you can prevent forest fires." Propaganda appeals are more emotional than rational. They can be viewed as attempts either to reduce the moral cost of adapting to a policy or to make compliance desirable by attaching positive values to policies.[123]

In administering policies, agencies may make modifications in policies or adopt practices that will contribute to compliance. Revealed inequities in the law may be reduced or eliminated, conflicts in policy standards may be resolved, or simplified procedures for compliance may be developed, such as simplified federal income-tax forms for lower-income earners. Administrative personnel may develop knowledge and skill in enforcing policy that enables them to reduce misunderstanding and antagonism. Consultation and advice may be used to help those affected by laws come into compliance without issuing citations.

Laws may be interpreted or applied to make them more compatible with the interests of those affected. The administration of policy on oil-import controls by the Oil Import Administration "was almost wholly in the interests of the petroleum industry."[124] They had little cause for complaint. Several hundred of the health and safety "consensus" standards initially issued by OSHA were later rescinded because of widespread complaints that they were outmoded, trivial, or of little use in protecting against health and safety hazards.[125] OSHA hoped thereby to reduce the antagonism of the business community toward itself by eliminating those standards.

Agencies will resort to sanctions when the sociological and psychological factors supporting obedience and other available methods fail to produce compliance. Sanctions are penalties or deprivations imposed on those who violate policy norms and are intended to make undesired behavior patterns unattractive. They directly punish violators and serve to deter others who might not comply if they saw violators go unpunished.

Sanctions can be imposed by either administrative agencies or the courts. Common forms of judicial sanctions are fines, jail sentences, award of damages, and injunctions. However, in most areas of public policy (crime policy is a major exception), administrative sanctions are used much more frequently because of their greater immediacy, variety, and flexibility. Among the sanctions that agencies may impose are threat of prosecution; imposition of fines or pecuniary penalties that have the effect of fines, as by OSHA; unfavorable publicity; revocation, annulment, modification, or suspension of, or refusal to renew, licenses; summary seizure and destruction of goods; award of damages; issuance of cease-and-desist orders; and denial of services or benefits.

To be most effective, the severity of sanctions must be geared to the violations against which they are directed. If they are too severe, the agency may be reluctant to use them; if they are too mild, they may have inadequate deterrent effect, as is the case with minimal fines often imposed by national and state agencies for pollution violations. In many instances, when fines are assessed, they are less than the economic benefits realized by the violators.[126] The Office of Education was handicapped in its early administration of Title I of the ESEA because the only sanction it had for state and local violations was to cut off funds totally. Because of the adverse reaction this penalty would have caused, the agency was politically reluctant to impose the penalty and chose not to do so. Agencies clearly need appropriate and effective sanctions to help ensure compliance with policy.

Agencies may also seek to induce compliance by conferring positive benefits on compliers and thereby bringing self-interest into support for compliance. This method can be referred to as the purchase of consent. Benefits may take such forms as favorable publicity and recognition for nondiscrimination in hiring, tax credits for industrial-plant modernization, and federal grants-in-aid for the support of state programs of medical aid to the indigent that meet federal standards.

It is often difficult, however, to distinguish rewards from sanctions. Does an individual comply with a policy to secure a benefit or to avoid losing it? Whatever the motives of persons seeking benefits, the government does use rewards extensively to gain compliance with policy. In many situations they are much more acceptable politically than would be a clear-cut prohibition or requirement of some action with penalties for noncompliance. Imagine the reaction if rather than using tax credits, businesses were required to modernize their plants or else be subject to fines and other penalties.

Clearly, then, compliance—or noncompliance—with public policies is a function of many factors. It is a complex topic that needs more explicit attention from policy analysts because of its importance for the implementation and effectiveness of public policies.

For Further Exploration

▌ *http://www.gpo.gov*
> This site contains links to issues of the *Federal Register* published since 1995, the *Code of Federal Regulations*, public laws, and administrative decisions.

▌ *http://www.osha.gov/index.html*
> The Occupational Safety & Health Administration's (OSHA) official website provides information in relation to workplace health and safety issues, and a collection of statistical data related to topics such as inspections and workplace safety.

▌ *http://www.whitehouse.gov/*
> This site provides numerous links related to the executive branch, including a link to presidential press briefings, radio addresses, and executive orders issued by the President.

Test Your Knowledge

Log on to the student companion website at

> *login.cengage.com*

to access tutorial quizzes, chapter outlines, crossword puzzles, and glossary flashcards that review chapter concepts and terminology.

 **Suggested Readings**

Cornelius M. Kerwin and Scott R. Furlong, *Rulemaking: How Government Agencies Write Law and Make Policy*, 4th ed. (Washington, DC: CQ Press, 2010). Thorough, readable, and replete with examples, Their book discusses the politics and process of federal rule-making.

Denise Scheberle, *Federalism and Environmental Policy*, 2nd ed. (Washington, DC: Georgetown University Press, 2004). An analysis of federal-state relations and what shapes them in some areas of environmental policy.

Dennis D. Riley and Bryan E. Brophy-Baerman, *Bureaucracy and the Policy Process* (Lanham, MD: Rowman and Littlefield, 2006). This text provides a thorough, in-depth, and readable look at the national bureaucracy's role in policymaking.

Francis E. Rourke, *Bureaucracy, Politics and Public Policy*, 3rd ed. (Boston, MA: Little Brown, 1984). This volume retains its usefulness as an examination of administrative agencies and their power, politics, and role in policy formation.

Ken Godwin, Scott H. Ainsworth, and Erik Godwin, Lobbying and Policymaking (Washington, DC: CQ Press, 2013). The authors provide an excellent empirical and theoretically guided look at lobbying, which is expecially valuable on regulatory agencies.

Kenneth J. Meier and John Bohte, *Politics and the Bureaucracy: Policymaking in the Fourth Branch of Government*, 5th ed. (New York: Harcourt Brace, 2006). A comprehensive and systematic treatment of the national bureaucracy as a policymaking organization, this book deals with structure power, politics, and policy.

Paul C. Light, *A Government Ill Executed* (Cambridge, MA: Harvard University Press, 2008). A master student of the federal bureaucracy, drawing on Federalist Paper #70, examines its decline and what can be done about it.

Philip B. Heymann, *Living the Policy Process* (New York: Oxford University Press, 2008). An outstanding treatment, utilizing case studies and more, of policymaking and implementation.

Notes

1. Peter C. Bishop and Augustus J. Jones Jr., "Implementing the Americans with Disabilities Act of 1990: Assessing the Variables of Success," *Public Administration Review*, Vol. 53 (March–April 1993), pp. 121–128.
2. Cf. Randall B. Ripley and Grace A. Franklin, *Policy Implementation and Bureaucracy*, 2nd ed. (Chicago, IL: Dorsey, 1986), pp. 4–5.
3. Charles S. Bullock III and Charles M. Lamb, eds., *Implementation of Civil Rights* (Monterey, CA: Brooks/Cole, 1984), p. 5.

4. Those political scientists interested in the government regulation of business had long been concerned with the implementation because of its policy consequences. See Emmette S. Redford, *The Administration of National Economic Control* (New York: Macmillan, 1952); and Marver H. Bernstein, *Regulatory Business by Independent Commission* (Princeton, NJ: Princeton University Press, 1955).

5. Jeffrey L. Pressman and Aaron Wildavsky, *Implementation* (Berkeley, CA: University of California Press, 1973). The book's subtitle is "How Great Expectations in Washington Are Dashed in Oakland: Or, Why It Is Amazing that Federal Programs Work at All, This Being a Saga of the Economic Development Administration as Told by Two Sympathetic Observers Who Seek to Build Morals on a Foundation of Ruined Hopes."

6. Representative studies of implementation include Eugene Bardach, *The Implementation Game: What Happens after a Bill Becomes Law?* (Cambridge, MA: MIT Press, 1977); David A. Mazmanian and Paul A. Sabatier, *Implementation and Public Policy* (Chicago: Scott, Foresman, 1983); Malcolm L. Goggin, *Policy Design and the Politics of Implementation* (Knoxville, TN: University of Tennessee Press, 1987); and Bradley C. Canon and Charles A. Johnson, *Judicial Policies: Implementation and Impact*, 2nd ed. (Washington, DC: CQ Press, 1999).

7. Paul A. Sabatier, "Top-Down and Bottom-Up Models of Policy Implementation: A Critical Analysis and Suggested Synthesis," *Journal of Public Policy*, Vol. 6 (1986), pp. 21–48.

8. Denise Scheberle, *Federalism and Environmental Policy*, 2nd ed. (Washington, DC: Georgetown University Press, 2004), well illustrates this.

9. Paul Berman, "The Study of Macro- and Micro-Implementation," *Public Policy*, Vol. 26 (Spring 1978), pp. 157–184.

10. Barry G. Rabe, "Power of the States: The Promise and Pitfalls of Decentralization," in Norman J. Vig and Michael E. Kraft, eds., *Environmental Policy*, 6th ed. (Washington, DC: CQ Press, 2006), pp. 49–50.

11. This account relies on Michael Kirst and Richard Jong, "The Utility of a Longitudinal Approach in Assessing Implementation: A Thirteen-Year View of Title I, ESEA," in Walter K. Williams et al., eds., *Studying Implementation* (Chatham, NJ: Chatham House, 1982), Chap. 6; and June A. O'Neil and Margaret C. Simms, "Education," in John L. Palmer and Isabel C. Sawhill, eds., *The Reagan Experiment* (Washington, DC: Urban Institute, 1982), Chap. 11.

12. Andrew Rudalevige, "The Politics of No Child Left Behind," *Education Next*, Vol. 3 (Fall 2003), pp. 62–69.

13. Brian Friel, "Damage Control for 'No Child Left Behind,'" *National Journal*, Vol. 36 (June 5, 2004), pp. 1786–1787; and Chester E. Finn Jr. and Frederick M. Hess, "On Leaving No Child Behind," *The Public Interest*, No. 157 (Fall 2004), pp. 35–56.

14. Bryan Shelly, "Rebels and Their Cause: State Resistance to No Child Left Behind," *Publius*, Vol. 38 (Summer 2008), pp. 444–468.

15. Scott Franklin Abernathy, *No Child Left Behind and the Public Schools* (Ann Arbor, MI: University of Michigan Press, 2007), esp. Chaps. 1, 2; and *The New York Times* (June 12, 2008), pp. Al, A21.

16. Charles T. Goodsell, *The Case for Bureaucracy*, 4th ed. (Chatham, NJ: Chatham House, 2003), Chap. 1.

17. See Harold Lasswell, Politics: Who Gets What, When, and How (New York: McGraw Hill, 1936).

18. Frank Goodnow, *Politics and Administration* (New York: Russell and Russell, 1900).

19. Martha Derthick, *Agency under Stress: The Social Security Administration in American Government* (Washington, DC: Brookings Institution, 1990); and Susan Gluck Mezey, "Policy-making by the Federal Judiciary: The Effects of Judicial Review on the Social Security Disability Program," *Policy Studies Journal*, Vol. 14 (March 1986), pp. 343–355.

20. George C. Edwards III and Stephen J. Wayne, *Presidential Leadership*, 6th ed. (Belmont, CA: Wadsworth, 2003), pp. 287–288.

21. See James E. Anderson, "Presidential Management of the Bureaucracy and the Johnson Presidency: A Preliminary Exploration," *Congress & the Presidency*, Vol. 1 (Autumn 1984), pp. 137–164; and David M. Welborn, *Regulation in the White House: The Johnson Presidency* (Austin, TX: University of Texas Press, 1986).

22. Peter Baker, "For Obama, a Tricky Balancing Act in Enforcing a Law He Viewed as Invalid," *The New York Times* (March 29, 2013), p. A17.

23. Robert Diclerico, *The Contemporary American President* (Boston, MA: Pearson, 2013), pp. 221–233.

24. Jonathan Weisman, "Congress and Country Fired Up after Hearings on IRS Abuses," *Congressional Quarterly Weekly Report*, Vol. 55 (October 4, 1997), pp. 2379–2384.

25. *Wall Street Journal* (December 9, 1999), p. A28; *The New York Times* (August 15, 2000), p. 1.

26. *The New York Times* (March 31, 1989), p. 8.

27. Louis Fisher, *Constitutional Conflicts between Congress and the President*, 4th ed. (Lawrence, KS: University Press of Kansas, 1997), p. 157.

28. Leroy N. Reiselbach, *Congressional Politics: Evolving Legislative System*, 2nd ed. (Boulder, CO: Westview, 1995), pp. 400–405.

29. David T. Stanley and Marjorie Girth, *Bankruptcy: Problems, Process, Reform* (Washington, DC: Brookings Institution, 1971), p. 172.

30. *Adarand Constructors v. Pena* (1995). Reported in *The New York Times* (June 13, 1995), p. A8.

31. See Samuel P. Huntington, "The Marasmus of the ICC: The Commission, the Railroads, and the Public Interest," *Yale Law Journal*, LXI (1952), pp. 470–509.

32. This discussion draws on Harold Seidman, *Politics, Position, and Power*, 5th ed. (New York: Oxford University Press, 1999), pp. 197–202. See also General Accounting Office, *Federal Advisory Committee Act* (Washington, DC: USGAO, October 1988).

33. Kay Lehman Scholzman and John T. Tierney, *Organized Interests and American Democracy* (New York: Harper & Row, 1986), p. 334.

34. Sheila Jasanoff, *The Fifth Branch: Science Advisers as Policy-makers* (Cambridge, MA: Harvard University Press, 1990), pp. 65–66.

35. James W. Davis Jr. and Kenneth M. Dolbeare, *Little Groups of Neighbors: The Selective Service System* (Chicago: Markham, 1968).

36. *CQ Weekly*, Vol. 59 (February 3, 2001), pp. 283–285; and Vol. 60 (November 2, 2002), pp. 2861–2863.

37. Seidman, op. cit., pp. 12–13.

38. Paul C. Light, *Thickening Government* (Washington, DC: Brookings Institution, 1995).

39. This account draws on Charles Noble, *Liberalism at Work: The Rise and Fall of OSHA* (Philadelphia, PA: Temple University Press, 1986), pp. 89–95.

40. This discussion draws some ideas from my *Politics and the Economy* (Boston, MA: Little, Brown, 1966), pp. 86–90.

41. *Wall Street Journal* (August 10, 1989), p. 1; and *The New York Times* (August 13, 1993), p. 1.

42. Cf. Matthew Holden Jr., " 'Imperialism' in Bureaucracy," *American Political Science Review*, LX (December 1966), pp. 943–951. This is a seminal article.

43. Richard Tobin, *The Expendable Future* (Durham, NC: Duke University Press, 1990), p. 98.

44. Interview with the author.

45. Holden, op. cit., p. 944.

46. Daniel McCool, *Command of the Waters* (Berkeley, CA: University of California Press, 1987), Chap. 2.

47. This discussion, and that in the first part of the next section, draws on Francis E. Rourke, *Bureaucracy, Politics and Public Policy*, 3rd ed. (Boston, MA: Little, Brown, 1984), Chaps. 4–5.

48. Ibid., pp. 106–107.

49. Ibid., p. 108.

50. On the separation of the ability to decide from the authority to decide in organizations, see Victor Thompson, *Modern Organizations* (New York: Knopf, 1961). See also James G. March, *A Primer of Decision Making* (New York: Free Press, 1994).

51. Theodore C. Sorensen, *Kennedy* (New York: Harper & Row, 1965), Chap. 25. On secrecy in administration generally, see Harold L. Wilensky, *Organizational Intelligence* (New York: Basic Books, 1967), Chaps. 3 and 7; and Symposium on "The Freedom of Information Act," *Public Administration Review*, XXXIX (July–August 1979), pp. 310–332.

52. See James A. Nathan and James K. Oliver, *Foreign Policy Making and the American Political System*, 3rd ed. (Baltimore, MD: Johns Hopkins University Press, 1994).

53. Rourke, op. cit., p. 108.

54. This story is told well by Richard E. Neustadt and Harvey V. Finebert, *The Swine Flu Affair* (Washington, DC: U.S. Department of Health, Education, and Welfare, 1978).

55. Stephanie Ann Lenway, *The Politics of U.S. International Trade* (Marshfield, MA: Pitman, 1985).

56. Florence Heffron, with Neil McFreely, *The Administrative Regulatory Process* (New York: Longman, 1983), pp. 226–235.

57. Cornelius M. Kerwin, *Rule-Making: How Government Agencies Write Law and Make Policy*, 3rd ed. (Washington, DC: CQ Press, 2003), pp. 89–90.

58. Heffron, op. cit., p. 239.

59. Kerwin, op. cit., pp. 63–67.

60. Ibid., p. 111.

61. Heffron, op. cit., pp. 227–230.

62. Clayton R. Koppes, "Public Water, Private Land: Origins of the Acreage Limitation Controversy," *Pacific Historical Review*, Vol. 47 (November 1978), pp. 607–636.

63. *Congressional Record*, Vol. 149 (January 7, 2003), pp. 551–552; and Doug French, "Water Is Gold," *Liberty Watch Magazine* (November 8, 2007). www.lewrockwell.com/french/french64.html.

64. A cease-and-desist order is an agency's civil directive to stop engaging in a practice held to be in violation of the law. Agencies such as the Federal Trade Commission and the NLRB are authorized to issue such orders.

65. Chuck McCutcheon, "Nuclear Waste Issue as Hot as Ever Despite Senate OK of Nevada Site," *CQ Weekly*, Vol. 60 (July 13, 2002), pp. 1880–1881.

66. Matthew L. Wald, "Future Dim for Nuclear Waste Repository," *The New York Times* (March 6, 2009), p. A17.

67. This discussion draws on Claudia Copeland, "Clean Water Act and Total Maximum Daily Loads (TMDLs) of Pollutants" (Washington, DC: Congressional Research Service, August 25, 2008).

68. Mark R. Powell, *Science at EPA* (Washington, DC: Resources for the Future, 1999), pp. 334–335.

69. *Federal Register*, Vol. 68 (March 19, 2003), p. 13608.

70. See Oliver A. Houck, *The Clean Water Act TMDL Program: Law, Policy, and Implementation*, 2nd ed. (Washington, DC: Island Press, 2002).

71. Walter A. Rosenbaum, *Environmental Politics and Policy*, 7th ed. (Washington, DC: CQ Press, 2008), p. 204.

72. James P. Lester, ed., *Environmental Politics and Policy: Theories and Evidence*, 2nd ed. (Durham, NC: Duke University Press, 1995), Chap. 3.

73. "Smokey Bear at 50: Still Going Strong," *National Woodlands*, Vol. 17 (April 1994), pp. 16–19.

74. This paragraph draws on Ann Schneider and Helen Ingram, "Behavioral Assumptions of Policy Tools," *Journal of Politics*, Vol. 52 (May 1990), pp. 510–529. See also their *Policy Design for Democracy* (Lawrence, KS: University Press of Kansas, 1997), Chap. 4.

75 Richard H. Thaler and Cass R. Sunstein, *Nudge: Improving Decisions about Health, Wealth, and Happiness* (New Haven, CT: Yale University Press, 2008).

76. Emmette A. Redford, *The Administration of National Economic Control* (New York: Macmillan, 1952), p. 104.

77. Stephen Breyer, *Regulation and Its Reform* (Cambridge, MA: Harvard University Press, 1982), pp. 90–95.

78. Donald K. Kettle, *Sharing Power: Governance and Private Markets* (Washington, DC: Brookings Institution, 1993), Chap. 3.

79. John David Skrentny, *The Ironies of Affirmative Action: Politics, Culture, and Justice in America* (Chicago, IL: University of Chicago Press, 1996), pp. 133–134.

80. Congressional Budget Office, *Contractors' Support of U.S. Operations in Iraq* (Washington, DC: Government Printing Office, August 2008).

81. Kenneth J. Meier, *The Politics of Sin: Drugs, Alcohol, and Public Policy* (Armonk, NY: M.E. Sharpe, 1994), Chap. 5.

82. Daniel P. Franklin, *Making Ends Meet: Congress Budgeting in the Age of Deficits* (Washington, DC: Congressional Quarterly Press, 1993), p. 23.

83. Charles Schultze, *The Public Use of Private Interests* (Washington, DC: Brookings Institution, 1977).

84. Paul R. McDaniel, "Tax Expenditures as Tools of Government Action," in Lester M. Salamon, ed., *Beyond Privatization: The Tools of Government Action* (Washington, DC: Urban Institute, 1989), Chap. 6.

85. Christopher Howard, "Tax Expenditures," in Lester M. Salamon, ed., *The Tools of Government* (New York: Oxford University Press, 2002), Chap. 13.

86. Budget of the United States Government Fiscal Year 2006, *Analytical Perspectives* (Washington, DC: Government Printing Office, 2014); *The New York Times* (March 15, 2013), p. A1.

87. Peter Woll, *American Bureaucracy*, 2nd ed. (New York: Norton, 1977), p. 95.

88. Peter S. May, "Social Regulation," in Lester M. Salamon, ed., *The Tools of Government* (New York: Oxford University Press, 2002), Chap. 5.

89. Martin C. Schnitzer, *Contemporary Government and Business Relations*, 4th ed. (Boston, MA: Houghton Mifflin, 1990), p. 242.

90. This discussion draws on Deborah A. Stone, *Policy Paradox and Political Reason* (Glenview, IL: Scott, Foresman, 1988), p. 225; and Schultze, op. cit.

91. Allen Kneese and Charles Schultze, *Pollution Prices and Public Policy* (Washington, DC: Brookings Institution, 1975), p. 89.

92. Stone, op. cit., p. 228.

93. Michael D. Reagan, *Regulation: The Politics of Policy* (Boston, MA: Little, Brown, 1987), p. 142. See also Steven Kelman, *What Price Incentives? Economists and the Environment* (Boston: Auburn House, 1981), pp. 27–28.

94. *The New York Times* (April 8, 1993), p. C2; and *Illinois Agri-News* (April 9, 1993), p. C7.

95. "Project Regulatory Reform: A Survey of the Impact of Reregulation and Deregulation on Selected Industries and Sectors," *Administrative Law Review*, Vol. 47 (Fall 1995), p. 476.

96. Robert N. Stavins, "What Can We Learn from the Grand Policy Experiment? Lessons from S0$_2$ Allowance Trading," *Journal of Economic Perspectives*, Vol. 12 (Summer 1998), p. 71. See also Richard Schmalensee et al., "An Interim Evaluation of Sulphur Dioxide Emissions Trading," *Journal of Economic Perspectives*, Vol. 12 (Summer 1998), pp. 53–68; and J. Clarence Davies and Jan Mazurek, *Pollution Control in the United States* (Washington, DC: Resources for the Future, 1998), pp. 140–141.

97. "Acid Rain Program 2007 Progress Report" (Washington, DC: Environmental Protection Agency, January, 2009), pp. 1–2.

98. James Kanter and Jad Mouawad, "Pipe Dreams and Politics," *The New York Times* (December 11, 2008), p. B1.

99. A. Denny Ellerman and Paul L. Jaskow, *The European Union's Emissions Trading System in Perspective* (Arlington, VA: Pew Center on Global Climate Change, May 2008).

100. John M. Broder, "Obama's Greenhouse Gas Gamble," *The New York Times* (February 28, 2009), p. A15.

101. Two exceptions are Kenneth J. Meier and David R. Morgan, "Citizen Compliance with Public Policy: The National Maximum Speed Law," *Western Political Quarterly*, XXXV (June 1982), pp. 258–273; and John T. Scholz and Neil Pinney, "Duty, Fear, and Tax Compliance: The Heuristic Basis of Citizen Behavior," *American Journal of Political Science*, Vol. 39 (May 1995), pp. 490–512.

102. R. Kent Weaver, "Forget Compliance: The Final Frontier of Policy Implementation," *Issues in Governance Studies* (Washington, DC: Brookings Institution, September, 2009), pp. 1–11.

103. This discussion draws on ideas in my "Public Economic Policy and the Problems of Compliance: Notes for Research," *Houston Law Review*, IV (Spring–Summer 1966), pp. 62–72.

104. Tom R. Tyler, *Why People Obey the Law* (New Haven, CT: Yale University Press, 1996), p. 178.

105. Anne Schneider and Helen Ingram, "Behavioral Theories in Policy Designs." Unpublished paper presented at the Midwest Political Association meeting (1989).

106. Herbert A. Simon, Donald Smithburg, and Victor Thompson, *Public Administration* (New York: Knopf, 1950), p. 479.

107. *Los Angeles Times* (March 1, 2002), part 3, p. 1.

108. David Cay Johnston, "Fearing for Jobs, I.R.S. Workers Relax Efforts to Get Unpaid Taxes," *The New York Times* (May 18, 1999), pp. A1, C11. See also his *Perfectly Legal* (New York: Portfolio, 2003), Chaps. 10 and 11.

109. *Newsday* (January 22, 2002), p. A26.

110. John D. McKinnon, "IRS Rides the Ups and Downs of Congressional Whims," *Wall Street Journal* (April 8, 2002), p. A28.

111. Robert Lane, *The Regulation of Businessmen* (New Haven, CT: Yale University Press, 1954), pp. 69–70.

112. 370 U.S. 421 (1962).

113. See John A. Murley, "School Prayer: Free Exercise of Religion or Establishment of Religion," in Raymond Tatalovich and Byron W Daynes, eds., *Social Regulatory Policy* (Boulder, CO: Westview Press, 1989), Chap. 1.

114. *Santa Fe Independent School District v. Doe*, 530 U.S. 1 (2000).

115. Timothy B. Clark, "Honesty May Become the Best Tax Policy If Tax Compliance Bill Becomes Law," *National Journal*, Vol. 14 (July 24, 1982), pp. 1292–1296.

116. Marshall B. Clinard, *Sociology of Deviant Behavior* (New York: Holt, Rinehart and Winston, 1957), pp. 168–171.

117. Ibid.

118. Robert E. Lane, "Why Business Men Violate the Law," *Journal of Criminal Law, Criminology, and Police Science*, XLIV (1953), pp. 151, 154–160.

119. John G. Fuller, *The Gentlemen Conspirators: The Story of the Price-Fixers in the Electrical Industry* (New York: Grove Press, 1962), pp. 88, 109–110.

120. G. Pascal Zachary, "The Minimum Wage Law Is Frequently Ignored in Some Industries," *Wall Street Journal* (May 20, 1996), p. 1. See also idem., "Many Firms Refuse to Pay Overtime, Employees Complain," *Wall Street Journal* (June 24, 1996), p. 1.

121. Lane, op. cit., Chap. 5.

122. Kerwin, op. cit., p. 81.

123. Simon, Smithburg, and Thompson, op. cit., p. 457.

124. Roger G. Noll, *Reforming Regulation* (Washington, DC: Brookings Institution, 1971), p. 65.

125. *Wall Street Journal* (May 19, 1977), p. 40; and Timothy B. Clark, "What's All the Uproar Over OSHA's Nit-Picking Rules?" *National Journal*, Vol. 10 (October 7, 1978), pp. 1594–1596.

126. General Accounting Office, *Environmental Enforcement: Penalties May Not Recover Economic Benefits Gained by Violators* (Washington, DC: USGAO, June 1991), pp. 5–10; and, generally, Marc Allen Eisner, *Governing the Environment* (Boulder, CO: Lynne Rienner, 2007).

7

Policy Impact, Evaluation, and Change

W hen it is viewed as a cycle or sequential pattern of functional activities, the final phase of the policy process is evaluation. As much an art as a science, policy evaluation involves the estimation, appraisal, or assessment of a policy, its content, implementation, goal attainment, and other effects. The policy evaluator wants to know whether and to what extent a policy has accomplished its goals or whether it has had other effects, intended or unintended.

Policy evaluation may also seek to identify factors that contributed to the success or failure of a policy. This, in turn, may lead to recycling of the policy process (problem definition, formulation, adoption, and so on) in order to continue, modify, strengthen, or terminate the policy. Put differently, information gained through evaluation feeds back into the ongoing policy process.

As a functional activity, evaluation can occur at any point in the policy process, not simply after some effort has been made to implement a policy. Thus, attempts are made to determine prospectively—to estimate or predict—the likely effects, or the costs and benefits, of policy alternatives prior to their adoption. Typically, however, policy evaluation "looks backward" to what has happened whereas the other stages of the policy process look forward to attaining a goal.[1]

Before proceeding further in examining evaluation, we need to pause and look at policy impacts, at the general sorts of effects or consequences that may ensue from policies.

Policy Impact

To begin, we need to distinguish *policy outputs* and *policy outcomes*. *Policy outputs* are the things actually done by agencies in pursuance of policy decisions and statements. The concept of outputs focuses attention on such matters as amounts of taxes collected, miles of highways built, welfare benefits paid, price-fixing agreements prosecuted, traffic fines collected, or foreign-aid projects undertaken. Outputs usually can be readily counted, totaled, and statistically analyzed. Examining outputs may indicate, or seem to indicate, that a lot is being done to implement a policy. Such activity, however, sometimes amounts to nothing more than what Professor William T. Gormley Jr. calls "bean counting." Agencies, under pressure from legislators, interest groups, and others to demonstrate results, "may focus on outputs, not outcomes, in order to generate statistics that create the illusion of progress."[2] If the percentage of students graduating from universities in a state increases, does this tell us anything about the quality of education that they are receiving?

Policy outcomes (sometimes called "results"), in contrast, are the consequences for society, intended and unintended, that stem from deliberate governmental action or inaction. Social-welfare policies can be used to illustrate this concept. It is fairly easy to measure welfare-policy outputs such as amounts of benefits paid, average level of benefits, and number of people assisted. But what are the outcomes, or societal consequences, of these actions? Do they increase personal security and contentment? Do they reduce individual initiative? Did Aid to Families with Dependent Children, now Temporary Assistance to Needy Families (TANF), have the effect of encouraging promiscuity and illegitimacy, or teenage pregnancies, as some alleged? Do welfare programs help keep the poor quiescent, as others contend?[3] Questions such as these, which are tough to answer, direct our attention to the societal effects of policies. Among other things, policy students should want to know whether policies are accomplishing their intended purposes, whether society is changing as a consequence of policy actions and not because of other factors such as private economic decisions, and whether it is changing as intended or in other ways. Policy impacts are an amalgam of outputs and outcomes.

The impact of a policy may have several dimensions, all of which should be taken into account either in the conduct of a formal evaluation or in the course of an informal appraisal of the policy.[4] They include the following:

1. Policies affect the public problem at which they are directed and the people involved. The target populations whom the policy is intended to affect must be defined, whether they are the poor, small-business people, disadvantaged schoolchildren, petroleum producers, or whoever. The intended effect of the policy must then be determined. If it is an antipoverty program, is its purpose to raise the income of the poor, to increase their opportunities for employment, or to change their attitudes and behavior? If some combination of such purposes is intended, analysis becomes more complicated because priorities should be assigned to the various intended effects. Typically, policies accomplish at least a portion of their goals or objectives.

Further, a policy may produce either intended or unintended (unforeseen or unplanned) consequences, or even both. Unemployment compensation may improve the economic situation of the unemployed, as designed by its proponents, but it may also cause them to delay in finding new jobs. A public-housing program may improve housing conditions for urban blacks, but it may also be so administered as to contribute to racial segregation in housing and neighborhood schools. The agricultural income and price support programs, intended to enhance farmers' incomes, also may lead to overproduction of supported commodities (only a few such as corn, wheat, and cotton are covered), to higher food prices, and to unearned increases in land values.

The causes of unintended policy consequences are multiple: the complexity of the issue being addressed; insufficient information on which to ground a decision; pressure to act quickly on a matter; too little consultation with other legislators or affected persons; partisan pressures and the politicization of issues; and, finally, human error. Also, statutory language needs mention. A law may be clumsily drafted, or too detailed, or too vague, and thus permit unintended interpretations.[5]

A good illustration of a policy with negative unintended consequences was financial deregulation (or nonregulation). The Financial Services Modernization Act (1999) permitted banks to combine commercial banking (deposits and loans), investment banking, and insurance services. Huge banking conglomerates developed, some of which became viewed as "too big to fail" because of their potential effects on the economy. The Commodity Futures Modernization Act (2000), which was slipped into a huge omnibus appropriations bill and enacted with no debate, prohibited regulation of credit default swaps (don't ask) and other financial derivatives. These statutes, and decisions by regulatory officials not to use the authority they did possess, because of a belief in self-regulating markets, contributed greatly to the near financial collapse of the American economy and the Great Recession.[6]

2. Policies may affect situations or groups other than those at which they are directed. These are variously called third-party effects, spillover effects, or externalities.[7] The construction of urban interstate highways is of much benefit to motorists and trucking companies. However, they also cause inconvenience, disorder, and social disruption for the neighborhoods through which they run, and they have helped produce urban sprawl. Clear-cutting in national forests, which is of benefit to timber companies and in line with the perspective of those who view forests as tree farms, is profoundly disturbing to environmentalists, nature lovers, and many sportsmen and women because it results in the destruction of wildlife habitat, the loss of aesthetic value, and the siltation of trout streams.

These two examples portray negative externalities, but externalities may also be positive. Public-education programs not only educate students but also provide employers with a more capable workforce and the community with better-informed citizens. A strong line of research supports a correlation between education and support for democracy. Those who contend that only those who have children in public schools should contribute toward their support ignore such positive externalities. Although pollution-control programs impose costs on many industries, they are a boon to the manufacturers of pollution-control equipment. Many of the outcomes of public policies can be most meaningfully understood as externalities that impose costs or provide benefits for third parties.

3. Policies have consequences for future as well as current conditions; for some policies most of their benefits or some of their costs may occur in the far future. Was the Head Start program—a preschool education program for the poor—supposed to improve participating children's short-term cognitive abilities or their long-range development and earning capacity? Did regulation of the field price of natural gas, a policy initiated in the 1950s and extending into the 1980s, really produce a shortage of gas in the 1970s, as some contended (notably petroleum-industry officials and their supporters, who had long been critics of price regulation)? Are we better off under deregulation?

The future effects of some policies may be very diffuse or uncertain. Assuming that patent and copyright policies do indeed stimulate invention and creativity, and that these activities in turn enhance economic growth and societal development, how does one measure their benefits, either qualitatively or quantitatively? Again, how does one appraise (with reasonable objectivity) the effects of the National Foundation on the Arts and the Humanities' support for literacy, artistic, and museum activities? Would the elimination of such policies as these have deleterious consequences for American society?

4. Just as policies have positive effects or benefits, they also entail costs. Economists seem never to tire of telling us that there is no such thing as a free lunch. Costs come in different forms. First, there are the direct costs for the governmental implementation of a policy or program. These are usually fairly easy to calculate, whether stated as the actual amount of money spent on the program, its share of total governmental expenditures, or the proportion of the gross domestic product devoted to it. Budgeting documents will yield such figures. If, however, a governmental expenditure serves multiple purposes, such as operating the space program and developing new technology, the allocation of costs becomes more perplexing.

Direct costs also include private expenditures that are necessary in order to comply with public policies, such as those for industrial health and safety and environmental-pollution controls. These may be more difficult to discover or calculate. Moreover, it is possible that some companies would have installed protective devices in the absence of policy, whether out of a desire to serve the public interest or to protect themselves from lawsuits. Should their costs then be assigned to the policy? In the absence of governmental subsidies, the direct costs of complying with regulatory policies initially fall primarily on the regulated, who have an ideological incentive to inflate claimed costs, deliberately making the policies appear more burdensome. Ultimately, of course, most compliance costs are likely to be shifted to consumers in the form of higher prices for goods and services.

This brings us to indirect costs. Public policies may cause reduced production, higher prices, or mental anguish or distress. Expenditures to meet coal-mine-safety requirements may cause a reduction in mine output. People called for jury services typically receive compensation that does no more than cover commuting costs. The consequence is lost wages, or lost production, or both. Many public policies have indirect or social costs of these sorts. Mental anguish may occur when one's hometown is flooded by a new impoundment. Financial compensation may be paid for one's childhood home, but what of the loss that occurs because, being under twenty feet of water, it can no longer be visited? The concept of indirect cost often calls for putting a price tag on intangibles. They tend to defy precise measurement.

Finally, there are opportunity costs, a concept that rests upon the fact that we cannot do everything at once and that resources used for one purpose (e.g., flood control) cannot be used for another purpose (e.g., public housing). "Opportunity cost is a decision making rather than an accounting concept."[8] It focuses attention on what one has to give up (or, alternatively, what one will gain) if resources are used for one purpose rather than another. Thus, economists argue that the United States' all-volunteer army will not attract needed recruits if the opportunity costs of military service are kept below those of civilian life. When the ranks of the military were largely filled by draftees, less concern had to be given to opportunity costs and the compensation of service personnel.[9]

5. The effects of policies and programs may be either material (tangible) or symbolic (intangible). The consequences of symbols are both important and hard to measure. Symbolic outputs, according to political scientists Gabriel A. Almond and G. Bingham Powell include "affirmations of values by elites; displays of flags, troops, and military ceremony; visits by royalty or high officials; and statements of policy or intent by political leaders." Consequently, they "are highly dependent on tapping popular beliefs, attitudes, and aspirations for their effectiveness."[10]

Symbolic policy outputs produce no readily discernible changes in societal conditions. No one eats better because of a Memorial Day parade or a stirring speech by a high public official on the virtues of free enterprise, however ideologically or emotionally satisfying such actions may be for many people. More to the point, however, policy actions ostensibly directed toward meeting material wants or needs may turn out in practice to be more symbolic than material in their effect.

This shift in policy tone is well illustrated by the Fair Housing Act of 1968. Enacted by Congress in part because of pressure created by the assassination of Dr. Martin Luther King Jr., the 1968 law prohibited discrimination in the rental or sale of housing because of race, color, religion, sex, or national origin. However, the Department of Housing and Urban Development (HUD), which was assigned primary responsibility for its enforcement, was authorized only to mediate disputes between a person who thought he or she had been discriminated against and the renter or seller. The Justice Department, in turn, could not act unless it found a "pattern or practice" of discrimination. As a consequence of these weak enforcement provisions, the Fair Housing Act in practice did not live up to its promise. The act, which one member of Congress called a "toothless tiger," was of little use in preventing discrimination in housing.

The Congress in 1988 reached a compromise agreement on legislation to strengthen enforcement of the Fair Housing Act. Now a person who believes he or she has been discriminated against can file a complaint with HUD, which, if it cannot settle the dispute, can issue a charge of housing discrimination. At this point either party to the dispute can choose to have it decided by either a federal district court or an administrative hearing. If either party chooses to go to the federal court, that choice prevails. This procedure was intended to put some real "teeth" into the enforcement of the act and give it material rather than merely symbolic effect. It has been partially successful, but complaints have been far fewer than actual incidents of discrimination.

Studies indicate that presidential level support for fair housing has varied from Johnson to Obama. So have enforcement actions by federal, state, and local agencies. Though some forms of discrimination have lessened, overall housing discrimination remains a problem in many cities and suburbs. Housing segregation and discrimination contribute to other problems—for example, segregated schools, limited job opportunities, and exposure to high crime rates in minority areas.[11]

Other public policies that appear to promise more symbolically than their implementation yields in material benefits include antitrust activity (especially as that involves "trust busting"), public-utility rate regulation, and equal employment opportunity. Even though the actual effect of a policy may be considerably less than is intended or desired, it nonetheless may have significant consequences for society. An antipoverty program that falls short of its mark may provide some assurance to people that the government cares about poor people and wants to reduce poverty. Legislation on equal employment opportunity informs people that their government, officially at least, does not condone discrimination in hiring on the basis of race, sex, or nationality. Apart from the effects such policies have on societal conditions, they may contribute to the maintenance of social order, support for government, and personal self-esteem, which are not inconsequential considerations.

The analysis and evaluation of public policy is usually focused upon what governments actually do, why, and with what material effects. We should not, however, neglect the symbolic aspects of government, despite their intangible and nebulous nature. The rhetoric of government—what governments say, or appear to say—is clearly a necessary and proper subject for the policy analyst.

Policy Evaluation

Policy evaluation, as a functional activity, is as old as policy itself. Legislators, administrators, judges, pressure-group officials, media commentators, and citizens have always made judgments about the worth or effects of particular policies, programs, and projects.

The Boston Tea Party, for instance, is often portrayed as an unfavorable evaluation of one of King George's colonial tax policies. In actuality, those most threatened were colonial merchants who sold tea smuggled into the country and enjoyed large profits. They were the organizers of the Tea Party, not consumers.

Many policy judgments have been of an impressionistic or intuitive variety, based at best on anecdotal or fragmentary evidence, and strongly influenced by ideological, partisan, or idiosyncratic valuational criteria. Thus, staunch conservatives may regard public-housing programs as socialistic and in need of repeal, regardless of their causes, necessity, or consequences; or Democrats may support higher taxes on corporations and the rich because they believe this will enhance their electoral opportunities. Unemployment compensation may be deemed a "bad" program because the evaluator claims to know "a lot of people" who improperly receive benefits.

Apocryphal stories about "welfare queens" who drive Cadillacs to collect their welfare checks are commonplace among welfare critics. Most of us are familiar with this style of policy evaluation and have perhaps enjoyed doing a bit of it ourselves. Much conflict results from this sort of evaluation, however, because different evaluators, depending upon their values or criteria, may reach sharply divergent conclusions on the merits of the same policy. The food stamp program is a recent example of this.

Another form of policy evaluation centers on process, on the operation or administration of a policy or program.[12] Although the terms *policy* and *program* are often used interchangeably, a line can be drawn between them. *Policy* is defined in this book as a course of action followed by government in dealing with some problem or matter of concern. A policy may spawn a variety of programs, a *program* being defined as a set of rules, routines, and resources intended to carry out a policy or a portion thereof. Programs, which give "direct, specific, and concrete expression" to the policies on which they are based, sometimes are marked out in legislation. More likely, however, they will be the handiwork of administrative officials. Thus, the Antitrust Division has created several programs to enforce the antitrust laws, such as the competition advocacy and anti-cartel enforcement programs.

A program, or several programs, conceivably could be eliminated without impairment of the underlying policy. In 2003, the Bush administration proposed eliminating several fairly specifically focused education programs because they were deemed unnecessary, duplicatory, or replaceable. However, the broad, underlying policy of federal support for public elementary and secondary education remained firmly in place. Most of the targeted programs were retained by Congress.

Questions asked about how a policy or program is being run may include: What are its financial costs? Who receives benefits (payments or services) and in what amounts? Is there unnecessary overlap with or duplication of other programs? Are legislatively prescribed standards and procedures being followed? Is the program honestly administered? This kind of evaluation, which may involve much monitoring of agencies and their officials, will tell us something about whether there is honesty or efficiency in the conduct of a program, but like the first kind of evaluation, it will probably yield little or nothing in the way of hard information concerning the societal effects (outcomes) of a program. On the other hand, process evaluation is often helpful to program managers wanting to improve the administration of their programs and reduce their potential for political criticism.

A third, comparatively new type of policy evaluation, which has been getting increasing attention in the national government in recent decades, is the systematic and intendedly objective evaluation of programs. This form of evaluation, which I will refer to as *systematic evaluation*, employs social science methodology to measure the societal effects of policies or programs and the extent to which they are achieving their goals or objectives.

The Departments of Labor, Health and Human Services, and Energy, for instance, have assistant secretaries whose responsibilities include program evaluation. Bureaus within these and other departments often include policy- and program-evaluation staffs. Moreover, they enter into many contracts with private research organizations, university scholars, and others for the performance of evaluation studies. More attention appears to be given to evaluating social programs (welfare, education, health, and nutrition) than most other areas of governmental activity. This preference probably arises from the proliferation of social programs in recent decades, their substantial financial costs, the controversies that swirl around them, and the dislike of "welfare."

Systematic evaluation seeks information on the impact of a policy or program on the public need or problem at which it is directed. Utilizing particularly the talents of social scientists (economists, political scientists, psychologists, and sociologists), it involves the specification of goals or objectives; the collection of information and data on program inputs, outputs, and consequences; and their rigorous analysis, preferably through the use of quantitative or statistical techniques.

Evaluation researchers use a variety of evaluation research designs, which are often coupled with high-powered statistical and mathematical techniques. The three evaluation designs discussed here—the experimental design, the quasi-experimental design, and the before-and-after study—are basic.[13] An examination of them will convey a notion of the problems involved in setting up evaluation studies.

The *experimental design* is the classic method for evaluating a policy or program. Two comparable groups—an experimental, or treatment, group and a control group—are randomly selected from the target population. The experimental group receives treatment through a policy or program; the control group does not. Pretests and posttests of the two groups are used to determine whether changes, such as improved reading scores or lower incidences of a disease, have occurred in the two groups. If the performance of the experimental group is significantly better than that of the control group, the program is held to be effective. A high level of validity and generalizability is accorded the results of experiments. An example is in order.

Several years ago, the Delaware Department of Labor conducted a field experiment[14] to assess the effectiveness of various activities in helping "dislocated workers"—"persons who have lost long-term, stable jobs due to an increased international competition and/or changing technology."[15] The goals of the program for dislocated workers, which was funded through the Job Partnership Training Act, were to help increase workers' earnings and reduce their need for unemployment compensation benefits. A coterie of 175 workers with comparable characteristics was identified; 65 were randomly assigned to the treatment group, with the other 110 becoming the control group. Members of the treatment group were provided counseling on job-search activities, assistance in locating openings, retraining, and other services. Both groups were monitored for a year. Comparison of their performance revealed that the control group did better than the treatment group in meeting the program's goals. It was concluded that "the program did not appear to improve participants' job prospects."[16]

Use of the experimental design may not be possible because of costs, time, and ethical or other considerations. The *quasi-experiment,* then, may be a useful alternative. The process of random selection is not used. Rather, the treatment group is compared with another group (a "comparison group") that is similar in many respects. Consequently, in the quasi-experiment there is greater likelihood that the performances of the two groups could be influenced by their internal characteristics rather than the program treatment. Quasi-experiments nonetheless are still seen as quite useful for many purposes.

A well-known quasi-experiment involves the Connecticut highway speed-control program.[17] Following a record number of highway traffic fatalities, the state initiated a crackdown on speeding. Initial data indicated that the enforcement program had significantly reduced fatalities. It was possible, however, that this resulted from other factors, such as differences in the weather or more safe cars in operation. To control for such possibilities, the Connecticut highway fatality rate per 100,000 people was compared with that of neighboring states where there had been no enhanced enforcement program. This showed that Connecticut's fatality rate was lower than those of the other states, thus supporting the inference that the Connecticut crackdown had a positive effect in reducing traffic deaths.

The *before-and-after study* of a program compares the results of a program after a period of implementation with the conditions existing prior to its inception. Thus, one might compare the quality of water in a river before and after a pollution-control program was put into effect. Before-and-after studies often have low costs and take less time to conduct. A major drawback, however, is that the changes that occur are open to rival explanations. Improved water quality in our imaginary river could be due to increased flow, voluntary action by polluters, or an economic recession's having caused reduced industrial activity. On the other hand, if a before-and-after study finds little change in the desired direction, then it is likely that the program is not having much effect.[18] Given all of this, it is still possible for before-and-after studies to produce useful information about a program that otherwise would be unavailable.

As this discussion indicates, systematic evaluation draws on experience in assessing the effects a policy or program has on the public need or problem at which it is directed. It permits at least tentative, informed responses to such questions as: Is this policy achieving its stated objectives? What are its costs and benefits? Who are its beneficiaries? What happened as a consequence of the policy that would not have happened in its absence? Consequently, systematic evaluation gives policy-makers and the general public, if they are interested, some notion about the actual impact of policy and provides discussions of policy with some grounding in reality. Evaluation findings can be used to modify current policies and programs and to help design others for the future.

Of course, evaluation studies can also be used for less laudable purposes. Professor Carol Weiss comments, "Program decision-makers may turn to evaluation to delay a decision; to justify and legitimate a decision already made; to extricate themselves from controversy about future directions by passing the buck; to vindicate the program in the eyes of its constituents, its funders, or the public; to satisfy conditions of a government or foundation grant through the ritual of evaluation."[19] In short, evaluators may be motivated by self-service as well as public service and by a desire to use analysis as ammunition for partisan or personal political purposes. Thus, the staff of the Federal Paperwork Commission was interested only in evaluations supportive of their goal of eliminating as much governmental regulation of business as possible, albeit under the guise of paperwork reduction.[20]

We now turn to some of the ways in which policy evaluation is handled in the national government.

Policy Evaluation Processes

Much policy evaluation is performed by nongovernmental actors. The communications media; university scholars and research centers; private research organizations such as the Brookings Institution, the Urban Institute, and the American Enterprise Institute; pressure groups; and public-interest organizations, such as Common Cause, the Audubon Society, and Ralph Nader and his "raiders" (a collection of public-interest activists) are examples; all make evaluations of public policies and programs that have greater or lesser effects on public officials. They also provide the general public with information, publicize policy success and failure, sometimes act as advocates for unpopular causes, and occasionally provide representation for those unrepresented in the policy process, such as the aged confined to negligently run nursing homes or exploited migratory farm workers.

Collectively, this aggregation of private evaluators of public policies has been designated by Professor Richard Hofferbert as the "policy evaluation industry."[21] We will take a look here at three of its components.

Many university scholars engage in evaluation on their own initiative, as members of university research centers, while under contracts with government agencies, or to gain academic advancement or fame. Many universities have graduate schools of public policy whose faculty have a more "applied" or practical orientation and are inclined to undertake policy research. Some of the research of university scholars is published in such journals as *Evaluation and Program Planning, Evaluation Review,* and *Journal of Policy Analysis and Management*. For the most part, though, university scholars are more interested in making theoretical contributions to their academic disciplines than in getting involved in current policy debates.

A number of private research organizations ("think tanks") devote all or most of their time to performing evaluation studies.[22] The Manpower Development Research Corporation uses funds from national, state, and local governments and foundations to research social welfare and employment programs. The RAND Corporation operates mainly as a contract researcher producing policy reports for the Department of Defense. Research organizations of this sort often can act more independently and be more critical of agency actions than can internal agency personnel. "Of course, contract researchers often face pressures to follow the agency line, especially if they are highly dependent on a single agency."[23]

In their reporting of the news when public policies are involved, the media tend to focus on policies and government actions that go awry. Some sort of policy scandal is even more "newsworthy." The operative assumption seems to be that that sort of reporting will attract more viewers or readers than will information about a successful program or the routine operations of government. Some years ago, one of the television networks featured an occasional series titled "The Fleecing of America" as part of its evening news report. The focus was on governmental blunders and misadventures. Coverage of this nature contributes to the (incorrect) notion that "the government can't do anything well." More positively though, it may also help to focus public attention on some matters that need examination and correction. Television and radio programs that recount public-policy successes are scarce. One does not hear much about soil conservation, brownfield restoration, railroad safety, or public housing.

Moving on, within the boundaries of the national government, policy evaluation is performed in numerous ways by officials and organizations. Sometimes these evaluations are rigorous and systematic; at other times, they are rather haphazard or sporadic. In some instances policy evaluation has become formalized, a regular component of the policy process; in others it remains essentially informal and unstructured. In the remainder of this section, we glance at a few forms of official policy evaluation—congressional oversight, Government Accountability Office (GAO) studies, the activities of presidential commissions, and "in house" evaluations handled within agencies.

Congressional Oversight   Although it is not specified in the Constitution, one of the primary functions of Congress is the supervision and evaluation of the administration and execution of laws and policies, which is commonly referred to as *congressional oversight*. Some, agreeing with the English political theorist John Stuart Mill, think that this is the most important function a legislature performs.[24] Oversight, however, is not a separable, distinct activity; rather, it is an integral part of almost everything that members of Congress do, including gathering information, legislating, authorizing appropriations, and being of service to constituents. It may be intended either to control the actions of agencies, as when they sometimes are required to clear actions in advance with particular committees, or to evaluate agency actions, as when individual members or committees seek to determine whether administrators are complying with program objectives established by Congress. It is the evaluative aspect of oversight that is pertinent here.

Oversight may be performed by a number of techniques, including (1) casework, that is, intercession with agencies as a consequence of constituents' demands and requests; (2) committee hearings and investigations; (3) the appropriations process; (4) approval of presidential appointments; and (5) committee staff studies.[25] In the course of these activities, members of Congress reach conclusions about the efficiency, effectiveness, and impact of policies and programs—conclusions that can have profound consequences for the policy process. Congressional oversight is in essence more fragmented and disjointed than continuous and systematic. Bits and pieces of information, impressionistic judgments, and the members' intuition and values are blended to yield evaluation of policies and those who administer them. On the whole, however, members of Congress are more likely to be involved with initiation and adoption of policy than with evaluation, at least in any systematic sense.

The congressional practice of enacting laws—for example, the Clean Air Act and the Head Start law—for determinate lengths of time builds evaluation into the legislative process. Periodically such laws have to be reauthorized by Congress, thereby creating opportunities to make changes in them on the basis of experience and available information. At the state level, sunset laws have a similar effect. These laws provide that state agencies will be terminated unless they are periodically evaluated and reauthorized. The programs of a terminated ("sunsetted") agency may be shifted to another agency. That opportunities for evaluation are created does not, of course, guarantee that they will be well exploited.

Government Accountability Office
The GAO, usually regarded as an arm of Congress, has broad statutory authority to audit the operations and financial activities of federal agencies, to evaluate their programs, and to report its findings to Congress.[26] The agency, which has several thousand employees, has become increasingly involved with the evaluation of programs and now gives only a minor portion of its attention to financial auditing.

The Legislative Reorganization Act of 1970, which revamped the congressional committee system, also directed the GAO to "review and analyze the results of government programs and activities carried on under existing law, including the making of cost-benefit studies," and to make personnel available to assist congressional committees in handling similar activities. A subsequent statute authorized GAO to establish an Office of Program Review and Evaluation. Because of its expanded evaluation activities, the agency hires many more people trained in the social sciences than it once did.

Evaluation activities may be undertaken by the GAO on its own initiative, because of directives in legislation, at the request of congressional committees, or sometimes at the behest of individual members of Congress. In the course of a year, the GAO produces several hundred evaluation studies, varying in length from several pages to a few hundred. The titles of four evaluation studies issued by the GAO in 2012 indicate the diversity and evaluative thrust of its actions: FDA's Food Advisory and Recall Process Needs Strengthening; Border Security: Additional Steps Needed to Ensure that Officers Are Fully Trained; Nuclear Safety: DOE Needs to Determine the Costs and Benefits of Its Safety Reform Effort; and School Bullying: Extent of Legal Protections for Vulnerable Groups Needed to Be More Fully Assessed. GAO officials are also frequently called upon to testify before congressional committees.

Copies of GAO studies are sent to members of Congress and the affected agencies. The agencies are required by law to report to Congress and the Office of Management and Budget (OMB) on actions taken in response to the GAO's recommendations or on why they did not act.

CASE STUDY   *The GAO and Food Safety*

A short narrative will help convey an understanding of the GAO evaluation process. Food safety is an ever-present problem in the United States. The federal Centers for Disease Control and Prevention estimated in 2011 that about 48 million people in the United States annually suffer from food-borne illnesses. These result in 120,000 hospitalizations and 3,000 deaths. In recent years, food poisoning outbreaks have been traced to lettuce, peanuts, hamburger meat, and jalapeno peppers. For example, in 2011, Listeria bacteria on cantaloupes grown in Colorado caused thirty-three deaths.

Fifteen federal agencies operating under more than thirty laws govern the U.S. food supply. Primary among them are the Food and Drug Administration (FDA) in the Department of Health and Human Services; the Food Safety and Inspection Service (FSIS), the Agricultural Marketing Service (AMS), and the Grain Inspection, Packers and Stockyards Administration (GIPSA) in the Department of Agriculture; and the National Marine Fisheries Service (NMFS) in the Department of Commerce. The FDA regulates some 57,000 food-processing establishments and sets standards of quality and identity for food products. The FSIS supervises more than 6,000 plants engaged in slaughtering and processing meat and poultry products. The AMS has jurisdiction over hundreds of egg and egg-product facilities. The NMFS provides voluntary (fee for service) safety and sanitary inspections for approximately 2,500 foreign and domestic seafood firms.

In 1992, at the request of a House subcommittee chair, the GAO undertook an evaluation of the consistency, coordination, and effectiveness of the federal food-safety inspection program.[27] Data and information for the study were acquired by interviewing agency officials; by analyzing agencies' inspection policies, procedures, and records; and by meeting with industry and consumer groups.

The GAO reached several negative conclusions about the food-safety inspection system. Food products presenting similar health risks were treated differently by the various agencies, duplicative inspections occurred, and coordination among the agencies was inadequate. The agencies' effectiveness was limited by inconsistencies and illogical differences, based on statutory authority and funding, in their approaches to food safety. Thus, plants processing meat and poultry were inspected daily by the FSIS, but food-processing plants under FDA jurisdiction were inspected once every three to five years.

Further, the agencies drew some narrow jurisdictional lines. For one, the FSIS handled inspection of open-faced meat sandwiches made with one slice of bread whereas the traditional sandwich made with two slices of bread was the FDA's responsibility. For another, pizza with meat topping was inspected by the FSIS, pizza without meat topping by the FDA.

Finally, meat and poultry plants were required to register for inspection with the FSIS before they could operate and sell their products. In contrast, food-processing factories were under no such mandate and had to be tracked down by the FDA.

To correct these and other problems, the GAO recommended the creation of a single food-safety agency. Because this was not a good political possibility, the GAO said a "more realistic" alternative would be the appointment of a panel of experts to develop an inspection model based on public-health risks and strong enforcement authority. This would provide a rational basis for improving the effectiveness of the food-safety system. No Congressional action was taken on the GAO's recommendations.

Since 1992, the GAO has produced dozens of studies regarding the food-safety system, calling for reform and the creation of a single, independent food safety agency.[28] Members of Congress have introduced bills calling for creation of a unified Food Safety Administration. However, because of resistance from committees with jurisdiction over various aspects of food safety, reservations about the creation of a consolidated agency, and lack of strong public concern, the single-agency idea has foundered.[29]

Some improvements have been made to protect the food supply. In 2011, the Food Safety and Modernization Act became law. It strengthens the authority of the FDA to regulate the way foods are grown, harvested, and processed. Inspections of food facilities will become more frequent and the agency was given authority to require food recalls. Also, the FDA's authority to protect against threats to the food supply under the Bioterrorism Act of 2002 was enhanced.

Generally, however, the food safety system continues to be characterized by fragmentation, duplication, and insufficient resources. The GAO's proposal for a single agency continues to be unacceptable to the Congress.[30] ∎

Presidential Commissions   Earlier we examined the presidential commissions' role in formulating policy. Now we will see that they can also be used as an instrument of policy evaluation. Whether set up specifically to evaluate policy or governmental management in some area or for other purposes such as fact finding, making policy recommendations, or simply creating the appearance of presidential concern, most commissions involve themselves in policy evaluation to some degree.

In November 1986, it was disclosed that the U.S. government, under the leadership of National Security Council (NSC) officials, had sold arms to the Iranian government and diverted some of the profits to the Nicaraguan rebels (the "Contras"). This news touched off a major political controversy. To inquire into this matter and to make recommendations for correction, President Reagan appointed the President's Special Review Board. Better known as the Tower Commission, it was composed of former Republican senator John Tower (from Texas) as chair; Edmund Muskie, former Democratic senator from Maine and secretary of state; and Brent Scowcroft, former national security adviser to President Gerald Ford (and later to President George Bush).

In its report issued early in 1987, the Tower Commission sharply criticized President Reagan and his administration for their conduct in the Iran-Contra affair. The NSC was depicted as carrying on operations outside its advisory realm, deceiving Congress, paying little heed to the law, and avoiding any effective oversight. The president himself was viewed as uninformed, detached, and not in control of NSC action, which ran counter to his administration's own policy of no arms sales to the Iranians. The commission's report made specific recommendations for bringing the NSC system under more effective presidential control and direction.[31] President Reagan accepted the commission's report and instituted some changes designed to prevent recurrence of such problems.[32]

A more traditional presidential commission was the sixteen-member Social Security Commission established by President George W. Bush to appraise the Social Security program and propose ways to strengthen it. Much as its Democratic critics contended it would, given its membership, the commission set forth three options for partial privatization of the program in its report.[33] It is not uncommon for commissions to reach conclusions agreeable to the appointing president. Some do not, however. A commission appointed by President Richard Nixon to recommend actions on marijuana surprised him by calling for its legalization. The President refused to even read the report.

It appears that the policy evaluations and recommendations made by presidential commissions often have little immediate influence on policymaking. For whatever effect they do have, the important variables are probably not the quality and soundness of their findings. Charles Jones concludes that an evaluation commission is likely to have the greatest effect when its report coincides with other supporting events and accords with the president's policy preferences, when it includes some members who hold important governmental positions and are committed to its recommendations, and when commission staff personnel return to governmental positions in which they can influence acceptance of its recommendations.[34] These conditions, however, are often not present.

Administrative Agencies   Many evaluations of policies and programs are produced within the administering agencies, either on their own initiative or at the direction of Congress or the executive. Agencies usually want to get some notion of how their programs are working and what can be done to improve them. Educational program evaluations are often labeled either *formative* or *summative*. Formative evaluations (also known as program monitoring) are designed to assist officials in making mid-course corrections or adjustments in programs to improve their operation. Summative evaluations are broader and more thorough in scope and are used to inform upper-level policy-makers of the overall effects of important policies and programs. They may lead to major program changes. There is not much reason to expect, however, that such evaluations will cause agency officials to recommend terminating favored policies or programs.

The Johnson, Nixon, and Carter administrations tried to build policy analysis and evaluation into the national budgetary process.[35] The Johnson administration instituted the Planning-Programming-Budgeting System (PPBS), which required agencies to search for the most effective and efficient (least-cost) means to achieve their goals. (Remnants of PPBS remain in a few agencies.) The Nixon administration replaced PPBS with Management by Objectives (MBO), a more modest effort requiring agencies to specify goals and measure progress toward achieving them. By the time the Carter administration came to town and installed Zero-Base Budgeting (ZBB), MBO had evaporated. The ZBB required agencies to specify different levels of funding and accomplishment for programs, including the "zero" base (defined not as nothing but rather as the funding level below which the program would have no real worth). By so doing, agencies would assess the worth of programs and indicate where spending would do the most good. ZBB did not survive the Carter administration.

These efforts at reform failed for several reasons. They were instituted on a government wide basis without much planning or testing, they conflicted with existing budgetary practices and habits, they were difficult and time-consuming to use, they were viewed as efforts to shift power to higher executive levels, and they lacked continuing presidential interest and support. They were not, however, without effect, for they left behind in the agencies a residue of interest and support for more systematic analysis and evaluation of agencies' activities. It has now become fairly standard practice for Congress to specifically direct agencies to undertake program and policy evaluations.

Agencies are not prone to evaluate themselves. The conduct of their programs and day-to-day operations take precedence over more "distant" concerns like program evaluations. Moreover, evaluation would divert scarce funds from current operations—issuing licenses, making grants, processing applications, inspecting products and facilities, and so on. If evaluation of program effectiveness were conducted, and it turned out unfavorable from the agency's perspective, it could be used as political ammunition by the agency's critics. In all, agencies do not have much incentive to evaluate themselves.

The Government Performance and Results Act (GPRA) (1993), supported by the Clinton administration and enacted by Congress with little controversy or public notice, is intended to shift the focus of agencies from inputs and processes to outputs and outcomes—or results.[36] That is, how do agency operations affect such matters as air quality, industrial safety, the employability of job trainees, or investment opportunities? This is a laudable aspiration.

To accomplish this purpose, agencies are directed to work with Congress and its committees in formulating five-year strategic plans. These plans are to include "(1) the annual performance goals for agencies' major programs and activities, (2) the measures that will be used to gauge performance, (3) the strategies and resources required to achieve the performance goals, and (4) the procedures that will be used to verify and validate performance information."[37] In 1999, after trial runs in a few agencies, the GPRA became effective for all agencies who annually report in March on their progress and results.

Successfully implemented, the GPRA should facilitate program evaluation and provide useful information for executive and congressional budget decision-makers. Initially, agencies had problems in putting GPRA requirements in place. Thus, the Department of Education's progress in attaining some of its outcome goals was difficult to appraise because of data shortages. In other instances, it showed little progress in achieving outcome goals.[38] For the Environmental Protection Agency (EPA), the GAO reported that "the annual performance measures established under GPRA are often selected on the basis of available data that focus primarily on outputs rather than environmental results [or outcomes] for which credible data are often lacking."[39]

The agencies have continued to wrestle with GPRA mandates. What has been accomplished?" Some believe that GPRA has followed the path of previous reforms—a big investment by agencies at the outset leading to the generation of vast amounts of paperwork that satisfy formal requirements but provide little evidence that the innovations have made a dent in behavior or decisions."[40] A less cynical view holds that GPRA has been beneficial. Some congressional appropriations committees, for example, have pressured agencies to include information on outcomes or results in their budget justifications.

In 2010, in an effort to strengthen the act, Congress enacted the Government Performance and Results Modernizations Act. Requirements for agencies to consult with Congress were enhanced. A new framework was specified aimed at getting agencies to take a more crosscutting and integrated approach to focusing on results and improving government performance. The GAO is to evaluate agency accomplishments.[41] Performance evaluation continues to be an appealing idea, if less than fully successful.

Problems in Policy Evaluation

The most useful form of policy evaluation for policy-makers and administrators, and for policy critics who want a factual basis for their positions, is a systematic evaluation that tries to determine cause-and-effect relationships and rigorously measures the results of policy. It is, of course, often impossible to measure quantitatively the effect of public policies, especially social policies, with any real precision. In this context, then, to "measure rigorously" is to seek to assess policy impacts as carefully and objectively as possible, using the best information available and making careful judgments. There is no reason to assume that only quantitative data and analysis are meaningful.

Determining whether a policy or program is doing what it is supposed to do, or doing something else, is not an easy, straightforward task, as some appear to assume. Snap judgments are easy to make but lack definitiveness. A variety of conditions raise obstacles or create problems for the effective accomplishment of policy evaluation. These include uncertainty over policy goals, difficulty in determining causality, diffuse policy impacts, and others, all of which are reviewed in this section.

Uncertainty over Policy Goals   When the goals of a policy are unclear, diffuse, or diverse, as they frequently are, determining the extent to which they have been attained becomes a difficult and frustrating task.[42] This situation is often a product of the policy-adoption process. Because the support of a majority coalition is needed to secure adoption of a policy, it is usually necessary to appeal to persons and groups possessing differing interests and diverse values. To win their votes, commitments to the preferred policy goals of these various groups may be included in the legislation.

The Model Cities Act, enacted during the Johnson administration, was a laudable attempt to confront urban problems. Goals of the Model Cities Act included rebuilding slum and blighted areas; improving housing, income, and cultural opportunities therein; reducing crime and juvenile delinquency; lessening reliance on welfare programs; and maintaining historic landmarks. No priorities were assigned to the various goals; nor, indeed, were their dimensions well-specified. Substantial funding was provided for Model Cities evaluation research, which was supposed to determine the extent to which the diverse goals of the act were being met. Limited in impact at best, the Model Cities program has been relegated to the dustbin of history.

Determining the real goals of a program can be a difficult or conflictual task. Persons occupying different positions in the policy process, such as legislators and administrators, or national and state officials, or possessing differing ideological or philosophical perspectives, may define goals differently, act accordingly, and reach differing conclusions about a program's accomplishments or success. Moreover, "because 'what you measure is what you get,' choosing the right goals to measure is essential."[43] Later in this chapter, we will see how the multiple goals of the Head Start program, and measurement problems, have complicated its evaluation.

Difficulty in Determining Causality   Systematic evaluation requires that societal changes must be demonstrably caused by policy actions. The mere fact that when action A is taken, condition B develops does not necessarily mean the presence of a cause-and-effect relationship. Other actions (or variables) may have been the actual causes of condition B. As we know, many common colds are "cured," not by ingesting medicines, applying ointments, or using nasal sprays, but by the human body's natural recuperative power.

Consider this example. Many states require periodic automobile safety inspections in an attempt to reduce highway traffic accidents and fatalities. Research indicates that states with mandatory inspection laws do tend to have fewer traffic fatalities than do other states. Other factors, however, such as population density, weather conditions, and percentage of young drivers might in fact have more power in explaining the difference. Only if such conditions are controlled in the analysis, and if differences remain between states with and without inspections, can it be accurately stated that a policy of periodic automobile inspections reduces traffic deaths. In actuality, such laws do seem to have a modest beneficial effect.[44]

To further illustrate the problem of determining causality, let us take the case of crime-control policies. The purpose, or at least one of the purposes, of these policies is deterring crime. *Deterrence* may be defined as the prevention of an action that can be said to have had a "realistic potential of actualization," that is, one that really could have happened.[45] (This assumption is required to avoid the kind of analysis that holds, for example, that consumption of alcoholic beverages prevents stomach worms since no one has ever been afflicted with them after starting to drink.) The problem here is that not doing something is a sort of nonevent, or intangible act. Does a person's not committing burglary mean that he or she has been effectively deterred by policy from so acting? The answer, of course, first depends upon whether he or she was inclined to engage in burglary. If so, then was the person deterred by the possibility of detection and punishment, by other factors such as family influence, or by lack of opportunity? As this example indicates, the determination of causality between actions, especially in complex social and economic matters, frequently is a daunting task.[46]

Diffuse Policy Impacts   Policy actions may affect groups other than those at whom they are specifically directed. A welfare program may affect not only the poor but also others such as taxpayers, public officials, and low-income people who are not receiving welfare benefits. The effects on these groups may be either symbolic or material. Taxpayers may grumble that their "hard-earned dollars are going to support those too lazy to work." Some low-income working people may indeed try to go on welfare rather than continue working at grubby, unpleasant jobs for low wages. So far as the poor who receive material benefits are concerned, how do benefits affect their initiative and self-reliance, family solidarity, or maintenance of social order? We should bear in mind that policies may have unstated intentions. Thus, an antipoverty program might have been covertly intended to help defuse the demands of black activists, or a program to control importing of beef may be intended to appease cattle growers politically but not really do much to limit foreign competition.

The effects of some programs may be very broad and long-range in nature. Antitrust policy is an example. Since the policy was originally intended to help maintain competition and prevent monopoly in the economy, how does one now evaluate its effectiveness? We can look at current enforcement activity and find that some mergers have been prevented and many price-fixing conspiracies have been prosecuted, but this record will tell us little about the extent of competition and monopoly in the economy generally. It would be pleasing to be able to determine that the economy is *n* percent more competitive than it would have been without antitrust policy. Because its goals are general and because measuring competition and monopoly is difficult, this determination just is not possible. Interestingly, after a century of antitrust action, we are still without agreed-upon definitions of monopoly and competition to guide policy action and evaluation. No wonder those assessing the effectiveness of antitrust policy sometimes come to sharply different conclusions.[47]

Difficulties in Data Acquisition As implied in some previous comments, a shortage of accurate and relevant statistical data and other information may handicap the policy evaluator, particularly when one's concern is with policy outcomes. Thus, an econometric model may predict how a tax cut will affect economic activity, but suitable data to indicate its actual impacts on the economy are hard to come by. Again, think of the problems in securing the data needed to determine the effect on criminal-law enforcement of a Supreme Court decision such as *Miranda* v. *Arizona*,[48] which held that a confession obtained when a suspect had not been informed of his or her rights when taken into custody was inherently invalid. The members of the President's Crime Commission in 1967 disagreed about its effect, the majority saying it was too early to determine results. A minority, however, held that, if fully implemented, "it could mean the virtual elimination of pretrial interrogation of suspects .... Few can doubt the adverse effect of Miranda upon the law enforcement process."[49] Absence of data does not necessarily hinder many evaluators.

The use of "Miranda cards" to inform suspects of their rights now has become standard police practice. A consensus exists among criminal-justice scholars and law-enforcement officers to the effect that this reform has had little adverse effect on law enforcement. Various field and quantitative studies support this view. Moreover, it is suggested that the Miranda rule has helped improve professionalism among the police.[50]

For many social and economic programs, a question that typically arises is "Did those who participated in programs subsequently fare better than comparable persons who did not?" Providing an answer preferably involves an experimental evaluation design utilizing a control group. The difficulty in devising a control (or comparison) group for a workforce program is summed up in this passage:

> A strict comparison group in the laboratory sense of the physical sciences is virtually impossible, primarily because the behavior patterns of people are affected by so many external social, economic, and political factors. In fact, sometimes the legislation itself prevents a proper comparison group from being established. For example, the Work Incentive Program legislation required that all fathers must be enrolled in the WIN program within 30 days after receipt of aid for their children. Therefore, a comparison group of fathers with comparable attributes to those fathers enrolled in the program could not be established. Even if all the external factors of the economy could be controlled, it would still be impossible to replicate the social and political environment affecting any experimental or demonstration program. Thus, it is easy for a decision maker to discount the results of almost any evaluation study on the basis that it lacks the precision control group.[51]

Because of problems such as those mentioned in the quotation, experimental designs frequently cannot be used. (This reason is apart from their often high dollar cost.) Second-best alternatives must then be utilized, such as a quasi-experimental design using a nonequivalent control group.[52]

Official Resistance   Evaluating policy, whether it be called policy analysis, measurement of policy impact, or something else, involves reporting findings and making judgments on the merits of policy. This is true even if the evaluator is a university researcher who thinks that he or she is objectively pursuing knowledge. Agency and program officials will be alert to the possible political consequences of evaluation. If the results do not come out "right" from their perspective, or worse, if the results are negative and come to the attention of decision-makers, their program, influence, or careers may be thrown in jeopardy. Consequently, program officials may discourage or disparage evaluation studies, refuse access to data, or keep incomplete records.

Within agencies, evaluation studies are likely to be most strongly supported by higher-level officials who must make decisions about the allocation of resources among programs and the continuation of given programs. They may, however, be reluctant to require evaluations, especially if their results may have a divisive effect within the agencies. Finally, organizations tend to resist change, and evaluation implies change. Organizational inertia may thus be an obstacle to evaluation, along with more overt forms of resistance.

A Limited Time Perspective   The time horizon of legislators and other elected officials often extends only as far as the next election. Consequently, they, and others who think like them, often expect quick results from governmental programs, even social and educational programs whose effects may take many years to fully appear. This being the case, short-run evaluations of program accomplishments may be unfavorable.

A good example is the New Deal's resettlement program, which provided opportunities for land ownership to thousands of black sharecroppers in the South during the late 1930s and early 1940s. It was judged as a failure and just another New Deal boondoggle by contemporary critics. A decades-later evaluation of the program by policy analyst Lester Salamon concluded, however, that it had significant, positive, long-term effects, although not as an agricultural policy.[53] At modest cost, it did transform "a group of landless black tenants into a permanent landed middle class that ultimately emerged in the 1960s as the backbone of the civil-rights movement in the rural South." If the time dimension is ignored in evaluation studies, the results may be flawed and neglect important long-term effects. The pressure for rapid feedback concerning a policy can then create a dilemma for the evaluator.

Evaluation Lacks Influence   Once completed, an evaluation of a program may be ignored or attacked as inconclusive or unsound on various grounds. It may be alleged that the evaluation was poorly designed, the data used were inadequate, or the findings are inconclusive. Those strongly interested in a program, however, whether as administrators or beneficiaries, are unlikely to lose their affection for it merely because an evaluation study concluded that its costs are greater than its benefits. Moreover, there is also the possibility that the evaluation is flawed.

Governmental programs are not terminated solely as a consequence of an unfavorable systematic evaluation, although such evaluations did contribute to adoption of the Airline Deregulation Act. Of course, evaluations frequently lead to incremental changes or improvements in the design and administration of programs. That is the intent of many program evaluations done by the GAO, for instance, which, perhaps, is all that should be asked or expected of most evaluations.

Policy Evaluation: The Use and Misuse of Cost–Benefit Analysis

Cost–benefit analysis is a formal, quantitative evaluation technique that requires identifying the costs and benefits of either a proposed or actual policy and translating them into monetary values for purposes of comparison. It assumes that society will be made better off only by policies (or projects, or programs) whose benefits exceed their costs. Cost–benefit analysis has been most frequently used to evaluate proposed policies.

Sometimes, though, it is employed to appraise existing policies. Thus, economist A. Myrick Freeman III used it to evaluate national air- and water-pollution-control policies. He found that the control of air pollution from stationary sources yielded benefits that were much greater than control costs. On the other hand, the costs of controlling industrial and municipal sources of water pollution were greater than the benefits realized.[54] In the following discussion, the focus will be on cost–benefit analysis primarily as a prospective evaluation technique.

The major steps in performing a cost–benefit analysis can readily be summarized.[55] First, one identifies all of the effects or consequences of a policy and categorizes them as costs or benefits for various groups. (Note that this requires establishing which groups are entitled to be considered in determining costs and benefits.) Both direct and indirect effects should be analyzed.

Second, dollar values are placed on various costs and benefits. This will be relatively easy for items that are customarily bought and sold in markets. For such matters as good health, the prolongation of human life, or scenic vistas, it will be much more difficult.

Third, some of the consequences or effects of a policy will be current or near-term, but others will occur many years in the future, or even the next generation. Hence, proponents of cost–benefit analysis call for a discount rate to equate the value of near and long-term effects. The basic assumption underlying the discount rate is that a dollar today is worth more than a dollar years from now. Inflation may reduce the dollar's value or purchasing power. Alternatively, the money could be invested and its value would increase. My guess is that most readers would prefer a thousand dollars today to a thousand dollars seventeen years from now. What is the explanation?

Fourth, the costs and benefits, direct and indirect, current and future, of the policy are compared. If benefits exceed costs, the policy is acceptable; conversely, if costs exceed benefits, it should be rejected, or a better way of doing it should be found.

So presented, cost–benefit analysis appears as a reasonably clear-cut method for appraising policies. In actuality, there are significant problems involved in its application, a few of which are examined here.

Good data on the costs and benefits of a policy are frequently difficult to come by. How, for example, does one calculate the value of the health benefits of cleaner air? Or of the esthetic benefits of reducing haze in national parks? How are dollar values to be assigned to such matters? The value of land flooded (a cost) for a reservoir can readily be determined by reference to the value of nearby land. But what of the value of an ancestral home located there? The data and dollar values on which a cost–benefit analysis is based can be of tenuous and arguable nature. Professor Frank Rourke states that "the numerical values assigned to both costs and benefits are more often the product of imagination than mathematical skill."[56]

It is, further, no easy task to identify the appropriate discount rate. It can be based on such criteria as the interest rate, the rate of inflation, or the opportunity costs of capital—that is, the rate of return that money would earn if devoted to private investment rather than public purposes. Despite its importance, there is no scientific way to decide on a discount rate. A low discount rate preserves the value of future benefits whereas a high discount rate can sharply reduce their value. During the Reagan years, the OMB advocated a discount rate of 10 percent. This discount rate meant that the value of future benefits, such as lives prolonged two or three decades hence by reducing the incidence of cancer, would have very low value. This, in turn, increased the likelihood that a cost–benefit ratio would be unfavorable, and that regulation would not be justifiable.

Cost–benefit analysis is based on the premise that efficiency is the primary, if not the only, value to be realized. Actions are evaluated on the basis of whether resources are used to improve the aggregate public good.[57] Little attention is accorded alternative or competing values—equity, human dignity, personal freedom, and equality, to name some. These are important to most people. The American system of criminal justice, for instance, is not very efficient because of our concern with equity and due process.

Another problem that arises in the course of many cost–benefit analyses is the need to place a value on a human life. Some take the position that life is priceless and that attempting to place a dollar value on life reduces it to just another commodity. In response it is argued that many policy decisions, such as industrial-safety standards and highway speed limits, have an impact in terms of human lives. It is better to objectively take into account the value of life. The EPA in 2008 determined that the "value of a statistical life" was $6.9 million in current dollars, nearly a million dollars less than five years earlier. This figure was calculated from opinion surveys asking people what they were willing to pay to avoid specified risks and what employers paid employees to assume additional risks. (Figure 7.1 displays some alternatives for valuing a human life.) The EPA has traditionally put the highest value on human life of any federal agency. Interestingly, all units within the EPA do not use the same figure.[58] Under the cost–benefit regimen, the less a life is worth, the less need for regulatory protection, and vice versa.

Finally, let us note that cost–benefit analysis emphasizes the consequences for society as a whole. As we know, however, public policies distribute advantages and disadvantages, or costs and benefits. Those who pay the costs of policies often do not benefit from them, and vice versa. Put differently, policies have distributive consequences that are of importance. People may appropriately be more concerned with who benefits from industrial-safety policies than whether their total costs exceed their benefits.

Problems such as those sketched here have not prevented cost–benefit analysis from being used as a tool in governmental decision-making for several decades. The Flood Control Act of 1936 specified that flood-control projects could be undertaken by the Army Corps of Engineers only "if the benefits to whomsoever they may accrue are in excess of the estimated costs." This standard must also be used for water projects handled by the Natural Resources

FIGURE 7.1

The Valuation of Human Life

Several techniques for the valuation of human life for cost–benefit analyses have been developed.* Four are presented here.

1. *The human capital approach.* This is sometimes also called *discounted future earnings.* This technique, which appears free of moral sentiment, holds that a person's value depends upon what he or she can earn in the marketplace during a lifetime of work, discounted to the present. Some analysts would subtract a person's living expenses from earnings to arrive at a net value. The more one earns, the more one's life is worth.

2. *Willingness to pay.* This may be determined in a couple of ways. Wage rates in risky occupations may be compared with those in less risky occupations. Wage differentials and differentials in the magnitude of risk involved are used to calculate a life's value. For example, if annual wages were $50 higher for a job that exposed someone to a 1 in 50,000 greater risk of death, that would yield a figure of $2.5 million.

The contingent valuation variant involves using surveys to determine how much people are willing to pay to reduce health risks. Based on their responses, a dollar value for life is assigned.

3. *Court case settlements.* Awards made by judges and juries in product liability and medical malpractice cases for the loss of life could be used to construct the value of a life. It must be noted, though, that these awards greatly vary in amount and that many potentially actionable cases of negligent deaths are not litigated.

4. *Individual appraisal.* Assuming that people are the best judges of their own self-interest, they might be surveyed on how much they would be willing to pay to avoid death. Alternatively, a person could be queried about how much he or she would accept in payment for his or her death. Whether this technique would yield much usable information is doubtful.

* This listing draws on Kenneth J. Meier, "The Limits of Cost-Benefit Analysis," in Lloyd G. Nigro, ed., *Decision-Making in Public Administration* (New York: Marcel-Dekker, 1984), pp. 43–63; and Thomas O. McGarity, *Reinventing Rationality: The Role of Regulatory Analysis in the Federal Bureaucracy* (New York: Cambridge University Press, 1991), Chap. 9.

Conservation Service and has been voluntarily employed by the Bureau of Reclamation. In the 1960s, cost–benefit analysis was first used in evaluating defense programs and then domestic programs as part of PPBS.

In the 1970s, Presidents Ford and Carter directed executive-branch regulatory agencies to prepare "inflation impact statements" and "regulatory analyses," respectively, in developing some proposed regulations. These statements involved analyzing their expected economic consequences. The Carter administration made it clear, however, that although regulatory agencies should consider the burdens and gains of proposed regulations, a cost–benefit test was not to be used in appraising them.[59]

A goal of the Reagan administration when it took office was to substantially reduce governmental regulation of private economic activity. People who were critical of the programs under their jurisdiction were appointed to regulatory positions. A second action involved issuing Executive Order 12291 in

February 1981,[60] which drew heavily upon the Carter administration's experience. The order required that proposed major regulations issued by executive-branch agencies (the independent regulatory commissions were exempt) must be accompanied by regulatory impact analyses assessing the potential benefits, costs, and net benefits of the regulations, including effects that could not be quantified in monetary terms, unless such calculations were prohibited by law. Some statutes ban the use of cost–benefit analysis for the programs they establish.

Major regulations were defined as those likely to have an annual impact on the economy of $100 million or more, to lead to major cost or price increases, or to have "significant adverse effects on competition, employment, investment, productivity, innovation, or the ability of U.S.-based enterprises to compete with foreign-based enterprises in domestic or export markets." The OMB was authorized to make the final determination of what was a major rule, to supervise the evaluation process, and to delay the issuance of proposed or final rules if it found the regulatory analyses were unsatisfactory.

Rules could be issued only if their estimated benefits exceeded their estimated costs. If a choice was available, the less costly alternative was to be selected. The burden of proof that this standard was met rested with the agency. An action by the OMB holding up a rule could be appealed to the President's Task Force on Regulatory Relief, which was staffed by the OMB and comprised several executive officials under the leadership of Vice President George Bush. (The word *relief* in the task force's title indicates its orientation.) Although the task force was phased out in 1983, all of this planning was intended to ensure, among other things, that "Regulatory Action shall not be undertaken unless the potential benefits to society for the regulation outweigh the potential costs to society." Thus, cost–benefit analysis was to be more than an analytical technique; it became a decision rule with a conservative bias.

The Reagan regulatory-analysis program was a center of controversy. Critics contended that it was used improperly to reduce the extent of regulation and to delay the issuance of rules rather than to improve the quality of regulations by encouraging better analysis. The OMB was also accused of improperly interfering in the regulatory process by usurping authority vested in the regulatory agencies. The administration denied such accusations. In practice, though, administration officials demonstrated much more vigilance about the costs than the benefits of regulation in trying to reduce the burden of regulatory activity on businesses.

The George Bush administration continued the regulatory-analysis program and in time created the Council on Competitiveness, an interagency committee chaired by Vice President Dan Quayle, to work with the OMB in perpetuating the use of cost–benefit analysis.[61] In the final two years of the George Bush administration, the Council on Competitiveness acted vigorously to represent the business community in the regulatory process and to reduce the number and strength of new regulations.[62] For the most part, it avoided publicity and sought to leave few "fingerprints."

The Clinton administration quickly abolished the Council on Competitiveness and later replaced Executive Order 12291 with its Executive Order 12866, entitled "Regulatory Planning and Review." The Clinton regulatory-review program continued to make use of cost–benefit analysis for major rules. Regulatory review, however, was conducted more openly and less stringently and intrusively than under the Reagan and George Bush administrations. Regulatory agencies experienced little to complain about.

The George W. Bush administration retained Clinton's executive order. The Office of Information and Regulatory Affairs (OIRA), however, now came under the direction of a true believer in cost–benefit analysis. Much of his activity at a university policy center had been funded by business corporations. In its first few months under the Bush administration, OIRA rejected twenty-one proposed regulations, more than had been turned down by the Clinton administration in eight years.[63] This was not surprising given the strongly conservative, antiregulation stance of the George W. Bush administration. OIRA continued for the next seven years to take a tough stance on proposed rules.

As the record here presented indicates, the uses of cost–benefit analysis, and presidential review of proposed regulations, have become regularized features of the regulatory process. They will continue under the Obama administration, albeit with softening modifications.[64] How they are implemented depends substantially upon the ideological leanings of a presidential administration. Clearly, cost–benefit analyses is a malleable evaluation instrument.

Fairly used, cost–benefit analysis may contribute to rationality in the decision-making process by aiding in the identification and appraisal of alternatives, helping to identify impacts or consequences, and otherwise developing information and insights that will assist persons in making reflective, well-considered decisions. A careful appraisal of the likely costs and benefits of a proposed action, and of the persons and groups upon whom they will fall, is certainly useful, regardless of whether all are converted into dollar figures, and without converting cost–benefit analysis into a decision rule.

Cost–benefit analysis, however, is open to manipulation to support the values and preferences of its users. In the instance of Executive Order 12291, because of the stoutly antiregulatory orientation of its implementers, it became a form of partisan political analysis dressed up as regulatory rationality.[65] Again, it is doubtful that the Army Corps of Engineers has ever been unable to undertake a rivers-and-harbors project that its officials really wanted to construct because a favorable cost–benefit analysis could not be contrived.

Policy evaluation, as our discussion indicates, is more than a technical or objective analytical process; it is also a political process. In the next section, a case study of the Head Start program illustrates how political factors can affect the conduct and results of an evaluation of a social program. The case also demonstrates that such evaluations, even when intended to be neutral or objective in form, become political because they can affect allocation of resources.

| CASE STUDY | *The Politics of Evaluation: Head Start* |

CASE STUDY *The Politics of Evaluation: Head Start*

In January 1965, President Lyndon Johnson announced that a preschool program named Head Start would be initiated as part of the Community Action Program (CAP) authorized by the Economic Opportunity Act of 1964. The Head Start program, which was designed to help overcome the effects of poverty on the educational achievement of poor children, included early classroom education, nutritional benefits, parent counseling, and health services.

Initially, $17 million in CAP funds was earmarked for summer 1965 to enable 100,000 children to participate in Head Start. The announcement of the program, however, produced requests for a much larger volume of funds from many localities. Officials in the Office of Economic Opportunity (OEO), who had jurisdiction over the program, decided to meet this demand. Ultimately, $103 million was committed to provide places for 560,000 children. To say the least, the Head Start program was highly popular, undoubtedly because it directed attention to poor preschool children, who readily aroused the public's sympathy, and to the goal of equal opportunity.

Late in the summer of 1965, Head Start became a permanent part of the antipoverty program. According to President Johnson, Head Start had been "battle-tested" and "proven worthy." It was expanded to a full-year program. In fiscal year 1968, $330 million was allocated to provide places for 473,000 children in summer programs and another 218,000 in full-year programs, making Head Start the largest component of the CAP. Essentially, Head Start was a multifaceted program for meeting the needs of poor children. More than a traditional nursery school or kindergarten program, it was designed also to provide poor children with physical- and mental-health services and nutritious meals to improve their diet. Further, an effort was made to involve members of the local community in the operation of the program.

With this background, let us turn to evaluation of the program.[66] The OEO was among the agency leaders in efforts to evaluate social programs because of statutory requirements. Within the agency the task of evaluating its programs for overall effectiveness was assigned to the Office of Research, Plans, Programs, and Evaluations (RPP&E). Some early efforts had been made to evaluate the effectiveness of Head Start, mostly by Head Start officials and involving particular projects, but by mid-1967, no solid evidence was available on overall program effectiveness. This lack was beginning to trouble OEO officials, the Bureau of the Budget, and some members of Congress.

The Evaluation Division of RPP&E, as part of a series of national evaluations of OEO programs, proposed an ex post facto study design for Head Start in which former Head Start children currently in the first, second, and third grades of school would be given a series of cognitive and affective tests. Their test scores would then be compared with those of a control group who had not been in the Head Start program. The Evaluation Division believed such a design would yield results more quickly than a longitudinal study that, although more desirable, would take longer to complete. (A longitudinal study examines the effect over a period of time of a program on a given group.)

Within the OEO, Head Start officials opposed the proposed study on various grounds, including its design, the test instruments to be used, and the focus on only the educational aspect of the program to the neglect of its other goals—health, nutrition, and community involvement. The RPP&E evaluators acknowledged the multiplicity of Head Start goals but contended that cognitive improvement was its primary goal. They agreed with Head Start officials that there were risks in making a limited study, such as possibly misleading negative results, but insisted that the need for evaluative data necessitated taking the risks. In the wake of much internal debate, the OEO director decided the study should be made, and in June 1968 a contract was entered into with the Westinghouse Learning Corporation and Ohio University. The study was conducted in relative quiet, but hints of its negative findings began to surface as it neared completion.

Early in 1969, a White House staff official became aware of the Westinghouse study and requested information on it because the president was preparing an address on the Economic Opportunity Act that would include a discussion of Head Start. In response to the request, OEO officials reported the preliminary negative findings of the study. In his message to Congress on economic opportunity on February 19, 1969, President Nixon referred to the study, commenting that "the preliminary reports…confirm what many have feared: the long-term effect of Head Start appears to be extremely weak." He went on to say that "this must not discourage us" and spoke well of the program. Nonetheless, his speech raised substantial doubts about Head Start among many observers in the public arena.

The president's speech also touched off considerable pressure for release of the study's findings. The OEO officials were reluctant to do this because what had been delivered to them by Westinghouse was a preliminary draft intended for use in deciding such matters as what additional statistical tests were needed and what data required reanalysis. From Congress, where hearings were being held on OEO legislation, claims were made that the study was being held back to protect Head Start and that the report was going to be rewritten. The pressure on the White House became sufficiently great that it directed the OEO to make the study public by April 14. A major conclusion of the report was that the full-year Head Start program produced a statistically significant but absolutely slight improvement in participant children.

The release of the report set off a flood of criticism from Head Start proponents, including many academicians, directed at the methodological and conceptual validity of the report. A sympathetic article on the front page of *The New York Times* bore the headline "HEAD START REPORT HELD 'FULL OF HOLES.'" Much of the ensuing controversy focused on the statistical methods used in the study and involved a broad range of claims, charges, rebuttals, and denials. The proponents of Head Start seemed to fear that their program was being victimized by devious intent. This fear had several facets. One was that persons within the OEO who favored Community Action over Head Start wanted a study that would spotlight Head Start's deficiencies. Another was that the administration was going to use the findings to justify a major cutback in Head Start. Finally, there was the fear that "enemies of the program" in Congress would use the negative results as an excuse for attacking it. Although there later appeared to have been little factual basis for these fears, they were real to the proponents of Head Start and contributed to the intensity of their assault on the evaluation study.

The methodological conflict that arose over the study focused on such standard items as sample size, validity of the control group, and appropriateness of the tests given to the children. An examination of these matters would be too lengthy and too technical to include here. An assessment of the study by liberal economist Walter Williams, however, provides a balanced view of the controversy:

> In terms of its methodological and conceptual base, the study is a relatively good one. This in no way denies that many of the criticisms made of the study are valid. However, for the most part, they are the kinds of criticisms that can be made of most pieces of social science research conducted outside the laboratory, in a real-world setting, with all of the logistical and measurement problems that such studies entail. And these methodological flaws open the door to the more political issues. Thus, one needs not only to examine the methodological substance of the criticisms which have been made of the study, but also to understand the social concern which lies behind them as well. Head Start has elicited national sympathy and has had the support and involvement of the educational profession. It is understandable that so many should rush to the defense of such a popular and humane program. But how many of the concerns over the size of the sample, control-group equivalency, and the appropriateness of covariance analysis, for example, would have been registered if the study had found positive differences in favor of Head Start? We imagine that this type of positive, but qualified assessment will fit any relatively good evaluation for some time to come. We have never seen a field evaluation of a social action program that could not be faulted legitimately by good methodologists, and we may never see one.[67]

Interestingly, the findings of the Westinghouse study were as favorable to Head Start as were the earlier evaluations of specific projects made by Head Start officials. These, too, showed that the program had limited lasting effects on the children. What the Westinghouse study, and the controversy over it, did was to inject these findings into the public arena and expand the scope of the conflict over them.

Despite the essentially negative evaluations of its accomplishments, the Westinghouse report recommended that Head Start be preserved and improved, at least partly on the ground that "something must be tried here and now to help the many children of poverty who may never be helped again." Head Start was, and is, a politically popular program. Congress and the executive have generally been favorably disposed toward the program, and it has suffered little of the criticism directed at other aspects of the antipoverty program. Children are a potent symbol in policy conflicts.

Ten years after the Westinghouse study was made public, the findings of another group of researchers on the long-term effects of Head Start were published by the Department of Health, Education, and Welfare. Based on a series of longitudinal studies, this study concluded that Head Start had significant, long-lasting social and educational benefits for its participants. Thus, children who had been in the program had much less need for remedial classes, were less likely to be retained in grade, and were half as likely to drop out of high school as were adolescents of comparable age who had not been in the program.[68] As a consequence, Head Start was now hailed as a success by the communications media. Why the substantial difference in findings by the two evaluations? The explanation rests primarily with the different methodological approaches. The Westinghouse study, using an experimental design, focused on short-run effects, especially as measured by intelligence-test scores. The second study focused on long-range effects.

In 1981, Head Start was designated part of President Reagan's "social safety net," which provided assistance to the "truly needy," and thus was not tagged for cutbacks in funding, as were several other programs that provided aid to poor people. In 1988, approximately 450,000 children were enrolled in Head Start, which now operated year-round, at a cost of $1.2 billion. Only about a quarter of the eligible children were actually enrolled in the program, however. Head Start continued to expand under subsequent administrations.

Research studies on the benefits of Head Start and early-childhood education have continued to yield inconclusive findings. Children who go through Head Start are found to have improved cognitive abilities, greater self-esteem, and improved social skills. On the other hand, various studies report that gains in academic achievement are not lasting. After a few years, when Head Start children are compared with non-Head Start children, the educational gains fade away.[69]

A major evaluation of Head Start published in the *American Economic Review* in 1995 illustrates these mixed findings.[70] Using longitudinal data for a sample of nearly 5,000 children, the evaluators examined the impact of Head Start on cognitive achievement, school performance (whether a child repeated one or more grades), utilization of preventive medical care, and health and nutritional status. Children who had been enrolled in Head Start were compared with their siblings who either had been enrolled in other preschool programs or had had no preschool experiences.

The evaluation found that Head Start had positive and persistent effects on the cognitive achievement and school performance of white children. In contrast, although there were positive effects on the cognitive achievement of African-American children, these effects soon disappeared. No positive effects were found on the school performance of African-American children. For both white and African-American children, Head Start had a positive effect on preventive health care, as measured by measles immunization rates. For neither did it have an impact on health and nutritional status, as measured by conformity with national height-for-age norms.

The results of evaluation studies have not lessened the political popularity of the Head Start program, and it has drawn bipartisan support from Congress and the executive. The program came up for renewal in 2003. The George W. Bush administration wanted to give the states more control over the program, to require standardized testing for four- and five-year-old enrollees in math and reading, and to permit faith-based Head Start providers to base hiring decisions on religious preference.[71] These proposals drew strong opposition from congressional Democrats and the National Head Start Association. No legislation was passed until 2007 when Congress, now under Democratic control, was able to break the impasse. The contested provisions were eliminated, eligibility for participation in the program was expanded, and increased funding for the program was authorized. Also, the legislation sought to improve the quality of Head Start teachers and to strengthen program accountability.[72]

Evaluations of Head Start continue to be done, and they continue collectively to yield inconclusive or divergent results. Supporters and critics of the program alike can search the many studies and find evidence to buttress their conclusions. Clearly, though, there is evidence here for the belief that policy evaluation is not an exact science.[73]

Head Start is perceived as a way to provide educational and social services to the truly needy—children in economically distressed families. Most Head Start families have annual incomes of less than $15,000. Perhaps, too, as many believe, the success of Head Start will lead to future reduced expenditures for other programs—those dealing with welfare, juvenile delinquency, and criminal justice, for example.

In 2012 Head Start had a budget of $8 billion and enrolled more than 900,000 children.[74] Nonetheless, hundreds of thousands of eligible children remained outside the program. ∎

Policy Termination

As noted in the preceding section, the evaluation and appraisal of a policy, dissatisfaction with its costs and consequences, and the development and expansion of political opposition may produce a variety of responses to it, including termination. Policies are only one set of targets for termination. Others are programs (e.g., the rural abandoned-mine program), projects (e.g., the cross-Florida barge canal), and agencies. More than half of the states, for example, have enacted sunset laws, which require the legislature to renew periodically the authorization for administrative agencies. If this is not done, agencies are automatically abolished. The termination of an agency, however, may mean only that its programs are shifted elsewhere.

Another possibility is that an abolished agency may be replaced by one or more new agencies. When the Interstate Commerce Commission, which had been established in 1887 to handle railroad regulation, was ended in 1997, its place was taken by the Surface Transportation Board. By then many of the duties of the ICC had been eliminated. Following the Deepwater Horizon disaster in April 2010, the Minerals Management Service, which many viewed as the captive of the petroleum industry, was terminated. In its stead appeared the Bureau of Safety and Environmental Enforcement, in charge of permits, inspections, and safety matters; the Bureau of Ocean Energy Management, to handle leasing, review development plans, and look after renewable energy; and the Office of Natural Resources Revenue, to take care of financial matters.

The focus here is on policies. Most of us can readily identify a number of government policies that we regard as wasteful, unnecessary, or inappropriate because they offend our ideological inclinations. Others, however, may not share our beliefs and instead may view these same policies as necessary and desirable, perhaps needing some change or improvement, but on the whole worth keeping. Perhaps these people directly benefit from the policies. Or their ideology may inform them that such policies are laudable uses of governmental power. Just as most policies arise out of conflict, so too there will be disagreement over their worth and retention.

If criticism of and opposition to a policy become sufficiently strong so that the policy-makers feel impelled to take action, a policy is more likely to be altered than terminated. An effort may be made to strengthen the policy to make it more effective, or portions of it that appear especially ineffective or offensive may be pruned away. This sort of adjustment is illustrated by the conversion of the Comprehensive Employment and Training Act of 1973 into the Job Training Partnership Act of 1982. Alterations were made in the administration of job training, and the public-employment program was jettisoned. Several years ago, the tobacco price-support program was separated from the general farm bill, and much of its cost was shifted to the private sector in order to save it; but only for a while. It later bit the dust.

Policy termination is difficult to accomplish for a number of reasons. Policies come into being because they have political support, and they typically retain some or all of that support. Though they may be few, the supporters of a policy or program probably will be strongly committed to it and may intensely resist change and ignore contrary evidence. The U.S. Army did not eliminate the horse cavalry until World War II, even though the cavalry had been obsolete for years because of military reliance on weapons such as the machine gun and rapid-fire artillery.[75] Some army officials could not comprehend an effective fighting force without the horse cavalry, reality to the contrary. The Tea Board consisted of three tea-tasters whose task was to ensure the quality of imported tea. Since its establishment late in the nineteenth century, it survived several efforts to abolish it, finally succumbing in 1996 after a U.S. senator from Nevada made its termination a personal cause, thereby saving the government a whopping $200,000 a year.[76]

The critics and opponents of a policy may be less intense in their feelings and may be both somewhat disorganized and diverse in their interests as well. It may also be quite difficult to weld together a coalition of sufficient strength to repeal a policy. The Tea Board was like a sitting duck. Some potential opponents of a policy may be most interested in preserving their own favored policies, and thus an attitude of "live and let live" may prevail. An intense minority often prevails over an indifferent majority in the democratic political process.

Within Congress, with its fragmented and dispersed power structures, those with jurisdiction over a policy are more likely than not to be its friends and supporters. They can then use their committee or subcommittee positions to protect the policy against attack, to fend off or stifle unwanted changes, and to block its termination, should that be proposed. Governmental structure favors those seeking to retain policies, just as it once favored those opposing their enactment. There is perhaps a rough equity in this arrangement.

Termination, moreover, is a severe action with unpleasant and negative connotations.[77] It has an undertone of admitting failure. Unpleasant consequences may ensue when a policy is terminated: people may suffer lost income and jobs, prices for services or products may increase, and communities may decline. Ill will and other political costs may be entailed. Most public officials thus prefer to be involved in creating new or better policies rather than terminating the old.

Although these factors may make policy termination controversial and difficult, successful termination does occasionally happen. Here are some terminated policies and their dates of demise.

Fair-trade legislation (1975). This legislation, adopted during the 1930s, permitted manufacturers of trademarked or brand-named products to set mandatory minimum resale prices for their products. It was intended to help small businesses. Over the years fair trade had become a tired, worn-out policy whose time had passed. Little support for it remained, and it was easily repealed.

Commercial airline regulation (1978). Almost all economic (but not safety) regulation was eliminated by the Airline Deregulation Act, the first major victory of the deregulation movement that began in the 1970s. Many policymakers became convinced, partly as a consequence of a multitude of policy studies, that market forces would more effectively control the airlines and protect the interests of users than would regulation.

Regulation of petroleum prices (1980). This policy, which always had much opposition, came into being as a consequence of the energy crisis in the 1970s. Difficult to administer, it was intended to prevent domestic oil companies from unduly profiting from high world oil prices. Its elimination in preference for market prices was coupled with a windfall-profits tax (see later discussion).

Synthetic-fuels research (1985). This policy was another product of the energy crisis. A costly program intended to develop commercial synthetic fuels as a substitute for fossil fuels, it had accomplished little by the time of its elimination, partly because of the length of time needed to get complex developmental projects underway. By 1985, the energy crisis and memories of it had ebbed, and the Reagan administration wanted more reliance on the market.

Revenue sharing (1986). Adopted during the Nixon administration, revenue sharing channeled billions of dollars annually to state and local governments, with few strings attached, partly to encourage them to be more creative in dealing with public problems. Large federal budget deficits were the ultimate reason for its termination, although congressional opposition to revenue sharing was always considerable.

Crude-Oil Windfall Profits Tax Act (COWPTA) (1986). Enacted in 1980, COWPTA was the price the petroleum industry reluctantly paid for oil-price deregulation, which permitted domestic oil prices to rise. From 30 to 70 percent of the windfall, the difference between the selling (or market) price of oil and a specified base price, was taxed away. A phaseout of the tax was to begin in January 1988, if $227 billion in revenue had been collected, or within one month following the collection of that amount, but in any event, no later than January 1991.

The price of oil, however, fell in the mid-1980s, and the tax ceased to produce revenue. An industry-supported effort to repeal the act failed in 1986. Success finally came in 1988, when a repeal provision was included in the Omnibus Trade and Competitiveness Act to pick up or solidify votes for that legislation. Time and events had thus made the windfall tax symbolic and readily expendable.

Agricultural production controls (1996). Restrictions on the production of many farm commodities had been a prominent feature of farm programs since their inception in the early 1930s. They had long drawn criticism from Republicans, conservatives, and some farm groups. Most production controls were terminated by the Federal Agricultural Improvement and Reform Act (FAIR Act), also called "Freedom to Farm," pushed through by the new Republican majorities in Congress. However, generous subsidies to enhance farm incomes were continued.

Glass-Steagall Act (1999). A 1935 response to the Great Depression, this act created bank deposit insurance and provided for the separation of investment and commercial banking. Banking deposit insurance became widely accepted; however, as the decades passed, the separation of investment and commercial banking came under increasing attack as an unnecessary hindrance to the financial business. Repealed in 1998, this action contributed to the financial crisis of 2007–2009.

Farm price support program for tobacco (2004). Put in place in 1938, the tobacco program used marketing quotas (mandatory limits on production) and nonrecourse loans to boost prices. Tobacco growers, worried about falling demand and lower prices for tobacco, and anti-smoking forces long opposed to the tobacco program, advocated its demise. A ten-billion-dollar buyout program for quota owners and tobacco growers helped gain their support. Many of those who were bought out ceased to grow tobacco.[78] Now anyone, wherever located, can grow and sell as much tobacco as they choose.

As these examples indicate, a number of factors may contribute to the termination of policies. A short list includes ideology, the urge to economize, altered political conditions, and clear policy failure. Systematic evaluation played a major role only in airline deregulation. Evaluators (mostly economists) over time were able to gather substantial evidence on the shortcomings of airline rate and route regulation and to effectively portray market regulation as an effective and satisfactory alternative. Most commonly, however, systematic evaluation has not been a critical element in policy termination.

Indeed, to emphasize a point made earlier, evaluation is more likely to reinitiate the policy sequence. Problems that emerge or become more intense during the implementation of a policy may be identified, alternatives for change or improvement may be formulated and debated, and so on, until perhaps the policy is modified in some fashion. It is also possible, of course, that those responsible for implementing a policy will act to make it more acceptable to complaining groups, as by speeding up the issuance of licenses or cracking down on certain kinds of law violations. Policy change, whether legislative or administrative in origin, is more likely to occur than policy termination.

CASE STUDY | *The Policy Cycle: Airline Regulation and Deregulation*

A case study of a public policy from its inception to its termination is an appropriate way to end a discussion of the policy process. National economic regulation of commercial airline service formally extended from 1938 to 1978, when deregulation legislation was adopted. Other forms of government involvement with the airlines—safety and air-traffic movement, security, airport operations, and financial assistance—continue. Laissez-faire did not come to the airlines after 1978, nor did they want it. This case study gives the reader an overall view of the policy cycle and an opportunity to identify and fit together the various phases of the policy cycle. It will also contribute to an understanding of why public policy on the airlines is what it is today, which is an interesting story in itself.

It is said that "policymaking is an extremely complex process without beginning or end." Complex it indeed usually is. However, one can fairly effectively date the beginning and end of policies like that of the Civil Aeronautics Act. To comprehend commercial airline regulation, one does not need to go back in time to Icarus's ill-fated flight or even the activities of the Wright brothers. The 1930s will do nicely. Economic regulation of the airlines ended with the implementation of the Airline Deregulation Act. Should dissatisfaction with conditions under deregulation lead to the reimposition of regulation, that would be another chapter in airline regulation, another cycle of the policy process, and reasonably distinct from the 1938–1978 era.

The American air-transportation industry began with the Air Mail Act of 1925, which authorized the Post Office Department to use competitive bidding to award air-mail contracts to private airlines.[79] Government payments to the airlines often exceeded the revenue produced by air mail. Nonetheless, many airlines suffered operating losses, and the possibility or abandonment of services arose. New legislation increasing the level of air-mail subsidies was adopted in 1930. Because passenger service was just beginning to catch on in the 1930s, carrying the mail continued to be a major source of revenues for the airlines. As a consequence of the Great Depression, by the mid-1930s, the airlines were once again in financial distress, and again there emerged a demand for favorable government action to bail them out.

It was widely agreed among industry and governmental officials that there was a need for new economic and safety regulation. Because it appeared that there were more airlines than could be supported by available revenues, it was feared that unregulated competition among the many small companies making up the industry would degenerate into "destructive competition." The airlines themselves were united in favor of restrictive legislation. Between 1934 and 1938, the enactment of legislation was delayed by problems in resolving two issues: whether regulation should be handled by the Interstate Commerce Commission, which was the position of President Franklin Roosevelt, or by a new independent commission, and whether the same agency should administer both economic and safety regulation. These issues were finally resolved by the Civil Aeronautics Act of 1938, which passed Congress by substantial majorities.[80] We will trace its history here.

The Civil Aeronautics Act, as modified by a 1940 presidential executive order, established the Civil Aeronautics Board (CAB) to handle economic regulation and the Civil Aeronautics Authority (CAA) in the Department of Commerce to administer safety regulation, to control air traffic, and to maintain a national airway system of guidance systems, airports, and the like.

In 1956, the collision of two passenger planes over the Grand Canyon led to questions about the adequacy of air-traffic control and safety regulation.[81] In response, Congress enacted the Federal Aviation Act of 1958, which replaced the CAA with a new independent agency, the Federal Aviation Administration (FAA), which was given a strengthened air-safety mandate. The FAA later became a unit in the Department of Transportation and continues to be responsible for air-traffic control and safety. We will not deal further with it in this case study.

The CAB, an independent regulatory commission, was headed by a five-member board serving six-year, staggered terms of office. Appointed by the president with senatorial consent, no more than a majority of the board members could come from the same political party. The CAB was authorized to regulate entry into the commercial airline industry by the issuance of certificates of "public convenience and necessity," which were also used to determine the particular routes that an air carrier could serve. The abandonment of service also required CAB approval. Airline rates had to be "just and reasonable" and could be changed by the CAB if it found them unjust or unreasonable because they were too high or too low. The CAB was also authorized to administer air-mail payments and operating subsidies. The act "grandfathered" the existing sixteen air trunk lines (carriers providing service between major cities) into the business. No new trunk lines were subsequently admitted to the industry by the CAB during the next forty years. This was often cited as a shortcoming of the airline regulatory system.

The Civil Aeronautics Act's declaration of policy directed the CAB to use its authority to "foster sound economic conditions" in air transportation; to promote "adequate, economical, and efficient service by air carriers at reasonable charges"; to ensure "competition to the extent necessary to assure the development of an air-transportation system properly adapted to the needs of the foreign and domestic commerce of the United States"; and, for good measure, to be concerned with the "promotion, encouragement, and development of civil aeronautics." Essentially, the act laid out a number of desirable objectives and then left to the CAB the choice of which ones it would emphasize. The agency's multiple mandate was a frequent target of critics.

Through its regulatory authority, the CAB significantly influenced the structure of the airline industry. Several categories of carriers were developed. The trunk carriers, whose numbers, through mergers, had been diminished to eleven by 1970, provided regularly scheduled service between major cities and accounted for the lion's share of passenger service. Local-service (or regional) carriers provided short-haul service between smaller cities (such as Piedmont and Ozark), and commuter airlines, operating small planes, provided service to places not reached by the larger carriers. The latter did not need prior CAB approval for their route and rate decisions. There were also all-cargo and charter airlines. A few intrastate airlines serving cities entirely within the boundaries of a single state also existed, and these were not subject to CAB regulation. The discussion here focuses on the trunk carriers.

During its forty years of existence, CAB regulatory policy fluctuated between pro- and anticompetitive tendencies, depending upon the economic situation of the airlines. When airline profits were high or "excessive," the CAB increased competitive route awards and encouraged the companies to reduce or discount airfares. Conversely, when profits were low, the CAB adopted an anticompetitive stance on new route awards and encouraged or approved fare increases to offset lower passenger traffic. Service competition—the frequency of flights, seating arrangements, food services, and other amenities—was left alone by the CAB. Barred from rate competition, airlines occasionally featured champagne flights and gourmet meals in their efforts to attract passengers. Both the airlines and the traveling public generally found the CAB's regulatory policies to be acceptable. Airline travel was mostly pleasant.

In the 1970s, a recession that reduced passenger traffic, rising fuel costs caused by the energy crisis, and inflation drove down airline earnings and propelled the CAB to take a strong anticompetitive position. A moratorium was imposed on the award of new airline routes, and substantial rate hikes were granted. Departing from previous policy, the agency also sought to discourage service competition. Further, a scandal erupted involving the CAB chair, who had accepted free trips and favors from the airlines.[82] Collectively, these events drew attention to the CAB; much criticism of the agency arose from both governmental and private sources. For many people it seemed clear that the CAB was the "captive" of the airlines, serving their interests rather than the public interest. The CAB, however, was not as fully under the sway of the airlines as the captive charge implied.

A number of studies conducted by economists in the 1960s and 1970s concluded that the CAB's policies protected inefficient airlines by preventing rate competition. The result was higher costs for the traveling public than would occur in an ideal competitive situation. This line of argument was supported, in turn, by other analyses comparing the operations of CAB-regulated interstate carriers with those of intrastate carriers in Texas and California that were not controlled by the CAB. The rates for the latter over similar routes were considerably lower.[83] Although these studies initially were generally ignored by the CAB and others, in time, they helped make deregulation a viable alternative to the CAB's regulatory regime.

In 1974 and 1975, airline regulation (and deregulation) reached the national policy agenda as a consequence of two sets of circumstances. First, in 1974, Senator Edward Kennedy (D, Massachusetts), chair of the Senate Judiciary Committee's Subcommittee on Administrative Practice and Procedure, decided to hold hearings on CAB regulation. These hearings, which actually took place in 1975, revealed much dissatisfaction with the CAB and publicized the large differential between the rates of CAB-regulated and nonregulated carriers.[84] There was no agreement on the specific direction that reform should take, however.

Second, in August 1974, Gerald Ford became president following the resignation of Richard M. Nixon. A conservative Republican, Ford took office confronted by double-digit inflation. Advised that government regulatory programs contributed to inflation by raising business costs and prices, Ford made regulatory reform part of his anti-inflation program. (This action also coincided with his dislike of big government.) Although there was not much public clamor for regulatory reform per se, inflation was an issue of high public salience. In October 1975, Ford sent an aviation regulatory reform bill to Congress that called for reduced CAB control of the airlines.

In 1977, Jimmy Carter replaced Ford as president. Although he had not said much about it while campaigning, Carter quickly made airline deregulation a high-priority item in his legislative program. Rather than introduce its own bill, however, the Carter administration chose to support legislation that was already being considered in Congress, hoping thereby to secure a quick and easy legislative victory. Carter officials also stressed the relationship between regulation and inflation. (In actuality, because they constituted such a small portion of gross domestic product, airfares set at the zero level would have had miniscule effect on inflation.)

In the Senate, Kennedy and Howard Cannon (D, Nevada), chair of the Subcommittee on Aviation of the Senate Commerce Committee, became the sponsors of a bill titled the Air Transportation Regulatory Reform Act. Not initially a supporter of aviation regulatory reform, Cannon at first had been irritated by Kennedy's hearings. However, he shifted his position and became a supporter of reform rather than be left behind by the surge for reform.

The Kennedy-Cannon bill provided for increased competition in the airline industry by making it easier for carriers to obtain authorization to serve new routes and giving them substantial leeway in setting fares. Other provisions authorized subsidies for small-community air service and compensation for airline employees suffering wage reductions or unemployment because of increased competition. These provisions were designed to counteract some of the opposition to regulatory reform, which we will discuss later in this section. The reform legislation under consideration in the House, where there was difficulty in getting agreement on a bill, was weaker than the Senate bill.

Supporting and opposing coalitions emerged.[85] Among the supporters of reform were several government agencies full of economists, including the Council on Wage and Price Stability, the Council of Economic Advisors, the Federal Trade Commission, and the Antitrust Division; many consumer groups; Ralph Nader; most economists; and such conservative groups as the American Farm Bureau Federation, the National Federation of Independent Business, and the National Association of Manufacturers. Also supporting reform was United Airlines, which believed that it had been unfairly treated by the CAB in its route decisions. The supporters of reform argued that greater competition would benefit both passengers and airlines. The former would get lower fares while the greater volume of passenger traffic these generated would yield larger profits for the airlines.

Opponents of reform comprised most of the larger scheduled airlines and their trade organization, the Air Transportation Association; airline employees' unions; and organizations representing the interests of airport operators and small communities. Diverse interests drew them together. The air carriers feared that major changes in CAB rate and route regulation would lead to "cutthroat competition" and instability in the industry. The unions saw deregulation as a threat to job security wage levels, and their status as employee representatives. Some airport operators were concerned that deregulation would mean reduced business, and small communities and rural states fretted about the possible reduction or total loss of air service.

At this point we need to pick up another facet of the deregulation story. In the course of a few years in the mid-1970s, the CAB was transformed into a leading proponent of deregulation. The change began with President Ford's appointment of John Robson in mid-1975 to chair the agency. Under Robson's leadership, the CAB began to review its regulatory policies and to shift to a more procompetitive position. Robson also testified before Congress concerning the need to replace the current aviation regulatory regime. This came as a surprise to many people.

The pace of change within the CAB accelerated in June 1977 when Carter appointee Alfred Kahn, a Cornell University economics professor, replaced

Robson as CAB chair. He was soon joined by economist Elizabeth Bailey as a board member. Kahn moved quickly to fill key CAB staff positions with supporters of deregulation. Then, under his skillful direction, various actions were taken to substantially reduce CAB control of airline rate and route decisions so as to increase competition in the industry. For instance, it was made much easier for airlines to obtain new routes and to initiate or terminate service on unprofitable routes at their own discretion. In all likelihood, some of the CAB initiatives violated the Federal Aviation Act (which had replaced the Civil Aeronautics Act).[86] Indeed, one airline sued the CAB in federal court, alleging that the agency had failed to meet its responsibilities under the act.

This administrative deregulation increased the odds in favor of the enactment of reform legislation for two reasons. First, the CAB itself was rapidly implementing many of the reforms proposed in the legislation being considered by Congress. Second, airline profits increased in 1977 and 1978. Whether because of the CAB's policy changes or improved economic conditions, this reduced the resistance of the airlines to regulatory reform. In fact, their opposition largely collapsed by the end of summer 1978.[87]

The Senate passed its version of airline regulatory reform in April 1978, but the House was not able to complete action on its bill until September. Included in the House bill was a provision calling for the termination of the CAB at the end of 1983. Initially included in a substitute bill by a strong advocate of "sunset review" (the periodic evaluation of agencies to determine whether they should be continued), it was incorporated in the final House bill as a concession to deregulation supporters in exchange for making milder reductions in CAB regulatory authority than in the Senate bill.[88] In the Conference Committee, however, the House yielded to most of the Senate's stronger reform provisions. The bill, now titled the Airline Deregulation Act, was passed by both houses and signed into law by President Jimmy Carter. "For the first time in decades," he said, "we have deregulated a major industry."[89]

The Airline Deregulation Act initially made it easier for airlines to enter new routes and gave them flexibility in setting fares. It provided for continuation of "essential air transportation service" to smaller communities, with subsidies to ensure such service, for ten years. Compensation was authorized for a maximum of six years for airline employees who lost their jobs, had their pay reduced, or were forced to relocate because of competition engendered by the act. Then, what is most significant, the act set forth a deregulation schedule. Unless Congress decided otherwise, the CAB's authority over domestic routes would end on December 31, 1981; its authority over domestic rates and fares would expire on January 1, 1983; and the board itself would be abolished on January 1, 1985. Its remaining authority would then be transferred to the Departments of Transportation and Justice and the U.S. Postal Service. All of this happened on the specified dates.

The Airline Deregulation Act marked a basic change in public policy on commercial airlines, a shift from detailed administrative regulations to reliance on the market and competition to control their economic behavior. It ran directly counter to the theory of economic regulation, which holds that "regulation is acquired by the industry and is designed and operated primarily for its benefit."[90] Although that theory is a plausible, but not fully convincing, explanation for the Civil Aeronautics Act of 1938, it is simply not applicable to airline deregulation (or to trucking and railroad deregulation either, for that matter), which was strongly opposed by most of the industry until there was little doubt that strong deregulatory legislation would be adopted.

What, then, accounts for the Airline Deregulation Act? Martha Derthick and Paul Quirk provide a good explanation.[91] First, there was wide support for deregulation in the academic world and in the political sphere. "Procompetitive reform...proved to have a broad appeal, engaging liberals (led by Senator Edward M. Kennedy), who stressed the benefits of lower prices for consumers and an end to government protection of business, and conservatives (led by President Gerald R. Ford), who stressed the benefits of reducing the burdens of government regulation in private markets."[92] Second, many public officials in leadership positions—presidents, committee chairs, CAB chairs—were advocates of deregulation. Third, much deregulation would have occurred even had Congress not acted because of the CAB, which, whatever its history, demonstrated in the mid-1970s that it was not the captive of the airlines.

Fourth, strong majorities in Congress, despite the opposition of most of the airlines, supported aviation regulatory reform. They acted not only in response to executive and legislative leadership but also out of a desire to produce policy that responded to public concerns about inflation and intrusive government. Fifth, economists and other policy analysts had produced myriad studies that portrayed reliance on the market and competition as a viable alternative to economic regulation. This was in line with the old adage that "you can't beat something with nothing."

Finally, the airline industry was unable to maintain a united front in opposition to major regulatory change. First United defected. Then other airlines split off, especially as the CAB's removal of controls accelerated. Finally, airline opposition collapsed, leaving the way open for Congress to enact sweeping deregulation legislation.

What has happened in the airline industry since 1978? Has airline deregulation been a success? The conventional wisdom says yes—air fares decreased initially, and competition on air routes increased. The record, however, is not that clear. Some developments in the airline industry and public policy are reported here. Whether they are all the direct consequence of deregulation is uncertain.

Following deregulation, many new airlines entered the industry, but within a few years almost all of them had either failed or been absorbed by major airlines. In the 1990s, a second wave of new carriers (e.g., Allegiant, Kiwi, Reno, JetBlue) entered the industry. Each, however, accounts for a miniscule portion of airline traffic. Some of them also have failed.

The control of domestic air travel has become more oligopolistic. Most major airlines in existence in 1978 (Braniff, Eastern, Pan American, Trans

World, National) have vanished because of bankruptcy or merger.[93] In 1999, the seven largest companies carried 89 percent of air passengers.[94] Afflicted by economic adversity, the airlines turned to concentration through merger as the remedy for their problems. Northwest's attempted takeover of Continental and a proposed United–U.S. Airways merger were stymied by the Justice Department.

However, in 2008 a merger of Delta and Northwest gained Justice Department (DOJ) approval, creating the then world's largest airline. Justice contended that it would produce "efficiencies" that would benefit consumers and would probably not "substantially lessen competition." This consolidation was followed by mergers of United-Continental (2010) and Southwest-Airtran (2011). Then, in early 2013, American Airlines proposed to merge with U.S. Airways, which would have yielded a new world's largest airline. This proposed merger hit a snag months later when DOJ's Antitrust Division moved to block it as anti-competitive and not in the best interest of consumers, who had been experiencing rising airfares and service fees since the prior mergers.[95] The outcome of this latest merger proposal is, therefore, uncertain. This can be said, however: the current oligopolistic airline industry is not what the proponents of airline deregulation promised.

The hub-and-spoke system, whereby flights from many "spoke" cities converge in a single "hub" city, has enabled one or two carriers to dominate service to and from most large cities. Thus, most of the passenger traffic moving through Atlanta is controlled by Delta.[96] United dominates traffic into and out of Houston, Chicago, and Denver. Through predatory rate-setting and provision of excess service, the airlines that dominate hub cities have been able to drive or keep most low-cost carriers out of their markets.

The picture concerning airfares is cloudy. Controlling for the effects on inflation, one study found that average passenger fares overall declined by nearly 25 percent between 1979 and 1989.[97] Many variations are concealed by averages, however. For instance, fares on long, highly traveled routes have declined whereas those on short, less-traveled routes have increased. Passengers at major airports dominated by one or two airlines pay substantially higher fares than do travelers leaving airports where more competition prevails.[98] Discount fares—such as for persons purchasing tickets fourteen to thirty days in advance and staying over Saturday night—enable leisure travelers to fly much more cheaply than business and other travelers who buy tickets on short notice and do not want to spend weekends away from home. The conditions attached to discount tickets, however, may create inconvenience for travelers.

Service also presents a mixed view. Much air travel has taken on the ambiance of intercity bus travel, especially for those flying in the economy or coach section. The number of seats and flights available to travelers has decreased, and the airplanes are more cramped and crowded. Meals on airlines are nonexistent and other amenities have been reduced. Fees for services or privileges have multiplied. Flight times on many routes have increased, as have delays.[99] Several members of Congress, responding to complaints about service and considering their personal experiences, have introduced bills providing for a passengers' "bill of rights." Nothing has come of these.

Since deregulation, and despite larger subsidies for local and commuter airlines under the Essential Air Service program ("temporary" when created in 1978), more than a hundred small cities have lost some or all of their air service or no longer receive jet service.[100] Despite fears that unregulated competition might cause airlines to skimp on costly maintenance and safety requirements, the safety of air travel appears to have improved.[101] A distinction here should be made between safety and security in air travel.

Some have called for a return of government regulation to address such matters as the domination of hub cities by particular carriers, deteriorating service, and sometimes-expensive and often-confusing airfares. Though such complaints have drawn some congressional attention and have found a low-level place on the agenda, the political climate has not presented a favorable setting for new regulatory programs.[102] On the other hand, when the declining financial situation of the airlines was exacerbated by a drop in air travel following the September 11 terrorist attacks, Congress quickly enacted a $15 billion bailout program of grants and loans. Some of the airlines, however, continued to have economic problems, including involvement in bankruptcy proceedings. Generally, the financial situation of airlines remains precarious.

More than three decades after its inception, what can be said concerning the success, or degree of success, of airline deregulation? This question presents a strong challenge for a policy evaluator. Obviously, competition, as measured by the number of competitors, has declined. So, also, has opportunity for choice. Beyond such concerns, what standards or criteria should be used? Some possibilities include levels of passenger fares, quality and convenience of service, and the economic condition and stability of the industry. How should these standards be measured? And their values compared? The deregulatory record does not permit easy responses to such questions. Whether airline deregulation has on balance been satisfactory calls for judgments based on careful review of the evidence and avoidance of ideological biases. Readers: Do you now find airline travel to be a pleasant experience?

Is airline deregulation here to stay, especially as the number of carriers decline? What would be required to restart the policy cycle? So far calls for "reregulation" have not produced action.[103] Would the development of a better, more extensive, rail passenger system be a good alternative? ■

For Further Exploration

▌ *http://www.brookings.org/*

The Brookings Institution, a moderate-to-liberal think tank, provides current, scholarly policy updates and briefs on both domestic-and foreign-policy issues.

▌ *http://www.gao.gov/*

The homepage of the Government Accountability Office provides users with access to evaluations of government programs and agency testimony before congressional committees.

▌ *http://www.urban.org/*

The Urban Institute's website provides a collection of recent reports evaluating social and economic policy problems from a more liberal perspective, along with discussing possible solutions to correct them.

Test Your Knowledge

Log on to the student companion website at

login.cengage.com

to access tutorial quizzes, chapter outlines, crossword puzzles, and glossary flashcards that review chapter concepts and terminology.

Suggested Readings

Amihai Glazer and Lawrence S. Rothenberg, *Why Government Succeeds and Why It Fails* (Cambridge, MA: Harvard University Press, 2001). Economic and political constraints that affect the success of government policies are discussed in this interesting study.

Anthony E. Brown, *The Politics of Airline Deregulation* (Knoxville, TN: University of Tennessee Press, 1987). This analytical study of the development, operation, and abolition of economic regulation of the airlines includes a discussion of deregulation strategies.

Carol H. Weiss, *Evaluation Research* (Englewood Cliffs, NJ: Prentice-Hall, 1972). This is a succinct and highly useful discussion of evaluation research methodology.

Mark R. Daniels, *Terminating Public Programs: An American Political Paradox* (Armonk, NY: M. E. Sharpe, 1997). Theory and practice in the termination of public policies and agencies are succinctly discussed in this monograph.

Roger W. Cobb and David M. Primo, *The Plane Truth: Airline Crashes, the Media, and Transportation Policy* (Washington, DC: Brookings Institution, 2003). Incorporated in this book is an evaluation of public policy pertaining to commercial airline safety.

Walter Williams, *Honest Numbers and Democracy: Social Policy Analysis in the White House, Congress, and the Federal Agencies* (Washington, DC: Georgetown University Press, 1998). Williams pulls no punches in this critical look at the partisan use of social policy analysis.

William T. Gormley and Steven J. Balla, *Bureaucracy and Democracy* (Washington, DC: CQ Press, 2004). This fine book surveys bureaucratic behavior, policymaking, performance, accountability, and more.

Notes

1. Charles L. Cochran and Eloise F. Malone, *Public Policies: Perspectives & Choices*, 2nd ed. (New York: McGraw-Hill, 1999), p. 52. See also Mark Bovens, Paul't Hart, and Sanneke Kuipers, "The Politics of Policy Evaluation," in Mickael Moran, Martin Rein, and Robert F. Goodin, *The Oxford Handbook of Public Policy* (New York: Oxford University Press, 2006), Chap. 15.
2. William T. Gormley Jr., *Taming the Bureaucracy* (Princeton, NJ: Princeton University Press, 1989), p. 5.
3. See Frances Fox Piven and Richard A. Cloward, *Regulating the Poor* (New York: Pantheon, 1971). Also Michael B. Katz, *The Undeserving Poor* (New York: Pantheon, 1989); and Paul Pierson, *Dismantling the Welfare State* (New York: Cambridge University Press, 1994).
4. Thomas R. Dye, *Understanding Public Policy*, 7th ed. (Englewood Cliffs, NJ: Prentice-Hall, 1992), pp. 354–358.
5. Denise Scheberle and Scott Furlong, "The Law of Unintended Consequences: Toward a Better Understanding of Why Laws Go Awry," *Comparative State Politics*, Vol. 19 (1998), pp. 17–38.
6. Simon Johnson and James Kwak, *13 Bankers: The Wall Street Takeover and the Next Financial Meltdown* (New York: Pantheon Books, 2010); and Richard A. Posner, *The Crisis of Capitalist Democracy* (Cambridge MA: Harvard University Press, 2010).
7. A discussion of externalities in public policy can be found in Randall G. Holcombe, *Public Sector Economics* (Belmont, CA: Wadsworth, 1988), Chap. 3.
8. Edith Stokey and Richard Zeckhauser, *A Primer for Policy Analysis* (New York: Norton, 1978), p. 152.
9. Roy J. Ruffin and Paul R. Gregory, *Principles of Economics*, 2nd ed. (Glenview, IL: Scott, Foresman, 1986), p. 734.
10. Gabriel A. Almond and G. Bingham Powell, *Comparative Politics: A Developmental Approach* (Boston, MA: Little, Brown, 1969), p. 199.
11. Charles M. Lamb and Eric M. Wilk, "Presidents, Bureaucracy, and Housing Discrimination Policy: The Fair Housing Acts of 1968 and 1988," *Politics & Policy*, Vol. 37 (February 2009), pp. 127–149; and Charles M. Lamb, *Housing Segregation in Suburban America since 1960: Presidential and Judicial Politics* (New York: Cambridge University Press, 2005).
12. Joseph L. Fisher, "Program Development Across Jurisdictional Lines," in Donald Bowen and Lynton K. Caldwell, eds., *Program Formulation and Development* (Bloomington, IN: Department of Government, Indiana University, 1960), p. 50.
13. The following discussion relies on Allen D. Putt and J. Fred Springer, *Policy Research: Concepts, Methods, and Applications* (Englewood Cliffs, NJ: Prentice-Hall, 1989), Chap. 11; and Carol H. Weiss, *Evaluation Research: Methods for Assessing Program Effectiveness* (Englewood Cliffs, NJ: Prentice-Hall, 1972), Chap. 4.

14. Laboratory experiments, which are also possible, are of a more artificial and contrived nature and have limited value.

15. Howard S. Bloom, "Lessons from the Delaware Dislocated Worker Pilot Program," *Evaluation Review*, Vol. II (1987), pp. 157–177. The quotation is on p. 157.

16. Ibid., p. 166.

17. Donald T. Campbell, "Reforms as Experiments," *American Psychologist*, Vol. 24 (April 1969), pp. 409–429. Although this study used time-series analysis, the focus here is on its comparative component.

18. Weiss, op. cit., p. 74.

19. Ibid., p. 14.

20. Stuart S. Nagel, *Public Policy: Goals, Means, and Concepts* (New York: St. Martin's, 1984), p. 414.

21. Richard I. Hofferbert, *The Reach and Grasp of Policy Analysis* (Tuscaloosa, AL: University of Alabama Press, 1990), p. 4.

22. R. Kent Weaver, "The Changing World of Think Tanks," *PS: Political Science and Politics*, Vol. 22 (September 1989), p. 567.

23. James Fallows, *Breaking the News: How the Media Undermine American Democracy* (New York: Pantheon, 1996).

24. John Stuart Mill, *Considerations on Representative Government* (New York: Liberal Arts Press, 1958). First published in 1861.

25. Leading studies of congressional oversight include Joel D. Aberbach, *Keeping a Watchful Eye* (Washington, DC: Brookings Institution, 1990); and Christopher J. Foreman Jr., *Signals from the Hill* (New Haven, CT: Yale University Press, 1988).

26. This discussion draws on Elmer B. Staats, "General Accounting Office Support of Committee Oversight," in Committee Organization in the House (panel discussion before the House Select Committee on Committees), 93rd Cong., 1st Sess. (1973), II, pp. 692–700. Staats was head of the GAO. See also Frederick C. Mosher, *A Tale of Two Agencies* (Baton Rouge, LA: Louisiana State University Press, 1984), Chap. 5.

27. General Accounting Office, *Food Safety and Quality: Uniform Risk-Based Inspection Systems Needed to Ensure Safe Food Supply* (Washington, DC: U.S. GAO, June 1992); Federal Food Safety and Security System: Fundamental Restructuring Is Needed to Address Fragmentation and Overlap (Washington, DC: U.S. GAO, March 2004); and Bioterrorism: A Threat to Agriculture and the Food Supply (Washington, DC: U.S. GAO, November 2003).

28. See, for example, Government Accountability Office, *Federal Oversight of Food Safety* (Washington, DC: U.S. Government Printing Office, January 2008).

29. Aliya Sternstein, "Food Safety: Stirring the Agency Mix," *CQ Weekly*, Vol. 66 (March 3, 2008), pp. 544–545.

30. Ranae Merle, "Lapses Spur Calls for Single Food-Safety Agency," *Bryan-College Station Eagle*, August 5, 2007, p. A4.

31. *The Tower Commission Report* (New York: Bantam Books, 1987).

32. George C. Edwards and Stephen J. Wayne, *Presidential Leadership: Politics and Policy-Making*, 3rd ed. (New York: St. Martin's, 1994), p. 441.

33. *The New York Times*, November 30, 2001, p. A17.

34. Charles O. Jones, *An Introduction to the Study of Public Policy* (Belmont, CA: Wadsworth, 1970), p. 118. Insight into the operation of a commission set up to appraise legislation regulating the political activities of public employees can be gained from Charles O. Jones, "Reevaluating the Hatch Act: A Report on the

Commission on Political Activity of Government Employees," *Public Administration Review*, XXIX (May–June 1969), pp. 249–254.

35. Donald Axelrod, *Budgeting for Modern Government*, 2nd ed. (New York: St. Martin's, 1988), Chap. 10, provides a succinct review of this reform effort.

36. Robert S. Kravchuk and Ronald W. Schack, "Designing Effective Performance Measurement Systems Under the Government Performance and Results Act of 1993," *Public Administration Review*, LVI (July–August 1996), pp. 348–358.

37. General Accounting Office, "Department of Education: Status of Achieving Key Outcomes and Addressing Major Management Challenges" (Washington, DC: U.S. Government Printing Office, June 2001), p. 5.

38. Ibid., pp. 6–15.

39. General Accounting Office, "Major Management Challenges and Program Risks: Environmental Protection Agency" (Washington, DC: U.S. Government Printing Office, January 2001), p. 8.

40. Allen Schick, The Federal Budget: Politics, Policy, Process, 3rd ed. (Washington, DC: Brooking Institution Press, 2007), p. 299.

41. William F. West, *Program Budgeting and the Performance Movement* (Washington, DC: Georgetown University Press, 2011), Chap. 6.

42. Carol H. Weiss, "The Politics of Impact Measurement," *Policy Studies Journal*, Vol. 1 (Spring 1973), pp. 180–181.

43. David H. Rosenbloom and Robert S. Kravchuk, *Public Administration*, 5th ed. (New York: McGraw-Hill, 2002), p. 319.

44. Edward R. Tufte, *Data Analysis for Politics and Policy* (Englewood Cliffs, NJ: Prentice-Hall, 1974), Chap. 1.

45. Charles F Bonser, Eugene B. McGregor, and Clinton V. Oster Jr., *Policy Choices and Public Action* (Upper Saddle River, NJ: Prentice-Hall, 1995), Chap. 12.

46. See Deborah Stone, *Policy Paradox: The Art of Political Decision Making*, rev. ed. (New York: Norton, 2002), Chap. 8.

47. See Kenneth J. Meier and E. Thomas Garman, *Regulation and Consumer Protection*, 2nd ed. (Houston: Dame Publications, 1995), Chap. 4.

48. 384 U.S. 436 (1966).

49. President's Commission on Law Enforcement and the Administration of Justice, *The Challenge of Crime in a Free Society* (Washington, DC: U.S. Government Printing Office, 1967), p. 305.

50. *Time*, Vol. 112 (July 18, 1988), p. 53.

51. Jeremy A. Lifsey "Politics, Evaluations and Manpower Programs." Unpublished paper presented at the Annual Meeting of the American Political Science Association (1973).

52. Carl V. Patton and David D. Sawicki, *Basic Methods of Policy Analysis and Planning*, 2nd ed. (Englewood Cliffs, NJ: Prentice-Hall, 1993), pp. 379–385.

53. Lester M. Salamon, "The Time Dimension in Policy Evaluation: The Case of the New Deal Land-Reform Experiments," *Public Policy*, XXVII (Spring 1979), pp. 129–184.

54. A. Myrick Freeman III, *Air and Water Pollution Control: A Benefit-Cost Assessment* (New York: Wiley, 1982).

55. For more extensive discussions of cost–benefit analysis, see Stokey and Zeckhauser, op. cit., Chap. 9; and David L. Weimer and Aidan R. Vining, *Policy Analysis: Concepts and Practice* (Englewood Cliffs, NJ: Prentice-Hall, 1989), Chap. 7.

56. Francis E. Rourke, *Bureaucracy, Politics, and Public Policy*, 3rd ed. (Boston, MA: Little, Brown, 1984), p. 176.
57. Weimer and Vining, op. cit., p. 15.
58. Seth Borenstein, "First Labeled Overweight, Now Overpriced," *Houston Chronicle*, July 11, 2008, p. A7.
59. See Thomas O. McGarity, *Reinventing Rationality: The Role of Regulatory Analysis in the Federal Bureaucracy* (New York: Cambridge University Press, 1991); and George Eads and Michael Fix, *Relief or Reform? Reagan's Regulatory Dilemma* (Washington, DC: Urban Institute Press, 1984).
60. *Federal Register*, Vol. 46 (February 19, 1981), pp. 13193–13198.
61. Kirk Victor, "Quayle's Quiet Coup," *National Journal*, Vol. 23 (July 6, 1991), pp. 1676–1680.
62. Barry D. Friedman, *Regulation in the Reagan-Bush Era* (Pittsburgh, PA: University of Pittsburgh Press, 1995), pp. 164–165.
63. Rebecca Adams, "Regulating the Rule-Makers: John Graham at OIRA," *Congressional Quarterly Weekly Report*, Vol. 60 (February 23, 2002), pp. 520–526. See also *Making Sense of Regulation* (Washington, DC: Office of Management and Budget, 2001).
64. Rebecca Adams, "The Costs and Benefits of Cass Sunstein "CQ Weekly, Vol. 67 (February 9, 2009), pp. 293–294. Cass Sunstein, a Harvard law professor and a fan of cost–benefit analysis, was appointed to head OIRA in February, 2009.
65. On partisan political analysis, see Charles E. Lindblom, *The Policy-Making Process*, 2nd ed. (Englewood Cliffs, NJ: Prentice-Hall, 1980), Chap. 4.
66. This account draws upon Walter Williams, *Social Policy Research and Analysis* (New York: American Elsevier, 1971); and Walter Williams and John W. Evan, "The Politics of Evaluation: The Case of Head Start," *Annals of the American Academy of Political and Social Sciences*, CCCLXXXV (September 1969), pp. 118–132.
67. Ibid. See Frank Fischer, *Evaluating Public Policy* (Chicago, IL: Nelson-Hall, 1995), pp. 47–66, for another discussion of the Westinghouse evaluation of Head Start.
68. See Department of Health and Human Services, *The Impact of Head Start on Children, Families, and Communities: Head Start Synthesis Project* (Washington, DC: U.S. Government Printing Office, 1985).
69. *The New York Times*, February 14, 1990, p. 1; March 4, 1992, p. B9; *Washington Post National Weekly Edition*, May 4–10, 1992, p. 31.
70. Janet Currie and Duncan Thomas, "Does Head Start Make a Difference?" *American Economic Review*, Vol. 85 (June 1995), pp. 341–364.
71. *The New York Times*, July 8, 2003, p. 1; and *Congressional Quarterly Weekly Report*, Vol. 62 (November 1, 2003), pp. 2706–2707.
72. *CQ Weekly*, Vol. 65 (November 19, 2007), p. 3486.
73. David Deming, "Early Childhood Intervention and Life-Cycle Skill Development: Evidence from Head Start" *American Economics Journal: Applied Economics*, Vol. 1 (2009), pp. 111–134; and *Head Start Impact Study: Final Report* (Executive Summary), Office of Planning, Research and Evaluation, Administration for Children and Families, U.S. Department of Health and Human Services, January 2010.
74. Office of Head Start, "Head Start Program Fact Sheet, Fiscal Year 2012," (Washington, DC, 2012).
75. Edward L. Katzenbach Jr., "The Horse Cavalry in the Twentieth Century: A Study in Policy Response," in Carl J. Friedrich and Seymour E. Harris, eds., *Public Policy*, Vol. 8 (Cambridge, MA: Harvard University Press, 1958), pp. 120–149.
76. *Wall Street Journal*, March 27, 1996, p. A20.

77. Garry D. Brewer and Peter deLeon, *The Foundation of Policy Analysis* (Homewood, IL: Dorsey Press, 1983), Chap. 13. See generally, Mark R. Daniels, *Terminating Public Programs* (Armonk, NY: M. E. Sharpe, 1997).

78. Jasper Womack, "Tobacco Quota Buyout," Congressional Research Service, Library of Congress, December, 2005.

79. Merle Fainsod, Lincoln Gordon, and Joseph C. Palamountain Jr., *Government and the American Economy*, 3rd ed. (New York: Norton, 1959), pp. 120–121.

80. Robert E. Cushman, *The Independent Regulatory Commissions* (New York: Oxford University Press, 1941), pp. 389–416.

81. Emmette S. Redford, Congress Passes the Federal Aviation Act of 1958, ICP case series: no. 52 (Tuscaloosa, AL: University of Alabama Press, 1961).

82. *The New York Times*, November 1, 1974, p. 1.

83. Anthony E. Brown, *The Politics of Airline Regulation* (Knoxville, TN: University of Tennessee Press, 1987), pp. 133–136.

84. Bradley Behrman, "Civil Aeronautics Board," in James Q. Wilson, ed., *The Politics of Deregulation* (New York: Basic Books, 1980), pp. 99–102.

85. Brown, op. cit., pp. 104–105.

86. *Wall Street Journal*, July 3, 1978, pp. 1, 7.

87. Brown, op. cit., pp. 116–119.

88. *Congressional Quarterly Almanac 1978* (Washington, DC: Congressional Quarterly, 1979), Vol. 34, pp. 496–504.

89. Quoted in Brown, op. cit., p. 2.

90. George J. Stigler, *The Citizen and the State* (Chicago, IL: University of Chicago Press, 1975), p. 114.

91. Martha Derthick and Paul J. Quirk, *The Politics of Regulation* (Washington, DC: Brookings Institution, 1985), pp. 238–245.

92. Ibid., p. 258.

93. Paul S. Dempsey and Andrew R. Goetz, *Airline Deregulation and Laissez- Faire Mythology* (Westport, CT: Quorum Books, 1992), p. 227.

94. General Accounting Office, *Aviation Competition* (Washington, DC: U.S. Government Printing Office, December 2000), p. 5.

95. *The New York Times*, August 14, 2013, p. 1; and August 15, 2013, p. B1.

96. General Accounting Office, *Airline Competition: Higher Fares and Less Competition Continue at Concentrated Airports* (Washington, DC: U.S. Government Printing Office, July 1993), p. 33.

97. Bonser, McGregor, and Oster, op.cit., p. 226.

98. General Accounting Office, *Airline Competition: Higher Fares and Reduced Competition at Concentrated Airports* (Washington, DC: U.S. Government Printing Office, July 1990), p. 1; and "Dominated Hub Fares" (Washington, DC: U.S. Department of Transportation, January 2001).

99. Don Phillips, "The Crowded Skies of Sardine Airlines," *Washington Post Weekly Edition* (June 26–July 2, 1995), p. 19; and *Congressional Quarterly Weekly Report*, Vol. 59 (June 23, 2001), pp. 1488–1492.

100. Paul Stephen Dempsey, "The Dark Side of Deregulation: Its Impact on Small Communities," *Administrative Law Review*, Vol. 39 (Fall 1987), pp. 454–459. Also *The New York Times* (January 10, 2009), p. B1.

101. Steven A. Morrison and Clifford Winston, *The Evolution of the Airline Industry* (Washington, DC: Brookings Institution, 1995), pp. 31–33; and Roger W. Cobb and David M. Primo, *The Plane Truth: Airline Crashes, the Media, and Transportation Policy* (Washington, DC: Brookings Institution, 2003), Chap. 3.

102. Jeff Plungis, "Lawmakers Wary of Unfriendly Skies Weigh Revisiting Airline Regulation," *Congressional Quarterly Weekly Report*, Vol. 58 (July 8, 2000), pp. 1671–1674. See also Merrill Goozner, "Air Piracy," *The American Prospect*, Vol. 12 (June 4, 2001), pp. 22–25.

103. Kathryn Wolfe, "Rough Skies for the 'Big Six,'" *CQ Weekly*, Vol. 63 (April 25, 2005), pp. 1068–1077; and Government Accountability Office, *Airline Deregulation: Reregulating the Airline Industry Would Likely Reverse Consumer Benefits and Not Save Airline Pensions* (Washington, DC: U.S. Government Printing Office, June 2006).

8

Reflections and Observations

n the preceding chapters I presented a general framework (or model), and a variety of concepts and ideas, for studying and analyzing the complex process of public policymaking. This framework—the policy cycle—depicts the policymaking process as a sequence of functional activities (problem definition, agenda setting, policy formulation, and so on). It is intended as neither a general nor causal theory of policymaking.[1] It is, rather, a useful way of dividing the policy process into manageable segments and of organizing and guiding examination of that process.[2]

Various theories designed generally to explain who makes or controls policy can be accommodated to this framework. Some of these theories are discussed in Chapter 1, "The Study of Public Policy." The various segments or phases of the framework are interrelated and sometimes meld together. What happens at one point in the policy process (or cycle) has meaning for action at later phases. Policy-makers often look down the road from one phase to another. Phases such as problem definition and agenda-setting, or policy adoption and implementation, may smudge together. Still, analytical distinctions can be made, as between policy formulation and policy adoption.

It would seem that the best advice for those hoping for the emergence of a general theory of policymaking is to be very patient. Not so long ago, political scientists spoke and wrote about the need to develop a general theory of politics.[3] Research projects were often justified in part as contributing to the development of a general theory. Politics and policymaking, however, are too complex to be explained satisfactorily by one grand theory, and so the quest for a general theory has been consigned to the disciplinary dustbin. These remarks are intended neither to disparage nor discourage theory development (or "building") in favor of descriptive or "factual" studies.

Theory is needed to help separate more important or relevant variables and facts from those less so in describing and explaining events. In building theories it seems advisable to focus on more manageable tasks, such as explaining why some policies are more successfully implemented than others, or why

FIGURE 8.1

Thoughts on Policymaking

1. Once underway, the formation of policy on most problems is continuous.
2. In a modern, pluralistic society, policymaking is likely to be complex, untidy, and perhaps unruly.
3. Policymaking in the United States tends to be adversarial, more characterized by conflict than cooperation.
4. Policy analysis has become more extensive and more utilized in the legislative and administrative venues.
5. Conventional wisdom holds that policymaking in the United States is mostly incremental.
6. Although conflict in policymaking attracts attention, there is also routine, low-visibility, low-conflict policymaking.
7. Change, sometimes designated as reform, is a constant feature of the policy process.
8. Despite frequent complaints about government or policy failures, public policies collectively accomplish much to resolve or ameliorate public problems.

© Cengage learning

only some distressful conditions out of all those existing in society become defined as public problems and reach policy agendas. These are challenging, worthy, and manageable tasks.[4]

In the remainder of this chapter, I will make some general observations and comments about the policymaking process. Also, some of the changes that have occurred in the policymaking process since the first edition of this book was published in the early 1970s will be noted (see Figure 8.1).

First, once the formation of public policy on most public problems—certainly those of any magnitude—gets underway, action tends to be ongoing. There may be lurches or fluctuations in the scope and intensity of action, however, and sometimes a matter may for a time drop below the political horizon. Much of the time something will be happening in some arena that has consequences for the content and impact of policy.

As the policy process unfolds, a problem is recognized, defined or framed, and wins a place on one or more governmental agendas; alternatives are developed, presented, and debated; a less than optimal alternative (the policy) is officially adopted; implementation begins; experience may reveal shortcomings, loopholes, or other defects in the policy, or some sort of formal evaluation and feedback may occur; legislative or administrative adjustments may be made in the policy; more implementation follows; evaluation and feedback again happen; infrequently, a policy may be terminated; and so on.

Somewhere along the way, changes in the policy environment may cause redefinition (or reframing) of the problem targeted by a policy. And the policy may shift in content. Farm policy has been a continuing concern of national policy-makers for most of a century, despite a major decline in the number of farmers and the farm population. In the early 1970s, the "farm problem" shifted from one of too much production, which drove down prices, to one of too little production. Farmers were then urged to plant "from fencerow to fencerow." Soon, however, surpluses emerged, and restrictions on production were strengthened. Then, in the mid-1990s, with Republicans in control of Congress, governmental limits on farm production were seen as the problem. "Freedom to farm" became a policy slogan. Farm legislation in 1996 abolished most restrictions on production, though this failed to "wean" farmers from subsidies, which in fact were increased by the 2002 farm bill and continued by the 2008 farm bill. The urge to buttress farm income continues as a focus of farm policy, although large commercial farmers are doing well.

A problem may also seem to disappear, at least for a time. An example is the energy problem. During the 1970s, the Nixon, Ford, and Carter administrations struggled to develop governmental solutions for the perceived shortage of fuels. The Reagan administration, however, contended that there was no scarcity of energy. When actions like these occur, the consequences may be substantial changes in the direction and content of some policies. Whereas the energy policy of the Carter administration stressed governmental action, conservation, and the development of new energy sources, Reagan administration policy called for less governmental action and more reliance on the market. This course of action on energy continued to prevail for several years, as the emergence of larger motor vehicles, higher speed limits, and cheap gasoline attest. In time, however, there was a shift back to energy shortages. The George W. Bush administration secured legislation intended to increase the supply of fossil fuels, especially oil. Support for production of biofuels has grown.

Policies in many areas often become settled and handled for the most part by routine administrative processes.[5] Often they will be dominated by subsystems and be characterized by low public visibility, only occasionally to be disturbed by some action that leads to identification of a new problem and that restarts the policy process. Examples include vocational education, soil conservation, railroad safety, and national weather services. It may be a change in socioeconomic conditions, as when the aging of the population creates a so-called crisis in Social Security financing. The AIDS crisis similarly created demands for change in medical-research policy, and the animal-rights movement sometimes threatens to do the same. Outbreaks of food poisoning periodically call into question the adequacy of the U.S. Department of Agriculture's meat-inspection program or the Food and Drug Administration's food inspection programs. In all, the policy process is best thought of as cyclical rather than linear, as something that recycles as new problems emerge, as continuous rather than finite in duration.

Second, in a large, modern, pluralistic society and political system, public policymaking is likely to be complex, untidy, and perhaps a bit unruly. Whether regularly or occasionally, many players, official and unofficial, participate, and many factors that help shape policy process are thus not sharply demarcated. Political authority and power are fragmented and dispersed by governmental structure, and by the social, economic, and ideological diversity of American society. In the early 1970s, power in Congress was further dispersed by being shifted from committees to subcommittees.[6] However, beginning in the mid-1990s a countertrend set in. Especially in the House, power became more centralized.[7]

Also, interest groups have proliferated in number and variety. The consequence is increased factionalism in policymaking. Factionalism, Professor Hugh Heclo says, is an old label but one that serves well to describe the current situation. The primary difference between the factionalism that James Madison wrote about in the *Federalist* No. 10 and the present factionalism is that "our factionalism has shaped itself around a governmental presence that is doing so much more in so many different areas of life."[8] As a consequence, government often seems too responsive to narrow group, sectoral, or regional interests and insufficiently concerned with searching out and caring for the public interest.

Decision-making in the congressional policymaking process, because of the fragmentation and dispersion of power, has long required logrolling and alliance building, negotiation and bargaining, and compromise. (These, in essence, are the ABCs of politics.) Delay in decision-making and moderation in action frequently flow from this situation. Action was delayed on such matters as family and medical leaves, child care, and food safety because of the time required to reach the necessary agreement.

In the last several years, because of intense polarization of the congressional political parties and unwillingness to compromise, especially on the part of the Republicans (examine the record), Congress has become quite dysfunctional.[9] Some major legislation (economic stimulus, health care, financial reform) was enacted when the Democrats had majorities in both houses, during the 111th Congress (2009–2010). Republicans contributed by extensive use of filibusters, requiring 60 votes for most major actions. The 112th Congress (2011–2012) accomplished little beyond passing legislation to name public buildings, enact commemorative resolutions, and after much squabbling, taking some actions on the budget deficit and national debt.

Several months into 2013, the prospects for legislative action seemed no better than they had been. So, readers, what should be done to bring about positive change? Of course, if you approve of the current congressional dysfunctionalism and minority rule in the Senate, nothing needs to be done.

On the other hand, the system sometimes can act quickly, even precipitously. Following the September 11 terrorist attacks, it took Congress only a few days to cobble together and enact a $15 billion "bailout" package to alleviate the economic distress of the commercial airlines. This was followed in a few weeks by the awkwardly titled Uniting and Strengthening America by Providing Appropriate Tools Required to Intercept and Obstruct Terrorism Act (the USA Patriot Act). Given cursory consideration at the time, this complex law increased the surveillance and investigative authority of U.S. law-enforcement agencies. Crises or emergencies, real or perceived, may jump-start the policy process.

In 1995, it initially appeared that a fundamental change might be underway in the policymaking process. For the first time in forty years, the Republicans took control of both houses of Congress. In the House, under the leadership of Speaker Newt Gingrich, a disciplined Republican majority, claiming a mandate from the voters, rammed through within a hundred days nearly all of the components of their radical "Contract with America." (The only exception was a proposed constitutional amendment providing for term limits.) The House bills, however, encountered opposition in the more moderate Senate and from the Clinton White House. By year's end, most of the Contract with America went unenacted. Moreover, the congressional Republicans and the president, who had the support of most Democrats in Congress, were stalemated over the issue of balancing the budget within a seven-year frame, although a balanced budget was later temporarily achieved. Once again, the separation and dispersion of power in the American political system complicated and tempered policy change.[10]

In all, the policymaking process in the United States is not easy to comprehend, describe, or explain. Those who offer quick, certain, or pat explanations as to why policies were rejected or adopted, or later proved unsuccessful, often oversimplify and at best provide partial explanations. Some historians assert that the Sherman Act of 1890 was adopted as a "sop to public opinion," an attempt to quell the public clamor for legislation against the trusts. Such explanations usually have within them a kernel of accuracy. Careful examination of the history of the Sherman Act, however, indicates far more than the "sop factor." There were real concerns about the effects of the trusts on the economy, society, and polity, and real differences in views about whether or not government should act and in what manner. Antitrust continues to be a basic regulatory policy, even if not always well-implemented.

Journalists and others (political scientists are not fully exempted here) sometimes explain legislative enactments idiosyncratically, as primarily the result of clever actions by this senator or that representative, or the machinations of a particular interest group.[11] Important executive decisions may be attributed to designated officials, acting almost alone and unaided, it would seem. People are important, they do make a difference, but they act within an institutional and societal context that also shapes, directs, and constrains action. The diversity of this context also adds to the complexity of the policy process.

If studies of policymaking are complex in substance and uncertain or tentative in findings and conclusions, it is not because political scientists and other policy analysts are at once obtuse and timid. Rather, it is more likely that the subject is complex, conclusive data are scarce, motives are unclear, influence is subtle, and policy impacts are uncertain. Accurately explaining human behavior is a tenuous and complicated task.

Third, the policymaking process in the administrative and judicial arenas in the United States tends to be adversarial, featuring the clash of competing and conflicting viewpoints and interests rather than either an impartial, disinterested, objective search for solutions to problems or a cooperative endeavor by interested parties to handle matters.[12] Nowhere is this conflict better illustrated than in the conduct of judicial proceedings, whether trial or appellate, and in the judiciary's extensive involvement in the policy process, which is brought about by those unhappy with decisions made by other governmental actors. Government-business relationships are also notable for their adversarial quality. Although it is occasionally urged that such relationships should be more cooperative, as they appear to be in Japan, so that the United States can compete more effectively in the world economy, not much changes.

The adversarial pattern is more congruent with American culture, its litigiousness, and its self-assertive values.[13] Most Americans prefer a more independent role for government as a guardian of the public interest. Also, some Americans have the notion that "government is not the solution to our problem. Government is the problem." Uttered by Ronald Reagan in his 1981 Inaugural Address, the mistrust of government that the statement reflects is a persistent element of American political culture.[14] It is not the stuff from which grow extensive cooperative relationships between government and others. Important interests, including that of the public, may be lost sight of in the clash of adversaries, however. What is good for banks, or for insurance companies, is not necessarily good for the public.

The Regulatory Negotiation Act (1990) provides an alternative to the adversarial pattern. The interested parties in a rule-making proceeding, including agency officials, can negotiate a proposed rule. They agree, once the rule is adopted, not to contest it. Negotiated rule-making has been used infrequently. Most interested parties believe they will fare better under the adversarial process.[15]

Fourth, policy analysis has become more widely practiced and its products more heavily drawn upon in the development of policies in the legislative and administrative arenas.[16] Policy evaluation, in its systematic variant, is also much more prevalent. Together, these developments have contributed to making the policy process more technocratic. The opposing sides in policy struggles trot out their experts and "objective" policy analyses to support their positions. "Good" science is juxtaposed to "junk" science. Science is ignored when it becomes politically inconvenient (see: George W. Bush administration).

More and more, policymaking threatens to become the domain of experts, into which ordinary persons ought not to intrude. Debates over arms control, for instance, are loaded with technical data about missiles and other weapons systems. Mathematical models are devised to estimate the likely responses of potential aggressors to possible actions. The average citizen often is baffled by this sort of analysis.

Policy analysis, however, is not the only cause of technocracy in policymaking. In Congress, the subcommittee system, which encourages specialization, and the rise of careerist legislators, some of whom have both incentives and opportunity to specialize, have also been contributory.[17] Of course, one must also recognize that some policy matters are by their very nature technical and complex. The treatment and disposal of hazardous waste is a good example. On the other hand, issues may be made deliberately to seem more technical than they are in an effort to exclude nonexperts from their consideration. Still worth remembering is the old public-administration adage that the expert should be on tap rather than on top.

Policy decisions ultimately remain political in tone, however, if for no other reason than that they distribute advantages and disadvantages. Sometimes it seems to be assumed that if enough research and analysis are conducted, and enough facts and data are gathered, answers to policy problems will appear upon which all people, or at least all reasonable people, can agree. If policy problems were only scientific or technical, this resolution might happen, as when vaccines are developed and generally administered to eradicate childhood diseases. No "pro-poliomyelitis" lobby campaigned against the Salk vaccine, for instance. Conflict may develop, however, over the administration of public vaccination programs. What should be done to combat AIDS is more than a technical or medical question.

Most policy problems, and certainly those of any magnitude, generate significant differences of view as to what is socially acceptable, economically feasible, and politically possible. Bargaining, negotiation, and compromise, not simply reliance upon the "facts," are then required to produce decisions. Policy analysis can inform, enlighten, develop alternatives, and even persuade to an extent, but by itself it is unlikely to yield consensus policy decisions. Room still remains in the policy process for generalists, who should be on top, according to the old adage.

Fifth, the notion that policymaking in the United States is essentially incremental is conventional wisdom among political scientists. Incrementalism can mean either that a new policy differs only marginally from current policies or that it resulted from a decision-making process involving limited analysis of goals, alternatives, and consequences. Some decisions are characterized by more analysis, others by less analysis, and none by complete (i.e., rational-comprehensive) analysis. To say that a policy was based on limited analysis is to say nothing that really differentiates it from other policies.

When our attention turns to the amount of change embodied in a policy, we find that often new policies make limited or marginal changes in existing policies and are therefore called *incremental*. This holds whether a change is an addition or deletion, although, accurately speaking, an increment is an increase. Incremental policies, which whittle away at problems, are typified by most educational "reforms."

Some policies, however, are of sufficient magnitude or impact, or make such a departure from the existing order, as to merit designation as *basic* or *fundamental*. They represent "breakthroughs" that yield lasting changes in the thrust of government action, expanding its scope and cresting new policy structures and relationships. Candidates for this category include the Social Security Act of 1935; the Marshall Plan, which provided massive economic aid to post–World War II Europe; the 1965 Voting Rights Act; the interstate highway program; the Clean Air Act (1970); and the Clean Air Act Amendments (1990), for its emissions trading system to control acid rain.

Although greatly exceeded in number by incremental policies, basic or fundamental policies significantly alter and shape the direction and effects of governmental action. The preoccupation of policy students with incrementalism as a descriptive or explanatory concept obscures the importance of these fundamental or breakthrough policies in the evolution of American public policy. Professors Frank Baumgartner and Bryan Jones, in their analysis of "punctuated equilibrium" in American politics, state that there have been long periods of incremental change in a policy area "punctuated" by brief periods of major change. Major change comes about when the opponents of the status quo devise and advocate new policy images (such as for nuclear power) and exploit the existence of multiple "policy venues" in the American political system.[18]

In time, it is true that significant changes in policies can occur incrementally. The progressive quality of the graduated income tax was gradually reduced by a plethora of laws creating deductions, credits, exclusions, and exemptions, mostly for the benefit of higher-income persons. By 1980, its progressive and redistributive effects were as much symbolic as material. In an incremental manner, a basic change was wrought in income-tax policy, without ever directly being considered on its merit. In the 1990s, some progressivity was restored via limited increases in marginal rates. More recently, the George W. Bush administration moved the pendulum in the opposite direction. In 2012, the highest marginal rate (39.6 percent) was restored for some taxpayers. Incremental action tends to mitigate conflict but the avoidance of conflict, if conflict helps to clarify issues and focus attention, is not wholly desirable.

Sixth, in the study of public policymaking and in the day-to-day observation of the governmental process, our attention usually focuses on conflict. Conflict attracts attention. Major public policies generate conflict and make news. They also draw scholarly attention. Consequently, one may come to believe that policymaking as a matter of course is always sharply conflictive. One can find some support in this book for such a conclusion, although a variety of references to less conflictive matters are provided. Environmental protection, tax reform, economic regulation, and Social Security reform have produced much conflict.

At the same time, however, there is what Professor Herbert Jacob calls the ongoing "routine policy process."[19] Although not devoid of conflict, it is characterized by such features as a narrow definition of the problem to be solved, low visibility, limited participation, low policy costs, and general compatibility between proposed and existing policies. The policies may be either regulatory or distributive, and they sometimes may be of considerable importance. Examples include the Animal Welfare Act, the Medical Waste Tracking Act, and the Dietary Supplement Health and Education Act, which exempted dietary supplements from most Food and Drug Administration regulation. At the state level, divorce-law reform is an example. All the states, without stirring much controversy, have revised their divorce laws. Now, along with other modifications in divorce law, no-fault divorce can be obtained in every state. The legalization of same-sex marriage is now gaining momentum.

In all, the routine policy process differs from the conflictive process more in degree than in genre. There is, for instance, public participation, but less of it. Disagreement occurs over what should be done on a matter, but efforts are made to muffle it. Much of the work in developing policy takes place at the subsystem level, which contributes to lower public awareness, although adoption occurs in the macro-arena. Of course, routine policy may also be studied using the sequential process framework.

Seventh, change is a constant companion of the policy process. Changes take a variety of forms, including alterations in the number and variety of participants or in their roles and relationships, in the manner in which some issues are handled, and in the procedures or techniques used to deal with problems. When change is deliberately designed and sought, when it takes the form of a deliberate effort to improve the operation of the policy process from some perspective, we often call it *reform*. When, however, it arises undesigned and unintended out of other events, we do not have a distinctive name for it.

Change in the policy process is more likely to be limited or incremental than sudden and sweeping in scope. The efforts of the Reagan administration to redirect the policy process, both in style and output, were soon referred to as the "Reagan Revolution." Changes did occur, but not to an extent sufficient to warrant the label "revolution." More executive control of administrative rule-making was installed, authorized by executive orders, and implemented by the Office of Management and Budget (OMB). The budget deficit, as a consequence of the large budget deficits incurred during the Reagan years, won a place at the top of the national policy agenda and complicated action on other policy matters. Some argue that large budget deficits were incurred deliberately by the president to make it difficult to adopt new spending programs. Not without a touch of plausibility, this line of argument attributes too much guile and strategic thinking to President Reagan. What actually occurred is better thought of as the unintended consequence of other actions, namely, tax reduction and greater defense spending.[20]

Changes in the policy process may occur for a number of reasons. I will focus here on three, which can be differentiated on the basis of causation, or what gives rise to them.

1. There are changes that are formally designed and adopted, and that operate generally as intended. An example is the creation by the Nixon administration in 1970 of the Environmental Protection Agency (EPA), which consolidated many environmental programs to enhance environmental protection. Though not a complete success, the EPA strengthened environmental administration.

2. Changes in the policy process may be the unintended consequences of actions taken for other purposes. The 1974 congressional budget legislation set up a budget committee in each house of Congress along

with a congressional budget process. This increased the rationality of congressional budget action and strengthened congressional control of the budget. It also unintentionally helped shift the role of the House Appropriations Committee from "defender of the Treasury" to protector of programs favored by committee members. The incorporation of the independent Federal Emergency Management Administration (FEMA) in the Department of Homeland Security was a factor in FEMA's ineffectiveness in responding in 2005 to Hurricane Katrina.

3. Some changes, because of broad or multiple driving forces, can best be regarded as responses to alterations in the policy environment. The increasing "technocratization" of the policy process is in point. This development stems from such factors as the shift in handling legislation from congressional committees to subcommittees, increased professional staff assistance for members of Congress, and the increasing complexity and technicality of policy problems. The technocratization of the policy process, in turn, makes meaningful participation by average citizens more difficult. One cannot identify a particular decision that, intentionally or inadvertently, produced this situation.

The conclusion to be drawn from this discussion is not that change is pernicious but rather that successful and intentional change in the policy process is not easily achieved. Term-limit advocates who suggested that members of Congress should serve for only six years (or twelve years) in order to reduce "careerism" and members' supposed unresponsiveness to the electorate probably had not thought deeply about all the consequences such a change would produce, both in the operation of Congress as an institution and in its participation in the policy process.[21] The political system, systems theory informs us, is composed of interdependent parts. A change in one part will affect the other parts and their roles and activities. Successful reform of the policy process requires adequate knowledge of the process and its operation. Such knowledge is not easy to acquire.

At the national level, there have been a variety of policy failures; that is, policies that have accomplished little or nothing. Examples include the Strategic Defense Initiative ("Star Wars"), the "war on drugs," the Nuclear Waste Policy Act, and wildfire suppression management.[22] Other policies have not accomplished what was hoped or expected. The collective governmental response to Hurricane Katrina (2005), the 2008 economic stimulus legislation, and consumer food protection are illustrative.

There are also policies that have produced great harm. Notable here is the recent deregulation and nonregulation of financial businesses. The Financial Services Modernization Act (1999) permitted banks to combine investment, commercial banking, and insurance services. Huge banking conglomerates came into being, some of which became viewed as "too big to fail" because of their potential effects on the economy. In 2000 the Commodity Futures Modernization Act, which was slipped into a huge omnibus appropriations act and enacted with no debate, prohibited regulation of credit default swaps (don't ask) and other financial derivatives. Collectively, these statutes, and decisions by regulatory officials not to use authority they possessed, contributed much to the financial devastation of the American economy.[23] After initially misdiagnosing the seriousness of the economic situation, strong action by Congress, the Treasury Department, and especially the Federal Reserve Board prevented a second Great Depression. Hundreds of billions of dollars were pumped into the financial system to resuscitate it.[24]

Because of the recklessness and avarice of many banks, bankers, and financial entities, the call for expanded regulation of the financial industry gained a prominent place on the policy agenda. However, as the economic situation improved and medical care reform pushed to the fore, financial regulation lost momentum. Bankers and their allies exerted much pressure in support of business, bonuses, and profits as usual. Estimates were that reform legislation would be moderate in tone. Even some of the national financial regulatory agencies have resisted creation of a new consumer financial protection agency to control financial abuses because it would encroach on their jurisdictions.[25]

In July 2010, the Wall Street Reform and Consumer Protection Act became law. It was a solid piece of legislation, though it did not do all that reform advocates wanted. Nothing like it had been enacted since the New Deal years. Hundreds of agency rules were authorized to spell out and implement its provisions. These agencies included the Treasury Department, Federal Reserve Board, Office of the Controller of the Currency, Federal Deposit Insurance Corporation, Securities and Exchange Commission, Commodity Futures Trading Commission, and the Consumer Financial Protection Bureau. Since its enactment, the financial community, its legions of lobbyists, trade associations, and conservative think tanks, and their congressional Republican allies, have conducted a continuous campaign to prevent, weaken, or delay agency rule-making. Once again, we see that the policy struggle does not end when "a bill becomes a law."[26]

Public policies collectively have accomplished a good deal, notwithstanding complaints about policy failures (which as indicated previously, are not without some validity) and allegations that public problems never get resolved. Crime, poverty, potholes, pollution, and diseases persist, although they may be lessened (or in the instance of smallpox, essentially eliminated). At the local level, however, garbage is regularly collected, fires are put out, public order is maintained, clean water flows from the tap, parks, recreation facilities are available, and most children learn to read and write (although it seems the public schools are never as good as they were).

People are often unaware of the existence of some public policies even if they benefit from them. These policies are part of what Professor Suzanne Mettler calls "The Submerged State."[27] She cites as examples the home mortgage interest and the employer-sponsored health insurance income tax deductions. As tax expenditures, each comes at a cost of more than $100 million annually to the U.S. Treasury. They have low public visibility. Another example involves lawsuits against job discrimination under the 1964 Civil Rights Act. Approximately 20,000 such lawsuits are filed annually in the federal courts, almost all of them by private enforcement of the law against job discrimination.[28]

Many national policies have been successful, yielding positive or beneficial outcomes. These include the Serviceman's Readjustment Act of 1944 (the GI Bill of Rights), the rebuilding of Western Europe by the Marshall Plan after World War II, the Voting Rights Act, Social Security, Medicare, and the protection of wilderness areas.[29] Government successes seem to be taken for granted. Accomplishments are minimized.

If few public problems are entirely resolved by government actions, many are partly or substantially solved or ameliorated. Employment problems remain, but are not as bad as they would be were there no job-training, economic-development, unemployment-compensation, and other employment-related programs. Consumers may still be misled and defrauded, but not with the frequency that they would be without consumer-protection programs. More wildlife survives than would have in the absence of fish-and-game laws, national and state parks, and wildlife refuges. Public-health and sanitation policies have greatly reduced the incidence of infectious diseases and contributed to greater human longevity. Civil-rights policies have done much to reduce discrimination and expand opportunities for minorities.

The goals of public policies are often stated in absolute rather than relative language. Thus, the streets are to be made safe (rather than safer) for all law-abiding people, or poverty is to be banished (not just reduced) from America. Absolute statements, because they are more appealing than conditional phrasing of goals, are used to garner public and interest-group support for policies. The Clean Water Act of 1972 set a goal of "zero" discharge of pollutants into the nation's streams by 1985. The goal obviously has not been met, although many streams are undoubtedly cleaner than they would have been without the act.[30] Has the act, then, "failed," as some allege?

Because of the intractability or persistence of many public problems, public policies may at best mitigate or reduce the target problems. The prevalence of heart disease can be lessened, for instance, or juvenile delinquency can be reduced. When goals are stated as absolutes, however, anything less than complete success tends to be construed as failure.[31] This masks the real accomplishments of many public policies, even those of which we may personally disapprove. Whatever their shortcomings, public policies have done much to improve the quality and comfort of modern life in the United States. How many fans of "limited government" would really choose to live in Somalia? Or Mongolia?

Notes

1. cf. Paul A. Sabatier, ed., *Theories of the Policy Process*, 2nd ed. (Boulder, CO: Westview, 2007), Chap. 1; and Debra Stone, *Policy Paradox*, rev. ed. (New York: Norton, 2002), Chap. 1.

2. It has been widely used. For examples, see Michael E. Kraft and Scott R. Furlong, *Public Policy*, 2nd ed. (Washington, DC: CQ Press, 2009); B. Guy Peters, *American Public Policy*, 7th ed. (Washington, DC: CQ Press, 2009). and Joseph Stewart Jr., David M. Hedge, and James P. Lester, *Public Policy; An Evolutionary Approach*, 3rd ed. (Wadsworth, 2008).

3. David Easton, *The Political System* (New York: Knopf, 1953). Also idem., *The Analysis of Political Structure* (New York: Routledge, 1990), Chap. 1.

4. But see Kim Quaile Hill, "In Search of General Theory," *Journal of Politics*, Vol. 74 (October 2012), pp. 917–931.

5. Donald F. Kettl, *The Next Government of the United States* (New York: Norton, 2009), pp. 33–38.

6. Burdett A. Loomis, *The Contemporary Congress*, 3rd ed. (New York: Bedford St. Martin's, 2003), Chap. 5.

7. Thomas E. Mann and Norman J. Ornstein, *The Broken Branch* (New York: Oxford University Press, 2006), Chap. 4.

8. Hugh Heclo, "The Emerging Regime," in Richard A. Harris and Sidney M. Milkis, eds., *Remaking American Politics* (Boulder, CO: Westview Press, 1989), p. 310.

9. Thomas E. Mann and Norman J. Ornstein, "Finding the Common Good in an Era of Dysfunctional Governance," *Daedalus* (Spring 2013), pp. 15–23. See also their *It's Even Worse Than It Looks* (New York: Basic Books, 2012).

10. John B. Bader, "The 'Contract with America'? Origins and Prospects." Paper presented at the 1996 meeting of the Midwest Political Science Association, Chicago, April 18–20, 1996.

11. As an example, consider Hedrick Smith's informative work on Washington politics and policymaking, *The Power Game* (New York: Random House, 1988). The power players discussed therein often seem to be acting within an institution-free context. Another example is Bob Woodward, *Maestro: Greenspan's Fed and the American Boom* (New York: Simon & Schuster, 2000). Greenspan, it turned out, had clay on his feet.

12. Robert Kagan, "Adversarial Legalism and American Government," in Marc K. Landy and Martin A. Levin, eds., *The New Politics of Public Policy* (Baltimore, MD: Johns Hopkins University Press, 1995), Chap. 4.

13. See Steven Kelman, *Regulating America, Regulating Sweden* (Cambridge, MA: MIT Press, 1981), pp. 133–141, 229–236.

14. Garry Wills, *A Necessary Evil: A History of American Distrust of Government* (New York: Simon & Schuster, 1999).

15. "Negotiated Rulemaking," http://en.wikipedia.org/wiki/Negotiated_Rulemaking.

16. John A. Hird, *Power, Knowledge, and Politics: Policy Analysis in the States* (Washington, DC: Georgetown University Press, 2005). Hird presents an insightful analysis of nonpartisan policy research in the American states.

17. Lawrence C. Dodd, "The Rise of the Technocratic Congress: Congressional Reform in the 1970s," in Harris and Milkis, op. cit., Chap. 4.

18. Cf. Frank R. Baumgartner and Bryan D. Jones, *Agendas and Instability in American Politics*, 2nd ed. (Chicago, IL: University of Chicago Press, 2009).

19. Herbert Jacob, *Silent Revolution: The Transformation of Divorce Law in the United States* (Chicago, IL: University of Chicago Press, 1988).

20. Cf. David A. Stockman, *The Triumph of Politics: Why the Reagan Revolution Failed* (New York: Harper & Row, 1986).

21. Gary C. Jacobson, *The Politics of Congressional Elections*, 4th ed. (New York: Longman, 1997), pp. 215–217.

22. George Busenberg, "Wildfire Management in the United States: The Evolution of a Policy Failure," *Review of Policy Research*, Vol. 21 (February 2004), pp. 145–156.

23. See Frank Partnoy *F.I.A.S.C.O.* (New York: Norton, 2009); and Dean Baker, *Plunder and Blunder: The Rise and Fall of the Bubble Economy* (New York: Polipoint, 2009).

24. Kevin Phillips, *Bad Money: Reckless Finance, Failed Politics, and the Global Crisis of American Capitalism* (New York: Penguin Books, 2009); and David Wessel, *In Fed We Trust: Ben Bernanke's War on the Great Panic* (New York: Crown Business, 2009).

25. *The New York Times*, June 18, 2009, p. B1; Peter H. Stone, "Financial Guns of August," *National Journal*, Vol. 41 (August 1, 2009), pp. 48–49.

26. Alan S. Blinder, *When the Music Stopped* (New York: Penguin Press, 2013), Chap. 11; and Haley Sweetland Edwards, "He Who Makes the Rules," *Washington Monthly*, Vol. 45 (March/April 2013), pp. 27–40.

27. Suzanne Mettler, *The Submerged State* (Chicago, IL: University of Chicago Press, 2011).

28. Sean Farhang, *The Litigation State* (Princeton, NJ: Princeton University Press, 2012).

29. See Paul C. Light, *Government's Greatest Achievements: From Civil Rights to Homeland Security* (Washington, DC: Brookings Institution Press, 2002); Milton J. Esman, *Government Works: Why Americans Need the Feds* (Ithaca, NY: Cornell University Press, 2000); and Edward Humes, *Over Here* (New York: Harcourt Books 2006). Humes's book analyzes experience with the GI Bill.

30. Paul R. Portney and Robert N. Stavins, eds., *Public Policies for Environmental Protection*, 2nd ed. (Washington, DC: Resources for the Future, 2000), Chap. 6.

31. Amihai Glazer and Lawrence S. Rothenberg, *Why Government Succeeds and Why It Fails* (Cambridge, MA: Harvard University Press, 2001). Also, see generally, Allen McConnell, "Policy Success, Policy Failure, and Grey Areas In Between," *Journal of Public Policy*, Vol. 30 (#3, 2010), pp. 345–362.

Index